STRANGE
EMPIRE

STRANGE

EMPIRE

A Narrative of the Northwest

JOSEPH KINSEY HOWARD

With a New Introduction by

Nicholas C. P. Vrooman

Teresa & Hal,
... our stories
bring us home.
As we share
our voices, this
is mine to you.
much love,
N.

Minnesota Historical Society Press
St. Paul

Grateful acknowledgment is made for use of quotations from
The Year of Decision: 1846 by Bernard DeVoto, reprinted by permission of Houghton
Mifflin Company, and from "Western Star" by Stephen Vincent Benet, copyright 1943 by
Rosemary Carr Benet, copyright renewed (c) 1971 by Rachel Benet Lewis, Thomas C.
Benet, and Stephanie B. Mahin, reprinted by permission of
Brandt & Brandt Literary Agents, Inc.

Picture credits: Minnesota Historical Society (cover); Montana Historical Society, Helena
(p. xxvii, xxviii); Private collection (p. xxx, Nicholas C. P. Vrooman, photographer)

Borealis Books are high-quality paperback reprints of books chosen by the Minnesota
Historical Society Press for their importance as enduring historical sources and their value
as enjoyable accounts of life in the Upper Midwest.

♾ The paper used in this publication meets the minimum requirements of the American
National Standard for Information Sciences—Permanence for Printed Library Materials,
ANSI Z39.48-1984.

Minnesota Historical Society Press, St. Paul 55102

First published 1952 by William Morrow and Company, New York
Copyright 1952 by Josephine Kinsey Howard
New material copyright 1994 by the Minnesota Historical Society

International Standard Book Number 0-87351-298-7
Manufactured in the United States of America

10 9 8 7 6 5 4 3 2 1

Library of Congress Cataloging-in-Publication Data

Howard, Joseph Kinsey, 1906-1951.
     Strange empire / Joseph Kinsey Howard.
          p. cm. — (Borealis books)
     Includes bibliographical references and index.
     ISBN 0-87351-298-7
     1. Red River Rebellion, 1869-1870. 2. Riel Rebellion, 1885. 3. Riel, Louis,
1844-1885. 4. Métis—Canada, Western—History—19th century. I. Title.
F1060.9.H7   1994
971.05'1—dc20   94-27626
                                                     CIP

To JEAN McREYNOLDS for whom, as for Rousseau,

"le bon n'etait que le beau mis en action."

That sun-dance has been blotted from
  the map,
Call as you will, those dancers will not
  come
To tear their breasts upon the bloody
  strap,
Mute-visaged, to the passion of a drum,
For some strange empire, nor the
  painted ghosts
Speak from the smoke and summon up
  the hosts.

Stephen Vincent Benet, "Western Star"

Sometimes there are exceedingly brief
periods which determine a long future.
A moment of time holds in solution ingredients which might combine in any
of several or many ways, and then another moment precipitates out of the
possible the at last determined thing.
The limb of a tree grows to a foreordained shape in response to forces determined by nature's equilibriums, but
the affairs of nations are shaped by the
actions of men, and sometimes, looking
back, we can understand which actions
were decisive.

Bernard DeVoto, *The Year of Decision: 1846*

"Nowadays a 'breed' is lower than a
dog. I went into a saloon with a dog
and they kicked me out and let the dog
stay."

Joseph Trottier, *Métis*

"Justice commands us to take up arms!"

Louis "David" Riel, *Exovede*

Table of Contents

Maps *by* IRVIN SHOPE

Introduction to the Reprint Edition

STRANGE EMPIRE is a compelling recounting of the story of the Métis people—age old in its plot, tragic in its drama, and profound in its significance. In this book Joseph Kinsey Howard tells of the struggle of Louis Riel and the Métis for control of the northwestern part of North America. Four decades after the book's publication in 1952, "it is," according to one historian, "still the only book that puts the story in international perspective."[1]

The name of the people—Métis—comes from a French word that translates as mixed-blood, that is to say, people of mixed racial heritage.[2] It is the French equivalent of the Spanish, Mestizo. In both cases the mixing is of Euro-American fathers and Amerindian mothers; both words derive from a Latin root, meaning mongrel, bastard, illegitimate. The words themselves give an idea of the deep-seated racism they imply. The Métis of the North are often referred to as French or French Canadians, and the Mestizos of the South are termed Latinos or Hispanics. They face continual discrimination as descendants of the first peoples of this continent.

The northern mixed-bloods are the descendants of Euro-American fur traders and Indian women. Throughout the eighteenth century when trappers and traders married the daughters of local tribal leaders, both Indian and white gained as trade deals were based on marital ties. Customarily, the children of mixed marriages were taken in either on their mother's side and taught Indian ways or their father's and schooled in Euro-American customs. By 1800 fur traders, although still intermarrying with full-blood women, were more frequently marrying the mixed-blood daughters of the fur trade marriages.

At the center of the continent, the blending of the races created the Métis. Primarily the fathers were French, although some were Scottish, Irish, or English, and the mothers were Cree or Ojibway. Their marriages were *à la façon du pays* or after the custom of the country, meaning without benefit of clergy. Most of the French fathers were traders with the North West Company.

The heart of the Métis settlement in the early nineteenth century was along the Red River of the North—the line of demarcation between the Woodlands and the Plains, which proved to be more than a division of ecosystems. The geography of the prairie determined much of the Métis identity. Where the canoe had been the vehicle of transport on the lakes and streams of the woodlands, on the prairie it was useless. The mixed-bloods developed and adapted the Red River cart, which may have been the first use of the wheel by indigenous people in the northwest. Based on medieval European design and modified by Indian intelligence to prairie circumstances, this innovation made possible the great buffalo hunts.[3] Buffalo robes and pemmican, a compound of dried buffalo meat, tallow, and dried berries, were the commodities of the barter by which the Métis made a living.

The development of the Red River carts was not the only instance where Indian and European technology and culture mixed. The Métis prided themselves on having the best of both worlds. Their European-style clothing was adorned in Indian fashion, often blending beadwork and tartan, symbols of their tribal and clan heritage. For entertainment they played the fiddle but employed a drum rhythm, and they danced the jig in an Indian manner. Deeply religious, they prayed to Jesus, yet sang medicine songs of healing. They wintered in cabins with pictures on the wall, slept in frame beds, and ate at tables. Into the retelling of medieval European fairy tales they introduced a native cast of characters. Freely they followed the yearly cycles of the hunt from the Red River to the Rocky Mountains, on both sides of the Canada–United States border. Indeed, for the Métis, as for the tribes, there was no border. From their two heritages, they created a new language—Michif—a beautiful blending of French nouns and Indian verbs. Their social structure was a mix of clan and European-style semimilitary organization. They were comfortable financially, the largest single population group on the Plains, larger than the Euro-Americans or the individual tribes, and the most powerful military force in the territory. These people also suffered the worst of both worlds—racism and prejudice from both sides of their heritage.[4]

The Hudson's Bay Company under charter from the king of England owned an area called Rupert's Land, which included most of western Canada and, until 1815, parts of what is now the United States (p. 30). The company's power and control were absolute. In 1811 Thomas Douglas, the earl of Selkirk, who held the controlling interest in the Hudson's Bay Company, secured from the company's stockholders a personal land grant he called Assiniboia (p. 33). As part of his plan to bring European-style agricultural development to the west, he founded the Red River settlement for white colonists near the present city of Winnipeg. Eighteen white women joined the colony in 1812. Twenty more soon followed.[5] The arrival of white women signaled the beginning of the end of life based on "custom of the country" alliances. Euro-American society pressed its claim for dominance.

The change came when Indian and mixed-blood women competed with Euro-American women for the same men and place in Red River society. In this struggle—played out in kitchens, drawing rooms, and bedrooms—race took ascendancy within the mixed-blood, cross-cultural economy, and the Euro-American women won. From 1816 on, economic, religious, and social pressures for racial purity increased to the point where mixed-bloods, men as well as women, no longer had full access to the white social or business world.[6]

Métis would thenceforward marry only Métis. The customs and lifeways that had been evolving became fixed and formed a distinct culture. What had once been an acceptable and successful union between peoples, marriage *à la façon du pays,* was in the 1870s declared by the Canadian courts to be null and void.[7] A whole people were deemed illegitimate, having no rights to property. The usage of the term Métis was applied by the Euro-Americans with new vigor and in a harsher tone.

For two decades prior to 1870 the Métis enjoyed economic success. The Hudson's Bay Company was losing its grip on its fur trade monopoly, and the Métis traded freely throughout the region and had more control of their own destiny. Both their sense of identity and political unity grew. But an action by the company threatened the Métis well-being; the company decided to divest itself of Rupert's Land.

Dreams were born and strategies hatched as the question of dominion over this vast tract of land remained unsettled. The United States wanted to extend its authority from the Louisiana Purchase to Alaska, effectively stopping Canadian expansion at Ontario's western border. Canada needed full access to the West Coast to solidify its national identity and economic potential. Left out of the discussion, of course, were not only the tribes but also the Métis.

The Métis believed they had as significant and rightful a claim to the area as anyone else. Their circumstances were different from those of the tribes, and their paternal heritage gave them a different political acumen. So began fifteen years of struggle for recognition and justice, an era capped on either end by armed resistance—at Red River in 1869–70 and in Saskatchewan in 1884–85.

A leader arose from among the Métis—Louis Riel, who gave voice to their cause and articulated their plight in a manner that forced Canada to take stock of its position. In November 1869 the Convention of the Peoples of Rupert's Land convened at Fort Garry and adopted a Bill of Rights. In the following month a Declaration of the Peoples of Rupert's Land and the North West was promulgated in the name of the "New Nation." The Bill of Rights gave the Métis "moral justification," and the declaration provided a legal basis for their movement (p. 153). These documents claimed sovereignty for the Métis people, who then elected Riel the president of the new nation. The last nation carved out of the continent was not the United States, Canada, Mexico, or even Texas, but a native nation, one that guaranteed equal rights to all whatever their heritage.

This conflict between the Métis and the Canadian government was not only a battle over native and Euro-American claims, but also an age-old fight between Catholicism and Protestantism, English and French, English and Irish, and English and American causes. But Canada, that is to say the English, won.

By June 1870 the Canadian negotiators agreed to meet the Métis terms for inclusion in the Ottawa government by passing the Manitoba Act, creating the province. The optimism of Métis victory did not last long. Within a year the Canadian government charged Riel with murder and treason (p. 182–85). In 1875 he was sentenced to exile, and he removed to the United States. What happened to Riel as an individual happened to the Métis as a whole. So began the Métis diaspora to the territories of Dakota and Montana and the areas of Saskatchewan and Alberta.

Desperate to supplement the buffalo hunt because the herds were diminishing quickly, the Métis continued their trading expeditions into the United States, although deemed illicit by Canada. In their new homes along the riverways of the west, they reestablished the centuries-old French style of agriculture—a system that they had previously used in the Red River settlement (p. 372). Along the United States–Canada border from Turtle Mountain to the Rocky Mountains, many Métis joined with their tribal relatives.

In 1879 Riel made his way to Montana, finally residing with a colony of Métis subsidized by the Catholic church at St. Peter's Mission west of Cascade.[8] He attempted to form an alliance between the Métis and the Indian tribes in the vicinity to launch a last, all-out surge to claim a nation for native peoples in Canada.

The tribes, as well as the Euro-Americans, distrusted the Métis. Riel's strategy having failed, in 1880 he turned to the United States federal government in hopes of creating a Métis reservation in Montana. That, too, was squelched by officials who refused to acknowledge individual rights and denied legitimate land claims.[9]

Riel's life changed drastically. He married and started a family, became a United States citizen, taught school, wrote letters to newspaper editors, and petitioned the territorial government to consider the rights of the Métis. Then one day in 1884 "Four Horsemen" rode into St. Peter's Mission—Gabriel Dumont and three companions. They had come at the request of the Métis people of Canada to ask Riel to lead them once again through a brewing conflict for the recognition of native rights in the Northwest.

The partnership of Riel and Dumont was symbolic of all that was Métis. Riel was the spiritual leader and statesman, Dumont the warrior and strategist. Together they were the head and the heart of the Métis nation. In a letter to his editor in 1951 Howard offered insights into the two men.

The Métis . . . regard the figure of Riel with awe, and some of them, . . . think he lives on . . .; but they love "ol' Gabe." They wined and dined him and treated him like a brother, rather than like a messiah. They never loved Riel, but they were dazzled by him. In their society he was a great man, but he would not have been one in ours; and I suspect that Gabriel would have been. I see Riel as a tragic figure, . . . but more in a sense of a symbol than as an individual; therefore I am rather pleased then [sic] otherwise that his tragic stature should emerge when it does—when, finally, he *establishes himself as a symbol* at the trial. Maybe I should have said this in the book instead of saying it in this letter. . . . Gabriel, on the other hand—though a symbol too—fought primarily because he liked to fight. The symbol attached to him was, so far as he was concerned, entirely incidental and unconscious. He was truly modest so far as assuming the role of leader of his people, but just cocky enough about his own ability as a fighter. Riel was just the opposite.[10]

The "trial" refers to the finale of Howard's *Strange Empire.* After the Métis forces coalesced around Riel and Dumont, formed alliances with the Cree, and fought and won four battles with the Canadian army, they were forced to surrender to the army after the battle at Batoche, Saskatchewan. Dumont escaped. Riel could have, but he allowed himself to be captured. He was tried for treason in Regina and hanged on November 16, 1885.

The immensity of the ill will and the power of the victors led to continuing persecution of the Métis following the resistance of 1885. North of the forty-ninth parallel several disbanded regiments of Canadian militia, which had been formed during the rebellions, raided unchecked across the prairie provinces. The lives of the Métis were made miserable, and many people were forced across the border into the United States. The rogue militiamen received land warrants for their service to the country during the rebellion. The land came from the Métis they uprooted. A virtual bounty situation existed: for every Métis killed or dispossessed and driven away, a parcel of land became available. Oral tradition preserves the story, and disparate documents testify to this expropriation.[11]

To the south, in a pattern that lasted for years, United States troops annually went on maneuvers rounding up the "breeds" along the Rocky Mountain Front and central plains of Montana and shipping them back to Alberta and Saskatchewan.[12] In a summer expedition in 1896, Lieutenant John J. Pershing, then assigned to Fort Assiniboine, led a regiment of buffalo soldiers (African Americans in the regular army) from Helena to Browning, rounding up Cree and Métis; 525 Métis were deported to Canada as "international vagabonds."[13]

Because of the coordinated harassment the Métis suffered, it is no wonder so few of the present-day generation know anything of their cultural heritage. For their grandparents to speak about who they were and where they came from put them in mortal jeopardy.

From 1885 to the 1930s the Métis lived, essentially, as refugees. They had, and continue to have, no land base. There are two exceptions: those Métis who found refuge and home among their relatives—the Pembina Chippewa (Ojibway)—for whom a reservation was created at Turtle Mountain in North Dakota; and eight colonies of Métis who gained legal status and land grants from Alberta during the 1930s.[14]

Yet all the while, on both sides of the border, a silent organization, the legacy of the Métis movement, began to resurface. In 1932 Joseph Dion piloted the formation of the Métis Association of Alberta, an organization that served as a model for Métis identity throughout Canada. He, with James P. Brady and Malcolm Norris, led the Canadian Métis for thirty years.[15] From the 1930s until his death in 1968, Joseph Dussome headed a similar effort in Montana. In large part due to his work, the state of Montana granted limited recognition to the Métis as a tribe, which became the landless Little Shell band. Legislation concerning Montana Indians since the 1930s has also included the Little Shell band.

From the 1930s to the 1950s, the Métis felt the impact of the Great Depression and World War II. Many relied on various government welfare programs for survival. Increasing contacts with the white communities frequently reinforced the discrimination the Métis encountered, leading Métis leaders to seek new solutions to old problems.[16]

The next phase of movement for recognition took place during the 1960s and 1970s when the growing Métis population shifted to the cities. As the civil-rights movement gained momentum, social services became more humane, more community organizations offered support, and new options for education expanded opportunities. Once again it seemed possible that justice for the Métis would be realized. The Métis became politicized, reinforcing their sense of national identity.

In 1967 in Winnipeg at the Indian and Métis Conference of the Community Development, Health, and Welfare Planning Council, which was an annual meeting sponsored by the Manitoba provincial government, J. Angus Spence proposed to separate the Métis from the Indians. Spence was able to point out the different circumstances and conditions of each group as distinct in its relationship to the Canadian government. From that meeting emerged the Manitoba Métis Federation. Spence served as the first elected president. The Métis Nations of Saskatchewan, Alberta, Ontario, and the Northwest Territories and the Pacific Métis Association of British Columbia followed suit.[17]

In 1982 an amendment to the Canadian constitution gave the Métis aboriginal rights. On this hopeful note, the Métis National Council was created, with offices in Saskatoon and Ottawa. This organization, led by President Gerald Morin in 1994, was comprised of forty-five provincial representatives, with the provincial presidents forming the executive board. The fact remains, however, that except for the North Dakota Métis and some of the Alberta Métis, the Métis of Canada and the United States were still considered nonstatus Indians and had no recognized legal relationship with Ottawa or Washington.[18]

In the 1990s the process of Métis legal recognition changed. As individuals or families came forward to proclaim their legitimate heritage as Métis, they were aided immensely by the genealogical records of the Métis people, which were remarkably complete. The Métis National Council was preparing to adopt a national standard for enrollment, based upon the Manitoba code, that had self-identification and self-declaration as the main criteria. The Montana Little Shell band employed this method as well.

In Manitoba, there were twenty-five thousand enrolled Métis in 1994. The Métis council conducted a survey; the results suggested this number represented but one-fifth of the families who could legitimately be identified as Manitoba Métis. Gordon Ranville, assistant director of Tripartite Self-Government Negotiations for the Manitoba Métis Federation, believed that the Métis may make up about half of the Manitoba population and be the single largest cultural group in western Canada.[19]

In the United States from 1981 to 1994 the Little Shell band rolls swelled from eighteen hundred to more than four thousand. Given the sense that the Métis still live with a legacy of mistrust and wariness and were only just beginning to acknowledge their heritage publicly, the state's actual Métis population may also be five times its enrolled figure, giving an estimate of twenty thousand. In North Dakota the Turtle Mountain Chippewa (Ojibway) Métis had about twenty-five thousand enrolled members, also an undercount.

The Métis resurgence was happening throughout the Northern Plains in conversations across kitchen tables as well as across the international border. The Canadians were learning about their beginnings in Michigan, Wisconsin, and Minnesota. Montana's Métis realized that half of their people were refugees from the north and the troubles of 1885, while the other half came from the east at Turtle Mountain and Pembina and the troubles of 1870.

The Métis in the United States have always felt their roots were in Canada and that they have been cut off from them. The political boundary that separated the two nations divided the Métis, resulting in a great loss of culture, community, family, and economic and political viability. Debbie Swanson, chairperson of the Little Shell band, said, "We are a developing nation, and there are real benefits to formalizing relationships with Canadian Métis organizations."[20] The Canadian Métis seemed to have a stronger sense of cultural and national identity than those in the United States.

The strengthening sense of cultural and national identity in the 1980s produced a flurry of "Métis Days" celebrations in many communities on both sides of the border. Métis components were part of Folklorama in Winnipeg, the Festival du Voyageur in St. Boniface, the Joe Dussome Annual Celebration in Havre, Montana, St. Ann's Days at Turtle Mountain, and Back to Batoche Days in Saskatchewan. New Métis heritage and dance groups were springing up in places such as Edmonton, Winnipeg, and Belcourt, North Dakota. Additionally fiddle contests, both local and national, and cultural performances, such as the Smithsonian's Festival of American Folklife on the Mall in Washington, D.C., and the Festival International de Louisiane in Lafayette, Louisiana, introduced Métis customs to new audiences.

The visual and artifactual legacy of the Métis that has recently come to light presents tangible evidence of the blending of Indian and Euro-American cultures. The larger state and provincial museums of the Northern Plains have major holdings, understood for their significance and used in public programming. But in the county and local museums and historical societies, as well as in Métis homes, a treasure-trove of Métis materials exists that is yet to be comprehensively identified, documented, and protected. Community self-documentation programs and cultural inventories, such as have occurred in Choteau, Montana, funded by the Montana Committee for the Humanities and the Montana Arts Council, have provided the Métis with material to assist in perpetuating customs and traditions.[21]

New curriculum materials under development reinforce Métis cultural heritage and identity. Educational organizations like Pemmican Publications in Winnipeg, the Gabriel Dumont Institute of Métis Studies and Applied Research in Regina, the Turtle Mountain Tribal College in Belcourt, the American Indian Higher Education Consortium of tribal colleges, the Canadian tribal colleges, the College of Great Falls Institute for Métis Studies and new groups like the Métis Cultural Recovery Trust, based in Choteau, have given real promise that the Métis story will survive.

Strange Empire is the legacy of Joseph Kinsey Howard, a compassionate man and a champion of the oppressed. Born in Iowa in 1906, Howard moved with his family to the province of Alberta when he was five. While in Canada he learned of the Métis plight and disenfranchisement and of the poor conditions and struggle of mine workers with whom his father worked—knowledge that would influence him throughout his life.

In 1918 his father left the family, leaving Josephine Howard as a single parent supporting her son. She was a Christian Scientist healer, who imparted to her son such qualities as compassion, tolerance, thoughtfulness, a reverence for ideas, and the notion that individuals could both better themselves and better the world.[22] Howard began to learn about the conditions of the oppressed and feel them from the inside out.

Howard and his mother moved to Great Falls, Montana, in 1919. He had been writing since early childhood, producing stories and newspapers. When he finished high school he went to work for the *Great Falls Leader* as a reporter. At age twenty he became an editor, a position he held until 1944 when he left the newspaper. By 1947 Howard was a free-lance writer.

He published articles in *Harper's Magazine*, *The Progressive*, *The Nation*, *Yale Review*, *Pacific Spectator*, *The Rotarian*, *Mademoiselle*, and the *St. Louis Post-Dispatch*, among others, and was a regular book reviewer for the *New York Sunday Times Book Review* and the *Herald-Tribune Sunday Book Review*, a correspondent for *Time* and *Life*, and wrote fiction for the *Saturday Evening Post*, *Esquire*, and *Collier's*. He wrote the seminal text, *Montana: High, Wide and Handsome*, which is still referred to by scholars, *Montana Margins: A State Anthology*, and, of course, *Strange Empire*, as well as contributing to a couple of regional books. K. Ross Toole, the preeminent Montana historian and then director of the Montana Historical Society, was quoted in a newspaper article found in Howard's papers that *Strange Empire* "missed the Pulitzer Prize for narrative history by one vote" in 1953. All of this in forty-five years.

Howard's writing and his friendship with Bernard DeVoto brought him to the renowned Breadloaf Writers Conference at Middlebury College in Vermont in 1947 where he studied the novel with John Ciardi and taught workshops on regionalism with Robert Frost. Through his friendship with A. B. Guthrie he became a lecturer at the University of Kentucky. He published contemporaneously in journals with Wallace Stegner.

Howard, with Baker Brownell and Paul Meadows, codirected the landmark Montana Study through the University of Montana in 1944. It was an early model of the nationally acclaimed "Small Town Renaissance." He crisscrossed the state lecturing and leading rural communities through cultural inventories, fueling his imagination on the possibilities of community. He became a founding member of the Montana Institute of the Arts, which gave birth to the Montana Arts Council. He conceived of and directed one of the most promising cultural movements of the Pacific Northwest, the Northern Rocky Mountain Roundup of Regional Arts. Howard was the first chair of the writer's group,[23] which evolved into the University of Montana Writer's Program. After Howard's

Joseph Kinsey Howard, late 1940s

Frederic Morton, Howard, Robert Frost, and Arnold Lott (left to right), about 1947

Howard and A. B. Guthrie (second and third from left) with a group of friends in Montana, late 1940s

death in 1951, the post remained vacant until poet Richard Hugo came to Montana.

Over the years Howard wrote about Indians. Great Falls, Howard's home, was also the site of Hill 57, a Métis settlement. He knew of their dreadful living conditions and was appalled by the treatment all Indians received in Montana. His first work on Indian topics appeared in 1929. He followed with newspaper reports, articles on Indian education, editorials on traditional Indian community structure and its applicability to rural life, and fiction in national magazines. His short stories in *Saturday Evening Post* ("Sun Dance," 1945) and *Collier's* ("A Cree Could Say Goodbye," 1948) are extraordinary in their perceptiveness and sensitivity; the latter was written in a Métis voice.[24]

In 1930 Howard purchased a cabin in the canyon of the south

fork of the Teton River on the Rocky Mountain Front west of
Choteau. Living in the cabin, which had been built by the Métis
who sought refuge in the canyon after fleeing Canada in 1885, reinforced Howard's appreciation and respect for the people whom he
admired and for the relationships of people to land and environment.[25]

Howard was well into his work on the Métis by 1940. In that
year Cecil B. DeMille produced *Northwest Mounted Police,* starring
Gary Cooper. The film purported to be an epic on the settling of
the Canadian West. Central to the plot was the Métis resistance of
1885. It was actually a glory-nod to expansionist dreams and the
Canadian Pacific Railroad, fraught with inaccuracies and half-
truths. Howard wrote a scathing letter to DeMille, published in
the *New York Times Review of Books,* that said the film should have
been left on the cutting-room floor. He ended the piece by saying,

Mr. DeMille, I think you should have taken that floor up and buried
under it yourself, the writers of the script, and the Mountie and ex-
Mountie who appeared in the "credits" as your advisors; and this is really
too gentle a penalty for these last two, who connived in this ungallant
treatment of a courageous foe, fighting in a just cause, the only foe which
ever licked the pants off the redcoats![26]

In 1943, Howard wrote to his publisher, "The questions about
Louis Riel and his Métis 'nation' amuse me because that's my next
book and the one I've been wanting to write and have been gathering material for several years."[27] Howard was primed. A 1945 letter
to his literary agent in New York provides a deeper understanding:
"I have to write this book—have had to since [I] first heard of this
story when I lived in Canada (aged 5–13) and I'll write it whether
anybody prints it or not. I did the Montana book as an obligation
because it was sold in advance; but all the time I was doing it I
wanted to get to this other; still do and haven't really had the
time."[28] In 1947 Howard received a Guggenheim Fellowship,
which was renewed in 1948. These subsidies allowed Howard to
devote the time he needed to complete his book on Riel and the
Métis.

After fire damaged the cabin he had bought in 1930, Howard and several Métis friends salvaged materials and built a second cabin, which still stood in 1994. Howard wrote much of *Strange Empire* here.

Ripley Schemm Hugo, a childhood friend and neighbor of Howard's on the Rocky Mountain Front, remembered that "Joe had a special belt and riding shirt and jeans that were kind of a ceremony for him. . . . Joe had the same dark eyes, dark hair and high cheekbones as the Métis. If it gives a man substance to have an image of himself and his relationship to the past, which I think Joe felt with the Métis, then that's very important."[29]

Beyond the fascinating history of the Métis remains the story and the lessons to be learned. These are found in the issues the book addresses: the ancient and destructive violence of greed, racism, sexism, and oppression. The scholarly discourse, as well as the common notion of Métisness, had been preponderately paternal and Euro-American in character.[30] The paternal side, at first glance, appears more obvious.

In the early 1980s, new research provided exceptional understanding of and insights into Indian-white relations. Sylvia Van Kirk, Jennifer S. H. Brown, and Jacqueline Peterson shed brilliant light on the maternal and Indian side of the blending in their essays and books on the Métis. These authors showed that the "things" of Métis life were Euro-American, but the "way" of things was Indian, thereby enhancing the understanding of the formal and informal workings of Métis social structure.[31] New doors of cross-cultural appreciation were opened.

Another area awaiting further study is the link between the British and the French on paternal sides of Métis who shared a Celtic heritage. The French fur trade workers were predominantly from Brittany and Normandy, the Celtic provinces of France. This Celtic nature superseded politics, religion, and race as a cohesive bond of custom and world view, tribal and clannish in form. Exploring this area might lead to a better understanding of the Fenian and Irish Republican Army involvement in what has been traditionally thought to be a French Catholic movement. Perhaps the Métis and Irish are not so very different, even today.

The perspective from the 1990s, with increased scholarly attention and new information, allows us to draw connections and understand a little more clearly this story. Empathetic as even Howard was to the Métis plight and as acute his comprehension of American history, by present-day standards his use of certain language as well as bias in some of his conclusions can be seen as bound by the limitations of his time and place.

Strange Empire ends with Riel's death. That moment, when the gallows rope sprung taut on a dream, marked the end of what might be called the first half of the Métis *l'histoire*. For some readers the core of the story is in the ongoing debate of whether or not schoolteacher, politician, prophet Louis "David" Riel was crazy. But the real questions are: shall a people be recognized, or not; is their claim crazy, or not; are mixed-blood people legitimate, or not. It is, in the end, a question of human rights. The claim of the legitimacy of the Métis movement rests on this issue.

For Howard's times schizophrenia was probably an accurate diagnosis of Riel's condition. In 1990s medical terms, Riel had a bipolar disorder and was manic depressive. But a cross-cultural understanding of the same information leads to a different conclusion. Perhaps he suffered because nobody understood him, that is to say, except all the Métis. Riel made perfect sense to them. The cross-cultural communication problem—present in 1870 and 1885—remains.

Riel had a vision, a vision of a new North America, the coming together of peoples and the end of racial purity as the denominator of human worth. Historically, in western culture, lineage had direct relationship to economic and social status. Property passed along "legitimate" lines. The property at the heart of the conflict among the Euro-Americans, the Métis, and the Indian nations was the whole Northwest.

That Riel evolved from a political leader into a spiritual one and prophesied a truly new North American native religion, blending the best of both worlds, was the last straw for the Euro-Americans and more than the Catholic church could bear. The church that Riel loved so much—and which was the basis for much of his inspiration—in the end betrayed him and his people. The ecclesiastical hierarchy chose treachery and gave up its flock to the redcoats in 1885, keeping their Métis souls Christian and pure, rather than allowing them to live with what the church thought was a mongrel form of the Catholicism. For society to make the ecclesiastical shift is to recognize and give cultural equity to the Indian side of spiritualism that was operative—and is still very much alive—side by side with the intense Catholicism of the Métis.

Howard was sure that if the virtues of Indian life were understood it would lessen the racial prejudice evident in our society. In a piece on Indian education he wrote: "Dignity and respect—they are today as they have always been, the primary goals of education in the Indian way."[32] Howard believed this applied equally to all peoples. He learned this from his mother, from the Indians, and from Riel.

Howard originally wrote this book as a novel that he called *Falcon's Song*.[33] The title refers to a chanson that was written to commemorate the Battle of Seven Oaks in 1816 where the Métis first fully conceived of themselves as a true and distinct people. In this case the truth of the telling far exceeded whatever fictional account Howard could imagine. The book needed to be nonfiction to give it the credibility it deserved. But Howard required that sense of emotion and passion that comes with the novel. In a way, his first intentions have come to pass. *Strange Empire* is, perhaps, best understood and appreciated as historically true storytelling. Howard subtitled his book a "narrative" because he knew that people learn by listening to stories.

NICHOLAS C. P. VROOMAN
Director
Institute for Métis Studies
College of Great Falls, Montana

The author wishes to thank Scott Mainwaring for editorial consultation; Bill Borneman and Rob Smith for the conversation; Tom Tracy for the Celtic connection; Gordon Ranville and Audreen Hourie of the Manitoba Métis Federation for Canadian insights; Debbie Swanson for faith in the Little Shell; all the Turtle Mountain folks; the Baudrillard Study Group, Helena; Montana

Historical Society staff; Sarah and Mary, the "Metchif Queens," Great Falls; Ron Haverlandt; the College of Great Falls; the Choteau Métis Cultural Recovery Trust; Ev Albers, North Dakota Humanities Council; Montana Committee for the Humanities; Sally Rubinstein for the "good work"; and, especially, White Corn Woman, Little Eagle, Eagle Heart, Braids, and the Thirsty Dancers.

1. Jacqueline Peterson, telephone interview by author, Apr. 5, 1994.

2. For a discussion of "Métis," see Jacqueline Peterson and Jennifer S. H. Brown, eds., *The New Peoples: On Being and Becoming Métis in North America* (Winnipeg: University of Manitoba Press, 1985), 4–6.

3. Rhoda R. Gilman, Carolyn Gilman, and Deborah M. Stultz, *The Red River Trails: Oxcart Routes Between St. Paul and the Selkirk Settlement, 1820–1870* (St. Paul: Minnesota Historical Society, 1979), 5.

4. Verne Dusenberry, "Waiting for a Day That Never Comes: The Tragic Story of the Dispossessed Metis of Montana," *Montana, The Magazine of Western History* 8, no. 2 (Spring 1958): 26–39; Julia D. Harrison, *Metis: People between Two Worlds* (Vancouver: Glenbow-Alberta Institute, 1985), 21, 26–32.

5. Sylvia Van Kirk, *Many Tender Ties: Women in Fur-Trade Society, 1670–1870* (Norman: University of Oklahoma Press, 1980), 179.

6. Jennifer S. H. Brown, *Strangers in Blood: Fur Trade Company Families in Indian Country* (Vancouver: University of British Columbia Press, 1980), 150–52.

7. Van Kirk, *Many Tender Ties*, 240–42.

8. Isabell Lewis Tabor, *Great Falls Yesterday, Comprising a Collection of Biographies and Reminiscences of Early Settlers* (Helena: Montana Historical Society Library, [1939?]).

9. Thomas Flanagan, "Louis Riel and the Dispersion of the American Métis," *Minnesota History* 49 (Spring 1985): 183–90.

10. Joseph Kinsey Howard to Helen King, Apr. 14, 1951, Joseph Kinsey Howard Papers, Montana Historical Society Archives, Helena.

11. Gordon Ranville, assistant director of Tripartite Self-Government Negotiations, Manitoba Métis Federation, interview with author, Mar. 24, 1994. The author is grateful to Audreen Hourie, provincial education coordinator for the Manitoba Métis Federation, for providing information from the Public Archives of Canada, Record Group 15, about land scrip issued to the militia for its service.

12. Dusenberry, "Waiting for a Day," 31–35.

13. Donald Smythe, "John J. Pershing at Fort Assiniboine," *Montana, The Magazine of Western History* 18, no. 1 (Jan. 1968): 20–22. The Métis were called Cree in the official records.

14. Joe Sawchuk, Patricia Sawchuk, and Theresa Ferguson, *Metis Land Rights in Alberta: A Political History* (Edmonton: Métis Association of Alberta, 1981), 187–88.

15. Harrison, *Metis,* 96–97; Sawchuk, Sawchuk, and Ferguson, *Metis Land Rights,* 188.

16. Harrison, *Metis,* 92–119.

17. Ranville interview, MAR. 24, 1994; Harrison, *Metis,* 134.

18. Harrison, *Metis,* 143–44; Sawchuk, Sawchuk, and Ferguson, *Metis Land Rights,* 8–9.

19. Ranville interview, Mar. 24, 1994.

20. Debbie Swanson, Havre, Mont., interview by author, Mar. 24, 1994.

21. For more on exhibitions on the Métis, see Bill Thackeray, ed., *The Métis Centennial Celebration* (Lewistown, Mont.: Métis Centennial Celebration Committee, 1979), Carolyn Gilman, *Where Two Worlds Meet: The Great Lakes Fur Trade* (St. Paul: Minnesota Historical Society Press, 1982), Turtle Mountain Indian Reservation, *St. Ann's Centennial: 100 Years of Faith* (Belcourt, N.Dak., 1985), and *Metis: A Glenbow Museum Exhibition/Une exposition du Glenbow Museum* (Calgary, Alta.: Glenbow Museum, 1985). Permanent exhibits have been installed at the Gray Nuns Museum, St. Boniface, Man.; State Historical Society of North Dakota, Bismarck; Montana Historical Society, Helena; Turtle Mountain Chippewa Heritage Center, Belcourt, N.Dak.; and Old Trail Museum, Choteau, Mont.

22. Jyl Hoyt, "Montana Writer Joseph Kinsey Howard: Crusader for the Worker, Land, Indian and Community," Master's thesis, University of Montana, Missoula, 1988, p. 12; Alice Gleason, Choteau, Mont., interview with author, Mar. 7, 1994; Howard Papers.

23. Paul Grieder, "Joseph Kinsey Howard: In Memorium," *Quarterly Bulletin of the Montana Institute of the Arts* (October 1951), copy in Howard Papers.

24. Norman A. Fox, "Joseph Kinsey Howard: Writer," *Montana, The Magazine of Western History* 2, no. 2 (Apr. 1952): 42.

25. Gleason interview, Mar. 7, 1994.

26. Howard to Cecil B. DeMille, undated, Howard Papers.

27. Roberta W. Yerkes, "The Last Rebellion," in *The Freeman,* Jan. 26, 1953, copy in Howard Papers.

28. Howard to Bernice Baumgarten, 1945, Howard Papers.

29. Hoyt, "Montana Writer Joseph Kinsey Howard," p. 15.

30. For an overview of Métis history, see Marcel Giraud, *The Métis in the Canadian West,* trans G. Woodcock, 2 vols. (Edmonton: University of Alberta Press, 1986), and George F. Stanley, *The Birth of Western Canada: A History of the Riel Rebellions,* 2d ed. (Toronto: University of Toronto Press, 1960).

31. Van Kirk, *Many Tender Ties;* Brown, *Strangers in Blood;* Peterson and Brown, eds., *The New Peoples.*

32. Hoyt, "Montana Writer Joseph Kinsey Howard," p. 136.

33. Fox, "Howard," 42–44. For a list of Howard's writings, see Bessie Sestak, comp., "Joseph Kinsey Howard Bibliography," *Montana, The Magazine of Western History* 2, no. 2 (Apr. 1952): 44–47.

STRANGE
EMPIRE

Joseph Kinsey Howard

JOSEPH KINSEY HOWARD died at Choteau, Montana, August 25, 1951, at the age of forty-five. With his death the West lost one of its few writers of the first rank and one of its most valuable citizens. The national letters knew him as the author of the most brilliant interpretation of the contemporary West anyone has written, *Montana: High, Wide, and Handsome. Strange Empire,* which he had just finished when he died, reveals him as a brilliant historian.

Both books are rooted in his love of the Western people and their country. He had elected to stay in the West, as most writers who are born there do not. For any writer the decision means a constant expenditure of energy resisting the forces which have transformed the West from an intensely individualistic society to one that puts a survival value on conformity, from the most cosmopolitan of American sections to one parochially assertive of its orthodoxies. For Joe Howard, who was born a fighter, an instinctive member of minorities, and a champion of the exploited and the oppressed, it meant a tumultuous and frequently bitter life. There would be no point in recalling here the details of the career that led the novelist A. B. Guthrie, Jr., to say of him when he died, "We have lost our conscience." Or in recalling details of the vigilantism with which a society inimical to the critical spirit fought back. Enough that he made himself heard, that castes and causes which had mercilessly assailed him came to solicit his support, that he won through to a position of acknowledged leadership and power. When *Montana: High, Wide, and Handsome* was published in 1943, you could buy it in some places in Montana only by such a back-room transaction as was required some years ago to buy a good novel in Boston. By the time its author died eight years later he came closer to being the spokesman of the West than any other writer has ever been. Indeed few writers of our time have so deeply or so visibly stamped their impression on their own place.

Thus summarized, it seems a triumphant career but Joe Howard had no sense of triumph: he had scars. His friends were aware of a deep melancholy in him, a deep loneliness, and he died a very tired man. American literature at large has no concern with the private pain in which books are forged, and cannot be troubled by the suspicion and contempt with which the West surrounds the practice of letters, so long as fine books come of it. There should be some concern, however, when a distinguished writer dies just as his talent reaches full maturity.

But that talent achieved full expression in *Strange Empire*. When Mr. Howard died he had finished revising the manuscript but had not begun to prepare it for the press. To do so has been my privilege as his friend and I must now render account. I have done nothing important enough to be called editing and I may fairly claim that what I have done is in accordance with his intent. Of the last month of his life I spent the first three weeks with him in Montana. I read much of the manuscript then and we spent a good many hours discussing it, as indeed we had done at intervals for some years.

It is on my responsibility that the book appears without notes. Mr. Howard intended to equip it with the usual citation of sources and the usual tangential amplification of remarks. Rosalea and Norman Fox, friends of his who have acted as his literary executors, found in his papers a mass of material which had been segregated for that purpose but he had not formulated any notes from it. There is no way of determining how much of it he intended to use, which sources he considered decisive, or what scholarly material he would have put in notes. No one can satisfactorily annotate someone else's book, in fact, and this one will not suffer through omitting one of the conventions. The text carries conviction: clearly the writer has mastered his subject, clearly he respects and observes the canons of historical writing, clearly he does not write without warranty and sanction. His authority is self-evident and anyone who wants to pursue any subject farther than the text carries it can get direction from the bibliography, which was compiled by Mrs. Fox.

The maps were drawn to my specifications. I was acting on my own knowledge of the terrain and on what I took to be Mr. Howard's intention, as shown by maps which he had marked and sketches which he had drawn. For the rest, my job has been to check the manuscript against a detailed report by his publisher's editor. She is Mrs. Helen King. She has done an enormous amount of work on this book, with touching devotion to a dead man's integrity as a writer. That my work on it would have been impossible without her does not matter, but I want formally to thank her on behalf of Joe Howard. I have cut out an occasional sentence, perhaps twenty all told. Following the editor's suggestions, I have arranged the opening paragraphs of three chapters in a different order. For another chapter I have written an opening page. And I have done what I would want a friend to do for me in the circumstances: I have remedied some awkward or obscure sentences which Mr. Howard would certainly have noticed and remedied if he had lived to read his manuscript again.

Nothing else needed to be done: it was the manuscript of a completed book. I do not need to remark that it is a brilliant and enlightening book. The subject that Mr. Howard found so congenial to his talent has been strangely neglected by historians and the momentous events it chronicles have, to an astonishing degree, faded from memory. Those events helped to determine the fate of the Plains Indians, especially in the United States. They solidified the separateness of Catholic Quebec in Canada, left their impress on Canadian society, and gave Canadian politics an alignment which still in part exists and in which their energy is still at work almost unrecognized. But, outside Manitoba and Saskatchewan, there is little public awareness of them in Canada and they have been but little written about in the twentieth century. A Canadian reader who knows about them only through such general histories as, say, Lower's or Morton's will have his conception of their importance radically altered by these pages. Even if he knows the small handful of modern treatises on the Métis, most of them in French and among them so far as I know only two historical studies of the rebellions, he will find here new matter and a new perception that will require him to change his ideas. In particular, he will be able for the first time to perceive their international importance. In the United States, Louis Riel, the Métis, and the events narrated here have not come to the attention of the general reader at all: they are barely within the awareness of historians. None of them are mentioned in the standard treatises on frontier and Western history or in the *Dictionary of American History*. Even in the work of monographers and Western antiquarians they are mentioned only incidentally, usually in relation to the Selkirk colony. This is the first book in English that describes the origin of the Métis, that unique people of mixed white and red blood, and there is only one work in French that describes it. It is the first book that traces in any detail the development of the great annual buffalo hunt which was the center of Métis life or that deals more than perfunctorily with the fascinating lore of the Red River cart. And it is the first book that has ever told for American readers the story of the two Métis rebellions that were so dramatic a menace to Canadian union and lighted such a strange hope of American expansion in Canadian territory. Before Mr. Howard no one has explored the possibilities of the primitive state that Louis Riel envisioned or has appraised the historical forces that created and then destroyed his vision.

Strange Empire, then, fills an important and surprising gap. The story it tells was part of the drama of American expansion and utilized some of its central energies. None were nearer the core of expansion than those which created the possibility I have already mentioned, that Canada might have lost her western and northwestern provinces and the United States might have gained them. That possibility was indeed slight, but its social and political implications were so explosive that to call them revolutionary falls short of the truth. Moreover, the Métis country, the Great Plains west of the Red River, is the one area of considerable extent where the remarkably coherent geographical unit that the United States occupies loses its sharpness and the unity becomes indeterminate. Between the Red River and the Rocky Mountains the forty-ninth parallel is much more nearly an arbitrary boundary than it is elsewhere. The Métis living on both sides of it crossed it with as little awareness of the change in sovereignties as they had of the earlier divergence in historical development that imposed it as a dividing line. Mr. Howard's is the first study of their dual citizenship, out of which they hoped to forge autonomy, and the first detailed examination of the geographical continuum as it affected history. The problem must be understood as posed by the approach of the agricultural frontier toward the Northwest Territories of Canada. If it had ever been forced to an issue, the wheat growers of Dakota Territory would have done the forcing and such Canadian support as they might have got, apart from the Métis, would have come from the wheat growers of

Manitoba and Saskatchewan. But whatever either of them might have done would have been previously conditioned by the fate of the Métis and the Indians. That tragic destiny is the subject of *Strange Empire*.*

I must point out, too, that *Strange Empire* belongs to a small group of studies that refuse to treat North American history as at best a dichotomy. The experience it deals with is common to Americans and Canadians and Mr. Howard has treated it as indivisible. In spite of John B. Brebner's brilliant work, this approach has been but little used, though it is certain to increase both nations' understanding of themselves and of each other.

But the great importance of the book is that it is a history of Indians, or rather of American primitives, and so enlarges a category so small it might almost be said not to exist. Most American history has been written as if history were a function solely of white culture—in spite of the fact that till well

* I venture to refer the reader to my discussion of the geographical problem in Chapter X of *The Course of Empire*. Mr. Howard confines his treatment of the possibilities to a neutral statement. Privately he believed that the forces making for separation were strong and would have grown stronger, and that it was the building of the Canadian Pacific that held the Northwest Territories for Canada. I cannot follow him, believing that the possibility had been extinguished before the Métis rebellions occurred. The westward expansion of Canada and the United States moved on parallel lines. As I see it, each nation had developed centripetal social energies of its own which made the forty-ninth parallel an inevitable compromise, rationalizing as it does a slight but tangible climatic and topographical distinctness. American expansion to Oregon was agricultural; Canadian expansion was a function of the fur trade. The difference in economic interest led both societies to cohere along the axes of their respective routes to the Rocky Mountains and the Pacific. Long before 1880 they had developed separate reflexes of growth, organic and very hard to change. Without the Canadian Pacific the Territories would have remained financially subject to St. Paul, but I cannot see financial dependence as a leverage sufficiently powerful to detach them from their society. It is not that war would have followed any formidable effort by either Canadians or Americans to separate them from Canada; rather, only a war could create the kind of disorganization that would have made any such effort formidable.

into the nineteenth century the Indians were one of the principal determinants of historical events. Those of us who work in frontier history—which begins at the tidal beaches and when the sixteenth century begins—are repeatedly nonplused to discover how little has been done for us in regard to the one force bearing on our field that was active everywhere. Disregarding Parkman's great example, American historians have made shockingly little effort to understand the life, the societies, the cultures, the thinking, and the feeling of Indians, and disastrously little effort to understand how all these affected white men and their societies.

In this book Mr. Howard writes the history of Indians and Métis organically—in three dimensions, in complete integration with history at large. This has required him to express the mind and personality of his primitives. No doubt his success is due to his instinctive championship of the exploited and his instinctive identification with the defeated. On page after page he is not a sympathetic white man depicting the Métis and the Crees: he has become a Métis or a Cree. Only once, I think, does his fervor take him a millimeter beyond the demonstrable. On modern reservations, he had seen fearful end products of the original injustices. So when he becomes a Cree and feels his feet shuffling in the purification dance and hears the voices in the council he succumbs to the vision of a finer justice which an independent primitive society north of the border would have made possible—and he believes that the primitives had a better chance of establishing it than historically they did.

But to find in his sympathy for the dispossessed an explanation of his achievement cannot dull one's realization of how remarkable an achievement it is. As nearly as in the modern world anyone is ever likely to come to it, here are the structure, the texture, the pattern, the pulse and informing spirit of primitive thought. Here are primitive emotion and primitive dream. Here is the American primitive, his par-

ticipation as a person and a society in the events of history,
and his world reaching its final collapse. In the whole expanse
of American historiography, there is very little writing about
the Indians of quality comparable with this. In regard to
the Plains tribes, which brought Indian society to its most
formidable power, there is nothing comparable: *Strange Empire* is unique, the best that anyone has written.

Finally, the book is very fine art. The hope of a small
company of writers is to bring history out of the seminar
and restore it to the living room, where it was once acknowledged to belong. Sacrificing none of the methods or the results of scholarship, they accept the heavy additional obligation of transforming scholarship into literature. That is what
happens here. Everything in *Strange Empire* conforms absolutely to the discipline of fact but an equally disciplined
historical imagination is at work, giving life to facts that
would be dead without it and the craftsmanship put at its
service. This is a drama of reality, not fantasy, of real men,
not imagined ones, but the reader is led to participate in it as
he might in the fictitious drama of the theater—to the end
that he may understand the deeds and the motives of men at
a decisive hour. Tense as narrative, very moving as tragedy,
it illuminates a part of the strange path that the people of
North America have traveled as they came to be what they
are. It increases understanding, it explains part of our heritage, and so it adds to our heritage. I am content to let those
words define the art of history.

                                              BERNARD DEVOTO

One Sure
and Certain Loyalty

THIS book was conceived more than thirty years ago in the "Cops and Robbers" play of a group of boys on the prairie of Western Canada. It was then that I first learned of the incidents which are the bare bones of this narrative.

A boy could comprehend the drama of those incidents. They were incidents of war, and boys play at war because they recognize in it, by unerring instinct, the most dramatic of human experiences. A philosopher has commented that, much as we hate to admit it, war gives "a sudden edged preciousness to values we had taken for granted, like light when night is falling, or conversation with a friend one knows is doomed to die." * I could understand that.

This war game was not concerned with the Kaiser and the conflict which was then raging far away in France. That struggle involved inconceivable masses of men and mysterious mechanical behemoths called tanks, and guns so big that they

---

* Irwin Edman, *Candle in the Dark.*

11

had to be moved about on railroad tracks. And poison gas. Such a war was beyond my comprehension and its aims were obscure—though, at twelve, I already was being drilled daily in school to take my place in that war, and went home with my arms aching from the weight of a Snider rifle as big as I was. Already men were returning from Ypres. They were not cleanly wounded by bullet or bayonet: they staggered, strangling, against the false fronts on Main Street and slumped there coughing their lungs out; they grew thinner and grayer every day until they disappeared.

One of these men told me that at Ypres the fabled "Princess Pats" who had looked so valiant, so invincible when the troop trains came through, had whimpered and choked and screamed when the gas got them, had sought desperately to survive by masking their faces with handkerchiefs soaked in their own urine. The story made me ill. No; surely not that war. It did not lend itself to boys' games.

But there was this other, this older war. It had been here —in the dry coulees, beyond that next innocent hummock, in the sparse groves of willow and poplar. This could be hand-to-hand with wooden gun and rubber knife. The prize of victory was familiar: the grass and the water and the cardboard cut-out peaks against the wide Western horizon where the snow lay all year, whence came the water. It was possible to love such a war, and hate another one.

Of course even in that older, simpler war there had been elements I could not begin to understand until I approached middle age. But meanwhile it was easy to recruit troops among my playmates for the game: we did not need to be concerned about the martyrdom of races, or power politics, or Manifest Destiny, to scrabble furiously in the dusty hardpan of the prairie and hollow out a rifle pit.

Best of all was the scouting, belly-flat in the crisp yellow grass with cap pistol in hand, worming forward inch by inch. One had to be careful, with one's eyes on the enemy position in that cave on the hillside, to avoid the buffalo chips (an identification that would have startled the placid milk cows who left them there) which often weren't as dry as they looked; and sometimes one was not careful enough. Hazard of war.

Choosing up sides was more difficult, but this usually was facilitated when, as the only fortunate owner of a "Mountie suit" in the whole town, I yielded the police uniform with appropriate show of reluctance to someone else. Such sacrifice inspired admiration and won me in return an adequate quota of warriors for my side, the "enemy" side. The truth, which I never dared to reveal, was that in this contest I was ashamed of the red coat; I alone was willing (worse, I was even eager) to adopt the role of traitor. No one else wanted to assume, even in play, the part of a member of the minority. That was the side that couldn't ever win, made up of people who—shamefully, somehow—weren't even white.

Decades later I was to find significance in these old choices. I had been the only "foreigner" among the participants in the game: an American, with a skeptical attitude toward our approved Canadian history texts. In the years which followed I learned that I had not been the first citizen of the United States to identify himself with the Dominion's enemies on the issues with which we had played at war. I discovered Manifest Destiny on the Northwestern frontier and read, with a thrill of recognition, about the Yankee dream: a State of Minnesota, or Territories of Dakota and Montana, reaching from the Great Lakes and the Missouri River to Alaska.

Moreover, I came to understand that this War for the West which had provided us with such fascinating afterschool adventures had been much more than a series of isolated skirmishes between strange "primitive" colored peoples and the "civilized" whites—that it had been, in fact, one of the most dramatic and most tragic social struggles in the history of the world. I grew up; I met and lived among the "primitives" who had lost the war; I discovered that they had a culture, too, and that the whites had not been quite as "civilized" as they pretended.

This book is about the period of transition in the North American West—Red River to the Rockies, in Canada and the United States. Some of the incidents with which it deals are familiar, others have been almost forgotten; a few, I think, have never before been put into a book. But that does not matter much; what does matter—at least to me—is that incidents heretofore reported as isolated, and perhaps of only local or regional significance or no significance at all, can be shown to have been related to each other and to the whole: the War for the West.

I believe it also can be shown that the West was a social and economic entity; that this war, though it took differing forms, raged on both sides of that "imaginary line," the forty-ninth parallel, at the same time; that the boundary, in fact, made very little sense to anybody on either side of it, and its elimination motivated some who were caught up in the bigger struggle of native against invader.

Philippe Régis de Trobriand, one of the most brilliant of the many intellectuals who were drawn to the far Western frontier, noted in his journal in 1867, "The destiny of the white race in America is to destroy the red race." Yet the native cause was not quite so hopeless as our histories have led us to believe. There were times when Manifest Destiny slid off the trail and bogged down. There were times when the defenders, given a little more skill, could have wrested a better bargain from white civilization.

This book tells of some of those lost opportunities. One arose in what is now Winnipeg, Manitoba, in 1870; few Americans have ever heard of the incident, but as a result of it the Sioux who annihilated Custer's command six years later could only count on refuge, instead of allies, across the international boundary just north of their Montana battlefield. The Sioux, in the treaty of 1868, had been the only enemy to wring from the United States an admission of defeat in war up to that time, and eight years later they won again. Had there been a native state north of the forty-ninth parallel —and there very nearly was—instead of a detachment of Northwest Mounted Police, the rested and reinforced Sioux would have come back.

American and Canadian military commanders knew that their task of subjugating or destroying the primitive peoples of the West would be hopeless, at least for many years, if the native races should unite. This idea came to Sitting Bull— too late; it came still later to the leaders of another but related people in Canada. Had there been time for them to act upon it there might have been independent, semiprimitive tribal societies in North America such as still exist on other continents as near neighbors to modern states.

Most of the crucial events on both sides of the boundary occurred within a span of fifteen years after 1870. It was a tortured time—a time of war, famine, disease, moral dissolution. It was a time when smallpox, whiskey, prostitution and the slaughter of buffalo did more to win an empire than bullets could; and perhaps the bullets could never have done it alone.

The native defenders of the West in this period were for the most part Sioux, Cree and Blackfeet Indians and their "cousins," the Métis or "half-breeds." Their "empire" was the great mid-continent buffalo range now designated the Northern Great Plains; as the Indians doggedly retreated from it, the Métis and whites moved in. But the Métis inherited all of the Indians' problems while the whites gained strength and cunning. The Métis therefore were the worst sufferers, and this book concerns itself chiefly with their nation because their tragedy climaxed and epitomized the whole struggle of red man, or brown, against white.

That nation evolved from what had gone before; like

many others it was conceived quickly and crudely, in a sudden urgency of history; it was born of violence and despair in the hearts of the wordless people, and reared to brief glory in the souls of two great men.

One of these men, perhaps against his conscious will, became a dictator, and there is interest in the study of dichotomy in the human soul—for this dictator, who adored God and feared and hated bloodshed, defied his priests to lead the people he loved into a suicidal crusade. It was said, of course, that he was mad; but mad or sane he grew to full stature as protagonist and symbol, personification, voice, and brain of a doomed race. He was supremely conscious of his historic role.

The comrade who shared his leadership was not concerned about God's justice or racial destiny or his own standing with posterity; he simply liked to fight. He was a practical man harnessed to an idealist and sometimes pulling hard against the traces. In this contest the practical man, for once, lost. But the war was lost, too.

When the Métis sought to achieve nationhood in the strange empire of the West, white men called it treason, the greatest of crimes.

More men went to trial for treason after World War II than ever before in history, and some were condemned for betrayal of their national allegiance on a law written in the Middle Ages, the same law that doomed the central figure in this book. Others died for an offense new to jurisprudence, for which a word had to be coined—*genocide*, destruction of a race, treason against the human spirit. The victors defined the crime, but victors and vanquished both knew that in the future there might be other trials, other culprits, and other judges.

The crime of genocide is older than its name, older than the judicial retribution now visited upon its practitioners.

The races with which we are concerned in this book were martyred in the name of Manifest Destiny or Canada First or an Anglo-Saxon God. There were no gas chambers then, but there was malevolent intention; and there were guns and hunger, smallpox and syphilis. And "backward" peoples, then as now, could be used as puppets in the power politics of dynamic "civilized" states.

Today, everywhere on earth, skilled secret police (and less skilled amateur "patriots") incessantly seek out the traitor, for loyalty now is a tenuous thing and one man's treason is another's sanctification. Treason can defeat the atomic bomb, and it is cheaper because men won over by ideas often do not have to be paid. But once, on our continent, treason was unable to defeat a crude machine gun and a half-finished railroad.

Discovery of the ultimate weapon, which can upset the elemental balance of the universe, has brought the demand that the world abandon, overnight, centuries-old concepts of national sovereignty. Lest civilization itself perish, old loyalties must be forsworn and new allegiances embraced. It is a momentous decision, but people have confronted it before. Those with whom this book deals clung to the old loyalties, defied science and the machine—and perished. Of course they were an illiterate people, primitive and unstable, not even white. And their spokesman and symbol, who believed the old values to be good, became thereby a traitor.

He died on the gallows and his nation died with him—his nation, and the dream of a strange empire in the West. The ideas from which the dream evolved live on among the remnants of his people, but they live feebly because the race is weak and dispersed and despised. The official histories read by other people have no room for them. Civilized man has achieved so much; there is no place for the dreams of a people who had no written literature, whose only art was that which adorned their garments or their homes, who built no cities, devised no economic theories. History cannot avoid, however, a grudging acknowledgment that this odd nation could produce men with a bent for politics and war, and that one or two of them may even have been geniuses in those fields.

But history is impatient with intangibles: the mystic meaning of a shadow pattern on a sacred butte, or that of the order of wild geese in flight. It cannot pause to describe the roar of the black wind, the Plains chinook, which is a welcome sound; or the silence of the white cold, which is terrible. It cannot bother to reflect upon why some men, primitive and civilized alike, should believe that in personal contest or communion with the elemental fury of a blizzard, the loneliness of the prairie or the aloof majesty of an unclimbed mountain, they may chance upon the essential core of truth and meaning of life, revealed to them in an instant of intuitive experience as a reward for superhuman effort.

Some incidents in this book may seem, to some readers, incredible; some acts may appear foolhardy rather than heroic. It is hard to believe, for instance, that the leaders of a people in the midst of a war and desperately beset could solemnly assemble to discuss the purposes of God and the reasonableness of eternal damnation. But such incidents occurred, whatever may be the modern judgment upon them. Even the words spoken by the people in this book are taken from the record: from contemporary accounts, official documents, or (in a few instances) from interviews with those who heard them spoken. There is no interpolated fictional dialogue.

As for the incidents, the reader must be persuaded that people can do strange things when, unlike himself, they have not yet established their right to pride in their race, their religion, or their "nationality"; when their skins are neither light nor dark but—most outlandish of all—just in between; when a way of life that has worked for generations suddenly will not work at all, through no fault of theirs; when all their dreams of things as they used to be and perhaps could be again are fashioned into passionate speech by a man on horseback, his upthrust hand grasping a cross.

People like that have one sure and certain loyalty. It is place. It may be as tiny as a burial ground where the bones of their forefathers rest; it may be half a continent whose landmarks bear the names their progenitors bestowed. Acre or empire, they will fight for it until the spirit is dead.

This is the story of such a place and why it was worth fighting for. Thirty years ago the tale was almost unbelievably romantic, losing thereby none of its attraction for an imaginative boy. Now it is less romantic, for the boy has grown up; there are no more games after school. Perhaps the imagination has atrophied, or perhaps romance cannot withstand the search for truth in political conflict. Romantic or not, the story still may be unbelievable. Yet this is the way it seems to have happened.

JOSEPH KINSEY HOWARD

Great Falls, Montana

PART ONE

Falcon's Song

Heart of a Continent

CHAPTER I

Heart of a Continent

GREAT LONE LAND

FROM the Red River of the North to the Rockies, winter ruled. In the winter the *chepuyuk,* the ghost dancers of the aurora, made a shuddering and swishing sound like that made by a throwing-stick when the boys played games on a windy day. It was customary for a man to shoot a few arrows toward the *chepuyuk* before closing the tipi flap for the night, to persuade them to keep their distance.

After a while the dancers gracefully withdrew and the strange sky-drumming which was the pulse of the universe grew faint. Then there was a little pause, and then came the wind. It was elemental force, homeless and heartless, rolling down from the far places, from the ice of Keewatin where the *chepuyuk* dwelt. The voice of *Kichemanito* was in it, reminding the man who had just knotted the tipi flap of his insignificance and his weakness. He shot off arrows to prove himself a man, a living thing and worthy of respect as were all living things (though no worthier than the living stone, or bird, or bison); but he knew always that nothing so puny

as he could intimidate the mighty spirits he had been permitted to glimpse briefly as they trod their endless, stately
measures into infinity.

Thus it was throughout the life of this man living in the
buffalo-skin lodge which he had learned to design so that it
would fend off the icy surf of the wind. First the drumming,
then a little rest while the gods gathered their strength, then
the gale; and finally the night swept clean. Then the man
could put aside the tent flap and come outside to look, to
stand erect but humble in a frozen instant of endless time,
taking peace to himself from the sudden quiet, seeing the
fixed glitter in the limitless sea of snow, seeing the sky full
of stars and mystery come down over the smoke hole of his
lodge.

The man, a Cree Indian, lived in the heart of the North
American continent, the great basin of the Red River of the
North. It extends from the river's source in south-central
Minnesota, near the South Dakota border, north 545 miles
to Lake Winnipeg. The river valley, once the bed of glacial
Lake Agassiz, is ten to a hundred miles wide. At its western
edge, elevated three hundred feet above the river channel,
lies a glacial drift prairie which reaches two hundred miles
west to the Missouri River Plateau.

Instinct drew the Indian here, as it was to draw many
others, even white men, after him; for this vast, well-watered,
almost treeless basin and the neighboring plain were rich in
resources to support man. The soil, a black loam four to
twelve inches deep, produced hardy, succulent grasses upon
which fed millions of buffalo. There were many rivers, and
where there are rivers there are furs. In fact, water was sometimes too plentiful: there were, and still are, floods thirty
miles wide.

Here three great river basins joined: the Nelson, draining
north to Hudson's Bay; the St. Lawrence, tumbling eastward
to the Atlantic, and the mighty Mississippi rolling slowly

southward to the Gulf. And only a little way to the west, across a ridge so low that travelers scarcely noticed it, lay the country of the Upper Missouri, full of furs and buffalo, too.

Today two of these rivers are Canadian, two are in the United States. But rivers, as Pascal said, are roads which move; they do not pause at customhouses. Nor did the men who lived by them and moved on them. The forty-ninth parallel, cutting east to west through the heart of the basin and the plain, was a conceit of congressmen, not of ecologists. It could not arrest the movement of men and ideas any more effectively than it could that of the buffalo herds.

This was the West, the last frontier, the country of contrast and conflict. Here for decades there was to be drama born of incessant struggle between men of irreconcilable races, faiths, and political principles, and between these men and Nature. Here there was to be political pandemonium of a type Americans are wont to attribute contemptuously to Europe's Balkan States, and religious and racial wars like those which reddened the sands of Africa.

Each of the four rivers which brought men to this crossroads of the continent brought also the political and cultural formulas by which the men were determined to live. And even in a basin of two million acres there was not room for any two of these systems to dwell together in peace.

The first river to contribute was the St. Lawrence, and the men it brought were French. Pierre Radisson may have entered the Red River country from the Great Lakes in 1659, but if he did so he immediately rejoined his partner Groseilliers at Lake Superior. French *voyageurs*, their names now unknown, reached Lake Winnipeg soon after the beginning of the next century, but the first white man to "stake a claim" on behalf of his race was the intrepid explorer-trader De la Vérendrye. He established Fort Rouge at the Forks of the Red River (the mouth of the Assiniboine) in 1738, and placed another, his headquarters, a short distance to the west. The city of Winnipeg, Manitoba, which has about a quarter of a million people, now stands at the Forks, and the site of the other post is occupied by the town of Portage la Prairie. They are the oldest communities established by white men in the Northwest.

Over the St. Lawrence canoe route the French brought their mystic piety, their thirst for adventure and for knowledge of what lay beyond the next hill, and a talent for military organization. They were almost free of racial arrogance, sincerely devoted to a faith which proclaimed all men equal in the sight of God but which demanded that every footloose Frenchman should be an instrument for conversion of the pagans of the New World. They were quite willing to marry in the Indian camps. It is small wonder that they were the most admirable of the newcomers in the eyes of the Indians, for their qualities were those which, in tribal tradition, made virile races.

Down from Hudson's Bay—but *up* the northward-flowing rivers—came the English and the Scotch, the meticulous merchants. They were proud of their white skin and their spotless linen and their heirloom china, arrogant and authoritarian, inflexible of faith, scornful of horizon-hunting when there was money to be made near at hand. And they were bred to firm dealing with "subject races." They were not very popular on the Western frontier a century ago, and—until acclimatized—they are not very popular yet; but they blundered through to victory in the War for the West. Dogged, the British.

The Mississippi contributed a new people, confident of their Manifest Destiny after they had survived a bloody Civil War. The Americans were money men like the British, but they were willing to gamble as the British were not, and they were determined to build an empire—whereas the British already had an empire which they were beginning to find a little tiresome. These men from the south whom the Indians called the Long-Knives were as certain as Americans have always been that their political system was divinely ordained, beyond criticism, and adaptable to all places and peoples. The Indians tolerated them, used them, and, on occasion, slaughtered them. The Americans never won the affection the aborigines freely gave the French or the tribute of fear and respect which they grudgingly accorded to the British.

Across the low divide to the west were the mountain men, the hunters and trappers of the Upper Missouri, closely associated with the Red River people and sharing their interests. Most of them were technically Americans, too; but they were fugitives from the newborn boosterism of the Mississippi Valley and from the political and social restraints which their compatriots to the east were busily fashioning. The big sky, the far horizon, drew them as it did the French; the hardships encountered in their seeking taught them respect for the elements and for elemental gods; and in their loneliness they learned to esteem the Indian wives they took "after the custom of the country." For the most part they got along well with their Red River neighbors and perhaps could have dwelt happily among them but for the fact that they could not abide a land which was so damnably flat.

Here in the heart of North America history moved south. The Indians came from Asia, across the land bridge which now is Bering Strait, and south on the long hungry trail through the Barren Lands. The men who ultimately were to conquer them came also from the north, from Hudson's Bay through the brush country to the Forks, and beyond to the open buffalo plains.

There, on the shores of the sea of grass, these men from the north and those from the St. Lawrence built a town which they called **Pembina.** The name, originally Pambian, was a French rendering of a Cree-Chippewa term for the high-bush cranberry, but it also meant "sanctified bread" because the berries were used in pemmican which was blessed by the priest.

Pembina still exists as a sleepy border village in North Dakota. It was an inhabited place in 1780 and thus is the oldest community in the American Northwest. But it has been neglected in all save the local histories, and somewhat neglected even there because so much has happened that not even the oldest residents could ever recall it all.

Few Pembina residents ever knew, for instance, that the first white children in the American or Canadian Northwest were born there. There were two, born in the same week; the parents of one came from Hudson's Bay, those of the other entered the country by the St. Lawrence. And Americans may find it odd that this American town was the first prairie headquarters of the thoroughly British Hudson's Bay Company, that it once was owned by a Scottish earl, and that it once was peopled almost entirely by German and Swiss mercenaries, veterans of some dog-eared European war.

But those distinctions are less important to us than some others. Pembina, a log-cabin village, was the first capital of a new race, the Métis or Red River half-breeds of the Northwest—in so far as a people who always shunned settlements could be said to have had a capital. It was the principal seat of their church, established in 1818 and served by a bishop whose diocesan boundaries (ignoring such political fictions as the forty-ninth parallel) were officially the Great Lakes, the North Pole, and the Pacific.

And, only eighty years ago, this village of Pembina was the scene of a political tragicomedy which determined the sovereignty of British North America and cost the United States its chance to acquire half a continent.

The map in *Morse's Geography,* a school text in the United States from its publication in 1789 until about 1812, labeled the country west of Lake Michigan as "little known," which indeed it was. But blank spots on maps are quickly filled by legend, and the mysterious mid-continent has always lent itself to wild tales.

There were, for instance, the "Welsh Indians" who dwelt just over the ridge, on the Missouri. They were the Mandans, and no more Welsh than were the Eskimos; but because, for Indians, they were light in color, lived in mud-and-brush huts instead of skin lodges, tended gardens, and spoke a strange tongue, they were reputed to be the descendants of Welsh colonists brought to America by the fabled Prince Madoc in the twelfth century. Vérendrye found the Mandans in 1738 and Lewis and Clark wintered among them in 1804-5; like all competent observers they reported that they were just Indians, though a friendly bunch. (Perhaps too friendly; the tribe is now extinct.) But the legend of Madoc persisted and crops up occasionally even now.

Another story, of more recent origin, may have greater validity. In 1898 a farmer living at Kensington, Minnesota, on the eastern edge of the Red River Basin, discovered an inscribed stone in the roots of an aspen tree. This, the famous Kensington Stone, has now been tentatively accepted by the Smithsonian Institution as authentic to the extent that the runes, the characters in which the inscription is composed, appear to date from the fourteenth century. The stone purports to give an account, written by a survivor, of the massacre of a group of Norse explorers by Indians at this site in 1362.

Supporters of the "Vinland" theory—that Norsemen visited North America in the eleventh and fourteenth centuries—hold that this stone and more than a dozen other relics such as swords, axes and mooring stones for boats, prove that the Vikings penetrated the interior of the continent more than a century before Columbus sighted San Salvador. Most of these relics have been found in the Red River Valley.

The tales have significance here only because of the locale.

Obviously, civilized man has found it incredible that such a bounteous empire as the northern mid-continent basin should have been uninhabited save by "savages" until Vérendrye's posts were established in the eighteenth century. Such neglect reflects somehow upon the white man's intelligence and initiative.

The crossroads of the continent needs no myth; its recorded history is romantic enough.

That history opens with the issuance of a charter, in 1670, by Charles II to "The Governor and Company of Adventurers of England Trading into Hudson's Bay." The Governor was Prince Rupert, cousin of the King, and the charter made the Company "true and absolute lords and proprietors" of all the lands drained by rivers entering the Bay. That domain —a third of a million square miles, though no one knew its extent then—was named Rupert's Land. Some of it lay south of the forty-ninth parallel, in what are now the states of Minnesota, North Dakota, and Montana.

But the "Adventurers of England" were incurious and unenterprising and their employees were timid. Only one, "the boy Henry Kelsey" who actually was a youth of twenty, could be induced to strike out from the Company's posts on the Bay into the prairie wilderness. Accompanied by an Indian, he went into the Assiniboine country, from Lake Winnipeg perhaps to what is now eastern Saskatchewan, in 1690, and spent almost two years. He was apparently the first white man to see musk oxen. Nearly a century passed before the Company, spurred by competition, established trading posts in the region he had visited.

Meanwhile a more vigorous rival, the "French" North West Company (actually its control was Scotch, but its headquarters were in Montreal and it favored French employees), established itself firmly deep in the interior of the fur country. Indians who chose to sell to the English firm had to spend

months every year traveling across the prairies to its posts on
the Bay. This was good for the furs because the long trek
left the animals undisturbed in summer when fur quality was
poor; but it was hard on the Indians, and the bulk of their
trade soon began to go to the more conveniently located posts
of the Nor'westers.

The strategic position of Pembina was recognized quickly
by everyone except the Hudson's Bay Company. A French
free trader established a post there in 1780, and in 1797 a
North West trading station was set up by C. J. B. Chaboillez.
The first Hudson's Bay post there was established in 1801 by
Thomas Miller; by that time the English firm had adopted
a policy of tagging around after its competitors. Because
Pembina was the favored point of assembly for buffalo hunters, it was to be the prairie headquarters of the Hudson's
Bay Company until 1823, when they were reluctantly moved
north to Fort Garry, now Winnipeg.

During this quarter-century the incompatible elements
which had been thrown together in the northern end of the
Red River Valley attempted to establish a new society, each
in its own pattern. None could succeed, and the forces gen-
erated in the effort were foredoomed to conflict. It came, this
opening skirmish in the War for the West, in about fifty years.

One of these elements was a new people, struggling to
create a nation. They succeeded—for ten months. There was
a country called Rupert's Land, and a flag the world had
never seen before, a banner with *fleurs-de-lis* and shamrock on
a white ground. And there was an anthem, called "Falcon's
Song" because it had been created by a man named Falcon.
It was not a very good song: the images were crude and the
sentiment not at all elevating; it was a hymn of hate and thus
like some other national anthems. But it was unique in this:
it was not written down. Pierre Falcon himself could not
write and his song was perhaps the only national hymn in
history which was transmitted exclusively by singing it. By

the time someone of another race got around to printing it, about fifty-five years after its conception, the nation which had sung it was singing no longer.

This was the nation of the Métis—or, as the song put it, the *Bois-Brulés,* the people whose skin was like scorched wood. "Sing the glory," the last line of "Falcon's Song" commanded, "of all the *Bois-Brulés!*"

ASSINIBOIA

The song was born on June 19, 1816. On that day, too, the nation was born in the minds of the people, if not yet in political fact.

These things occurred on a bloody battleground called Seven Oaks, now a park on the outskirts of Winnipeg, while the Métis, momentarily reverting to savagery, hacked with skinning knives at the bodies of twenty-two white men they had slain at the bidding of other white men. "Falcon's Song" was introduced at the celebration of the "victory" that night. It did not tell how the Métis had mauled, like dogs, the bodies of their victims; it said the whites were to blame for the incident, and some whites certainly were, though not the ones named by the simple Pierre.

The victims were Robert Semple, governor of Hudson's Bay Company territories in America, and a group of colonists who had been sent to the Red River by the Earl of Selkirk.

Selkirk's philanthropic venture was inspired by an economic revolution in the Scottish Highlands, when large-scale sheep raising superseded tenant farming and left thousands of families without means of support. In 1803 he sent several hundred settlers to Prince Edward Island. Then he won control of the Hudson's Bay Company, which was sadly ailing; it had lost its European markets in the Napoleonic Wars and was losing its trade to the Nor'westers in the fur country. In 1811 he wrested from his reluctant fellow stockholders, who feared that settlement would wreck the fur business, a grant

of 116,000 square miles in the Red River Valley upon which
to establish, at his own expense, an agricultural colony.

This grant was defined as the "District of Assiniboia." It
extended from Lake Winnipeg south to the divide between
the Red River and Mississippi Basins, and from the Lake of

Assiniboia

the Woods on the east to the source of the Assiniboine River
on the west. Nearly half of the area was within the limits of
what are now the states of Minnesota and North Dakota, but
this southern portion did not become American territory
until 1815 when the Treaty of Ghent, concluding the War of
1812, was ratified.

Selkirk's project was bitterly fought within the Company
by the "winterers"—the partners working in the field as post
factors, who shared the profits but had no voice in determin-

ing policy—and by Sir Alexander Mackenzie, chief London
director of the North West Company, who had also bought
into the rival firm. Savage attacks were launched in the press,
in the countinghouses, and at meetings of stockholders. The
Red River Valley, one of the world's most fertile regions, was
pictured as a desert to frighten off immigrants; Selkirk was
denounced as an "American land-jobber" and a megalo-
maniac bent upon creating a private empire.

The first colonists reached the Forks, which Selkirk had
chosen as the site of his Fort Douglas, capital of Assiniboia,
in 1812. There were only twenty-three. On September 4 their
leader, Miles Macdonnell, formally took possession of the
district in the earl's name, reading the land patents and his
commissions from Selkirk and the Company at a public ceremony. Those who attended had their ears cocked nervously
for the drum of horses' hooves; a few days earlier they had
been thoroughly frightened by an ominous incident. A
yelling horde of Métis, garbed as Indians and flourishing war
axes, had swept down upon the little tent colony to inform
the newcomers that agricultural settlement would not be
permitted in the heart of the buffalo country.

The demonstration had been inspired by the Nor'westers,
whose Fort Gibraltar was across the river. They had told the
Métis that Assiniboia belonged to the natives, the Indians and
half-breeds; the Nor'westers, interested only in furs, would
never dispute their claim. But farmers would drive them out.

The Métis had never before concerned themselves about
"ownership" of the country, for this was a concept foreign to
the Indian or Métis mind. With the urging of the whites,
however, the mixed-bloods were quick to catch on. Some of
their Indian relatives rather indifferently accepted the new
idea, but they never did make as peremptory a claim to the
country as the Métis made for them.

Selkirk sent more colonists and the Nor'westers stepped up
their campaign of terrorism. Métis horsemen raided the

farms, threatened and occasionally pillaged. And in April, 1815, a number of the Selkirk people deserted to the enemy. Meanwhile the efforts of Macdonnell to establish an embargo on foodstuffs had added to the fury of the rival firm and had increased the alarm of the Métis. The colony in its first years was always on the verge of starvation and its people spent the winters in Pembina, where buffalo meat could be obtained from the Métis hunters. Macdonnell established a post there, Fort Daer.

The Nor'westers managed to arrange for Macdonnell's arrest and removal to Canada for trial on charges emanating from his embargo proclamation, and he was succeeded first by Colin Robertson and then by Semple. The latter, born in Boston, was a Loyalist who had settled in England after the Revolution; he was a writer and gentleman of culture, and the colonists he brought with him were superior to most of those who had come before.

Lord Selkirk, setting out on his first visit to the colony, brought with him about a hundred former soldiers whom he planned to settle there. Most of the men were from the DeMeuron Regiment—Swiss, German and Italian mercenaries who had fought for Britain in the Napoleonic Wars, had been sent to Canada in 1812, and discharged at the conclusion of the war with the United States. But the earl and his troops did not reach the colony in time to prevent the tragedy of Seven Oaks.

The Métis "army" which participated in the massacre was organized at a North West Company post at Qu'Appelle, 250 miles west of Fort Douglas, by Alexander Macdonnell, a Nor'wester and cousin of Selkirk's lieutenant, Miles Macdonnell. Field command was assigned to Cuthbert Grant, son of a Scotch "wintering partner" of the North West Company and a Cree woman. Cuthbert was twenty-three and had had some education in Scotland. His sister married the "Métis minstrel," Pierre Falcon.

Grant's prairie cavalry took the field early in June, seized

a Hudson's Bay supply brigade and a post halfway to Red
River, and established new headquarters at Portage la Prairie.
On June 18, Grant and about sixty-five of his riders left there
for Fort Douglas and in the early evening of the following
day they were sighted from the fort's watchtower.

Unarmed settlers who had been working in their fields fled
to the fort, crying the alarm: "The half-breeds! The half-
breeds!" Semple left the fort with twenty-six men to greet the
Métis and learn the purpose of their visit. He could not bring
himself to believe that the visitors were unfriendly, so his
little party was inadequately armed.

There was a brief altercation, a clatter of gunfire. Grant, as
was the invariable Métis practice, had dispersed his men in
a wide circle, completely surrounding the Selkirkers. Semple
and twenty-one of his party were killed; the Métis lost one.
The governor, wounded in the thigh, had appealed to Grant
to have him carried to the fort and Grant agreed but was
called away; while he was gone someone shot the helpless
Semple through the heart.

The terrified colonists penned up in the fort opened the
gates to a survivor, sent by Grant with an ultimatum: Get
out of the district at once, or be destroyed. They grabbed
food and clothing and fled, to seek shelter at Hudson's Bay
Company posts on the trail north to the Bay.

In Portage la Prairie the malevolent Alexander Macdonnell
got the news from a swift Métis courier and called his followers together. "Good news!" he shouted. "Twenty-two
English have been killed!"

But Grant's men were enraged because Colin Robertson,
whom they wanted most, was absent from the fort at the time
of the attack. "He called us blacks!" one of the Métis cried.
"He will learn that our hearts can be as black as our bodies!"

The Nor'westers—and Robertson, if he was guilty as
charged—had done their work well. The new nation had
been born, and like all infants it had quickly adapted itself

to the pattern of its elders' thought. It had learned that land and water, the resources by which men lived, could be privately owned. And it had learned about race and color.

The Earl of Selkirk re-established his colony. There were to be more disasters, more hunger and bloodshed, and some would quit; but the colony survived. The earl's wards, who already had endured so much, had still to learn about drought and locusts and floods; they had to establish communication and commerce with their aggressive neighbors to the south without forfeiting their political sovereignty; they had to learn to live with the touchy new nation of the Métis. All these they managed to do, and the dream of the young Scottish lord was at last realized.

But the conspiracy against him, in which the Nor'westers had enlisted even the British Colonial Office and the courts, had its hoped-for result: Selkirk's health collapsed. Added to his discouragement and fatigue was his bitterness when it became apparent even to him that union of the warring fur companies, as desired by the Colonial Office, was the only solution. He had once been willing to consider this, but after Seven Oaks he refused to go into partnership with butchers. In 1820 he died in the south of France, at the age of forty-nine. His twenty-year struggle to establish the colony in the face of implacable opposition even from his government had cost his personal estate one hundred thousand pounds.

Less than a month before, Sir Alexander Mackenzie of the North West Company had died. The two greatest figures of the fur trade were gone and union of the companies followed quickly. Their war had cost the Hudson's Bay Company about forty thousand pounds in addition to Selkirk's own losses; the rival's costs were even greater. Both were hard-pressed, but Selkirk's militant policy left the Hudson's Bay in the stronger position; before he died the earl had the satisfaction of learning that the wintering Nor'westers were angling secretly for a deal by which they could sell out their London and Montreal partners.

The Hudson's Bay Company, whose name was assumed by the consolidated firm, repurchased Assiniboia in 1834 from the Selkirk estate for stock in the Company valued at fifteen thousand pounds. This repaid only a fraction of the losses of the lord of whom Sir Walter Scott, a close friend, once said, "I never knew a man of more generous distinction."

When Thomas Douglas, who was to become Earl of Selkirk, was seven years old a privateer named John Paul Jones raided the Selkirk estate on St. Mary's Isle at the mouth of the River Dee in Scotland. That was in 1778 and Captain Jones was the first naval officer to reach European waters under the Stars and Stripes. He had been born in the village near the Selkirk estate and there was some mystery about it: he grew up convinced that he was an unacknowledged and neglected son of one of the earls of Selkirk.

Captain Jones had intended to kidnap Thomas Douglas's father but the earl was not at home; instead, against Jones's wishes, the Yankee crew carried off some of the family plate. (Captain Jones bought it back from his men and restored it to the Selkirk family.)

The rough seamen had also threatened Thomas Douglas, a sensitive and timid child, and for the rest of his life he disliked and distrusted Americans.

When he died he was the owner, by Hudson's Bay Company grant, of a sizable chunk of the United States. The task of establishing the family's title fell to his son. The Selkirk attorney was the best to be had in America; probably he was too good, for he dreamed of being President, and he might have diminished his popularity by pressing a case for foreigners. Therefore Daniel Webster did nothing for his clients and the Selkirks finally had to relinquish all claims to their lands in two of the United States.

WAGON MAN

Half wagon, half man. That was how the *Bois-Brulés,* forever on the move, appeared to their half-brothers, the Indians. The Crees devised a sign to describe them: forefingers of each hand circling each other (wagon wheels), then the extended forefinger of the right hand drawn down the front of the body from the right side of the head.

But the sign came late, after the appearance of the Red River cart about 1800. There were *Bois-Brulés* long before that: they visited Sault Ste Marie as early as 1654 and "made a rendezvous" at Mackinac before 1670. These first "half-breeds" were literally that, probably the offspring of Frenchmen from Champlain's company, which established Quebec in 1608, and of Indian women among the Huron and Algonquin tribes.

These first men of the new race, and the French, Scotch and English who followed them to the Western frontier married among the Crees and "Saulteux." The latter really were Chippewas, named from their Sault Ste Marie headquarters. The Crees were especially favored because the white men found their women more attractive, more dependable morally—they eagerly embraced Christianity—and more intelligent than those of other tribes. Half-breed girls were especially desirable; early travelers reported they were often "of classic beauty."

The proportion of Indian blood in the children gradually dwindled and the term "half-breed," already invidious, became inaccurate also; a better word, and the one favored by the people themselves to the present day, was the French *métis*—mixed-blood.

There were comparatively few of these people until the middle of the eighteenth century, when the French invasion of the Plains began in earnest, a movement accelerated by Britain's conquest of Canada in 1760. The fur companies encouraged unions of their *engagés* and Indian women: love helped to induce men to put down roots in the country, and their Métis offspring were pledged, as a matter of course, to the service of the companies. Extensive immigration was discouraged because it would be bad for the fur business; and natives were more tractable and more efficient than newcomers.

Even before Quebec fell to the British and the dream of New France collapsed, Métis in the company of Indians or in little bands of their own had explored the continent as far west as the Rockies. A century after the conquest there were at least thirty thousand of them in the West; though their numbers by no means equaled those of the Indians, west of the Great Lakes they often outnumbered the whites.

During the great struggle for the prizes of the fur trade in the first half of the nineteenth century and for two or three decades thereafter the Métis were dominant on the rivers and prairies. They were the wanderers of the wilderness—the best boatmen, best guides, hunters, trappers and traders. They devised a system of freight transport for the Plains which established a new industry and made St. Paul the capital of Minnesota and the commercial center of the Northwestern frontier. Their knowledge of the country—much of it instinctive and thus inexplicable to white men—made them indispensable in development of the West, as did the fact that most of the Indians welcomed them as relatives and friends.

The Métis, a new people, were the cultural and economic intermediaries in the "civilizing" of a continent. Without their help the process would have been much bloodier than it was. They also were the inheritors of the Indians' culture, and with it, the Indians' problems.

At first the Anglo-Saxon visitors found them charming. Speaking of his French-Canadian *voyageurs*, who undoubtedly included some Métis, Colin Robertson reported, "They think themselves the happiest people in existence, and I believe they are not far mistaken." This was in 1812, but as late as 1859 the Earl of Southesk commented admiringly, at the expense of his own countrymen: "They are a fine race," he wrote; "tall, straight, well proportioned, lightly formed but strong and extremely active and enduring. Their chests, shoulders and waists are of symmetrical shape so seldom found among the broad-waisted, short-necked English or the flat-chested, long-necked Scotch."

Everyone agreed that they were merry, hospitable, honest and commendably pious—submissive to their priests, better Christians and better citizens than most of the white frontiersmen. But they lacked moral discipline in some respects; they loved exhausting dancing parties and drinking bouts.

Métis were fruitful in shifts and resources on the trail. They observed minutely all details of the landscape and never forgot them. Their endurance in the service of their English and Scotch masters was especially praised: they could travel fifty to sixty miles a day on foot or with a dogsled, and thirty on snowshoes.

One Canadian observer summed it up: "A harmless obsequious set of men, and will, I believe, be very useful here when the country gets filled up."

But, to the hurt astonishment of their white admirers who had so artlessly accepted the responsibility of overlordship, the Métis turned out to be neither harmless nor obsequious. The judgment of the whites thereafter reflected the exasperation of a superior race whose mastery has been repudiated by an inferior people who don't know what is good for them. After 1870 the Métis became, to Anglo-Saxon commentators, a race of greasy rebels, worthless vagabonds, bloodthirsty murderers and unhung felons.

They were neither so childlike as they appeared to the early visitors nor so villainous as they were subsequently said to be; they were just people, shaped by heredity and environment. As hybrids they found adjustment to any social scheme more difficult than it is for longer established racial castes. Their conception of their own role in society, the chief factor in determining "racial personality," was conditioned by emotional tension: they were superior in education to one social group, inferior to the other and smarting under its social taboos. Inevitably there developed a tendency to compensate: Métis leaders became egocentric and chauvinistic, and the people found comfort in pretentious formalism or defiant debauch.

Few peoples have had a more difficult adjustment to make. Members of two mutually exclusive groups, they were rebuffed by both. The "personality" which emerged from this inner conflict was not a biological consequence of the mixture of blood, but the product of social and psychological factors.

Métis education varied with the environment and the cultural standards of the parents, especially the father. Many children were sent east to church schools, removed during their formative years from the primitive region of their birth, but nearly all of them returned to adopt the roving life of their people. The youngsters were naturally quick and intelligent but lacked the discipline for sustained application; moreover, because of the free movement of their communities, they could rarely be collected in one place long enough for an integrated course of instruction. As a result few Métis could read or write.

They were, however, exceptionally apt linguists. Most of them spoke at least two languages, French and Cree, and many quickly added other Indian tongues and English. Some even learned German while they were in contact with Selkirk's DeMeuron veterans. Their own patois, still spoken by them throughout the West, is a mixture of French and Cree or Chippewa with some English words. The base is an obsolete French of a type said to be still heard in Normandy and Picardy, and a large vocabulary of terms applying to the prairie has been added. Words French in origin have been given new meanings.

French was the "official" language, used in letters and documents. It was also favored over English for spoken intercourse with whites and is still preferred by the elder Métis and widely used by them in Canada and the United States. As used in their own homes, however, the patois is more Cree than French.

Cree is fairly easily learned (at least by Métis) and it is expressive, rhythmic and euphonious. Like other Algonkian tongues it is rich in vowel sounds, shuns harsh consonants and is strongly aspirated; the manipulation of the "rough-breathing" termination of a syllable often changes the meaning of a word. Whole sentences or more of English can be put into one word of Cree; what other "civilized" languages achieve through the declension or addition of nouns is often done in Cree by altering the verb. For this reason one scholar has termed the language "one gigantic verb."

Cree is not, actually, one language, but three: there are Woods Crees, Swampy Crees, and Plains Crees, and the dialects differ considerably; but the base is the same everywhere. It is dramatic (January is the Moon of Exploding Trees) and vivid (August is the Moon of the Flying Up of Young Ducks), and just the sort of speech to appeal to a wagon man.

The unions of white men and Métis women were often casual and temporary, but just as often they were permanent. Many travelers commented upon the "tender attachments" which developed, and nearly all white visitors, including some who had not been away from home long enough to impair their judgment, found the mixed-blood women uncommonly pretty and provocative. They were frequently fairer of skin than the men, often as fair as Englishwomen; they were gay companions, industrious helpmeets, affectionate wives and devoted mothers. They were considered eligible for marriage at fifteen, though their brothers usually waited about five years longer.

The esteem in which the white men held their wives and children had much to do with what happened when the races finally clashed, for without the tacit support of many whites the Métis tragedy would have been even more severe than it was.

But of greater significance when the reckoning came was the regard the Métis had for themselves—their conception, slowly developed after Seven Oaks, of their race as unique and dynamic. This was the basic determinant of their destiny and it created a sense of solidarity which quickened the people and sustained their leaders. When the crisis came, Métis of all origins stuck together much better than might have been expected. The Scotch and English "breeds" were almost as numerous in the settlements, though not on the Plains, as their French cousins, and they were Protestant and docile; the French were Roman Catholic to a man and as wild, temperamentally, as antelope. But the Scotch and English supported their unruly kinsmen when the shooting started.

The attempt to resolve the conflict between loyalty to the "inferior" Indian progenitor and the desire for identification with the "superior" white was not made consciously, of course, by the average simple Métis. He was doomed to lose his function, his home and his life without ever knowing what had happened to him, to shed his blood for a slogan and a preposterous faith.

But the conflict was acknowledged by the man who coined the slogan and fashioned the faith. The greatest leader of the Métis touched upon it in one of his many analyses of the problem he put to himself: how to inspire in his people that pride with which one builds a nation and a race:

It is true that our savage origin is humble, but it is meet that we honor our mothers as well as our fathers. Why should we concern ourselves about what degree of mixture we possess of European or Indian blood? If we have ever so little of either gratitude or filial love, should we not be proud to say, "We are Métis!"?

"We are Métis!" It was a cry destined to echo for a few decades across the lakes, the wind-whipped grasslands and hidden coulees of the West, to be flung defiantly at the ghost dancers in the winter night; and then to be borne off by the gale and forgotten.

CHAPTER II

Freedom Road

THE BOUNDARY WAS ABSURD

THE old trails from the Forks of the Red River to
Pembina and St. Paul which were the caravan routes of the
New World are lost now in fields of tawny wheat as flat and
square and trim as deep-pile carpets laid out to freshen in
the sun. They almost became roads of empire, as caravan
routes often have; but because that was not to be their destiny, the commerce of the continent, which might have moved
efficiently north and south, was doomed to develop extravagantly east and west.

A trail linked Selkirk's Fort Douglas to Pembina and the
site of the future St. Paul at least as early as 1812. Selkirk
himself traveled over it in 1817, observing that "our people
might draw their supplies of many articles by way of the
Mississippi & River St. Peter's * with greater facility than
from Canada or from Europe." Such traffic could develop
into an important industry, he believed, so he wrote to John
Quincy Adams, Secretary of State, urging that the United

---

* The St. Peter's is the Minnesota River.

46

States encourage it by providing trade passports and other inducements.

Within a half-century the commerce he had foreseen amounted to more than two million dollars a year, shared by St. Paul and Winnipeg, the two major cities on the Red River trails. And it reached this total in the face of active obstruction by political and monopolistic business elements on both sides of the boundary.

"Pig's-Eye" Parent, christened Pierre, an ill-favored and dissolute half-breed, founded the city of St. Paul on June 1, 1838, when he erected a cabin in which to resume a sure-fire business which had got him into trouble elsewhere—the sale of liquor to soldiers and Indians.

When he chose a site commanding both a creek and a river, his querulous customers said the smaller stream would be just about adequate for dilution of his merchandise and the other would be handy for his getaway, but despite their opinion of him they were eager to settle in convenient proximity. Nor did they object when the new community was given his name; but in 1841 the village was renamed by the priest who conducted its first religious service. The Minnesota *Pioneer,* a nearby newspaper, recorded the metamorphosis:

> Pig's-Eye, converted thou shalt be, like Saul;
> Arise, and be, henceforth, St. Paul!

The community which was quickly to become the commercial capital of the Northwest was late getting started. "Pig's-Eye" Parent had already prospered in, and been expelled from, Sault Ste Marie, founded in 1668; Prairie du Chien, dating from 1685; St. Louis, 1764, and St. Peter's. The last, which became Mendota, Minnesota, was established about 1819. It was the headquarters of John Jacob Astor's American Fur Company and became the successor to St. Louis as outfitting headquarters when the fur trade moved north,

only to yield its pre-eminence within a quarter-century to
neighboring St. Paul. And as for Pembina—a whole generation of Métis had grown to maturity there before St. Paul
came ingloriously into being as a scattering of huts and tipis
around an illegal saloon.

Selkirk made possible the first important business venture
on the new north-south trail. In the spring of 1819, after a
grasshopper scourge had virtually wiped out his colony's
crops, an expedition went south to Prairie du Chien and returned with wheat, oats for seed, peas and chickens.

In 1820 a Métis, Alexis Bailly, drove a herd of cattle north
from Prairie du Chien and sold it profitably to the Selkirkers.
Others tried this subsequently with less success. Maj. Stephen
H. Long of the United States Army traversed the trail in 1823
en route to Pembina to place the first international boundary
marker west of the Great Lakes. He provided the first detailed
account of travel on the route, and disclosed that freighting
by oxcart was already being tried.

Nudged by John Jacob Astor, Congress in 1816 prohibited
trading with the Indians south of the boundary by anyone
other than an American citizen. To protect American rights,
the first military post on the Northwestern frontier was established three years later by Lieut. Col. Henry Leavenworth;
it was Fort Snelling, and from it developed the city of Minneapolis. Five dissatisfied Swiss families who abandoned the
Selkirk colony in 1821 settled at Fort Snelling, becoming the
first permanent residents of what would be the State of Minnesota. Several hundred more Selkirkers, most of them Swiss,
followed in the next five years, after stops of varying periods
in Pembina.

Paper work in Congress and even the establishment of a
military post failed to impress the intractable fur traders.
Some of them made cursory obeisance to law by acquiring, in
various devious ways, American citizenship papers; others just

didn't bother. Maj. Lawrence Taliaffero, a phenomenally in-
corruptible Indian agent, denounced them as "Mississippi
demi-civilized Canadian mongrel English-American citizens."
He could not become reconciled to the fact that, except among
officials and the military, citizenship had no meaning on this
frontier.

The forty-ninth parallel, that "imaginary line" drawn
across an open plain, was a wholly artificial boundary; the
idea of a purely political barrier which should obstruct the
free movement of men and goods was regarded as absurd on
both sides. The dominant racial elements were Métis and
Indian, footloose folk who might have been taught to respect
a boundary sharply defined by recognizable topographic features, but not a line they could not see. And the new, aggressive whites had found that their interests were identical north
and south.

So the boundary just did not make sense, and doesn't yet.
It sought to separate the sparse populations of a hazardous
frontier, to stay the essential interchange among people whose
needs were similar and who were socially compatible. Therefore the people ignored the line, flouted the law, and dodged
the enforcement agents.

For many years the conviction of interchangeable citizenship, or no citizenship at all, persisted. Even today, with customs and immigration patrols grimly awaiting a misstep,
border residents regard "the line" as merely a nuisance which
slightly delays their arrival at Saturday night dances. During
the rationing period of World War II, American housewives
in border villages crossed daily to buy meat for the evening
meal, and some still do this to take advantage of Canada's
lower prices.

Boundary red tape is incomprehensible to Indians and
Métis. They are continually in trouble because they cannot,
or will not, provide proof of their citizenship. But such proof
was not easily obtained by the last generation. A half-breed

born during a buffalo hunt had a hard time determining
which country could claim him if the hunt occurred, for instance, along the Milk River—or the Red, the Souris, Poplar,
Pembina, or other streams which flow in both Canada and
the United States.

The problem was further complicated by the fact that the
priest who accompanied the hunters and listed births and
deaths invariably filed this record at his home mission—which
might have been Pembina, on the American side, but just as
often was Portage la Prairie or St. Boniface, in British Northwest America. If a priest from north of the line officiated at a
christening, the odds were strong that the infant would become automatically a subject of the Queen.

The peripatetic character of the Church had an important
part in establishing the Métis and Indian concept of dual
citizenship. Its very birth had been binational. At the instance
of Selkirk and his Catholic lieutenant, Miles Macdonnell,
Fathers Norbert Provencher and Sévère Dumoulin and
Teacher William Edge arrived at Fort Douglas from Montreal in 1818. But that fall, at the request of the colonists who
were forced by hunger to move to Pembina, and of the Métis
hunters already settled there, Father Dumoulin went to Pembina and built a church. His congregation was about three
hundred, six times as large as that at Fort Douglas, where
Provencher in 1820 built the first church of St. Boniface. The
first school also was at Pembina, serving sixty children.

In 1823 the Hudson's Bay Company became convinced
that Pembina was on the American side of the line and insisted that the church and school there be abandoned as a
means of forcing residents of that community to move north
to Fort Douglas, which about this time became Fort Garry
and ultimately the city of Winnipeg. Provencher, become a
bishop, had to yield: the church could not survive without
Hudson's Bay Company support. Father Dumoulin, heart-

broken, returned to Quebec, and Pembina was served only by mission priests for about thirty years.

Not all of the Métis moved to British territory, and those who did insisted that they had been coerced and therefore had not forfeited any rights they might have possessed at Pembina—an argument arrived at instinctively but perhaps legally sound. The priests, also resentful because they were accustomed to crossing the boundary freely with the Métis on the hunt, shared the attitude of their parishioners and held the technical detail of citizenship to be of little importance.

Left-handed recognition of this "dual citizenship" finally came from the Government of the United States. It was recognition by default, and it came, ironically, when the Métis who established the tradition were least anxious to have it affirmed.

AN INDESCRIBABLE SOUND

There were three Red River trails. The two longest were the fastest because they were on the open prairie; the third, dodging into the woods to avoid possible contact with the ever hostile Sioux, was slower going. Ultimately one of the prairie trails became the favored route and was chosen for the first stage line and the first railway.

Except for sporadic Indian attacks, they were peaceful trails. The few violent incidents were furtive affairs having little in common with the theatrical outlawry on the longer, gold-spangled highways of the Upper Missouri. The people of Red River were a law-abiding lot except when it came to such annoyances as boundaries, embargoes and customs duties.

There were, however, other hazards. In the winter, when the trip was made by dogsled, there were the sudden deadly blizzards—and there were fleas. One traveler reported that when snowblindness forced interruption of his journey he spent several days in a one-room cabin with five men, ten dogs and two thousand fleas.

In spring and summer there were flash floods, thunderstorms, blistering heat—and mosquitoes.

Wind-borne swarms of mosquitoes, often preceding thunderstorms, bore down upon the cart brigades in such numbers that horses, dogs and drivers were overwhelmed within a few seconds. While the horses pitched and screamed under the attack of the savage insects and the dogs writhed in agony on the ground, the men fled under their carts and wound themselves, head to foot, in blankets, though the temperature might be in the nineties. The torment might last only a few minutes, but it frequently killed horses and dogs and disabled the men for days.

Sometimes the approaching swarm could be heard: a high, unbroken and terrifying hum. This gave the drivers time to throw wagon sheets over their animals. Mounted men would attempt to outrun the flying horde. Though they were almost always overtaken, the breeze created by their horses' panic flight saved them from the worst agony; but they pulled out of the gallop, miles away, with faces and arms streaming blood and with the insects six deep on their ponies. Animals heard or sensed the approach of a swarm before men could, and horses sometimes broke into a dead run without warning, unseating their riders.

Another dread enemy was fire. In the hot summer months the long prairie grass was always ablaze somewhere, and if fire broke out along the trail the consequences to a Red River train could be disastrous. The worst danger was shortage of feed, because the shaggy little ponies or the oxen which drew the carts lived off the country. Forced marches might be necessary to get out of a burned area and the feet of men and animals could be badly burned in the hot black ashes. (The Blackfeet Indians, farther west, got their name from the stain left on their white buckskin moccasins by the coal-black ash of burned prairie grass.) Lightning started most of these fires, which often raced across the plains with such speed that no animal could escape; but Indian and Métis hunters occasionally set them to drive the buffalo.

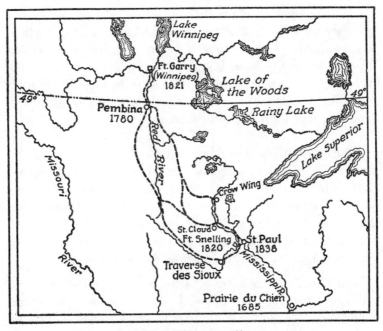

Red River Trails

The distance from Fort Garry to St. Peter's by the longest trail, the one farthest to the west, was about six hundred miles. A cart brigade was on the road more than a month, since fifteen miles was a fairly good day's run. This trail followed the Red River closely to Pembina, then swung to high ground twenty miles west to avoid the flood basin. It left the Red to run roughly parallel with the St. Peter's River as far as the village of that name or, later, St. Paul. Rivers too deep or too swift to be forded were crossed by raft or log bridge.

The heaviest traffic was in the spring and rain was encoun-

tered. This meant flooded streams and a marshy track; carts
were mired and had to be unloaded, lifted out of the muck
and loaded again while brush was put down to give them
footing. The train proceeded always in single file. Ten carts
made a "brigade," each of which usually had three drivers, so
each man handled three or four carts, making the entire
journey on foot. These men and the captain of the whole
train walked a thousand miles a season, endured tortures from
insects, faced the hazards of storm and fire and the back-
breaking labor of extricating the carts from gluey gumbo
potholes, almost without complaint. They were traditionally
as cheerful as their *voyageur* forebears.

The origin of the Red River cart and the year of its "birth"
are obscure. Some have credited its "invention" to Alexander
Henry the Younger, North West Company trader who arrived at Pembina in 1801. Other sources say the cart was
known in the region as early as 1784. Henry himself did not
claim to have designed it, but his journal entry of November
15, 1801, may be the first mention of the new vehicle:

Men now go again for meat, with small carts, the wheels of
which are one solid piece, sawed off the ends of trees whose
diameter is three feet. Those carriages we find more convenient
and advantageous than it is to load horses, the country being so
smooth and level that we can use them in every direction.

Henry became more and more enthusiastic about the cart.
"This invention," he wrote in 1803, "is worth four horses to
us, as it would require five horses to carry as much on their
backs as one will drag in each of these large carts."

Henry was English but the cart was definitely French.
Similar vehicles had long been in use in Quebec, whose inhabitants had modified the design they had known in France.
But the Red River cart was a product of evolution and adapta-
tion, built for the prairie, as was a similar one which evolved

on the Argentine pampas somewhat later. No one could be said to have "invented" it, nor did the design remain unchanged. The cart became lighter and stronger, until it could carry a load of five hundred pounds and make fifty miles a day when drawn by a pony, or carry nine hundred pounds fifteen or twenty miles a day when drawn by an ox.

The solid flat wheels of which Henry wrote were replaced by "dished" wheels with four or more spokes. The wheels could be quickly removed and attached under the cart or at its sides so it could be floated over a river. After spokes became popular, the felloes which formed the rim were wrapped with wet rawhide; shrinking and hardening as they dried, the leather strips bound the segments of the rim firmly together.

The cart was built entirely of wood and the noise of its wheel hubs as they rubbed on the axle, which usually was an unpeeled poplar log, was a tooth-stabbing screech which was never forgotten by anyone who heard it; it was as if a thousand fingernails were drawn across a thousand panes of glass.

The wheels were so high that even in a runaway the outfit seldom overturned. Wood was used exclusively even after metal became available, because trees were accessible in the watercourses along the trail and repairs could thus be made easily; also wood was light, so the cart could be lifted out of the mud, and would float.

The brigades wound across the prairie like a great snake, the extra horses or oxen fanning out beside the carts to get out of the dust; this herd usually numbered a tenth to a fifth as large as that actually pulling the carts. The start was made at daybreak, with a rest at noon, and a day's run lasted about ten hours.

The wheels could not be greased because dust would coagulate and cement them to the axle. Drivers and their animals just had to get used to the interminable shriek of the grinding wood, and soon did—though tenderfoot visitors found it incredible that anyone could. Most of the prairie

"tourists" came away affirming that the noise was indescrib-
able, then set out immediately to try to describe it—and had
to fall back upon such adjectives as "hellish" or "horrifying"
or "nerve-wracking."

The Red River cart brigades never sneaked up on anybody.
On a still day you could hear them coming for miles, and see
the great cloud of yellow dust they raised; and if the buffalo
of the plains did finally flee into holes in the ground as the
Indians believed—well, it was no wonder.

LONG LIVE LIBERTY!

The Red River trails linked two frontiers and two political
systems. A bewildering mélange of cultures flowed over them:
British, French, American, Swiss; Indian and white and
Métis; Catholic and Protestant and pagan.

They freed trade from the restraints which governments
and private monopoly sought to impose upon it, and they
changed, for a time, the direction of commerce. They could
have changed the political destiny of half of the continent,
and almost did.

Initially the flow of goods to the frontier was from east to
west: Montreal to Red River by canoe; from New York to
Mackinac. But about 1830 the movement began to shift,
with the cargoes originating in the north and south. When
the Hudson's Bay Company absorbed the Nor'westers, London got the business of supplying the empire's outposts and
the goods came in by way of the Bay; on the American side
at about the same time the fur companies began shipping
supplies from St. Louis up the Mississippi to St. Peter's.

The Red River trails had been in use for several years for
occasional unscheduled transport before they became a vital
link in the new north-south chain of communication. In 1843
the first regular cart service was inaugurated between Pembina and St. Paul by Joseph Rolette, Astor's agent at Pembina. Half a dozen carts then sufficed to take the furs south
and bring back trade goods, implements, and whiskey; but

by 1851 more than a hundred were making the trip and in 1858 the number had grown to six hundred. This meant that a sizable share of the fur trade had been diverted, illegally, from the Hudson's Bay Company to the aggressive Yankee traders of St. Paul and New York, for there were not enough furs south of the boundary in the region served by the carts to make possible shipments on this scale.

Freight traffic over the prairie route reached its peak in 1869 when twenty-five hundred screeching carts raised a cloud of dust which hung over the trail for three months. Next year political troubles began and trade was interrupted; then, in 1873, the first steamboat came up the Red, and in 1878 the first railroad was completed. The old trails were finished.

But they had done their job. Among other things, they contributed more than any other factor to the break-up of the best-entrenched political and industrial combination that ever existed, the Hudson's Bay Company. The Company of Adventurers could absorb and disarm its most enterprising competitors; it could dictate to bishops and shift populations; it could stave off investigations and audits and other governmental interference—but it could not close the Red River trails.

The new nation being born on Red River owed much of its raison d'être to smuggling, as had other nations before it. Much of the commerce upon which St. Paul and other cities of the American frontier were built was illegal. But the laws that were broken were mostly Hudson's Bay Company laws, and few persons on either side of the forty-ninth parallel recognized the right of a chartered company to make and enforce legislation. Legally the Company did have governmental authority, but it could not convince its own "subjects," let alone other nationals, of that fact. Resistance to its decrees was sometimes active, sometimes passive, but constant.

The governmental authority was the Council of Assiniboia,

serving with the Company's local governor and selected by
him. In 1835 this group, using as an excuse the need for
money to be spent on "public works" (none of which developed), levied a duty of seven and one-half per cent on all ex-
ports and imports. The Métis reaction was so alarming that
the impost was soon cut back to four per cent, where it had
originally stood, and other measures were tried. Public flogging was ordered as punishment for theft, and theft could be
defined as removal of furs from the Company's jurisdiction
without an export license. But this could not be enforced,
either, without risking an uprising, so the law was repealed.
In 1840 the Company's men began searching homes and cart
trains for contraband furs, and a new land deed was devised
binding homeseekers not to trade in furs or import goods
from the United States.

The smugglers just took a wider cut across the prairie to
Pembina, and the settlers "squatted" without bothering about
titles. Their numbers were soon so great—more than five
thousand, most of them Métis, by this time—that the Company did not dare to try evictions.

The furs flowed south along the Red River trails, and
goods came back. St. Paul could supply pots and stoves and
tools and whiskey much more cheaply than cargoes could be
brought from London to the Bay and then south by boat to
Fort Garry. And the American traders gave two to four times
as much for furs as the British paid. Mink sold for ten pence
a skin at Fort Garry, forty cents at Pembina; buffalo robes,
for which the Company gave only five shillings, brought
$2.50 when smuggled south; and the American price for
beaver, $3.25, was double the sum offered by the British.

Moreover, the buffalo could not be persuaded to pay any
attention to the international boundary. They ranged freely
across it, but they preferred the country which was to become
Dakota and Montana; and where they went the hunters had
to follow. En route home, they sold the robes, tongues, and

some of the pemmican to the Americans at **Pembina**. As buffalo became scarce the Hudson's Bay Company was virtually
forced out of the market by the better-paying Yankee traders.

When smuggling increased the Company resorted to more
and more desperate measures, including even censorship of
the mails—which merely encouraged the people to smuggle
their letters, too, across the boundary to be carried by cart
to St. Peter's.

The Métis, slow to wrath, began to come to a boil. They
petitioned the Company for a definition of their rights and
were told, in effect, that they didn't have any: "Conditions of
land tenure have always been understood to prohibit any
infraction of the Company's privileges." They sent a few
petitions to American officials, to sound them out on the possibility of establishing themselves south of the boundary;
nothing came of these appeals, either. They sent complaints
to London which were vigorously prosecuted by Alexander
Isbister, a London attorney who was himself of Métis stock;
but after some steps were taken toward a governmental inquiry, the matter was dropped.

The mounting unrest frightened the Company and Her
Majesty's Government. An imperial regiment was brought to
the colony and martial law was imposed, but the Métis bided
their time. The troops were withdrawn after two years, and
in 1849 the people and the Company had it out. The Company lost.

Five hundred armed Métis surrounded the courthouse the
day Guillaume Sayer and three others were tried for illegal
trading in furs. Their leader told the Company's magistrates
that if the men were sentenced they would be forcibly freed.
The court yielded; the verdict was guilty but no penalty was
imposed.

A Métis, standing in the doorway, shouted the news: *"Le
commerce est libre! Vive la liberté!"*

The slogan spread like fire across the plains of Red River

south along the rutted trail to Pembina and St. Paul. The Métis sang and danced, the Yankee traders grinned; the Company of Adventurers had been cut down to size. Enforcement of its monopolistic decrees was never seriously attempted again. One could buy a Red River cart for ten dollars or make one for less, and the trail to St. Paul was open and free.

MILLER OF THE SEINE

The Métis leader who threatened the court and emerged to shout the good news to his colleagues was Louis Riel, called "the Elder" because his son of the same name was to attain great fame. He was known also as "the miller of the Seine," because he had built a flour mill on that little tributary of the Red near St. Boniface, the French settlement across the river from Fort Garry. Almost single-handed, he had dug a nine-mile channel from another creek to divert more water into the Seine to turn his wheel.

He was born in 1817 at Isle à la Crosse, a fur trade post in what is now northern Saskatchewan. His father, a Hudson's Bay Company trapper and trader, was white, a French Canadian among whose forebears there had been an Irishman who lived in St. Peter's parish, Limerick, in 1700. Riel's mother was a Métisse, half French, half Montagnais. The Montagnais were moose hunters, a Northern tribe which once triumphed spectacularly, with Champlain's help, over the mighty Iroquois.

Riel was educated in Berthier, Quebec, and studied for the priesthood, but like many others he found that his religious resolution could not withstand the call of the prairies. He came back to the Northwest in 1843 to join the buffalo hunt, and that fall he married. Though he was a natural leader, well-educated, intelligent and unusually enterprising, this marriage contributed as much as any of his personal qualities to his selection by the Métis as their spokesman and chief.

His bride was Julie Lajimodière, daughter of the revered "first white woman in the Northwest," sister of the "first white child."

In 1807 in her native Three Rivers, Quebec, Marie Anne Gaboury, destined to become the first white woman in the Northwest, was noted for her beauty—but at twenty-five she was still unwed, and there was talk about it in the parish, and head-shaking, and in the bosom of the family a little prayer. Marie Anne was waiting, and in Three Rivers many girls had waited, to their sorrow, until the steady young farmers of the neighborhood had gone elsewhere for brides.

The farmers made dependable but unexciting mates, whereas Three Rivers had produced another breed of men, wild and reckless and romantic, who wooed tempestuously, won—and departed. They were the *coureurs de bois,* the bush rangers; the first had come with Champlain when he established Three Rivers near Quebec in 1633. As lovers, these men were worse risks even than the fishermen, because there were women in the wilderness. The few women whom the men had brought back to Three Rivers were dark, unlovely creatures, sullen or dumbly meek, not at all like the dainty maidens who were primly trained by the sisters of the village. Nevertheless they were women, and the men married them—"after the fashion of the country," as they put it. Marie Anne sometimes worried about this.

But she—alone, perhaps, among all the pretty girls in town —need not have worried. After five years in the West, Jean Baptiste Lajimodière came home, as he had sworn he would, and he came alone—save for the sights and sounds and smells of the prairie which he brought into the trim little white cottages along the St. Lawrence. In April, 1807, they were married.

Before the honeymoon was over the bridegroom was talking about returning to the Northwest to make their fortune.

Marie Anne had observed that abandoned wives were no happier in Three Rivers than apprehensive sweethearts, even if their social standing was superior. If she could not crowd the wilderness out of her husband's heart, she could make certain of her own place in it, and incidentally show the heedless men of Three Rivers that courage and enterprise were not exclusively masculine virtues. She packed a little leather trunk and instructed Jean Baptiste to reserve her a place in his canoe with the fur brigade. She was going along—a thousand miles into the wilderness where no white woman was known to have gone before.

Jean Baptiste was horrified. He protested violently; so did her family, her friends, and the priest. But Marie Anne went.

She was not to be, after all, the first white woman—and incredible indeed are the coincidences of history.

About a year earlier, in the Orkney Islands off the Scottish coast, an unhappy girl had cut off her hair, donned boy's clothing and embarked as cabin boy on a ship bound for Hudson's Bay, in pursuit of a vanished lover. Traveling south on the rivers which emptied into the Bay and through the lakes, she reached the Red River country, the secret of her sex still incredibly undiscovered by most of her associates.

In December, 1807, she gave birth to a son at Henry's post in Pembina. This was the first white child born in the American or Canadian Northwest, and no one has ever known his name. There is no record of whether the Orkney girl found her faithless lover or took another; but her son was white. Henry, astonished when "the Orkney lad" suddenly began having labor pains after having asked permission to rest awhile in the trader's cabin, recorded the event in his journal—without the young mother's name. She went home on the next ship from Hudson's Bay, taking her baby with her, unaware—like so many others—that she had made history.

Just eight days after the "Orkney lad's" astonishing per-

formance at Pembina, Marie Anne's first child was born, and
in the same place.

This child was a girl. Because Marie Anne and her daughter lived out their lives in the Northwest (Madame Lajimodière died in 1878 at the age of ninety-six) they have been
regarded historically as the first white woman and first white
child.

There is no record of a meeting between the two young
mothers, but it is reasonable to assume that they did meet.
Marie Anne was in a hunters' camp and the Orkney girl was
at the North West Company post, but they were the only
white women in thousands of square miles and were likely
to have heard of each other's presence.

Marie Anne named her daughter Reine—the Queen—because she was born on the fete day of the Kings of the Magi,
January 6, 1808. The child was born in a tipi. Three Indian
and Métis women, as was the custom, helped. They drove two
long stakes into the earth floor and to these they lashed a
cross bar which came to Marie Anne's chest when she knelt
on a mat of moss. They whittled handholds in the bar and
told her to grasp it with both hands, to strain against it and
dig her moccasined feet into the pad of moss. The incessant
prairie wind whipped the taut skins of the lodge and the
snow pattered against them and swept on; but inside it was
warm and safe, and Marie Anne did not hear the wind because the women talked. The musical Cree phrases, though
she could understand only a few of them, were comforting.

Soon it was over. Reine was bathed in warm ashes and
wiped clean with moss and a powder made by pulverizing
rotten wood. The midwives clucked over her and gave her
a chunk of hardened fat, smoothly tapered at one end, to
suck until the mother would be permitted to nurse her, the
second day after birth. A moss bag was made; in this Marie
Anne could carry the baby on her back, or she could hang

the bag in a tipi and swing it gently, as other white mothers rocked a cradle.

The white girl from Three Rivers never forgot the kindness of her dark sisters of the wilderness. Years later when her husband was dead and her older children dispersed and she faced a trying time alone, she did not go back to the village on the St. Lawrence as she could have done; she went again to live among the Indians until a son came back from the plains to make a home for her.

The fortune Jean Baptiste had been so sure of obtaining was won and lost several times: it never seemed quite large enough to justify their return to Three Rivers. But after a few years that did not matter because neither of them had any desire to go back. He became a renowned guide and woodsman and messenger for the Earl of Selkirk. Their daughter Reine married Joseph Lamère (originally probably Lemieux), one of the French who chose the country south of the imaginary line, and died in the United States in 1894. More children were born to Marie Anne, including another daughter, Julie.

Julie Lajimodière grew up among Indian and Métis children; there still were few white youngsters during her childhood and they were Swiss or Scotch, alien to Julie by tradition, religion and language. She spoke Cree and French as did the Métis, dressed as they did, and in 1843 married one.

Julie's Louis was a restless, ambitious man; the flour mill on the Seine was only one of his many ventures, and the only one that was successful. Farming bored him and he was full of business schemes, one of them the establishment of a woolen mill. But the Hudson's Bay Company, the only source of capital in Rupert's Land, was not interested in promoting business ventures which might some day weaken its own commercial monopoly, and it refused to help Louis Riel.

The miller grumbled as he ground the farmers' wheat, and he found sympathetic hearing both among the Métis and the whites. So long as the Company retained political sovereignty, everyone agreed, business enterprise would not be encouraged. They were lucky to be able to sneak their furs south to Pembina for sale to the Americans. Down there, in the country of free competition, things were happening; markets were expanding, prices were good. There was a lot to be said, the miller told his customers, for the Yankee system.

CHAPTER III

Manifest Destiny

SPIRIT OF CHANGE

THE judgment of Louis Riel the Elder, the obscure Métis miller in Rupert's Land, was supported by that of a distinguished English intellectual to whom the United States was host in 1861.

As he approached St. Paul in the new State of Minnesota (it had been admitted to the Union in 1858), Anthony Trollope reviewed his conclusions about the "frontier American," who was something new in his experience. His research had been difficult. The traditional aloofness of the Briton, he decided, was a fiction: for downright surly taciturnity, give him a Western Yankee every time. "A Western American man is not a talking man. He will sit for hours over a stove with a cigar in his mouth and his hat over his eyes, chewing the cud of reflection."

But these Westerners, Trollope warned his countrymen, were highly intelligent. More, they were "energetic and speculative, conceiving grand ideas, and carrying them out almost with the rapidity of magic. Everybody understands

66

everything, and everybody intends sooner or later to do everything."

Take, for example, this city of St. Paul. Its site was "almost romantic," and fourteen thousand people had already settled upon it. But its hotel was what had really impressed the visitor. No sound and solid Englishman, he said, would dream of building an establishment of such size and luxury in a place five times as big.

In all of it the Briton read ominous portents for the Empire. Hatred of England was general throughout the Northern states; "to us the danger is very great." One possibility could not be ignored—that the Union Army, if victorious in the struggle with Secession, might turn upon Britain's North American colonies to avenge English affronts to the pride of the United States. And if that did not happen, he foresaw still another hazard—filibustering by discharged troops. A million men had been under arms south of the forty-ninth parallel, and some of them would not readjust easily to the humdrum life of the farm. Thinking it over, Trollope decided that this filibustering might develop into the most serious threat to their security that the British North American colonies had ever faced.

There was talk of forming a federal government for Canada, linking the independent provinces of Upper Canada (now Ontario), Lower Canada (Quebec), New Brunswick and Nova Scotia. Trollope believed such a confederation would be of great advantage. It might even be given a king, he suggested, for "we are rich in princes." At present the colonists were loyal, but at one time some years before there had been outspoken sentiment for annexation to the United States, and now the pressure from south of the line was constant: "aggression, braggadocio, insolence" on the part of the Americans, and among the Canadians a dangerous dependence upon Yankee transport facilities and Yankee business enterprise.

A good reporter and perceptive political analyst, Trollope was not alone in recognizing the threat to British North America from the new, aggressive, industrialized United States which might emerge from the Civil War. His book,

Canada, Before Confederation 1867

published in 1862, probably helped to promote Canadian Confederation, but there had been many other and earlier voices. Confederation came on July 1, 1867, the effective date of the British North America Act of the imperial Parliament. Sir John A. Macdonald and other Canadian negotiators in London had tried hard to create, as Trollope had urged, "the Kingdom of Canada," and to found a new British monarchy.

But Britain feared this would vex the Americans; with their Union saved at the cost of half a million lives, they were touchier than ever about their republicanism. So the "Dominion" of Canada was born, uniting Quebec, Ontario, Nova Scotia and New Brunswick, and a governor general, instead of a prince, represented the Crown.

From the first the sponsors of Confederation had had their eyes upon the Northwest. It was there that American "aggression" was most to be feared. As much as ten years earlier, annexation of Rupert's Land by Upper and Lower Canada had been proposed, but the provinces had lacked the cash and could not command the credit to buy out the Hudson's Bay Company.

The struggle for Oregon in the forties, the invasion of the goldfields of the crown colony of British Columbia in the fifties by California prospectors, the piratical practices of Yankee traders in the Red River Basin in the sixties, and the westward thrust of the Union Pacific, the first transcontinental railroad, completed in 1869—all contributed to the conviction that unless Britain bestirred herself, the West would soon be lost. Development now centered in the mid-continent: Minnesota, a Territory with only 6,000 people in 1850, was a State with 172,000 people ten years later.

While the Canadian negotiators were busy in London, Secretary of State William H. Seward and Senator Charles Sumner managed to put over American purchase of Alaska from the Russians; Seward then announced publicly that the whole continent sooner or later would come within the confines of the American Union. Similarly Presidents Johnson and Grant and the latter's Secretary of State Hamilton Fish made no secret of their annexationist ambitions.

It had been apparent for a decade that the Hudson's Bay Company could not hold the British Northwest for the Crown. It had tired of judicial and administrative responsibilities. It was harassed by Métis smugglers and American free traders and its costs were rising. Stockholders in London begrudged the expense of nonbusiness functions; the fur trade was no longer profitable enough to support the provision of governmental services by a mercantile company.

Canada, After Confederation 1867

In December, 1867, a series of resolutions was introduced in the Dominion Parliament by William McDougall. He was Minister of Public Works in Prime Minister Sir John A. Macdonald's first Cabinet of Confederation, and he had been one of the men who had participated in negotiations for Canadian union in London a year earlier.

To promote the prosperity of the new Dominion and to strengthen the Empire, the resolutions said, the time had come to extend Canada to the Pacific. The vast territory which lay between the Lake of the Woods and the Rockies must be wrested from the relaxing grip of the Hudson's Bay Company, which had shown itself wholly unable to control the Indians, those half-savage Métis, or the Americans who moved freely north and south along the Red River, Upper Missouri and British Columbia trails. Canada would pay the Company, in return for relinquishment of all its title, three hundred thousand pounds sterling, would reserve to it some blocks of acreage around each trading post, and give it one-twentieth of the land in each township opened to settlement.

It was an ambitious scheme, because the Dominion was weak and opposition to Confederation was still vociferous. Prince Edward Island, Newfoundland, and British Columbia had not come in at all, and there were strong blocs even in the four united provinces who viewed the Dominion with suspicion. Moreover, despite the attitude of the Company's London stockholders, there was angry opposition within the chartered firm to the surrender of any of its privileges. This came from the "wintering partners," the chief factors and chief traders who owned no stock but earned an annual share of the profits. They were the kings of the wilderness, and human enough to enjoy it; and they were understandably annoyed because no provision had been made to give them a share of the money Canada would pay for the Company's domain. And, finally, there was the problem of the money itself: it would have to be borrowed from the British Government, for the new Dominion was broke.

But none of these obstacles loomed large enough to obscure the vision or check the ambition of William McDougall.

It was unfortunate, Sir John Macdonald confessed to his intimates, that a man of McDougall's ability should have, politically speaking, so little sense.

McDougall, a Member of Parliament from Ontario, had

been trained for the law but preferred journalism and politics. He distinguished himself quickly in both fields: the newspapers called him "an eloquent young man." But the gossips

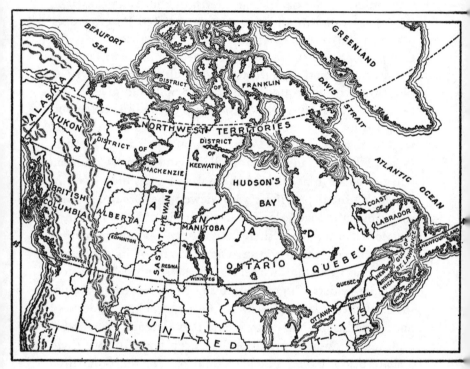

Canada Today

said he was unpopular even among his colleagues and that
Sir John was eagerly anticipating an opportunity to "kick
him upstairs."

The Minister of Public Works was disdainful of such
political prattle; he had more important concerns. He
brooded over the map of British North America and drafted
ill-tempered letters to the Colonial Office in London.

The transfer of the Northwest to the Dominion must not be delayed, he wrote on December 28, 1867, "by negotiations or correspondence with private or third parties whose position, opinions and claims have heretofore embarrassed both Governments in dealing with this question." That meant the Americans and the Company's winterers, reluctant to yield their influence or power. McDougall, athirst for power himself, was impatient of such concerns in others; and anyway it was no business of his how the Company cut the pie. But he had consented to the insertion of some placatory phrases in the resolutions. It had been deemed expedient to offer some reassurance to the winterers and to the natives—the Indians and Métis upon whom the winterers exerted, unfortunately, very strong influence. So the address to the Queen urging the annexation of the Northwest by the Dominion included a pledge to respect the rights of individuals and to settle Indian claims "in conformity with equitable principles which have uniformly governed the British Crown in its dealings with the aborigines."

That should make the natives easier to handle, McDougall reflected, when he arrived among them to assume his duties as the first Lieutenant Governor of Rupert's Land. For he was going upstairs—Sir John had promised him the post if he could put this over. He had done well in politics, but a Cabinet portfolio need not be the end. He had not been able to obtain, as yet, any record as an administrator. Rupert's Land would provide that. Then, perhaps, a title; and ultimately, why not the Prime Ministry?

William McDougall's cupped hands enclosed on the map the empire which he was to rule. Two million square miles! But the "eloquent young man" was now forty-five years old; somehow he must convince the Colonial Office that there was need for haste.

His finger traced the forty-ninth parallel from the western boundary of Ontario, on the ninety-fifth meridian, to the

Rocky Mountains, on the hundred and fifteenth—two thousand miles of unguarded frontier. He tapped the map sharply at the Red River, and turned back to his letter:

The recent proposals in the Congress of the United States in reference to British North America, the rapid advance of mining and agricultural settlement westward, and the avowed policy of the Washington Government to acquire territory from other powers by purchase or otherwise, admonish us that not a day is to be lost in determining and publishing our policy in regard to these territories.

That bit about "purchase or otherwise" might waken the Colonial Office to its responsibilities. Perhaps it was not strictly accurate; the Washington Government, in so far as it had avowed any policy at all, had mentioned only purchase. But the border men, the intriguers in Pembina and St. Paul, were not so circumspect. And how about those outrageous Fenian Raids last year?

Trollope's prophecy of filibustering by jobless veterans of the Civil War came true about five years after he wrote it—in June, 1866, when the first of the fantastic Fenian Raids upon Canada was staged by Gen. John O'Neill of the Irish Republican Army.

The Fenian movement, organized in the United States to seek freedom for Ireland by harassing Britain or her colonies, recruited thousands of skilled American soldiers, including O'Neill. He was born in Ireland in 1834, had been an Indian fighter in the Second U. S. Cavalry, and fought in the Peninsular campaign in the Civil War. He was seriously wounded and was officially noticed as "an unusually daring and active officer." After the war he became United States claim agent at Nashville and threw himself into Fenian activities.

O'Neill led a thousand men, most of them Civil War

veterans, in the first raid. They were ferried across the Niagara River from northern New York and defeated an ill-organized, outnumbered and ineptly led force of Canadian volunteers to capture Fort Erie, Ontario. Ten thousand more Fenians waited in the Buffalo area for O'Neill to secure the bridgehead, but the United States belatedly intervened and cut off his supplies and reinforcements; after two days the invaders withdrew.

Blame for Canada's disaster at Fort Erie fell upon Lieut. Col. John Stoughton Dennis, who commanded an Ontario militia detachment which he led into the trap set by O'Neill. Half of Dennis's command was lost and some of his men claimed he had disgracefully deserted them under fire. Finally, at Dennis's own request, a military court of inquiry sat in judgment upon him. Cowardice was not proven, the court decided, but it was a close thing: the court's president, in a separate opinion, judged Dennis guilty of inexcusable recklessness and inefficiency.

Dennis had shown courage and initiative by forcing a showdown. The whispers about his alleged desertion might have wrecked his career; as it was, the incident barely interrupted it. He was surveyor of public lands in Ontario; when a new assignment came from his old friend William McDougall, he was ready for it. It took him a thousand miles west to Pembina, where many trails crossed, and led him into ventures so desperate that his horrified Government sought to expunge his follies from the official record. And on his heels, traveling the same Pembina trail to his final, fatal humiliation, came his conqueror, Gen. John J. O'Neill.

GENIAL GEOPOLITICIAN

Seven years after Trollope's visit, while William McDougall and Sir George Cartier of the Canadian Cabinet dickered in London for the purchase of Rupert's Land, the progressive people of St. Paul had begun to listen seriously to an apper-

ceptive thinker who had introduced them to geopolitics and
made them like it. He was James Wickes Taylor, born in
New York state, two years older than McDougall and like
him a lawyer and journalist. Taylor was an "eloquent young
man," too, first winning notice as such when he delivered a
funeral oration over the body of a fraternity colleague at
Hamilton College.

Before he arrived in St. Paul to open a law office, Taylor
had written a novel, a history of Ohio, a school manual, and
scores of letters and articles for newspapers. He had made
himself the foremost authority on the geography, economics
and social conditions of America's northern frontier. His reports on the commercial and political relations of the British
Northwest and adjacent American territories and states had
been used by legislatures and by Congress.

In 1868 Taylor was nearing the end of ten years' service as
a special agent of the United States Treasury, charged with
investigating trade with British North America and transport
facilities. He was a scholar and a gentleman, gifted with an
easy grace of manner which charmed everyone he met. Many
never discovered his shrewdness and few realized until long
after his death the full scope of his learning and the prescient
quality of his thought. He was the author of half a dozen
painstaking studies of the timber, mineral, agricultural and
water resources of the American prairies, the British Northwest and even the remote Mackenzie Basin. As early as 1860
he pointed out the economic and strategic interdependence
of the United States and British possessions to the north and
urged a customs union.

The dual citizenship of the Western frontier reached its
finest expression in James Wickes Taylor. Though at one
time he was a secret agent of the United States in Canada—
to all intents and purposes a spy—Canada knew him as a
wise counselor and considerate friend. It was no secret that
he dreamed of American annexation of the British North-

west and worked hard for it, but nowhere in his public utterances or private papers is there any indication that he would have countenanced military conquest. Annexation was to come only by the consent of the people of Red River, freely given. It was a long time before Taylor and less scrupulous men associated with him in the movement were to be convinced that this consent would never come.

Geopolitician Taylor had a great deal to say and nearly all of it was worth listening to. But it could not always be said briefly and sometimes his listeners tired. It is possible that not all of those who heard him one evening in February, 1868, in St. Paul, were fully alert to what he was proposing.

That evening he presented to the Chamber of Commerce the draft of a memorial to Congress which he suggested that the Chamber endorse and send to Washington. It was several thousand words long and innocently titled; it appeared to be a petition for immediate establishment of triweekly mail service by stagecoach from Minnesota to the new goldfields capital, Helena, Montana. This service would mean the beginning of overland transport from St. Paul to the Rockies.

It sounded like an excellent idea. Why should not St. Paul divert some of the profitable Montana business which had all been going down the Missouri River to St. Louis? A casual voice vote approved Taylor's resolution.

The press next day carried the full text, obligingly provided in advance by Taylor. Reading it, some who had perfunctorily recorded their votes of approval wondered if they had been indiscreet. They recalled Taylor's passing reference to the purchase of Alaska; but what had followed that reference had not sounded quite so audacious as it now looked, in print:

If the country at large shall acquiesce, a public sentiment, already manifested quite distinctly in San Francisco, will become general, that the intervening territories [between St. Paul and

Alaska], if possible, shall be annexed to the United States. Their
inhabitants, largely emigrants from the United States, will never
consent to be transferred by Parliamentary edict and without
a popular vote to the distant and feeble Confederation of Canada. . . .

The reader may have paused here. "Largely emigrants
from the United States" was putting it a bit strong; St. Paul
had many customers across the line who were loyal subjects
of the Queen. Perhaps the "American element" about which
the border people talked so much was somewhat exaggerated.
There were the half-breeds, of course. But were they American? Were they anything?

"We speak without reserve," Taylor's resolution continued, and the reader may have thought, we do indeed:

Our fellow citizens of the Pacific Coast and the people of the
Northwest States have resolved that the Dominion of Canada
shall find its western boundary on the 90th meridian of longi-
tude. . . .

The St. Paul Chamber of Commerce had officially, and on
the record, unanimously, demanded the annexation of British
Northwest America. And Minnesota's conscientious Senator
Ramsey promptly ran with the ball Taylor had ingeniously
passed to him. In July, 1868, the Senate adopted Ramsey's
resolution instructing the State Department to inquire into
the possibility of purchasing the vast domain of the Hudson's
Bay Company.

The St. Paul business community had taken its first dip in
the treacherous pool of power politics. It was not the first
venture, however, for Taylor or Ramsey. Taylor had proposed annexation in 1866, in a trade relations report which
Congress had asked of him, and his ideas were incorporated
in a bill introduced soon thereafter by Gen. N. P. Banks,
chairman of the House foreign relations committee. But
Banks's bill caused such an uproar in the Canadian colonies

that it was permitted to die without debate. Late in 1867 Ramsey offered another resolution suggesting negotiations for annexation; this, too, was on its way to oblivion when Taylor's St. Paul maneuver enabled the senator to revive it and get it passed.

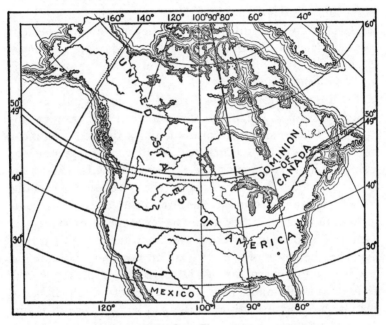

Yankee Dream

The Taylor and Ramsey proposals and the Senate's action in July, 1868, preceded the adoption by the Canadian Parliament of its own resolution authorizing absorption of the Northwest by the Dominion. In point of time, therefore, the Americans had a good argument: they were at least as eager as the Canadians were to extend the protection of their flag and the benefits of their commerce to the sparsely peopled prairies. And, as usual, the Yankees had more money.

The United States talked of paying the Hudson's Bay

Company ten million dollars, as against Canada's paltry million and a half, and undoubtedly the Americans also could have been induced to reserve land grants similar to those the Company won from the Dominion. There would be money for the disgruntled winterers—or at least some of them were persuaded that there would be. And the United States would start immediately to build a Northern Pacific railroad, an undertaking which surely would be beyond the power of the poverty-stricken Dominion for a hundred years. (Actually Canada managed to do it in twenty, much to the amazement of her southern neighbor.)

But the American proposal really was presumptuous and almost insulting. It ignored the community of political interest of Britain and its Dominion, and it ignored the fundamental British rights which had been won by exploration, conquest and settlement. The deal gave Canada little as an inducement to abandon its claim, and gave Britain nothing at all. To the Dominion the Americans offered (as compensation for a boundary fixed forever at the western edge of Ontario!) the boon of free trade, boasting that this would increase the value of every Canadian farm and business by ten per cent, overnight. To Britain the Yankees offered shadow, not substance. They would scale down their Alabama claims, growing out of losses sustained by Northern shipping from Confederate vessels fitted out in British ports. These claims had not been adjudicated, and an offer to reduce them was merely an attempt to sell a pig in a poke.

But all these considerations of international barter were of little concern to the people of St. Paul. They were humanly interested in the simple and familiar: the fate of their neighbors on Red River. The American proposals for annexation recognized the interests of the present inhabitants and their right to a voice in their destiny. That was more than the Dominion, apparently, intended to do.

The people up north, Taylor's resolution had said, "will

never consent to be transferred by Parliamentary edict and without a popular vote to the distant and feeble Confederation of Canada." That was dogmatically phrased; it might have been wondered how Taylor knew.

CONSPIRATORIAL CRIPPLE

It is likely that he knew because Enos A. Stutsman told him.

Enos Stutsman, like other featured players in the Northwestern drama, was a lawyer and journalist. In 1868 he was forty-two, younger than either McDougall or Taylor but of their generation and sharing to some extent their attitudes and ambitions.

With that, however, similarity ended; for Enos Stutsman had no legs.

The mere fact of this man's survival on the crude Western frontier in the sixties when life was difficult even for those with a full complement of strong limbs, tells more than volumes could about his courage and persistence. He was born without legs and never was able to stand erect or move except with crutches, yet at seventeen he was supporting himself as a teacher. He died at forty-eight, but he had made himself a prominent political figure and, by shrewd real estate investments, a prosperous man. He could have become an American hero if Washington had been less timid. If the United States had acquired the British Northwest, an area larger than that of the Louisiana Purchase, he would have done as much as anyone to bring it about, as much even as Taylor.

It would be easy to picture Stutsman as another Gloucester, an embittered and unscrupulous intriguer, craving power, loathing his own malformed body and despising his physical betters, a man without charity or love. But he was not such a man. He was generous and companionable, popular, competent. Like Taylor he loved the prairie, and he did not permit his physical handicap to keep him indoors. Above the waist his body was well-formed, as large as that of a two-hundred-pound man, and his arms possessed unusual strength. He was handsome, his young face framed by the "burnsides" affected by men of his time; his gaze was clear and direct, his mouth somewhat sensitive, with a delicate look about it.

Stutsman never married. He took care of himself without fuss and without complaint. His agility as he swung himself from his crutches into his buggy and even, occasionally, into a specially made saddle, was the marvel of the musclebound frontiersmen who watched him. He rode and drove alone, setting out fearlessly on long trips in uncertain weather.

The cripple came of pioneer stock. His father, a Pennsylvania German, had lived in three states before Enos was born in Indiana; the son, scorning physical disability, pressed on still farther, to the outermost western limits of civilization. In Coles County, Illinois, where the Stutsmans were neighbors of Abraham Lincoln's father, the eager young student prepared himself for teaching, law, and politics; in 1856 he moved on alone to Sioux City, then an outpost on the Indian frontier, and started the real estate business which he conducted successfully for the rest of his life. This work took him to Dakota Territory. There he helped to establish the town of Yankton and became a territorial legislator.

In 1866 Stutsman was appointed a customs agent for the United States, assigned—legs or no legs—to the risky and unpopular job of checking smuggling on the Red River trails. He moved to historic Pembina, the only port of entry in the Territory. There, in addition to performing his governmental function, he practiced law, built a hotel, and was elected several times more to the legislature.

When Enos Stutsman died in 1874 the press of Dakota Territory, St. Paul and other Western cities eulogized his skill, his geniality and his honorable record. He had won respect and admiration on the frontier, the papers said; there was no one who would not mourn him.

But there was one who did not mourn, one who by this time had been mercifully forgotten by the American press.

There would be no title for William McDougall and he would never become Prime Minister, nor even, again, a Cabinet minister, because Enos Stutsman, the legless schemer of Pembina, made him the laughingstock of a continent.

McDougall outlived the brilliant cripple by thirty-one years, but he never lived down the story of his bungling, of his futile rage born of frustrated ambition, which Stutsman poured into the columns of the newspapers for all the world to read. And McDougall could never be certain that he might not have succeeded and ruled the empire of which he dreamed if it had not been for the intrigues of the American whom he had mistakenly regarded, with pity edged with contempt, as only half a man.

CHAPTER IV

Chance of Glory

THE SUPERIOR INTELLIGENCE

DROUGHT and grasshoppers ruined the Red River crop in 1868 and the buffalo herd unaccountably vanished, as it often did. The colony again faced starvation. Relief funds were solicited by Catholic Bishop Taché and the Protestant clergymen; the Hudson's Bay Company gave six thousand pounds, about five thousand dollars came from the United States, nearly all of it from St. Paul, and the Province of Ontario, with much fanfare, pledged five thousand dollars which it never delivered.

The crisis was a God-given opportunity for McDougall and his chief, Sir John. Negotiations in London for the transfer of Rupert's Land to the Dominion inevitably would be slow; meanwhile Canada's position in the West could be consolidated by sleight of hand. McDougall offered "work relief" to the desperate men of Red River in the form of jobs on the Dawson Road. This was a route from the Lake of the Woods to Fort Garry surveyed some years before by S. J. Dawson; no work had ever been done on the western end.

No one seems to have accepted McDougall's offer, but he sent men anyway to launch his project. Later, when the question of the legitimacy of their mission was raised, the Minister said the Company had consented; but the record showed that Chief Factor William Mactavish, Governor of Rupert's Land, had protested the intrusion. Mactavish, however, was slowly dying of "consumption." He was bedridden much of the time, and he was resentful, as were all the winterers, because he had not been considered in the negotiations with Canada. He could hardly have been expected to take aggressive steps to safeguard the Company's interest.

McDougall's chief agent was John A. Snow, chosen to direct construction of the road. Snow established fifteen dollars a month as the going wage for laborers he engaged to clear brush and trees from the right-of-way. Low as this was (there were rumors that Canada had budgeted eighteen dollars and that someone was pocketing the difference), it was paid not in cash but in purchase orders on the project store at Oak Point, reputedly owned by the leader of the colony's "Canadian party," Dr. John C. Schultz. Prices at this store were outrageously high: flour cost eighteen dollars a barrel there, fifteen in Fort Garry. The work, moreover, was hard and equipment was inadequate. Men had to carry felled trees on their backs. And sometimes Snow was slow with the pay orders.

The Métis workers, Snow acknowledged, were as efficient as any he had ever encountered, and were tractable; but he found the Canadians—his own people—and the Americans, some of them deserters from the United States Army, much harder to handle. One day a group of white workmen demanded a raise in pay and when Snow refused it they manhandled him and almost threw him into a river. Their ringleader, subsequently fined for the assault, was an irascible young Canadian, Thomas Scott. He soon became one of the most important figures in the history of the West, merely by getting himself shot.

Snow's assistant was Charles Mair, perhaps the only poet in the history of literature whose work so aroused his critics that they set upon him in the local post office and beat him up. (The critic who got in the best licks was Mrs. A. G. B. Bannatyne, wife of the postmaster.) Mair, whose incendiary composition had been newspaper prose in this instance, apologized abjectly, abandoned journalism, and thereafter confined himself to epic verse.

He had produced a volume of poetry shortly before his arrival in Rupert's Land and it had been ecstatically received by the press of his native Ontario; at twenty-eight, the newspapers said, Mair had become "the Canadian poet." The press hung upon his words, and so it happened that without his permission his private letters from Red River to friends at home found their way into the columns of the Toronto *Globe*.

Mair had quit the hotel, he wrote, to move in with Dr. Schultz and thus escape "the racket of a motley crowd of half-breeds." He commented with amused condescension upon the "jealousies and heartburnings" which developed from racial tension in the colony:

Many wealthy people are married to half-breed women who, having no coat of arms but a totem to look back to, make up for the deficiency by biting at the backs of their white sisters. The white sisters fall back upon their whiteness, whilst the husbands meet each other with desperate courtesies and hospitalities, with a view to filthy lucre in the background.

After his chastening interview in the post office with a group of enraged women, the poet did his best to make amends. He admonished the friends who had made his letters public and wrote a placatory piece for the *Globe*. Thereafter he managed to stay out of trouble—but his boss, Snow, was not so lucky.

With Mair, Schultz and others of the Canadian group, Snow schemed to get in on the ground floor of the land boom which they anticipated after the Dominion took over. Snow started dickering with the Indians for property to which the Métis or the Company had equal or greater right, and one of his favorite mediums of exchange was whiskey. He was promptly caught, brought before the Company's court, and fined ten pounds.

This incident confirmed the swiftly developing fears of the Métis that the alien invaders intended to push them out of the country. There had been eight years of reckless talk and mounting tension. The only newspaper, *The Nor'wester,* established in 1859 by Canadians, had continually demanded annexation to the Dominion. "The wise and prudent," its editors wrote, "will be prepared to receive and benefit by them [the changes to be made when Canada assumed sovereignty] whilst the indolent and careless, like the native tribes of the country, will fall back before the march of a superior intelligence."

At the time of Snow's arrest the newspaper was controlled by Dr. Schultz and was more outspoken than ever. It had reported, with vigorous approval, the negotiations in London. But no official notification of these negotiations had ever been given to the people whom they affected, nor had their opinion ever been asked by the newspaper or by anyone else. Governor Mactavish had not been officially informed of the impending change in his status by Canada or even by his own company, though he was the head of such government as existed.

"Enlightened" Canadians subsequently acknowledged that all this constituted incredible bungling by Sir John A. Macdonald, the revered "Father of Confederation." But none of the apologists dared strike to the heart of the matter—the social attitude which had made such bungling inevitable. There was no need to inform "the natives": the lords of

Ottawa and the lords of London would decide what was good for them.

About a year later—too late—Sir John found it necessary to send a commissioner to explain the Dominion's intentions. Then he made his thinking quite clear in a letter:

We must not make any indication of even thinking of a military force until peaceable means have been exhausted. Should these miserable half-breeds not disband, they must be put down, and then, so far as I can influence matters, I shall be very glad to give Col. Wolseley the chance of glory and the risk of a scalping knife.

The fact that the "miserable half-breeds" had a better claim than anyone save their Indian cousins to ownership of the country was of little concern to any Canadian, from the head of the Government all the way down to Dr. John C. Schultz.

NORTHERN LIGHT LODGE

That was a long way down. Schultz was an ambitious meddler, western archetype of the political physician. He was ruthless and bigoted, but he was also a big man of superb physical strength, handsome, an effective speaker, intelligent and courageous. Sir John thought him "clever, but exceedingly cantankerous and ill-conditioned." Donald A. Smith of the Hudson's Bay Company, the future Lord Strathcona, was more blunt: he called Schultz a man "of very indifferent private character."

The doctor was an old Ontario friend of Minister McDougall and they kept in touch with each other by correspondence or through visits to Ottawa by Schultz. For a long time McDougall's only knowledge of conditions in the West came from Schultz. Later, when one of McDougall's own agents sent him an accurate appraisal of Red River sentiment coupled with an urgent warning, the Minister ignored it.

Schultz was born in 1840 and started the practice of medicine when he was twenty. He came west at about that time, busied himself in political agitation and soon seized leadership of the Ontario faction, the "Canadian party." Though he had a head start on others in his profession, he neglected medical practice to run a store and to become a partner in the newspaper, which was abusively anti-Métis and anti-Company as long as he was connected with it.

In 1868 the doctor sold his newspaper interest to a dentist whom he could depend upon to follow the Canadian line. In that year, too, he broke finally with the Company by successfully defying its legal authority. Imprisoned because he refused to pay a judgment imposed by the local court, he broke out of jail with the help of his wife and friends, then produced a witness whose story enabled him to go free. By the time Snow and Mair arrived and moved into his home he regarded himself as the biggest man in Assiniboia and made no secret of the fact that he expected political preferment when Canada assumed control.

Medicine, merchandising, politics and journalism were not enough, however, to fill the life of this indefatigable Canadian. Early in 1864 he took on another responsibility— leadership of the first Masonic lodge in the Northwest.

Several members of a company of United States troops temporarily stationed in Pembina were Masons, and in January, 1864, they established the "Northern Light" lodge in the border town. (Masons in a Montana gold camp had an earlier dispensation but did not get around to the formal organization of their lodge until a couple of years later.) Dr. Schultz led a group of candidates to Pembina from north of the boundary and in the spring he became acting master of the lodge. After the American troops withdrew from Pembina in October the lodge was moved to Fort Garry. It lasted only five years, but it gave Schultz much influence over the Protestant white element. His newspaper hinted tantalizingly

of ancient secrets known only to its editor and a select circle
of his friends, and reported with smug flourishes the frequent
Masonic meetings and social affairs.

The Catholic priests knew little about Masonry but feared
the worst. They jittered and gossiped and communicated
their alarm to the credulous Métis. Some of the clergy's
suspicions were fantastic, but they did have cause for worry:
many if not most of Schultz's Masonic colleagues were also
affiliated with the Loyal Orange Institution.

Orangemen, implacable foes of Catholicism, were an important and sometimes dominant political force in Ontario,
which was honeycombed with their lodges. The earliest
Canadian immigrants brought the creed to Red River and it
contributed strongly to the social tension. The community
was half Catholic, and to add a complication the Catholics
were French; the Irish political aspects of Orangeism were
incomprehensible to them and mysteriously evil. Owing in
no little part to the naive boasting of Schultz and a few others,
Masonry was soon bracketed in the Catholic mind with this
earlier and more bigoted arrival.

Masonry also alienated the Métis and other humble settlers
because it sought to set up an elite social group. The standards of the new West were built upon achievement, not upon
breeding or social standing, and upon skills rather than upon
wealth. The scholar and aristocrat and the prosperous were
respected if they could prove their usefulness to the community, but it behooved them to acknowledge the social equality
of their neighbors: many a "gentleman" owed his life to an
illiterate half-breed guide.

Most of the newcomers had fitted fairly easily into the new,
liberal social pattern until the arrival of the militant "Canadian party" in the sixties. The Selkirk colonists had been farmers, artisans, military mercenaries—all poor and of varied racial stocks. The Americans had long since rejected the aristo-
cratic tradition and now ostentatiously despised it. Only a

small group, dubbed by one observer "a few Canadian snobs" —never more than a hundred individuals in a population of twelve thousand—found it insupportable that they should have to put aside their starched dickeys in favor of the sweat-stained buckskins of the frontier.

The development of a new social concept was illustrated by an incident which occurred in 1857 when Henry Youle Hind, M.A., F.R.G.S., was exploring the Red River country. He visited the farm of John Gowler, nine miles from Fort Garry, and was invited to stay for lunch. Mrs. Gowler set only one place. Her husband seated the guest, then asked, "Where is my plate?"

"Oh, John!" his wife remonstrated. "You would not think of sitting at table with a gentleman!"

John Gowler glanced about the room. His son-in-law and his children were watching silently.

"Give me a chair and a plate!" he said. "Am I not a gentleman too? Is not this my house, and these my victuals? Give me a plate!"

The tinder for the fire was nearly all assembled now, in a remote prairie outpost where few contemporary observers could recognize the forces which had contributed fuel for the blaze.

Here were a new people, wild and free and in love with their land, unsure of themselves but proud of their traditional skills, timid now and brave tomorrow, gentle and savage.

Here were a few ambitious men of ability who wanted fame or money, or needed to recapture lost prestige; and a few who were merely foolhardy, who would never have been heard of in another, more populous setting.

Here were brilliant and aggressive men who would have thrust the boundaries of the reinvigorated United States north to the Pole, in obedience to the dictates of Manifest

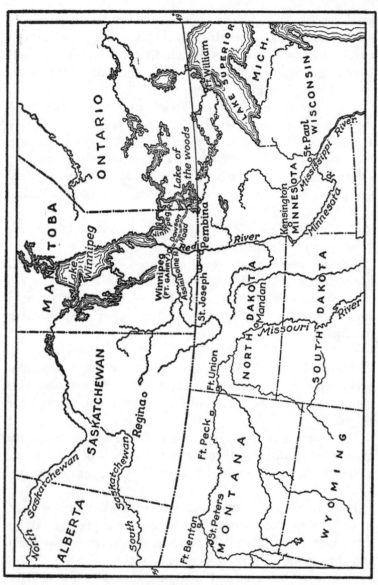

Area of *Contention*

Destiny; and one who was bitterly dying, William Mactavish, who would have held that empire for the Company of Adventurers trading into Hudson's Bay.

A new ideal of social equality had been born here, permitting John Gowler to sit at table with a gentleman; but it was threatened with destruction before it had a chance to establish itself.

Many languages were spoken, but only two which had been imported from Europe—French and English—could no longer be spoken quietly, in friendship. Here, where there were almost no Irish, there were nevertheless Orangemen and Fenians who would recruit allies to help them bloody the soil in ancient alien quarrels. Where all men once had worshiped the sun, two irreconcilable foreign faiths reached for the wounding word, gingerly edged and kept ready to hand under the cassock.

Only a little more fuel was needed, and a spark. They were provided by Minister McDougall and Col. John Stoughton Dennis.

THE MOST DESIRABLE EMIGRANTS

By March, 1869, Canada's delegates had reached general agreement with the Hudson's Bay Company on the terms of transfer of Rupert's Land. But the pact would not be signed until November, and even then the territory could not be formally acquired until the Crown approved the transaction and the Queen issued a proclamation. The Dominion hoped to have that proclamation dated December 1.

Meanwhile the impatient Minister of Public Works could see no reason to wait upon legal formalities. In July he issued an order to Colonel Dennis:

Referring to the subject discussed at our interview yesterday, I now request you to proceed without delay to Fort Garry, Red River, for the purpose, as explained to you, of selecting the most

suitable localities for the survey of townships for immediate settlement. . . .

The American system of survey is that which appears best
suited to the country, except as to the area of the section. The
first emigrants, and the most desirable, will probably go from
Canada, and it will therefore be advisable to offer them lots of a
size to which they have become accustomed. This will require
you to make the section 800 acres instead of 640, as on the American plan.

Dennis was instructed to confer with Governor Mactavish
—but only because the latter "should be able to help." Mc-
Dougall actually was sending an agent into a sovereign foreign state to select lands for settlement predicated upon a
transfer of authority which had not yet occurred and which
was bitterly opposed in the affected region. The United States
would have been hardly more presumptuous if it had chosen
to regard the annexation bills introduced in its Congress as
excuse to send its surveyors into British North America.

But arrogance was not the only significant characteristic
of Dennis's orders.

"The most desirable emigrants," McDougall wrote, "will
probably go from Canada," and the survey should be of a type
familiar to them—but by Canada he meant Ontario, because
Quebec and the Maritime Provinces had not been surveyed
on the plan he suggested to Dennis. Thus the new Northwest,
ostensibly to be a Territory of the Dominion, really was to be
an extension of Protestant Anglo-Saxon Ontario.

And the newcomers, not the settlers already established,
were to be accommodated by the survey. There were twelve
thousand people in Rupert's Land and all of them had some
sort of claim, no matter how informal; hundreds held legal
deeds from the Hudson's Bay Company to property which
had been surveyed on a different basis.

McDougall's decision that the American system was "best
suited" had greater historical importance than he could have

realized. That system was unknown in Rupert's Land. It was difficult to explain to the settlers, and when it was explained, many of them, including all of the Métis, said flatly that it wouldn't work; it took no account of the basic element of life in the semiarid West—water. The American rectangular township had originated in humid regions, where one could farm anywhere, where distance from a river didn't matter.

The system which had been in use on the Red River was French, adapted from that of Quebec. It provided each settler with a small river frontage and appurtenant water rights, and with a "hay privilege" extending back from the river two miles on the open prairie. This "hay privilege," though uncultivated, was an integral part of each farm, used for the grazing of cattle or sheep or horses on the nutritious native grass. The river lot itself was only a small part of the settler's property. The "hay privileges" were unfenced and generally were used in common by neighboring landholders, but there was no question about each man's legal right to two miles of land behind his own farm.

This ribbon-like land pattern was designed for small, self-sufficient farmsteads with a livestock base, requiring little cultivation. It was thus ideally suited to the needs of the Métis, who were long absent on the hunt; the domesticated herds could fend for themselves while the elders of the community tended the gardens and small fields of grain. And it had not been in the Company's best interest to establish farms so large that they would divert the natives' energies from the hunt for furs and robes.

But the American system which McDougall sought to impose was designed for large-scale grain production on plowed soil. Without access to the river one could not raise cattle or garden crops; this would be satisfactory to "the most desirable emigrants," who would be farmers; but it was anything but satisfactory to the Métis, the nomadic herdsmen, the hunters and adventurers. McDougall might not have been

daunted even if he had known what he was doing, but undoubtedly he did not realize that he was attempting to alter,
arbitrarily, the whole way of life of thousands of people.

To do him justice, he was not acting solely on his own initiative. Sir John, the Minister explained later in his own defense, had urged him to send twenty surveyors to Assiniboia
"to gratify our friends who wanted employment"; he had objected, had sent only three or four. "We had no authority
until the transfer to make surveys at all," he admitted, and
said he had called this to the attention of his chief.

But now, to accomplish the Government's purpose, Mc-
Dougall even overrode the objections of his own agent, Colonel Dennis. After the catastrophe at Fort Erie there had been
some question about Dennis's obedience to command; this
time he did his best. When he discovered, the day he arrived
at Fort Garry, that McDougall's orders were infeasible and
fraught with peril for the Dominion, he reported promptly
and urged the Minister to take steps to placate the outraged
Métis. McDougall ignored the appeal. Then Dennis, for once
in his life using excellent judgment, worked out a compromise which was approved by McDougall. But it was too late;
a little blunder started the fire.

Dennis arrived at Fort Garry on August 20, 1869, accompanied by the ubiquitous Dr. Schultz, who had met him en
route. That was Dennis's first mistake, for anyone who entered the colony under Schultz's auspices or in his company
was immediately suspect. The colonel wrote McDougall the
next day. "I find," he said, "that a considerable degree of irri-
tation exists among the native population in view of surveys
and settlements being made without the Indian title having
been first extinguished." He went on:

You will, no doubt, have become aware that the half-breeds
lately in a public meeting called the Company here to account
in the matter of the money paid for the transfer to Canada.

Whatever may have been the views of the Government as to
the character of the title to be conveyed by the deed of transfer . . . I am satisfied that the Government will, in the first
place, have to undertake and effect the extinction of the Indian
title.

This question must be regarded as of the very greatest importance.

Any hostility whatever on the part of the half-breeds would
seriously obstruct settlement, Dennis warned, so no time
should be lost before starting negotiations. The situation
would become grave if the "discontented parties" had the
opportunity during the winter to "brood over, and concert
measures in opposition." The Métis were "a turbulent element" and already had threatened violence if surveys were
attempted.

A week later he wrote McDougall again, remarking the
"uneasy feeling" and reiterating his appeal to the Dominion
to negotiate with the established settlers. Because of the tension and the fact that most of the colony's fields were still in
crop, he reported that he was starting the surveys at a distant
point, near the boundary marker at Pembina. He had tried to
reassure the Métis, but had been left without an argument
when they asked by what right he was making surveys at all.
He recognized the justice of this inquiry, for in his second
letter he mentioned the danger of work which might "anticipate an approval which may not be confirmed."

Accordingly Dennis instructed his men not to resurvey the
farm lots on the Red and Assiniboine Rivers, but to confine
their work to "the broken sections against the rear limits of
such ranges so as to leave the same intact as independent
grants." This directive was approved by McDougall without
comment, but he still made no move to comply with Dennis's
urgent request for negotiations with the Métis.

The work went forward, and though the half-breeds grumbled constantly, there might have been no serious trouble

had it not been for the hay privilege. One of Dennis's crews, ignorant of the real character of this strip of uncultivated range and therefore misinterpreting his directive about the "rear limits" of the settlers' property, trespassed upon pasture land behind the farm of André Nault.

Nault was white, a French Canadian; but he had married into the Riel family and thus had become a member of the Métis community. When he encountered the surveyors on his hay privilege, he protested vigorously, but he could speak only French and could not make them understand that the lot and section lines they were drawing, if they were continued across his farm, would separate his buildings. He ran to get help.

Sixteen unarmed Métis led by a stocky, curly-haired young man who at first glance appeared, like Nault, to be white, accompanied the aggrieved landholder back to his farm. With his ragged, dirty troop straggling along behind him, the young man marched up to the surveyors and put his moccasined foot on their chain. "You go no farther," he told them calmly, in English. The Métis lined up beside him and stared silently, expressionless as fish, at the little survey crew. The two or three Canadians expostulated, but the young man only repeated his words. The surveyors left, and were instructed by Dennis to attempt no further work in Métis neighborhoods.

MOROSE YOUNG MAN

The leader of Nault's rescue party was Louis Riel the Younger, son of "the miller of the Seine" and his successor as "chief" of the Métis colony.

Young Louis had last seen his father in 1858 when the latter was returning from a prairie trip. They met at Pembina; the boy, then fourteen, was en route to Montreal to enter the Sulpician college and study for the priesthood, as his father had. Archbishop Taché of St. Boniface had been struck by the youngster's intellectual precocity and religious

ardor during his elementary schooling there and had suggested college. The family could not afford it, so the archbishop had found a generous patron; she was Mme. Joseph
Masson of Terrebonne, wife of the former Lieutenant Governor of Quebec.

Young Louis had been born at St. Boniface and had never
before left home; he was already homesick by the time he
reached Pembina, and uneasy about the reception he would
encounter when he reached "civilization" a thousand miles
to the east. His father comforted him, recalling his own
memories of Montreal. He cautioned the boy to take full
advantage of his unusual opportunities and to be grateful to
his benefactors. They parted—Louis Riel *père* riding north,
to die within six years, when only forty-seven; Louis Riel *fils*
riding east to prepare himself for his Messianic mission, leadership in the War for the West.

When he learned of his father's death, Louis sent home a
grief-drenched letter which does not wholly escape the appearance of an exercise in priestly rhetoric. But he was justifiably proud of his name, and he sincerely loved his father.
"Let us love the Hand of God," he wrote his mother, the
widowed Julie, "no matter what happens; it is always paternal. . . . Papa always acted with wisdom; he will therefore
be glorified."

Seminaries are never gay establishments, but so somber was
the mien of young Louis Riel that it caused comment even
there. He was admired by his colleagues as an unusually intent and serious scholar, but they were repelled by his taciturnity and his heaviness of mood, even before his father's
death. After this bereavement he deliberately shunned the
company of others, whereas before he had been merely aloof
and impatient. He was regarded, in short, as brilliant but a
bit odd. His masters could not question the depth and sincerity of his faith, but they wondered if he had the qualities

of forbearance and human sympathy which he would need
as a missionary or parish priest.

One-eighth Indian, he was not identifiable as a Métis by
anyone who did not know his antecedents. At this time he
was solidly built, strong, and youthfully handsome. His face,
somewhat sallow but not darkly pigmented, had not yet acquired the morose dignity which was to distinguish it later,
but the intensity of his gaze had already been remarked by
observers. His deep-set brown eyes were always to be his most
forceful physical feature.

He was a couple of inches under six feet. However, as
always occurs when many witnesses describe a great popular
leader, there is more divergence of opinion about his height
than about anything else. His hair was brown, becoming
darker as he grew older; it swept back in luxuriant waves
from a broad forehead. In youth his lips and jaw and nose
had a tendency to heaviness which was accentuated by the
"burnsides" he then affected; later his face thinned out and
he grew mustache and full beard.

Hostile witnesses who met him in the West regarded him
as vain and egotistical in manner, but they acknowledged that
his relationship to the honored Julie and his obvious intellectual superiority in the crude frontier environment set him
apart. He accepted as his due the deference with which the
ignorant and illiterate almost always view the man possessed
of learning and a facile tongue.

In a face which even an unfriendly visitor testified was
"remarkable—the more so, perhaps, because it was to be seen
in a land where such things are rare," the one unpleasant feature was the nervous mouth. The gaze was direct, even fright-
eningly so sometimes, but the mouth was often twisted and
agitated.

It is strange that the eyes were still, because nervousness
was characteristic of the whole man. When others were present he could not sit quietly for long, but had to stride rest-
lessly about the room, picking up objects and setting them

down again, gesturing, interrupting others' talk—or as suddenly becoming silent in the midst of some tirade of his own, and abruptly quitting the room.

In Montreal he lived with an uncle and often secluded himself for days, ostensibly engaged in study, prayer or meditation. But a friend discovered that he was writing French verse. The single example of his poetry of this period that has survived reflects preoccupation with self which even in a poet seems somewhat morbid. The protagonist of the poem, a man of thoughtful face and sorrowful air, wanders lonely and misunderstood in the heedless crowd: "In pain he consumes his days, abrim with bitterness."

The poem's gloom normally could be dismissed as a product of adolescent melancholy, but its author was in his middle twenties when this was written and his mood of dejection, on the testimony of his associates, was maintained too continuously to be wholly a pose. It is apparent that Riel was already acquiring the conviction of his singularity which was to become unhealthily dominant later in his career. Yet this early verse contained no trace of obsessive racial consciousness, and that was to be one of the major driving forces of his life. A sense of inferiority probably evoked the poem's naive conceit, and this may have been born of racial insecurity, as yet unrecognized; it may also have indicated that Riel—several years after his arrival in the city—still had not recovered from his abrupt removal at too early an age from his accustomed environment. This adjustment proved difficult for all of the better-educated Métis.

The poem was not a success. It was all of a piece with the letter he had written some time before to his mother, after his father's death: it attempted to become a keening cry but instead came perilously close to blubbering.

Louis spent ten years in Montreal. When his widowed mother sent word that she needed him, he returned to the Northwest without completing his religious education. His

abandonment of a career in the Church probably was greeted
with relief by his teachers, but there is no evidence that he
was actively discouraged from entering the priesthood, as
was later alleged.

He was eager to get back to the prairies despite an unusually strong call to the religious life. He was reluctant to submit to ecclesiastical discipline and his poet-mystic's mind was
impatient of dogma and canon law; but in some ways he was
better trained and better suited temperamentally for the cassock than many who wore it.

En route home in 1868 he stopped off in St. Paul for several months, taking a job as a sales clerk in a general store
to earn some money to take to his mother. He was courteous
and efficient. He sold yard goods and hardware and spent his
evenings in excited talk with the Métis of the Red River
brigades, who brought him news of mounting unrest north
of the boundary. An obnoxious little group of white men
calling themselves the "Canadian party" were causing trouble, they told him. A man named McDougall had negotiated
the transfer of Rupert's Land from the Hudson's Bay Company to Canada, and nobody had asked the Métis how they
felt about it. There were a couple of Americans he must meet
—one Taylor, here in St. Paul, and Enos Stutsman in Pembina; what a man, that Stutsman! Both good friends of the
Métis, these Yankees.

And there was another he should know, a teacher in the
College of St. Boniface at Red River, named O'Donoghue.
It was said he was training for the priesthood, but not with
much heart for it. He brooded all the time about the wrongs
of Ireland, where he was born. He had lived in New York,
too, and had been mixed up with something called the Fenians. Did Louis know about Fenians? Very *drôle;* one did
not know what to make of them. But they hated the British
and Canadians and therefore might be useful.

It was almost twenty years since the Sayer trial had freed

the trail to St. Paul. A Louis Riel was needed again on Red River.

By mid-December Louis was home. He moved in with his mother in Julie's comfortable little cottage in St. Vital, on the Assiniboine near the St. Boniface cathedral and school. She was overjoyed; Louis had always been the favorite. Such a brilliant mind, such piety—and withal, so handsome! It was almost as if he had, after all, become a priest. She submitted humbly to his interminable lectures, to his long, pretentious prayers; their rhetoric impressed her, but she was sometimes frightened to see how deeply moved Louis could be by his own words. Truly he was possessed of a spirit, and it went without saying that it was the Spirit of God.

The incident on the Nault farm occurred October 11, 1869. Bishop Taché was in Quebec, where he attempted again (he had tried once before in July) to convince members of the Government that their policy in Rupert's Land would bring about a fatal collision with the Métis. His warnings were shrugged aside, even by Sir George Etienne Cartier, a French Catholic—the prelate was so cavalierly treated by this statesman that for some time he refused to have further communication with him. Fearful and despairing, Taché sailed for Rome to attend an ecumenical council.

Governor Mactavish also had attempted several times to awaken the Government to its peril. His final appeal, presented by Taché, brought some response, but not the kind the Governor and bishop had hoped for. The press of Ottawa announced that when the new Canadian lieutenant governor set out for Rupert's Land he would take with him three hundred Enfield rifles.

This news reached Fort Garry swiftly over American telegraph lines to St. Cloud, Minnesota, and thence by prairie courier. Only shortly before this the seething Métis had learned who their new ruler was to be. In September William

McDougall had been appointed Lieutenant Governor of Rupert's Land—McDougall, who had negotiated the transfer of
the country without consulting its inhabitants, who had sent
Snow and Mair and Dennis to survey lands the Dominion
did not own, who had persistently disregarded appeals for
fair play even from his own agents, who was a personal friend
of Dr. John C. Schultz.

On that day, October 11, McDougall was in St. Cloud, waiting for his luggage—and three hundred rifles—to catch up
with him and be transferred to wagons and carts for the prairie journey north to Fort Garry.

The Governor-designate of Canada's hoped-for new territory could not even approach his domain on Canadian soil;
until the Dawson Road should be completed there was no
access to the country by land save through U. S. territory.
And though the transfer of sovereignty could not possibly
occur before December 1, McDougall and his chief, Sir John,
had not been able to wait. The "eloquent young man" had
a precious document in his pocket, one he had worked for
hard and long. It instructed him to "proceed with all convenient speed to Fort Garry in order that you may effectually
superintend the preliminary arrangements for organization
of the Government and be ready to assume the Government
of the Territories on their actual transfer to Canada."

John H. O'Donnell, a physician also en route to Fort Garry,
encountered McDougall and his party at St. Cloud. Dr.
O'Donnell had come west with a letter of introduction to a
man who was beginning to make a name for himself in Red
River transportation and trade, James J. Hill of St. Paul.
Hill had provided him with a guide for the trip north; he
also had told him that McDougall would never see Fort
Garry.

O'Donnell relayed this information to McDougall when
they met. Oh, there had been many such rumors, the Gov-

ernor-designate said calmly; they were "wild and contradic-
tory" and he had no intention of heeding them.

Two days out of St. Cloud, at Sauk Centre, two travelers
from Fort Garry talked with O'Donnell. They agreed with
Jim Hill. Again O'Donnell informed the executive party, but
McDougall said there would be no trouble. His friend,
Charles Mair, had joined the group. Mair knew the Red
River people and he was not concerned about the rumors.

So, Dr. O'Donnell said, "all faced the North cheerfully, as
if on a pleasant outing."

PART TWO

New Nation

CHAPTER V

Gentlemen in Pembina

"THAT BLASTED FENCE!"

In the Northwest October is a lazy month and wayward. To the Crees it is the Moon of Migration before the Freezing-up Moon, a time when creatures move but the seasons pause—for a week, perhaps, or for the full month. The blizzard may come in October, but first there is the Little Summer of St. Luke.

At sunset in October the sky is suddenly aflame and pulsing with the bugle chorus of wild geese flying. Pond and plain and hazy hill throb with color—so much of it to be crowded into so little time, before the long night. Winter soon will be relentless ruler of this land, but now he sends his scouts secretly, under cover of the dark, and in the morning the grass is beaded for an hour and the air is clean and sharp.

In the Northwest October can be glorious, a time that lifts up the heart.

William McDougall and his companions enjoyed their ride to Pembina. The trail was dry, the sky bright and cloudless. Thousands of ducks, geese and swans rested on the lakes.

One member of the party had a splendid fowling piece, double-barreled, exquisitely chased and carved, a noble British gun. After luncheon one day he went hunting, and spied two mallards. Dr. O'Donnell, who had tagged along, watched with interest.

"After adjusting his monocle," the doctor reported, "he took good aim and fired one barrel at a bird sitting, and the other as the flock rose, but not a feather was ruffled."

The hunter's "more intimate friends chaffed him unmercifully," not about his poor marksmanship or his monocle, but because he had fired on a sitting bird, which was not sporting. However, Dr. O'Donnell thought the culprit was a match for his persecutors: "He accepted the badinage with that stoical, cynical smile, always an excellent weapon of defense used by the refined English gentleman."

The evenings gradually grew colder and there was ice on the river at dawn. The company began to move a little faster. It was snowing and cold the day they met the Honorable Joseph Howe on the trail north of Fort Abercrombie, Dakota, and neither party wanted to waste much time in talk. Howe was Secretary of State for the Provinces in the Dominion cabinet and had visited Fort Garry unofficially, hoping to familiarize himself with the new Territory which would come under his jurisdiction. He was sixty-five years old, the rigors of the long journey had told on him, and now he was anxious to reach shelter.

In later years the disgruntled McDougall blamed Howe for much of his trouble, even charging him with inciting the Métis to resistance. This was absurd, but it is true that Howe, alone among Canadian notables who visited Rupert's Land, shunned the society of Dr. Schultz and requested the Canadian faction not to raise their homemade (and incorrect) flag in his honor. Nor had he visited the Canadians' stronghold,

Portage la Prairie; he had heard, he said, that it was so windy there it took two men to hold one man's hat on.

Subsequent developments seem to have convicted Howe of bad judgment in his determination to maintain the fiction that he was merely a tourist, for this prevented him from issuing any conciliatory statement in the name of his Government. He made himself well-liked during his short sojourn and might have been able to persuade the Métis that Canada would deal fairly with them. But he had no way of knowing that they had met secretly before his departure to plan their strategy, and he may have felt that he should report in Ottawa before making any official move.

Howe did know that there was serious unrest, and in his brief talk with McDougall on the snow-swept trail he cautioned the Governor-designate to anticipate hostility and to tread lightly in exercising his commission. But McDougall still could not bring himself to credit the alarms. He was counting heavily upon the good offices of his personal secretary, J. A. N. Provencher, whom he intended to appoint as Secretary of the Territory. Provencher was a nephew of the first Bishop of St. Boniface at Red River.

At one of the villages en route a nondescript half-breed had sidled up to McDougall and handed him a slip of paper, which the Canadian had discarded unread. It may have been the same man O'Donnell had noticed in St. Cloud, watching the transfer of McDougall's personal luggage, furniture, government files—and guns—to sixty wagons and carts which were to be spread out on the trail for weeks. O'Donnell approached the man and asked if he were "a member of the Governor's party." The Métis smiled and said courteously, *"Non, monsieur."* Long before McDougall reached the frontier, Métis scouts had reported at Fort Garry upon every detail of his equipment and upon the names and personalities of his companions. His slow-moving train was passed several times by half-breeds riding hard for the North. Métis "intelligence" was remarkably good: even the exact contents and significance of official Canadian communications leaked quickly to their "high command." But McDougall, it should be noted, was on hostile ground where everyone save the members of his own party (and perhaps one or two of those) was against him.

McDougall reached Pembina on October 30 and at the American customhouse was handed a note by a Métis courier. This one he read, flew into a rage, "addressed the messengers in contemptuous and insulting language," and threatened them with dire penalties for their insolence. The note, written in French, said:

Dated at St. Norbert, Red River, this 21st day of October, 1869.

SIR,

The National Committee of the Métis of Red River orders Mr. William McDougall not to enter the Territory of the Northwest without special permission of this Committee.

By order of the President JOHN BRUCE.

LOUIS RIEL, *secretary*

The letter had been drafted at a meeting of the Métis nine days after the survey incident. At the same meeting the National Committee had been organized and a call issued for mobilization of the manpower of the half-breed community. Within two or three days five hundred armed men, most of them mounted and all of them skilled marksmen, had reported for duty.

The Métis had had long experience in organization—for the hunt, for emergencies such as Indian attacks, for the complex administration of cart trains which were months on the trail. Their processes were democratic in that leaders were selected by vote; but family prestige, education and eloquence, as in Riel's case, were often weighty factors. Despite the almost worshipful regard in which Riel was held, however, he would never have been chosen to lead the movement (Bruce, a mild and almost illiterate but popular man, was merely a figurehead and soon resigned) had they not felt that his talents specially fitted him for the task. He would never have been selected to lead a war party. The Métis needed a statesman, a facile speaker and writer to present their case to their neighbors in Rupert's Land and to the foreign power which they had good reason to believe intended to subjugate them. Unquestionably they chose the best man they had; and they did not demur merely because the election occurred on the eve of his twenty-fifth birthday. He was young to lead a "new nation," but the Métis, like the American colonists, respected youth.

It is significant that the note to McDougall did not forbid him to enter the country: it merely informed him that he could do so only with the committee's permission. It therefore invited him to institute the negotiations which Canada should have undertaken long before. But McDougall had no intention of treating with people whom he insisted upon regarding as "rebels."

That was the official view in Canada, too, until the shock wore off and the Dominion's legal experts began to study their situation. At first it was "rebellion," fomented by a handful of ignorant, headstrong (later, also bloodthirsty) "natives."

But the Métis movement was not rebellion; it was not even insurrection, the milder term favored by some of Riel's apologists. Both of these words mean an uprising against duly constituted authority. The Métis movement was simply a resistance; there is no better word for it in English, possibly because nothing quite like it had ever happened before. The duly constituted authority, until the Queen proclaimed the transfer to Canada, was the Hudson's Bay Company. But the Company had signed away its authority and its embittered agents had virtually ceased to govern. For all practical purposes the state no longer functioned; Rupert's Land, for a brief time, was anarchic. The new Government which McDougall was attempting to impose and against which the Métis "rebelled" did not exist either, and the "Governor" had no more right in the country than any private citizen. He was not even entitled, at the moment, to the courtesies due a visiting dignitary, because he was no longer a member of the Canadian Cabinet.

No matter how his orders read, McDougall's mission was one of conquest. The people whom he expected to govern had had no voice in his selection, in the type of government he would impose, or in its administration after he assumed office: Rupert's Land was to be a Territory ruled by officials appointed in Ottawa and a council appointed by Lieutenant Governor McDougall in Fort Garry. To be sure, the Hudson's Bay Company's government, structurally, had been just as autocratic, but actually the governors usually had named to their councils the men selected by the inhabitants, and there was no hint that McDougall had any intention of doing that. Even at that, the Hudson's Bay regime had been far from satisfactory; the Métis put up with it only because much of their time was spent on the plains under command of their own elected captains.

But for a long time now there had been talk at Red River of a new kind of government, one which resembled in many ways the Métis system on prairie and trail, one in which the people elected their leaders at regular intervals, were permitted even to choose their own judges. This was the American way, and Americans in Rupert's Land were always boasting about it, especially that remarkable man in Pembina, Enos Stutsman. He had moved from the customs office to the United States land office and had more free time now, time to swing himself into his buggy or into the saddle—never-ending marvel!—and drive or ride the seventy miles to Fort Garry for chats with his friends the Métis.

The Americans had brought free trade to the Red River and as a result the Métis had profited on the hunt and in the transportation of goods. The American system was good business: even Métis could become rich. And Americans did not undervalue Métis skills, did not regard them as "natives" to be thrust out of the way, did not threaten their religion. In America—or so Stutsman said—a half-breed could be equal to anyone, especially if he were rich. There were many Métis in America. They, or their French-Canadian forebears, had established settlements which had become splendid cities: Chicago, Detroit, St. Louis, St. Paul, Pittsburgh, Peoria, Sault Ste Marie, Green Bay, Prairie du Chien. . . .

On September 22, 1869, at about the time trouble began over the survey, Enos Stutsman had had an enjoyable all-day conference with leaders of the Métis community at their homes on Red River.

William McDougall brushed the Métis couriers out of his way, summoned his companions and drove on from Pembina proper to the Hudson's Bay Company post two miles north of the boundary. There he paused to write a report to Ottawa and to rest and think.

Capt. D. R. Cameron of the Royal Canadian Artillery, who had come west just for the ride but had ambitions to become Minister of Militia in the new Territory, was outraged by the delay. Canadian authority, he said, must be established at once. McDougall commissioned Provencher to proceed to Fort Garry, notify Governor Mactavish that he was waiting to enter the country, and demand his protection. Cameron insisted on going along, taking his wife and two servants in his own surrey and their luggage in another vehicle, in the face of McDougall's strongly expressed displeasure. The trip, McDougall warned him, "may cause some embarrassment . . . by provoking a collision." He put his disavowal of responsibility on record, though he acknowledged that he had no authority to forbid Cameron to go.

Provencher got away alone and drove swiftly, but the irrepressible Cameron caught up with him at St. Norbert, nine miles south of Fort Garry. Provencher had been stopped at a barrier erected by the Métis where the road entered a narrow cut between two patches of timber and two rivers.

While Provencher was still trying to argue himself through the gate, Cameron drove furiously up to the Métis guards. He jumped to his feet in his carriage, jerked his monocle to his eye, and bellowed:

"Remove that blasted fence!"

The Métis stood open-mouthed for a moment; then they came forward quietly, grasped the bridles of the horses drawing the two carriages, led the animals around gently until they faced in the direction they had come, smacked them on their rumps, mounted their own horses and escorted the Cameron party and the unlucky Provencher back to Pembina. Most of Cameron's luggage was left behind.

The same day, November 2, an armed patrol of Métis led by six-foot-three Ambroise Lépine, the National Committee's "adjutant general," called upon McDougall at the Hudson's Bay post and gave him until sundown to get back across the boundary. He obeyed.

STIFF NECK IN A COLD CLIMATE

It was hard for McDougall to understand. He had been assured by Schultz, Mair and Dennis that the "loyal" people of Rupert's Land would greet him with wild cheering. There even had been talk of sending an escort of Canadians to accompany him from the border.

As he rode angrily back to Pembina he pondered the letter from Colonel Dennis which had been handed to him on his arrival there. It indicated that someone had badly miscalculated.

There was a disposition among the English-speaking inhabitants, Dennis wrote, "to receive the new Government with respect, but there is no enthusiasm." This did not apply to the militant Canadian party—but what that group had in enthusiasm it lacked in numbers. The majority, though deploring the "outrageous proceeding" of the Métis, had indicated that they shared their French neighbors' resentment. Dennis quoted their own words:

We could hardly justify ourselves in engaging in a conflict which would be, in our opinion, certain to resolve itself into one of nationalities and religions, and of which we could hardly at present see the termination. . . .
We feel this way: we feel confidence in the future administration of the Government of this country under Canadian rule. At the same time, we have not been consulted in any way as a people in entering into the Dominion. The character of the new Government has been settled in Canada without our being consulted.

The English-speaking people, Dennis concluded ruefully, would accept the new regime and obey its laws when and if it established itself; but they had lived in peace with the French up to now and they were "disinclined" to take up arms against them.

The spirit of John Gowler was abroad in the land. The people of Red River were of a mind not only to sit at table with gentlemen but even to take issue with them!

Word of the astonishing events in the Northwestern wilderness did not reach the centers of civilization until November 9. On that day the St. Paul *Press,* closest to the scene of any important newspaper, carried a rumor story apparently obtained from travelers who reported "ominous news from Red River." The first factual account did not appear in the *Press* until November 16. It was dated at Pembina November 4 and had been carried by hand to the nearest telegraph point.

The story was headed, "EXCITING EVENTS; Progress of the Red River Rebellion; The Decisive Blow Struck; Five Hundred Insurgents in Arms." Written by "Spectator," who was probably Stutsman, the regular Pembina correspondent for the *Press*, it described the ouster of McDougall by "a company of Red River cavalry." A private letter which was printed as a "follow" to the main dispatch reported the formation of the "provisional government." The next day the *Press* reprinted an account taken from the *Nor'wester* of Fort Garry. This piece was violently anti-Métis.

McDougall and his entourage settled down in Pembina—showing, Stutsman sneered in the *Press,* "true British spunk." This was not easy for a company of gentlemen, especially since there were women and children in the party. The wives of Mair and Cameron, McDougall's daughter, his twenty-one-year-old son and his two younger boys made the task of finding quarters somewhat difficult. Pembina had nothing to offer fastidious tourists except a choice between log cabins and sod huts.

Most of the Canadians made the best of their uncomfortable and embarrassing situation. With the exception of their chief, Stutsman informed the *Press*, they were "social and pleasant," but "Mr. McDougall's neck seems too stiff for this climate."

But McDougall could be forgiven for feeling considerable annoyance. He had arranged in advance, through Dennis, to occupy "Silver Heights," one of Fort Garry's few large and well-built houses, and had paid some rent. Now, while his executive mansion stood untenanted seventy miles to the north, he was forced to move with his family into a twenty-by-twenty-five-foot log cabin owned by a Chippewa half-breed. It had only one room, but McDougall had partitions fashioned from canvas and ordered another cabin of the same size built directly behind it, at a cost of ninety pounds to be paid by the Dominion.

Secretary Provencher became a paying guest in the home of
Joe Rolette, Jr., renowned Pembina trader, and Attorney
General Albert Richards found a bed in the home of Rolette's
father. Cameron had to install his wife, who was the daughter
of a Member of Parliament, in a cabin sixteen feet wide,
twenty-four feet long and six feet high. Alexander Begg, a
Fort Garry merchant and collector of customs under the
Hudson's Bay regime, probably could have penetrated the
Metis barrier, but chose to remain for some time at Pembina
to see what happened. He went to Coulombe's "hotel," but
announced he would leave as soon as he could find other
quarters because Coulombe's beds were too hard. Begg was
not connected with McDougall's administration; he knew the
country, was generally liked, and was more amused than
otherwise by the Canadian's troubles. Later he became a
major historian of the period.

Stutsman's agile brain teemed with plots. On November
18 the *Press* reported that chiefs of the Chippewa tribe were
demanding a council in Pembina with the Governor-designate
to learn what he intended to do about their "rights." According to other Pembina sources, Stutsman himself had dreamed
up this enterprise as one more way to harass the unhappy
McDougall, and had attempted to talk the apathetic Indians
into it without much success.

"Nothing short of a very liberal government, independence,
or annexation to the United States will satisfy the whole
people," Stutsman's dispatch said that day. It was the first
mention of American hopes on the frontier, and the first
newspaper story purporting to disclose what the Métis were
after.

MR. TAYLOR IS CLAIRVOYANT

But the Métis themselves didn't know what they wanted.
They were, in fact, terrified by their own temerity.

The barrier at St. Norbert had been constructed half a mile

from the home of the Rev. Noel Joseph Ritchot, Catholic priest. Father Ritchot strolled over to ask what was going on and was told that messengers had been sent to Pembina "to invite Mr. McDougall not to enter the country." The priest's face showed surprise and concern.

"Are we doing wrong?" a Métis spokesman asked.

Father Ritchot had to weigh his words. "You seem to me," he said, "to be engaged in a very dangerous pursuit." But he felt that he should do nothing which might estrange his flock, and his judgment was upheld when Governor Mactavish asked him to remain among the Métis because he could exert a moderating influence.

The apathy of the majority of the English-speaking citizens was known to the half-breeds, but with good reason they anticipated violent reaction sooner or later from the militant Canadian group. Dennis was organizing this faction to resist and the *Nor'wester* was clamoring for a "loyal" uprising to put the "rebels" in their place.

In the minds of Riel and his followers, one word loomed large—"rifles." McDougall had three hundred of them packed in twelve cases, waiting at Fort Abercrombie. Three hundred and ninety were stacked in the arsenal at Fort Garry, which also had thirteen six-pounder cannon. Though many of the Canadians boasted militia experience, they were inadequately armed and would stand little chance against the sharpshooting Métis cavalry unless they could get possession of these guns.

For this reason, though traffic was permitted on the Pembina road, a rigorous search of all freight was instituted as soon as the barrier was erected, lest McDougall attempt to smuggle arms to his supporters. But there still was the supply in the fort to worry about. So on November 2, the same day McDougall was ejected from the country, Riel and 120 of his men seized Fort Garry.

Governor Mactavish, confined to his bed, and his staff expostulated. Riel told them he had acted to preserve order, that the Canadians otherwise might have seized the fort and precipitated a civil war—which might well have been true. He confined the Company men to their quarters and posted guards.

The Canadians angrily accused the Hudson's Bay officials of complicity in the coup. Riel had been virtually invited, they said, to move in: the gate had been wide open and, though some Canadian militia pensioners had offered to garrison the fort, no defense measures whatever were taken.

The Métis themselves always said that they had had at least tacit support from the Company's local employees, and one of them claimed that he carried a message from Mactavish to Riel in which the Governor suggested that the Métis take the fort. The evidence is far from conclusive, especially since Mactavish publicly condemned the Métis movement soon after seizure of the fort; but unquestionably the Governor originally had much sympathy for the desperate half-breeds. He had grievances of his own: as a representative of the winterers he had gone all the way to London to try to get them a share of the money to be paid to the Company by Canada, and had failed; besides, he despised McDougall.

"As one man to another," he said in a revealing letter, "it is a question whether Mr. McDougall should not be starved out for his arrogance." Then he continued:

Only I strongly advise you to risk nothing for the greedy London directory, from whom we are not likely to receive any thanks, but who will themselves receive full compensation for the stores, etc. . . .
As for Riel, he is every day strengthening himself, and all our work-people are with him.

The Métis helped themselves to supplies in the fort, but at Riel's insistence they kept strict account. About fifteen years later the Dominion paid the Company some ten thousand pounds in settlement of its claims for goods taken by the

Métis and expenditures the Company had been forced to make during the Riel "occupation."

The twenty-five-year-old strategist now set out to maintain order in the community and to establish a broad-based democratic government. He exacted an oath from his troops to shun liquor; they kept their promise for some time, but as the months wore on there were frequent levies upon the fort's stock of rum. He appointed a night watch of ten men for the streets and roads of the settlement, and instituted censorship of the mails. His patrols and gendarmes were strictly charged to be civil and managed it pretty well, even in the face of such provocation as that offered by the self-important Captain Cameron.

On November 6, Riel issued a proclamation inviting the residents of the English-speaking parishes to elect twelve representatives to form one body with his council of French Métis, also consisting of twelve. A meeting of the joint council would be held, he announced, in the courthouse at Fort Garry ten days later.

This proclamation was submitted to the *Nor'wester* for publication but the newspaper's irreconcilable publisher, Walter Robert Bown, refused to print it. The Métis thereupon threw him out of his plant, drafted a printer, and issued it themselves. The Canadian group promptly asserted that few, if any, of the English parishes would deign to notice Riel's invitation. But again they miscalculated; all of the parishes responded and elected delegates.

The first Convention of the People of Rupert's Land assembled, as scheduled, on November 16.

That day, in St. Paul, James Wickes Taylor wrote a letter to Secretary of State Hamilton Fish, Washington:

The attempt to extend the Canadian Confederation over Selkirk Settlement and the districts thence extending to the Rocky Mountains meets with armed resistance from the French population, mostly of mixed Indian blood, who are more than equal in number to the English, Scotch and American settlers. I estimate the French element at 6,000, capable of sending 1,000 men into the field. Of the latter, fully one-half, mounted and armed, occupy the roads and fords between Pembina on the international frontier and Fort Garry.

He went on to give an accurate report of the banishment of McDougall and the grievances of the Métis. He concluded with a summary of what the people of Rupert's Land would demand as the price of submission to Canada: the right to elect their own legislature; recognition of titles to all existing land claims; a homestead system; the American system of land grants for schools, roads, and public buildings; modification of the Canadian tariff. If these demands should be refused, "or in any event," especially the dispatch of Canadian troops, Taylor anticipated "a strong and determined movement in favor of annexation to the United States." He concluded: "If Central British America remains Canadian, it must be only as the result of a peaceful adjustment among the people interested."

At the time Taylor wrote these words the people of Rupert's Land had just assembled in their first convention five hundred miles from St. Paul. They had not even begun to draft demands. But a bill of rights was adopted two weeks later, and it incorporated all of the items listed by Taylor except one, tariff reduction, and that was inferentially covered by another clause.

This would seem to have been an astonishing instance of clairvoyance were it not for the fact that Enos Stutsman of Pembina possessed a pass through the Métis lines and had been in close touch with Riel and his council ever since the barrier went up at St. Norbert. The Stutsman-Taylor intelligence team functioned so smoothly and so swiftly that Secretary of State Fish had more and better information about

Canada's predicament in the first month than Ottawa got
until it was all over.

IN THE NAME OF THE QUEEN

But Sir John and his Government learned enough to convince them that they were in very hot water indeed.

McDougall wrote, on November 13: "Until the transfer of
authority has taken place, and I am notified of it, I shall not
assume any of the responsibilities of government." He added
that the Métis leaders "understand perfectly that I have no
legal authority to act or to command obedience until the
Queen's proclamation is issued." A day or so later he reported
that this resolution did not meet with the approval of the
militant Canadians, who were bringing pressure upon him to
issue a proclamation at once asserting his authority.

From Ottawa, Howe wrote that the privy council approved
McDougall's judgment so far and would deeply regret any
incident which might lead to bloodshed or any "hasty or
intemperate exercise even of lawful authority which should,
in the transfer of the country, array the feelings of any large
portion of the people against your administration." He cautioned McDougall specifically:

As matters stand you can claim or assert no authority in the
Hudson Bay Territory until the Queen's proclamation, annexing the country to Canada, reaches you through this office. . . .
You had better inform Governor McTavish that you are only
proceeding to Fort Garry on the presumed consent of the Company and its officers, and, having stated the facts, await his
answer. If he either declines to admit you, or is powerless to give
you safe conduct, stay where you are until further advised.

But McDougall had long since advised Mactavish of his
plight and had demanded the latter's protection; he also had
insisted that Mactavish issue a proclamation announcing the
change of government and ordering the Métis to abandon
their resistance. He was infuriated when Mactavish replied

frankly that he could not guarantee McDougall's safety and he thought it might be a good idea if that gentleman went home. As for a proclamation, the Company's man felt it would do no good, and he reminded McDougall that "up to this moment we have no official intimation from England or the Dominion of Canada of the fact of the transfer, or of its conditions, or of the date at which they were to take practical effect upon the Government of this country."

As the council met at the call of Riel on November 16, however, Mactavish changed his mind and issued a proclamation to be read to the delegates. He still thought it would do no good, but it might (and it did, briefly) placate McDougall. Besides, Mactavish was worried about the talk that he and his subordinates were parties to the Métis "plot." The proclamation was mild, somewhat fatherly in tone: it deplored the unlawful occupation of the Company's fort, interference with the mails, and ouster of "certain gentlemen from Canada" from the post at Pembina. It urged the Métis to disperse and attain their objectives through "constitutional" means. It nowhere mentioned McDougall's name.

Anxious conferences were held in Ottawa. It was three weeks after McDougall's ejection before the ministry could bring itself to reveal its plight to the imperial Government in London. The fledgling Dominion, barely two years old, had seriously mismanaged its first major venture and confession was painful. On November 23 a brief summary of events was cabled to London, followed by a letter containing details and the Ministry's defense: "The most extravagant misstatements have been circulated about the intentions of the Canadian Government, and misapprehensions created which there will be some difficulty in removing." The Dominion had now decided to send commissioners known and liked by the Métis to persuade them to submit—a step which should have been taken several months before.

London replied that the Queen had learned of the incident with "surprise and regret," attributed the resistance by "misguided persons" to "misunderstanding or misrepresentation," and urged her dissatisfied subjects to present their grievances to the Governor General, as her representative in Canada.

Under the circumstances, Ottawa told London, perhaps the Queen's proclamation annexing the Northwest Territories to the Dominion of Canada had better be postponed. Things had not worked out quite as Sir John A. Macdonald had anticipated when he wrote a friend the previous June: "We hope to close our session this week, and a very mountainous session it has been! We have quietly and almost without observation annexed all of the country between here and the Rocky Mountains. . . ."

To William McDougall, left out on a long, long limb, went another warning. "I have it in command to express to you," Howe wrote on November 29, "the anxious desire of the Governor General in Council that all collision with the insurgents may be avoided, and that no violation of the neutrality laws of the United States shall give a pretext for the interference of their Government."

The caution came too late. That same day McDougall had written to Howe complaining that he had not received any instructions to guide him on and after the day of the transfer —untrue, since he had been ordered to do nothing at all until an official copy of the Queen's proclamation reached him through the office of the Secretary of State for the Provinces. He was preparing, McDougall said, a proclamation announcing surrender of the Territory by the Hudson's Bay Company as of December 1, the date originally set—though it must have been apparent to him by this time that postponement was likely.

Bewildered, angry and humiliated, surrounded by hostility in an alien community, fair game for the venomous Stutsman and other Yankee schemers, and gravely handicapped by the difficulty and slowness of communication, McDougall reversed his position of two weeks before and succumbed to the pressure exerted by his only friends, the Canadian bloc at Fort Garry.

His decision once made, a mad frenzy possessed the "eloquent young man," onetime journalist and lawyer and radical politician, advocate of universal suffrage and of abolition of property qualifications for Members of Parliament, Sir John's good right hand in annexing the British Northwest "quietly and almost without observation."

With all the literary flourishes he could command, McDougall wrote a proclamation appointing himself—"our trusty and well beloved William McDougall"—Lieutenant Governor of Rupert's Land. To that proclamation he forged the name of his Queen.

CHAPTER VI

The Whole
Unbounded Continent

RUFFIANS IN ROBBERS' ROOST

THE twenty-four delegates to the first Convention of the People of Rupert's Land, assembling on the morning of November 16 in the snow-packed courtyard of Fort Garry, found there an "honor guard" of a hundred and fifty armed Métis. The clatter of rifle fire and the booming of twenty-four guns, intended by Riel as a salute to the convention, did not sit well with the English; but the only delegate to protest was an Indian. Henry Prince, Christianized chief of the Saulteux, who had been elected from an English parish, rebuked his half-brothers, the Métis: "When we hold a council of peace, we go without guns in our hands."

The English were somewhat mollified when they saw that Britain's ensign still flew over the fort, but the friendly feeling caused by this was soon dissipated. J. J. Hargrave, Governor Mactavish's secretary, presented Mactavish's proclamation and asked that it be read as the first order of business.

The French, led by Riel, refused to permit this lest it wreck the convention at the start by shaking the resolution of the English delegates. When the latter insisted upon hearing it, a compromise was reached; the proclamation was read at the close of the day's session.

Nothing was accomplished that day or the next. Riel's party, unsure of itself and inadequately prepared for parliamentary processes, was reticent about its objectives, and the English had no program of their own. After two days the convention adjourned on call, to permit the Company's judges to hold the quarterly session of court, with which the Métis had not interfered.

Sessions were resumed November 22—on which day, incidentally, Stutsman again appeared in Fort Garry for conferences with the French. The convention broke up once more, however, this time in a dispute over a motion offered by an English delegate to permit McDougall to enter and hear the demands of the people after he reached Fort Garry. To this Riel retorted that McDougall would enter Rupert's Land only over the bodies of himself and his troops.

Finally, on December 1, the convention adopted a bill of rights. The French proposed that it be taken to Pembina and that McDougall be required to guarantee its acceptance; if he lacked authority to do this, they insisted that he obtain the pledge from Ottawa before he should be admitted to the Territory. The English, knowing that it would be legally impossible for McDougall to grant anything, refused to accede to this plan. Technically the English were right, but the dispatch of delegates to Pembina and conferences with McDougall might have opened the way to negotiations and might have eased the dangerous tensions in Fort Garry. About a fortnight later, in fact, the thoroughly chastened McDougall himself urged just such a meeting as the French had proposed, but his activities in the meantime had so alienated the Métis that his plea was ignored.

The bill of rights for Rupert's Land was a remarkable document. Though native peoples overwhelmed by whites in North America had often prepared "demands" as the basis of negotiations, they had little in common with the bill drafted by and in behalf of the Métis of the Northwest.

The Indians, acknowledging inevitable defeat, had invariably asked for land, money and schools. The Rupert's Land bill, although its sponsors were part Indian, was a politically sophisticated document which abjured any note of supplication in laying claim to the rights of self-government and economic development. A self-respecting, undefeated and unchastened people offered alliance, not submission.

The bill of rights was notable in another respect. It offered a feasible program for union with the Dominion and at the same time managed to protect the interests of virtually all elements of an unusually heterogeneous community: no Englishman, Canadian, Frenchman, American or Indian could justly complain that his traditions, ideals or economic needs had been slighted.

The bill made the following demands:

The right to elect a legislature which could override a veto by the Executive.

The right to approve or reject, through the Territory's representatives, any Dominion legislation which directly affected the Territory.

The right to elect sheriffs, magistrates and other local officials.

A free homestead law.

Land grants for schools, roads and public buildings.

A guaranteed railroad connection with the nearest existing line. (A significant item: the nearest existing line was in the United States.)

Payment of the Territory's governmental expenses for the first four years from the Dominion treasury.

Recruitment of any military force to be stationed in the Territory from among people already living there.

Treaties with the Indians to preserve peace.

Use of the French and English languages in the legislature, in all public documents, and by judges of the Superior Court.

Respect for all privileges, usages and customs which had existed before the transfer of sovereignty.

Full and fair representation in the Parliament of the Dominion of Canada.

The English delegates voted with misgivings because they had not been specifically authorized by their parishes to approve any demands, but reaction of the community was generally favorable. The conditions were regarded as reasonable by everyone except the Canadian party, who thought any demands whatever were presumptuous. The small American faction, on the other hand, pronounced the bill moderate.

There is no doubt that Enos Stutsman had a hand in preparing it, and probably he hoped that Canada would reject is peremptorily. He and the other Americans pointed out that most of these rights could easily be obtained by a Territory joining the American Union and, with some negotiation, probably all of them could be obtained by a State—though even in the United States the bilingual items, on which the Métis set great store, would take some finagling.

These discussions clarified for the Métis the difference in the American pattern between Territorial status and Statehood and induced them to investigate the Canadian structure more thoroughly. The decision that if Rupert's Land ever became a part of Canada it would do so only as a full-fledged, self-governing Province probably was born at this time.

Meanwhile, spurred by reports from Stutsman and scholarly analyses of them by Taylor, annexation fever was mounting daily in St. Paul and on the frontier, and Washington was eagerly watching developments.

Stutsman wrote President Grant early in November. "I should be deficient in my duty both as an official and as an

American citizen," he said, "if I did not solemnly call your attention to the situation as it exists in this part of the continent of North America and the opportunity it offers for instant and decisive action on the part of the Government of the United States." Rupert's Land was virtually without a government and Stutsman believed "a majority" of its inhabitants were favorably disposed toward American annexation.

He exaggerated pro-American sentiment north of the boundary, as he and Taylor always did; but south of the line Manifest Destiny was on the march again. The newspapers reminded Minnesotans of the bloodless conquest of Oregon by a few thousand American settlers; there were now (1870) four hundred thousand people in Minnesota. It was recalled that President Johnson publicly, in a message to Congress, had approved annexation of the British Northwest. The rapacious Yankees had a favorite couplet, now recalled, with which they long had been scaring the daylights out of their weak northern neighbor:

> No pent up Utica contracts our powers;
> The whole unbounded continent is ours!

William McDougall, in Pembina, nervously reported to Ottawa that he was hedged about with conspirators. Even the United States postmaster in the village, Charles Cavileer, was in league with the Métis, he complained, and was conniving in their interference with the mails. He feared an aggressive expedition, official or otherwise, from St. Paul.

At first, Sir John Macdonald scoffed. "The Yankees would like to have a finger in the pie, I dare say, and so would the Fenians, but the march of four hundred miles from St. Cloud to Fort Garry and the carriage of provisions for such a force is quite sufficient protection from that quarter."

Eighty years after the event it is difficult to determine how much justification McDougall had for his concern; but there is considerable evidence to indicate that in this one instance his judgment was far better than Sir John's. The latter's statement was unrealistic: a four-hundred-mile trek obviously would be much less difficult for Americans on their own soil and aided by a sympathetic population than would be a march of twice that distance by Canadians on hostile ground. The Prime Minister was appallingly ignorant of Western conditions and even appeared to have forgotten some fairly recent history. He was taking it for granted, for instance, that the American interference McDougall dreaded could only be an official move, countenanced by Washington.

But what McDougall was disturbed about—and he was not the only one to report this development—was that sinister forces of freebooters were gathering around him in the Pembina region. The Canadian Government, which had been protesting for more than forty years about the depredations of American "border banditti," should have heeded his warning long before it did.

The United States and Canada ostensibly had been at peace since 1814, but during the succeeding half-century there had been several invasions of Canadian soil by filibustering bands. Purported "secret societies" sparked by rebellious Canadian elements had attacked from American bases in 1837 and 1838, and the Fenian campaigns started in 1866. All of these movements, though they were initiated by self-styled patriots, recruited their troops from the footloose and lawless adventurers who gravitated naturally to the boundaries and frontiers, who would enlist in any campaign which promised to provide excitement, wages, or loot.

In Kansas and Missouri such men became bushwhackers. In the Northwest they were buffalo hunters, smugglers, whiskey runners, wolfers, rustlers and road agents. Many were deserters from the United States Army; some were Métis outlawed by their communities for criminal offenses—usually theft—committed during the annual prairie hunt. Through conscienceless use of liquor they maintained uneasy alliances

with a few corrupted Indian bands which provided secure
hideouts and occasionally joined in raids. They were skilled
marksmen and had learned the science of guerrilla warfare on
the prairies from the Indians and Métis.

Throughout the seventies the "border banditti" straggled
westward, moving always just beyond the end of steel, plundering Indians and whites indiscriminately. They had their
own communities hidden in trackless coulees, often moved
overnight; they were in the Dakota hills called the Turtle and
Pembina Mountains, in the Cypress Hills just north of the
boundary, in the Bear Paw, Little Rockies and Highwood
Mountains of Montana, and in the labyrinthic, unmapped
and rarely visited "breaks" of the Upper Missouri and Yellowstone Rivers. They operated scores of log forts—so-called,
actually whiskey posts—which they threw up hastily on the
prairie between Fort Benton, Montana, head of navigation
on the Missouri and contraband capital of the West, and the
Indian settlements in the British Northwest. These were
short-lived; frequently their builders fled for their lives while
the posts were burned by the Indians they had debauched,
for hell had no fury like that of an Indian with a hangover
who was refused (because supplies were exhausted) a hair of
the dog that bit him.

Driven finally from Canadian soil by the North West
Mounted Police, which was organized to combat them, this
bloody company made their last stand along the Missouri
and Yellowstone in Montana. There they were destroyed or
dispersed by citizen "vigilantes" in the eighties.

These were the men to whom W. F. Sanford, a competent
Canadian observer, referred in a warning letter to Howe in
Ottawa. Sanford was traveling in Minnesota and Dakota in
November, 1869, while Riel was assembling the council in
Fort Garry. He wrote:

On my arrival in St. Paul, and when passing through St. Cloud, I found a great many rough men collecting and preparing for the prairies, just the class who would only be too ready to filibuster, and knowing that in a week they would be out of the way, I put into the paper the account of Mr. McDougall's safe arrival at Fort Garry . . . which, I have to confess, had not one word of truth in it.

Similar worries were bothering Donald A. Smith of the Hudson's Bay Company. Though he was in the East, he was far better informed, through his Company connections, than Sir John. A few days after Sanford's report to Howe, Smith sent off a letter to Governor Mactavish. His chief fear, he said, was that Riel's party might become "the prey or the associates of hordes of filibusters even now ready to pour into the Territory."

According to official testimony given some time later by Bishop Taché of St. Boniface, more than four million dollars had been pledged by unidentified Americans, in addition to men and guns, to support any movement to annex Rupert's Land to the United States. And Donald A. Smith told the Canadian Parliament, twenty years after the Métis incident, that a half-million at least had been offered by Minnesotans. "There was unquestionably a very great danger at that time," he said, "of the country being absorbed into the United States." He went on:

The fact was brought to my recollection by a gentleman of high position in Minnesota whom I met the other day as I passed through the country, who stated that he knew of persons then ready to place a very large sum of money at the disposal of Mr. Riel and his friends, upwards of half a million dollars, with the view of having the country annexed to the United States.

Smith reminded his listeners that at that time there had been bitter feeling between the United States and England and her colonies, and that "without railways, with a trackless wilderness and some five hundred miles to traverse, it was impossible in less time than two months" for Canada to get a single soldier into the Territory.

To men like Sanford and Smith, the fact that a nondescript frontier village of log and mud huts known as Pembina was booming was not without significance. McDougall watched anxiously as more and more of the villainous-looking new-comers assembled in the Robbers' Roost, Dead Layout, and Ragged Edge saloons; he cursed his irresolute superiors in Ottawa, and gratefully swallowed the boasts of the Canadian handful at Fort Garry that they were more than a match for "a few ignorant rebels."

THE VOICE OF MINNESOTA

But the fever was not confined to the ragged frequenters of the Ragged Edge and other shady grogshops on the fron-tier. There were the ambitious and well-heeled businessmen of St. Paul, and there were the politicians. Among the latter there was Ignatius Donnelly.

Donnelly in 1869 was completing a term in Congress. He was "the Voice of Minnesota," already well-known for two decades as a land speculator, farmer, journalist and orator, subsequently to become a great leader of the Populist and agrarian movements. He had been Lieutenant Governor of Minnesota in 1859, a year after the State was admitted to the Union.

On November 24, the St. Paul Chamber of Commerce in-vited him to address the public on "The Red River Revolu-tion." Donnelly responded with such enthusiasm that he was unable to resist giving most of his speech in advance in a letter of acceptance to the press.

The present moment, said "the Voice," was fraught with the weightiest consequences. Americans had nothing in com-mon with the "ludicrous and burlesque aristocracy of Canada" (after the Cameron incident, he had something there) which was attempting to establish a feudal state in the wilderness. Settlement of the Red and Saskatchewan Valleys by Americans was dictated by Minnesota's "geographical necessities"—a new phrase for Manifest Destiny. Minnesota should be heard at this crisis:

> Such a state of feeling should be aroused in the nation as will prevent General Grant from giving permission to the red-coated soldiers of England to cross the soil of our State to reduce to subjugation men whose aspirations are for liberty and whose entire sympathies are with the American people.
>
> If the revolutionists of Red River are encouraged and sustained by the avowed sympathy of the American people, we may within a few years, perhaps months, see the Stars and Stripes wave from Fort Garry, from the waters of Puget Sound, and along the shores of Vancouver.

After all that the speech itself was somewhat anticlimatic. About all Donnelly had to add was a reminder to the audience which packed Ingersoll Hall that the United States had ample precedent for recognizing "rebel" governments, and might well get busy on it. Also there was a bit of rhetoric which indicated he had been reading the papers: "This country [Rupert's Land] belongs to us, and God speed the Fenian movement or any other movement that will bring it to us!"

The Fenian reference had been inspired by Stutsman's latest reports from Pembina. There was "a tincture of Fenian inspiration" in the Métis movement now, he said, and "a young Irish priest supplies the brains and much of the stimulus." It was the first mention of one whose name would seldom be omitted (as it was this time) from news stories thereafter—W. B. O'Donoghue, the young mathematics teacher at St. Boniface College who abandoned his training for the priesthood to join Louis Riel.

Senator Alexander Ramsey of Minnesota had a resolution ready for the opening session of Congress a few days after Donnelly's speech. It requested a full report from the State Department on McDougall's attempt to assume authority in Red River in the face of the inhabitants' resistance. It was passed, and the annexation bloc led by Ramsey, Senator Banks and Anglophobe Zachariah Chandler, began to plan their next move—land grants to speed completion of a railroad to Pembina as a major branch of the projected Northern Pacific transcontinental line. They had been convinced by James Wickes Taylor that if Rupert's Land were given this economic tie to the United States political absorption would follow almost as a matter of course.

It was this economic threat, rather than McDougall's fears of a filibuster in Pembina, which finally lit a fire under Sir John. C. J. Brydges, manager of Canada's Grand Trunk Railroad, wrote the Prime Minister that the Americans hoped to carry their railroad so near the boundary that feeder lines into Rupert's Land would "injure, if not prevent, the construction of an independent line in British territory." He was convinced that the Washington Government was "anxious to take advantage of the organization of the Northern Pacific Railway to prevent your getting control for Canada of the Hudson's Bay Territory."

Macdonald replied rather more promptly than he or his associates were wont to answer their frantic colleague in far-off Pembina. It had now become evident to him, he wrote Brydges, that the Americans would do anything "short of war" to acquire the British Northwest, "and we must take immediate and vigorous steps to counteract them." Canada must show that it was resolved to build its own Pacific railway, and to do it at once. The Prime Minister had caught up with James Wickes Taylor, who had been saying for years that neither England nor Canada could hold the West without establishing transcontinental railroad communication.

Out of all this, Taylor, who had been functioning happily for a decade as an agent of the United States Treasury Department, reporting on commercial relations in the West, got a new job.

On December 30 Secretary Fish secretly commissioned the Minnesota geopolitician as a "special agent" of the State Department, to investigate the trouble in Rupert's Land and keep Washington advised. Taylor was charged not to reveal the nature of his commission, which was forwarded to him through Senator Ramsey; and during part of the six months he served under it, when he was working on Canadian soil, he was by any reasonable definition an American spy. He visited Rupert's Land and Ottawa, acquired a competent staff of correspondents, and finished his work in Washington, where he wrote studies of the crisis which were so detailed and so accurate that they still constitute some of the best sources for historians.

Washington was cautious but hopeful. There had long been signs of growing impatience with imperialism in London. Colonies as distant and valueless (for England still knew virtually nothing of the West's potential riches) as Rupert's Land were a nuisance, and the United States had been assured several times that Britain would not attempt to hold any colony against its will. Sir John had had trouble even at home persuading his colleagues to support annexation; he had a good deal more trouble in Whitehall and now his situation, in view of the resistance in the West, was precarious. He wanted a military expedition to Rupert's Land after the controversy was settled, to preserve peace; and he insisted that it contain a detachment of imperial troops in addition to Canadians, to convince the American people that England would not abandon her colonies and was not wholly indifferent to the future of the West. He finally won his point, but only at the cost of loss of much popularity in London.

Rumors of apathy in London were joyfully enlarged upon

in St. Paul. The voice of Minnesota swelled, and finally the *Press* managed to identify it with the voice of God:

. . . Whenever the people of the Northwest Territory, after having successfully vindicated their liberties and maintained their independence against Canada, shall declare themselves in favor of annexation to the United States, the United States, they may rest assured, will welcome them with open arms and England will gladly avail herself of such a providential opportunity to settle the Alabama claims with the cession of a country whose destinies God has indissolubly wedded to ours by geographical affinities which no human power can sunder, as He has divorced it from Canada by physical barriers which no human power can overcome.

The barriers to which the *Press* referred were the sterile pine lands, the marshes and rocks of the "Canadian shield," the Pre-Cambrian wasteland which lay between the settled portion of Ontario and Rupert's Land. This still is a formidable obstacle to Canada's communications; it is not very practical, for instance, to travel by automobile from Toronto to Winnipeg on Canadian soil. But the *Press* exaggerated, as usual, when it said that "no human power" could conquer the barrier.

THE BITTER WIND

But in 1869 the inhospitable, lonely wilderness east of Red River contributed importantly to McDougall's troubles. Because of it, all of his communications with Ottawa had to go by a roundabout route through the United States.

His letter of November 29, in which he told his superiors that he was preparing a proclamation "annexing" the Territory as of the original transfer date, December 1, was not answered by Howe until December 17—more than two weeks after McDougall had made the move he had said he was going to make. Howe's useless reply said McDougall's dispatch had "created some apprehensions that you were about to issue a proclamation announcing the formal transfer of the Territory, which has not yet taken place, and to organize or countenance movements which, however well intended, would have been without the sanction of the law."

McDougall had already done all this. On November 30 Colonel Dennis had posted on several walls in Fort Garry the copies of a proclamation given him by McDougall, dated December 1, 1869.

Headed "Victoria, by the Grace of God, of the United Kingdom of Great Britain and Ireland, Queen, Defender of the Faith, &c.," this document purported to give William McDougall, "Companion of Our Most Honourable Order of the Bath," governmental authority over the Territory as of that date. McDougall followed it with another, signed by himself, formally assuming command and deposing Mactavish, the Company governor. The decrees instructed all of Her Majesty's subjects "and all others whom these Presents shall concern," to take notice and govern themselves accordingly.

Louis Riel was reasonably certain, however—perhaps because his agents had had access to McDougall's official correspondence—that no such proclamation had been issued by Queen Victoria; and he knew that until it was, transfer of sovereignty could not occur. He said publicly that McDougall's proclamations were fraudulent and would not be honored by the Métis council.

McDougall may well have anticipated this; at any rate he knew some dramatic gesture was called for. He had said that he would not perform any official act on American soil; his assumption of sovereignty, therefore, had to occur north of the boundary. He did the best he could. . . . But the incident of December 1, 1869, intended to be imposing, turned out to be comic. His performance that night convulsed America, horrified Ottawa, and ruined him forever in the West.

It was bitterly cold that night—twenty below zero. A blizzard blotted out the sky, the cabins of Pembina, the trails and landmarks. The inhabitants of the frontier village huddled indoors and built up their fires. The Métis boundary patrol were in their comfortable homes sixty miles to the north.

At ten o'clock seven men slipped stealthily from their cabins and stumbled through the snow to a couple of carriages. Cursing their stiffening fingers, they harnessed teams, heaved themselves clumsily into the rigs, and drove furiously north into the blinding snow. Two inquisitive, loyal but very uncomfortable pedigreed sporting dogs—pointers—trailed behind, whining as the snow turned to wedges of ice in their pads.

The owner of the dogs, Governor-designate William McDougall, led the little company across the international boundary to the deserted Hudson's Bay post two miles within British territory. The horses were tied, the men gathered in a shuddering little ring in front of the post buildings, and the dogs curled up together in the shelter of a cabin.

McDougall fumbled with his heavy overcoat, found a Dominion flag, handed it to an aide. The latter held it with some difficulty, for the gale tugged at it incessantly and whipped it across his stinging face.

McDougall stepped into the center of the circle, wrestled again with his coat and drew out a sheet of parchment. A man stepped forward with a lantern and the others moved in to shield their chief from the icy wind.

The parchment scroll was hard to hold through the big fur mittens, and in spite of them McDougall's hands shook with the cold. He fumbled the sheet, lost his place, reread; but somehow "the eloquent young man" got through it, shouting his forged proclamation to the heedless wind.

A little to his rear, out of the direct range of his vision, stood the saturnine Alexander Begg, who had come along

just for the hell of it, the only one of the company who knew
how to be comfortable in a blizzard. While the ceremony
proceeded, he sucked happily on a bottle of Scotch.

McDougall rolled up his parchment, put away the flag,
called the dogs. The men scrambled back into the carriages
and rode solemnly home. Before they were back in Pembina
the wind and snow had effaced their tracks in Rupert's Land.

It was a day or so before anybody in Pembina, even Stutsman, ventured outside and heard about the expedition to
take over the Northwest for the Dominion. Word of it thereafter immediately reached Fort Garry, where the delighted
Métis immortalized the incident in a song. "Let us sing the
glory of McDougall," the crude little ballad urged; "he shows
the people across the frontier that he dares to face the bitter
wind."

Stutsman, describing the adventure of the "intrepid little
band" for the St. Paul *Press,* had a field day with the pointer
dogs, an old-fashioned Colt pistol carried by one member of
the party, and Begg's bottle. A kindlier commentator could
have read some pathos into the incident, but not Stutsman;
his account was pure farce. The dash across the frontier, after
it was determined that "all, save the firmament, was clear";
the scene in the post yard, McDougall screaming into the
wind, the whole group "shivering like frightened puppies"—
Enos Stutsman's clever pen dripped acid, and a delighted
America laughed. A bumptious aristocrat was getting his
comeuppance.

It was almost the end of the road for McDougall. The legless young man of Pembina, sliding in for the kill, had a
slavering pack behind him. The shrewd, scheming Yankees,
nursing their bitterness toward all that McDougall represented, were in the forefront of the hungry ring, but a still
deadlier company crouched behind. These were the luckless
McDougall's distinguished colleagues in Ottawa, the men

who had bungled the affair from the start, led by unctuous Sir John, who shared McDougall's bigotry and imperialistic visions but would never forgive his failure. Sir John and his crowd had to get out from under, and there never lived a more perfect scapegoat than eager, loyal, stupid William Mc-Dougall. When the pack was through with him he had been stripped of dignity, career and hope.

McDougall was not quite finished yet, however. On December 2 he issued another proclamation whose consequences might have been more serious for all the whites in the West than his initial forgery proved to be for him. By virtue of the commission which he was (illegally) exercising and because armed resistance was being maintained to his assumption of office, he chose to appoint John Stoughton Dennis as his "Lieutenant and Conservator of the Peace" for Rupert's Land and the Northwest Territories. The proclamation authorized Dennis—whose military judgment and conduct under fire had once been the subject of official investigation—to raise and equip a force to disperse the rebels, to fire upon any stronghold in their possession, to purchase or confiscate supplies, cattle, horses or vehicles, to attack even any private home "in which said armed men may be found."

The same day, McDougall sat down and wrote Ottawa about what he had done. He had given, he said, "large powers" to Dennis. He had indeed; he had commissioned that none-too-sound officer to start a civil war.

For his part, Dennis set out eagerly to obey his orders. He had been commissioned to raise "a sufficient force," and though he was ashamed of the English (one of the Canadian party wrote McDougall that "they are cowards, one and all of them") he did find some ready recruits at hand, anxious to get British guns and supplies. They were Indians.

With the aid of an Indian band, Dennis seized and established his headquarters in Lower Fort Garry, the "stone fort" of the Hudson's Bay Company about twenty miles north of the Forks where stood the community of Fort Garry proper. This was in violation of his orders, because Lower Fort Garry was not, and never had been, in possession of the Métis. Here he hired Joseph Monkman, an English half-breed, for ten shillings a day to recruit Indians for his command.

Word that Dennis was recruiting Indians and supplying them with arms caused an uproar when Pembina sent it on to St. Paul. Memory of the Sioux outbreak in which 650 Minnesotans had perished in 1862 was painfully fresh, and angry protests sped to Washington and from there to Ottawa. A Pembina dispatch reported McDougall had been sternly called to account by the white and Métis inhabitants of that community for enlisting Indians, and had said he "didn't think we'd have to use them." Again beset in St. Paul, he denied that he had approved the use of Indians "except the Christianized Chippewa or the English and Scotch half-breeds." Taylor charitably decided that McDougall was not fully cognizant of his "lieutenant's" desperate measures.

When the St. Paul interview occurred, William McDougall was on his way home, beaten. No one save Dennis had heeded his proclamations, and Dennis had been unable to organize the "loyal" demonstration the Canadians had promised on a scale sufficient to indicate that the new regime could establish itself. Riel and his council ruled Rupert's Land, and had disdained to reply to McDougall's last despairing gesture—a personal letter to Riel pleading for a meeting at Pembina.

Now the pack moved in. Ottawa's reply to McDougall's report on his issuance of the proclamations had to catch up with him en route, for he had already left Pembina when it was sent. Signed by Howe, it was a cruel and crushing—even if deserved—repudiation of McDougall and all his acts. Point by point it went over his blunders.

McDougall had "used the Queen's name without her authority, attributed to Her Majesty acts which she has not yet performed, and organized an armed force within the Territory of the Hudson's Bay Company without warrant or instructions." He had risked military action despite "the fearful consequences which might ensue were the Indians, many of them but recently in contact with the white inhabitants of the neighboring States, drawn into the conflict." The Ministry could not conceal from him "the weight of responsibility" McDougall had incurred, especially since it had learned of the "reckless and extraordinary proceedings" of Colonel Dennis. The latter, Howe said, "appears never to have thought that the moment war commenced, all the white inhabitants would be at the mercy of the Indians, by whom they are largely outnumbered, and divided as they would be, might be easily overpowered."

The Government regretted that McDougall should have been represented in Rupert's Land by "a person of so little discretion" as Dennis. That gentleman (and, by implication, his chief, McDougall) "would have to answer at the bar of justice for every life lost by such an assumption of authority." Finally, the disgraced Governor-designate was reminded that "the illegal seizure of an American citizen would at once provoke interference in the quarrel and lead to very serious complications."

Pursued by a vulgar Métis song and followed by sixty loads of gear, McDougall dragged sadly home. *"Adieux, château d'Espagne,"* the Métis minstrels mocked. McDougall had lost his crown, the song said; and now his only throne was a seat in a privy.

In Ottawa, Sir John washed his hands and wrote a little note to a colleague. "McDougall is now at St. Paul's and leaves this morning for Ottawa. He has the redoubtable Stoughton Dennis with him. The two together have done their utmost to destroy our chance of an amicable settlement with these wild people."

CHAPTER VII

A People . . . Free to Choose

THE ABILITY OF M. LOUIS RIEL

ALL the fear and fury of the "wild people" fought for control of the mind and soul of their twenty-five-year-old leader Louis Riel, erstwhile poet, almost priest.

Most Métis matured early, but Louis had had little experience on the hunt, where men were made, and had known few hardships. He was a mediocre horseman. He was clumsy and his hands were undexterous; many men of his race caught in prairie blizzards with no tool save a knife could survive, but he would have committed his soul to God and died. He could not shoot straight: he knew nothing of firearms and he dreaded and shunned them all his life. Living among people who drank to excess whenever they could, he used liquor sparingly; he had enemies who claimed they had seen him drunk, but as many friends swore he was a teetotaler. As for women, not even his enemies could make out a case against him. Either he had resigned himself to the priestly vow of chastity or he was unusually discreet, and he was nearly forty when he married.

But to his colleagues of the council and to the Métis people he was the brain. More than that, he was their voice: the only man they had ever produced who could fashion a philosophy from the crude materials of their semiprimitive way of life, the only one whose eloquence could become a sort of alchemy, transmuting frontier expedients into eternal human values, shaping standards out of habits. The forlorn people, facing the loss of land and livelihood, learned from him that the old ways had been good and the new ways were evil, that their struggle was significant.

Out of that struggle the Métis hero emerged: Louis Riel, symbol and spokesman of the oppressed but gallant minority; revolutionist, leader, and lord. It was "lord" in lower-case, for even to his most ardent admirers he was still just a skilled politician. Messiahship, the capital *L,* came later.

But the people did not know that the young hero doubted, even as they did, and was often afraid.

In public he was fluent, and assured to the point of being arbitrary. His poise cracked only when he was crossed; and on such occasions his outbursts of rage betrayed how meager were his reserves of tolerance, how slight, actually, his self-esteem. The youth was unsure of his adult role, and even his garb betrayed it: for his "audiences" with visitors he wore the starched shirt and collar, the silk cravat, black frock coat and black trousers of the Anglo-Saxon statesman—but there were moccasins on his feet.

He was harassed, threatened, cajoled and flattered by the counselors he had chosen himself, and a score who had descended upon him uninvited—Métis, Fenian, American, English, even a renegade Canadian or two; and the priests. He had to argue with them and negotiate in three languages—French, Cree, and English—and words change their meanings swiftly in the flight from tongue to tongue. He had no precedents to guide him, no tradition and no text, because his "revolution" was unique. He borrowed, compromised, improvised.

And he did astonishingly well. Consider the testimony of Capt. W. F. Butler, F.R.G.S., an Irishman in England's uniform who despised the Métis—"nobody could tell who or what they were." At the height of Riel's reign the captain visited Fort Garry. He thought some of his experiences there were comic, but he paid sincere tribute to the hero of the half-breed cause:

> It is almost refreshing to notice the ability, the energy, the determination which up to this point had characterized all the movements of the originator and mainspring of the movement, M. Louis Riel. One hates so much to see a thing bungled that even resistance, although it borders upon rebellion, becomes respectable when it is carried out with courage, energy, and decision.

There were times, however, when that courage, energy and decision were hard to come by. Then young Louis wondered why he had so eagerly accepted the responsibility his people had thrust upon him; then he feared and fumbled and wished he could turn back. He had no idea of what lay ahead except that one alternative—independence—definitely was not feasible. Though this was what many Métis wanted, he knew that the little Western colony could not maintain itself against Canada or the United States. But for the moment he appeared to have freedom of choice between these two predatory powers.

The American element grew bolder. Every conceivable pressure, including the offer of bribes, was exerted by the Pembina plotters, chief of whom were Stutsman and Joseph LeMay, United States collector of customs, and by the

Yankee contingent in Rupert's Land, ably led by one of
Riel's lieutenants, the Fenian O'Donoghue. For two months
the fate of British North America hung upon the whim of
Louis Riel. But Louis Riel refused to forswear his allegiance
to the Queen.

SHOWDOWN WITH SCHULTZ

The day of decision for Louis Riel was December 7, 1869.

On the flimsy excuse that "government stores" in his possession required protection, Dr. John Christian Schultz had
gathered forty-five members of the Canadian faction, armed
them, supplied four hundred rounds of ammunition, and
stationed them in his house, which he quickly converted into
a fort. To enroll this force had taken him several days, and
the move was made in defiance of explicit orders from Colonel Dennis, McDougall's purported "Conservator of the
Peace." Entrenched in the "Stone Fort" north of Fort Garry,
Dennis had sent word to Canadian sympathizers in the major
settlement to remain quiet and not to provoke the touchy
Métis. On December 4 he again urged, in a note to the group
in Schultz's house, that the Canadians disperse, warning that
he had no force at his command sufficient to rescue them if
the Métis attacked. His attempts to recruit a "loyal" army,
Dennis confessed, were not succeeding. "You speak of enthusiasm," he wrote Schultz; "I have not seen it yet with anybody but Prince's men [Indians]."

But the exasperated Canadians were determined to bring
matters to a head. They ignored Dennis, barricaded the doors
and windows of the house, christened it "Fort Schultz," and
virtually defied the bewildered Métis to come and get them.
Two or three members of the group, apparently couriers,
were captured by Riel's guards outside the house and were
lodged in prison quarters at Fort Garry. One of these men
was Thomas Scott, the obstreperous young Ontario Orange-

man who had had trouble with Snow, his boss on the survey for the western end of the Dawson Road.

Riel increased the number of Métis guards on the streets, and on December 7 he summoned them for review in front of Schultz's "fort." He read the illegal commission which McDougall had given Dennis, threw it in the snow and trampled upon it. Then he gave notice that he would not permit the organization of armed companies such as the one now lodged in "Fort Schultz" because they constituted a threat to peace.

The more level-headed citizens of the community now saw that open warfare was imminent. Led by A. G. B. Bannatyne, merchant and postmaster, they attempted to persuade Riel to let the Schultz party leave the house without molestation; but Riel insisted upon unconditional surrender. Nor were the peacemakers much more successful with Schultz when they went to see him: the reckless doctor gave them a long list of "conditions" to which he demanded that the Métis accede before he led his "soldiers" out.

Riel's answer was prompt and decisive. He sent Bannatyne into the house with an ultimatum expiring in fifteen minutes, surrounded the place with three hundred armed Métis, and set up two cannon aimed at the front door.

Dr. Schultz and his men were to yield their arms and surrender themselves, in which event their lives would be spared. If they chose to reject these terms, their wives and children (several had their families with them) and any English halfbreeds or Indians who chanced to be in the house would be permitted to depart unmolested before the Métis opened fire.

Riel's curt note, with its demand that every besieged Canadian humble himself by signing the surrender terms, suddenly brought home to the foolhardy company that Schultz had maneuvered them into an impossible position. Up to now, despite Dennis's warning, they had only played at war; but the menacing attitude of the Métis and the presence of the cannon left them with little doubt that Riel was ready to annihilate their "fort" and everyone in it. And their mad venture had no legal excuse: even if Dennis's commission had been valid, he already had condemned their resistance. The doctor's homemade Canadian ensign, flying from a staff in front of his "fort," flew without warrant.

Schultz's duped companions also realized now, with justifiable alarm, that they had committed their lives to the whim of the one man above all others whom the Métis loathed. Dr. John O'Donnell, no friend of his medical colleague, was the first to speak up: they were trapped and had no recourse save to yield. He stepped forward and signed the surrender note; the others quickly followed.

When all had signed, Bannatyne delivered the note to Riel. The chastened "garrison" marched out of the house between sullen rows of Métis standing with their rifles at ready, and were escorted to Fort Garry to be jailed. Mrs. Schultz, Mrs. Mair and Mrs. O'Donnell courageously chose to accompany their husbands; Mrs. Schultz, ill, could not walk to the fort and was borne there on a sled drawn by her husband. In Fort Garry the married couples were permitted to occupy the apartment of the Company accountant, and to share another with William Cowan, the chief factor, and his family, until the wives were persuaded to accept the freedom offered them by Riel.

Riel's summary, if bloodless, reduction of "Fort Schultz" almost eliminated the "loyal" movement, which, it was now apparent, had been built upon bluff.

Colonel Dennis gave up and issued a "peace proclamation." In a printed broadside, he ordered the "loyal party" to "cease further action under the appeal to arms made by me." The French party, he declared, had indicated willingness to negotiate a settlement with Canada; under the circumstances he was ready to help the cause of peace by dispersing his forces.

With that, Dennis left Red River behind him forever. It took him four days (according to some contemporary accounts he disguised himself as a squaw) to reach Pembina and join McDougall.

THE LAW OF NATIONS

The morning after he had jailed the Canadian militants, Louis Riel posted on the walls of public buildings his answer to McDougall's fraudulent proclamation of a week before, claiming sovereignty for the Dominion of Canada.

Dated December 8, 1869, the "Declaration of the People of Rupert's Land and the North West" was an unequivocal document. In the name of the council, Riel set forth the rights to which the people were entitled *as British subjects*. And, though the declaration was bitterly critical of Canadian policy, it asserted, "We hold ourselves in readiness to enter into such negotiations with the Canadian Government as may be favorable for the good government and prosperity of this people." The resistance, it was made clear, had been solely against establishment of Canadian authority "under the announced form."

The authorship of this eloquent declaration has long been a subject of dispute. Contemporary commentators, remarking its "Americanisms," were prone to attribute it to Stutsman; and the spelling of such words as "neighboring," "honor" and "favorable" in the first printed copies in English indicated that the typesetter, at least, was American. But a Catholic, violently pro-Métis historian and pamphleteer, the Rev. A. G. Morice, testified that authorship of the statement was acknowledged to him by another literary priest, Father Georges Dugas.

It is almost certain that Riel did not write the declaration himself. Probably he dictated most of its content to Dugas, drawing to some extent upon the ideas of his American friends. It is most unlikely that he gave the priest a free hand in composing this first general statement of principles of the "New Nation" of the Métis.

No matter who wrote it, the declaration was remarkable on several counts—not the least of these the fact that it might well have been written by Sir John A. Macdonald. Its major thesis and even some of its phrasing resembled strikingly what Macdonald said in a letter he wrote to McDougall on November 27. (Riel could not have seen this letter. Even if his spies had obtained a copy of it, as they probably had of others, it would have been impossible to get it to Fort Garry within ten days of the date it was written in Ottawa. The original reached McDougall too late to do any good.)

Sir John's letter warned the Governor-designate against crossing the boundary and assuming authority because such action would destroy the sovereignty of the Hudson's Bay Company. If McDougall still were barred by the Métis after he took this step there would be no legal government; anarchy would follow, and "no matter how anarchy is produced, it is quite open, by the law of nations, for the inhabitants to form a government *ex necessitate* for the protection of life and property." Such a government, Macdonald continued, would have certain rights in law "which might be very convenient for the United States, but exceedingly inconvenient for you."

What happened was just what Macdonald had feared. McDougall did assume authority, the Company did relinquish it—and Riel's provisional government, in Sir John's own words, was legal.

That was what the "Declaration of the People" set out to prove. "It is admitted by all men as a fundamental principle," the statement began, "that the public authority commands the obedience and respect of its subjects. It is also admitted

that a people, when it has no Government, is free to adopt
one form of Government in preference to another, to give
or to refuse allegiance to that which is proposed."

In accordance with these principles, the people of Rupert's
Land had respected the authority of the Hudson's Bay Company even if it had been "far from answering the wants of
the people." But, "contrary to the law of nations," the Company had transferred to Canada "all the rights which it had
or pretended to have in this territory, by transactions with
which the people were considered unworthy to be made acquainted."

The argument so far, including reference to "the law of
nations," almost duplicated the statements in Sir John's
letter. The declaration went on to draw the logical conclusions:

1st. We, the Representatives of the people in Council assembled at Upper Fort Garry on the 24th day of November, 1869,
after having invoked the God of nations, relying on these fundamental moral principles, solemnly declare in the name of our
constitutents and in our own names, before God and man, that
from the day on which the Government we had always respected
abandoned us, by transferring to a strange power the sacred
authority confided to it, the people of Rupert's Land and
the North-West became free and exempt from all allegiance to
the said Government.

2d. That we refuse to recognize the authority of Canada, which
pretends to have a right to coerce us and impose upon us a
despotic form of government, still more contrary to our rights
and interests as British subjects than was that Government to
which we had subjected ourselves through necessity up to a
recent date.

3rd. That by sending an expedition on the 1st of November,
ult., charged to drive back Mr. William McDougall and his
companions coming in the name of Canada to rule us with the
rod of despotism without a previous notification to that effect,

we have but acted conformably to the sacred right which commands every citizen to offer energetic opposition to prevent his
country being enslaved.

4th. That we continue and shall continue to oppose with all
our strength the establishing of the Canadian authority in our
country under the announced form. And in case of persistence
on the part of the Canadian Government to enforce its obnoxious policy upon us by force of arms, we protest beforehand
against such an unjust and unlawful course, and we declare the
said Canadian Government responsible before God and men
for the innumerable evils which may be caused by so unwar-
rantable a course.

Be it known, therefore, to the world in general and to the
Canadian Government in particular, that as we have always heretofore successfully defended our country in frequent wars with
the neighboring tribes of Indians, who are now on friendly
relations with us, we are firmly resolved in future not less than
in the past, to repel all invasions from whatsoever quarter they
may come.

And furthermore, we do declare and proclaim in the name of
the people of Rupert's Land and the North-West, that we have
on the said 24th day of November, 1869, above mentioned, established a Provisional Government, and hold it to be the only
and lawful authority now in existence in Rupert's Land and the
North-West, which claims the obedience and respect of the
people.

That meanwhile we hold ourselves in readiness to enter into
such negotiations with the Canadian Government, as may be
favorable for the good government and prosperity of this people.

In support of this declaration, relying on the protection of
Divine Providence, we mutually pledge ourselves, on oath, our
lives, our fortunes, and our sacred honor to each other.

The declaration was signed by John Bruce as President
and Louis Riel as Secretary. Two weeks thereafter the figurehead Bruce resigned and Riel assumed the title of President,
whose functions he had been exercising from the start.

Dr. Tupper, a physician and member of the Canadian Parliament, came all the way from Ottawa to get his daughter, the wife of the lordly but inept Captain Cameron, and take her home. South of Pembina he met McDougall, Dennis and most of the rest of the "Governor's" dragtail company. Mr. Richards, who had expected to be attorney general, told the newcomer that he had not had his clothes off for fully two months and had lived in hourly terror of losing his life.

Arriving at Pembina on Christmas Eve, Tupper found his daughter asleep. She sat up in bed and demanded, "What did you come for?" He told her he had come to recover her effects (in possession of the Métis since the incident at the St. Norbert barrier) and to accompany the Camerons home.

It would be as much as his life was worth, the Canadians had told Tupper, for him to go to Fort Garry. Rubbish, said Tupper. He went to Stutsman, told him what he wanted, and was instructed on how to get through the Métis line. He bribed and bullied a young half-breed guide into taking him north. There was a foot of snow on the trail, they were lost in a frozen fog, and the temperature was thirty below. For one night they took refuge in the cabin of a Métis settler who greeted them cordially, provided venison and tea with biscuits and real butter.

At Fort Garry the Canadian M.P. was courteously received by Riel and his request for the restoration of Mrs. Cameron's property was promptly met. Tupper said he got back "half a ton" of his daughter's trunks; "nothing had been taken from them." He also met Riel's sister, who was a nun at St. Norbert, and she sang for him in Cree. He found her to be a charming and dedicated young woman, and he corresponded with her, after she took up a teaching mission among the Indians at Isle à la Crosse, until her death.

On the whole Tupper was favorably impressed by Riel, though he could not, of course, countenance the latter's policies, and did his best on the way back to Pembina to

persuade Father Ritchot and the American Joseph LeMay
that the half-breeds should yield to Canada without further
ado. He thought he made some headway toward convincing
them that the United States would never actively intervene.
But he acknowledged Riel's strength. He had been conducted
to his interview in Fort Garry past two hundred armed
guards, and the attitude of the young head of the Provisional
Government had been poised and confident.

Louis was even more self-assured, if somewhat less courteous, when a blustering busybody who identified himself
as Colonel Rankin insisted upon an audience. The Métis
chief asked him to state his business, "in as few words as
possible." Well, Rankin admitted, he held no official position; but he was "in close touch" with the Dominion Government and anything he might report in Ottawa "would
have great weight."

Riel's implacable eyes pierced the pompous windbag who
had expected to confront an ignorant Indian whom he could
easily overawe. As always when he was on his dignity, Riel's
retort was stilted; but it was effective.

"You may say officially," he told the stunned Rankin, "that
you had an interview with Riel, the leader of the Métis, and
he said you had but twenty-four hours to get out of the
country, and further that if after that you are taken north
of the forty-ninth parallel, you will be arrested and tried
by court-martial and dealt with according to the findings of
the court. You say you are a military man; it will not be
necessary to explain to you what that means. Baptiste, show
this gentleman out!"

For the time being young Louis had quieted his own
doubts; his control over Rupert's Land was never more absolute, and he knew it. About sixty of his most dangerous op-
ponents—the forty-five captured at Schultz's house and a
dozen of Dennis's men picked up later—were languishing

in jail, and the other English-speaking citizens, most of whom felt that Schultz had brought his troubles on himself, were surprisingly complacent. Only at the village of Portage la Prairie was there left a nucleus of opposition. It was led by Maj. C. W. Boulton, who had been a member of one of the Canadian surveying parties.

And his government was not only legal and secure; it also worked. It was tested in two Indian scares—the approach of a band of the dreaded Sioux, probably lured to the settlement by Dennis's rash attempt to recruit tribesmen to fight the Métis; and a threat by a band from another tribe to seize Dawson Road supplies which were in the possession of Snow, superintendent of that survey. Riel and some of his Métis went out to meet the Sioux in council, presented gifts of tobacco, and persuaded the unwelcome visitors to return to their distant camps; and on an appeal from Snow, Métis guards were assigned to protect his stores—although the goods were owned by the Government they were resisting, and although Snow himself was a member of the Canadian bloc.

Riel had accomplished a great deal in two months. The bill of rights had established the moral justification for the Métis movement, and the declaration gave it a sound legal base. The usurper McDougall had been driven home; the reckless Dennis, unable to precipitate a civil war, had fled. Riel had kept his own volatile countrymen under control, and though hundreds of his men walked the streets armed, no one had been attacked and no one had been robbed. The community's morals—not altogether to its liking—were safeguarded; during the Christmas-New Year week the sale of liquor was prohibited by Riel's presidential decree. Canada had been forced to appoint commissioners and start them west to negotiate with him. He had won the respect—and more than respect, if he chose to avail himself of it—of his powerful neighbor, the United States.

It all added up to noteworthy achievement for a lonely, unhappy intellectual of twenty-five, and he could be forgiven a few new fripperies in his dress, a few somewhat pathetic flourishes in speech or statecraft which he hoped would give dignity to himself and his people. Nor could dignity ever be an insignificant concern to a new race whose color and culture had foredoomed it to exploitation by arrogant whites.

But there were other concerns; Riel could not pause to congratulate himself upon a few successes.

A government had to have a press. He had suppressed the consistently hostile *Nor'wester* and its successor, the Red River *Pioneer*. Now he extorted a loan from the Hudson's Bay Company and invested part of it in purchase of the *Pioneer*'s plant; on January 7, 1870, the first issue of *The New Nation* appeared. Riel entrusted the editorship to an American, Maj. H. M. Robinson, and this worthy made full use of his opportunities by editorializing vigorously for "independence" and ultimate union with the United States. Riel permitted this for several weeks, perhaps to enhance his bargaining position by exaggerating the pro-American sentiment in the settlement; later, however, he clamped down on Yankee agitation and ultimately Robinson lost his job—becoming vice consul and then acting consul for the United States.

(In Washington on January 15, Minnesota's Senator Ramsey called upon President Grant. The Red River resistance to Canada could be maintained indefinitely, he said, if $25,000 were put at the disposal of the Métis. He thought it would be a good investment for the United States. President Grant refused.)

The newspaper represented just one phase of Riel's overall strategy in the drive for political stabilization. The time had now come to dicker, to see how far an alarmed if not yet wholly docile Dominion could be pushed.

Canada's "peace commissioners" were Lieutenant Colonel
de Salaberry, Vicar General Thibault of the Montreal Catholic diocese, and Donald A. Smith, manager of the Hudson's
Bay Company's Montreal district. They arrived late in December, went before Riel's council separately, and sought
to win the Métis over with the aid of letters from Howe in
Ottawa specifically disowning the "acts of folly and indiscretion" which had been committed by persons purporting
to represent the Dominion.

De Salaberry and Thibault were primarily "goodwill am-
bassadors"; Smith, who had been sent west a week later with
more detailed instructions, took the lead in negotiations.
Riel was friendly to the first two men, but he distrusted the
shrewd, taciturn Smith. Smith had secreted his official papers
in Pembina; a struggle for possession of them ensued and was
won by Smith through the intervention of the dying Mactavish and a group of Métis friendly to the visiting Company
official.

Facing a split in his council, Riel finally assented to a public meeting at which Smith could present his documents and
argue Canada's case before the people. Louis had not actually
been opposed to this very strongly from the first, but he was
disgruntled because he was unable to get a look at Smith's
documents before the mass meeting.

Suddenly there was serious division within the Provisional
Government's inner circle. O'Donoghue was intriguing vigorously for American annexation, and another faction, in Riel's
opinion, was far too friendly with Smith if Louis were to
have the free hand in bargaining which he wanted. This pro-
Smith group he correctly judged to be more dangerous to his
cause than O'Donoghue and the Yankee wirepullers, so for a
time he appeared to be aligning himself with the Americans.
But to the one or two who had his confidence throughout, he
made it clear that he had never wavered in his determination
ultimately to reject the United States bid for Rupert's Land.

Intrigue was not his only problem. Discipline had begun
to pull loose at the seams in Fort Garry. He had to arrange
frequent furloughs for the guards and summon new companies by recruiting them at the church door after Sunday
masses. The Métis disliked sustained effort of any kind and
the novelty of policing the settlements and guarding the
prisoners had begun to wear off. The jailers got drunk and
prisoners escaped. A major break occurred January 9 when
twelve, including the rambunctious Orangeman Thomas
Scott, got away; most of them were recaptured, but Scott was
not.

(And Mrs. Schultz, her health improved, had smuggled a
pocketknife and a gimlet into her husband's cell.)

Worst of all, there was Major Boulton, working quietly—
but more effectively than had anyone else—to organize resistance among the English-speaking element. Boulton,
though no less guilty than others of occasional recklessness,
was the most competent and most honest of Riel's enemies,
and, but for Schultz, the most feared by the Métis. Rumors
reached Fort Garry that at Portage la Prairie he had managed to reassemble the shattered nucleus of the Canadian
party, was arming volunteers, and was even winning over
many of the hitherto neutral Englishmen, displeased because
Riel was holding the prisoners for an unreasonably long
time.

Louis was on weak ground in this matter of prisoners and
knew it. But they were his hostages, and he was determined
to keep them under restraint until his government was
secure. He looked now to the mass meeting called to hear
Donald Smith; it could bring about consolidation of all
elements of the community and provide assurance that until
his deal with Ottawa was completed the Métis would live in
peace.

CHAPTER VIII

Mr. Smith Wins an Empire

THE GREAT ASSEMBLY

JANUARY 19, 1870: an important day in the Northwest. That morning, under a bright sun, men began to assemble in a great open field within the settlement which surrounded Fort Garry—now slowly becoming known as the town of Winnipeg, taking its name from the big lake to the north.

Newcomers came every few minutes, milled around the field, soon had the foot-deep snow packed hard. By the hundreds they came—horseback, in wagons, on sleds, walking—from the villages scattered for miles up and down Red River; from Kildonan and St. Andrew's and Headingly; from St. Boniface, St. Norbert, St. Vital; from hamlets whose names evoked sober memories of the decorous and diligent parishes of the Old Country, and from others whose names sang of adventure and romance in New France.

Some had a long way to come. Headingly, for instance, was fourteen miles from Winnipeg. The distance once had been "stepped off" by a Métis runner hired by Englishmen to

163

settle a bet. (He was gone all night; when he got back the pedometer strapped to his leg registered more than a hundred miles. He explained that he had found a dance under way at Headingly, had stopped over to spend the night gaily doing the Red River jig, and at sunup had set out unwearied on the return hike.)

It was a long way to come, and distance is relative: a mile is shorter some days than it is on other days. Today the miles were long. The temperature was twenty degrees below zero.

By midmorning more than one thousand men and scores of women stood in the big field. The snow crunched under their feet as they shifted position and stamped to keep their blood circulating. They yanked off their mittens to thrust freezing hands under their blanket *capotes* and under their shirts to their warm armpits. They tested the brittle air between their teeth, sucking it in slowly and thinly lest the cold stab into their lungs—for such knife-thrusts of the cold could kill.

The people of Rupert's Land had been summoned by Louis Riel to meet in this field—there was no hall large enough—to hear Donald Smith present his case for Canada and decide what they wanted to do. Swift Métis runners had carried Riel's proclamation calling the meeting to the most remote corners of the scattered settlements. It was too bad that it was twenty below, but they were used to that; and affairs of state in the Northwest could not wait upon the weather.

There were at this time in the Red River settlements north of the boundary about twelve thousand people. Half were Métis and about four thousand were English half-breeds; there were only fifteen hundred whites and about six hundred Indians. Of the whites, seven hundred had been born there, three hundred were from Canada, and the others had come from Scotland, England, or the United States. And—though most of them had had less than a day's notice, though their sled runners shrieked on the wind-buffed snow surface of the trails and the astringent air burned their nostrils and throats—despite all that, ten per cent of the population had come to the meeting.

The people stamped their feet and gossiped. Their breath spurted in wisps of frosty mist; it was good to get a chance to talk. Winter was a lonely time, and after the Christmas and New Year parties, families shut themselves in and built up the fires and shunned dangerous travel. So they talked, and stared at the flag which flew from the tall staff of Fort Garry, a banner with but one figure, a bold *fleur-de-lis* in gold on a pure white field. Many of them had never before seen this flag of the Provisional Government of Rupert's Land, which replaced the red ensign with the union jack in the canton and the white letters *H B C* in the field, the banner of the Company of Adventurers. The new flag had been raised December 10, while the band of St. Boniface College, a bunch of youngsters who made up the only musical organization in the British Northwest, flung itself fiercely upon French folk songs and hymns, and a Métis guard of honor fired a ragged volley.

Now there was a clatter of rifle fire from the fort: a salute, or as near as the Métis, never very easy to regiment, could come to one. *Monsieur le président* Riel was coming, with his council, Donald Smith and others of the official party.

The people stood tiptoe: none of them had seen Smith, and many did not know Riel. The tall, well-built Scot walked with dignity beside the stockier Métis, saying nothing, biding his time. The people saw an imperturbable, long-nosed face, eyes calm but keen. They had heard about this man who had distinguished himself in his twenty years as administrator of the Company's Labrador district, had married a Red River white girl after dissolution of her earlier union with a fur trader, and had become manager of the Montreal district. He was now fifty, this was his first trip to the West, and he was on the threshold of fame. A seat in Parliament awaited him, then governorship of the great Company, elevation to the peerage as Lord Strathcona, and "empire building" as a founder and financial backer of the Canadian Pacific Railway.

The Scot looked benignly over the crowd and kept silence while the nervous Riel chattered. Together they climbed upon the platform the Métis had erected. Now the crowd could get a better look at Riel. Those who knew him observed that he had aged and grown heavier. His face looked somewhat sallow and puffy, but he was still handsome: the big head, broad forehead and mass of curly brown hair set him apart. The eyes had not changed—piercing, truculent, deep-set under heavy straight brows. His mustache was small and neat, angling sharply down to the corners of his mouth, fixing upon it the quality of sternness which the young leader so consistently affected. His cheeks were clean-shaven and he was carefully, perhaps a little too elaborately, dressed. He was short and stocky, or he was medium height and well built—none could ever agree on that; it was the head one looked at.

Louis spoke now, calling the meeting to order. His voice was clear and even, though this was the biggest audience he had ever faced. He did not shout, nor did he need to: even little sounds seemed loud in this thin cold air.

He proposed Thomas Bunn, a respected member of the English community, for chairman, and Bunn was dutifully elected. Colonel de Salaberry nominated Riel as translator and he was chosen by acclamation; it was a key role and a test of a man's honesty. (Donald Smith subsequently testified that Riel's translation, faithfully reported in *The New Nation*, was "sufficiently exact.") Judge Black, a Company magistrate, was elected secretary.

Smith read his commission, started on his mass of letters and other documents he had brought with him. Riel translated swiftly. The crowd was attentive and quiet, but for the incessant stamping of feet and swinging of arms. Heavy frost now rimmed the faces sunk in the hoods of the blanket *capotes* or buffalo coats. Several small fires had been started and people took turns warming themselves while small boys were kept busy gathering wood.

Squabbles broke out on the platform over lost or strayed papers, but ultimately all that Smith demanded were produced. He read on: Ottawa's cautionary messages to Mc-Dougall, proclamations, letters designed to prove Canada's good faith and her willingness to grant all rights "that the people may prove themselves qualified to exercise."

The sun faded in the southwest and the cold became almost intolerable, but Smith still read; and Riel, with hardly a pause, converted the stilted ambiguities of statecraft into the people's vivid French. The thousand people stamped and shuffled and stood still and listened—for five hours. . . .

Just before adjournment a Canadian shouted from somewhere in the slowly freezing mass: "Release the prisoners!"

Riel halted in midsentence, glared. "Not just now," he said coldly, and went on with his interpreting.

Others took up the cry. "Yes! Yes! Release the prisoners!"

Riel jerked his head, continued translating. On the outskirts of the crowd scores of Métis guards grasped their rifles and began to shove toward the center of the disturbance. The hecklers subsided.

That was the only untoward incident. The meeting was adjourned, to be resumed at ten the next morning.

On January 20 the crowd was even larger, and it was still twenty below. Most of the people had had to walk or ride miles to their homes and come back. That did not matter; the destiny of a new frontier, of generations of their descendants would be determined on the snow-covered field today, and the citizens had been invited to help decide what that destiny would be.

Mr. Bannatyne was chosen secretary; Judge Black, annoyed

by a brief clash with Riel the day before, declined to serve
again. Father Lestanc, administrator of the Catholic diocese
in the absence of Bishop Taché, who was still in Rome,
opened the meeting: "We have been good friends to this day
in the whole settlement, and I want to certify here that we
will be good friends tonight." Cheers crackled in the still air.

More documents were read, interpreted, discussed. And
finally Donald A. Smith, crafty, deceptively amiable (he was
to withstand, cheerfully, more personal abuse than any other
man ever involved in Canadian public life), played his trump
card.

The future Lord Strathcona was well aware that his personal destiny, as well as that of Riel and of Rupert's Land,
hung upon what he could accomplish at this instant. The
meeting was nearing the end of another five hours and
shadows were edging across the frozen field. Not even the
hardy people of Rupert's Land could stand much more, and
another day of it was unthinkable. So this was the moment.
Now Donald Smith—and probably only Donald Smith—
could win an empire for Canada.

McDougall had miserably failed. Sir John had lost face
in London. But a man who had started as an apprentice clerk
in a fur trading post thirty-two years ago, counting stinking
muskrat skins, could save the Dominion from disgrace, rescue
the Northwest from the greedily reaching fingers of the
Yankees, earn the gratitude of the Crown.

Smith came forward on the platform and obtained the
chairman's permission to make a personal statement—his
first in the two days of talk. His voice was friendly, his words
carefully selected, simple.

Much of what had been read concerned Mr. McDougall,
he said. He would like to make it clear that he had never
known that individual, had never seen him except for a few
minutes when they met on the trail as McDougall was on his
way out of the country. The people cheered.

He deprecated the fact that he was not well known here; but his wife was a native of Rupert's Land and the country was very close to his heart. (Cheers.) He represented Canada, but he would press her interests only in so far as they were in accord with the interests of the Northwest. (Hear, hear, and cheers.) Under no other circumstances would he have consented to act.

True, he was connected with the Hudson's Bay Company. (He was to hold its highest office for twenty-five years!) But he would resign from the Company at this moment if that would help Rupert's Land. (Cheers.)

The speech was short. "I sincerely hope," he concluded, "that my humble efforts may in some measure contribute to bring about, peaceably, union and entire accord among all classes of the people of this land."

Grimly but meticulously, hating every word, Riel translated. There were more cheers, this time from the French. Louis watched bitterly as Smith nodded and smiled to the crowd. For the first time the young Métis, master of political rhetoric in the Northwest, had met his match.

Smith stepped aside and Riel took the center of the stage. He moved that a Convention of Forty be held, starting January 25, to consider Smith's commission and what would be best for the welfare of the country. Twenty delegates would be elected by the Scotch and English, the same number by the French. The motion carried.

"But," someone in the crowd objected, "that sounds as if doubt were being cast upon the validity of Mr. Smith's commission!"

Louis Riel was silent for a moment. He looked out over the shivering thousand, over the snow and the great buffalo plain, and the free, wild, uncompassionate land of the Métis. He glanced at the fort and the flag he had designed: the golden symbol of medieval France on the pure white banner which had been borne westward by Champlain. He thought of the new nation whose flag it might have been: haven for wanderers of the wilderness, red or brown or white—the Cree who watched the ghost dancers in the winter night, a dainty and dauntless grandmother, Marie Lajimodière, the hunters, and *voyageurs*, and dusty wagon men.

Louis's answer to the cry from the crowd came slowly; his words were flat, indifferent.

"We accept the commission as genuine," he said. "We are merely to consider what is to be done under it."

Canada had won the Northwest.

THE CONVENTION OF FORTY

Night after night Dr. Schultz arose from simulated sleep in his dark, cold cell on the second floor of the prison building in Fort Garry, dragged the buffalo robe from his bunk, spread it on the floor and laboriously cut it into strips with the knife smuggled to him by his wife.

On Sunday, January 23, he was ready. That night he ripped the strips from the shaggy hair of the robe which had concealed his knife work, and braided them into a rope. It was too short to be secured to stationary objects in the room, so he screwed the gimlet his wife had brought him deep into the window casing and tied the rope to it. Then he scrambled over the sill of the high, unbarred window, squeezed his huge body—he was six feet four inches tall—through, grasped the rope and started down hand-over-hand.

The gimlet pulled out of the casing.

Schultz plunged two stories, the whole weight of his body dropping on one twisted leg. He lay helpless in the snow, gasping and cursing as the pain surged through him. He would freeze in a few minutes; the temperature was still about twenty below. He tested the leg gingerly; it was badly bruised and he would be lame, but it was not broken. He braced himself with his bare hands in the crusted snow, struggled erect. He could not put his weight on the injured leg; dragging it, he reached the wall of the fort.

Here his height helped him, and there were boxes; but it took several tries. His hands were stiff and bleeding, his body ached from the fall, and one leg was useless. But somehow he got over the wall and fell heavily on the other side.

Crippled, thinly clad and almost blinded by drifting snow, the big man staggered up the road toward Kildonan, the Scotch-English community four miles north of the fort. There were few guards about—it was too cold—but once or twice a burly figure in a buffalo coat loomed up ahead; Schultz broke into a stumbling run and threw himself down behind a cabin. He fell several times, almost fainting with exhaustion and pain, but he rose each time and scrambled on. At dawn he reached Kildonan.

Feeble but insistent knocking finally wakened Robert MacBeth. When he opened his door the gaunt, half-frozen fugitive fell into his arms.

MacBeth, who had been a member of the Company's governing council, had no reason to love Schultz; the doctor had led the opposition to the Company in the settlements and had heaped vituperation upon the council in his *Nor'wester* editorials. But the Scotch, no less than the Métis, had a tradition of hospitality. Schultz was thawed out, fed, and put to bed. At the risk of his own life, MacBeth hid the fugitive in his home for two days while he arranged secret transportation for him to the Stone Fort, where the doctor could be secreted indefinitely.

Riel was furious. Fort Garry's guards got a tongue-lashing the like of which they had never heard before, and were sent scampering throughout the settlements to hunt down the Canadian. Their orders were to shoot him on sight.

The red-blanketed horses of the Métis cavalry streamed past MacBeth's house. Schultz and his host peeked at them from an upstairs window. The doctor was determined not to be taken alive, and as he watched each patrol approach he hefted a pistol in each hand.

The homes of his known friends and associates were searched; horsemen, wagons and sleighs were stopped on all the roads. But MacBeth's house was not entered.

The French delegates were slow in assembling for the Convention of Forty, so proceedings did not start until January 26, 1870, one day late. On Riel's motion Judge Black was elected chairman, and French and English secretaries were chosen. Smith came to read portions of his papers again, explain them, and uphold Canada in the discussion. A committee of six, three from each faction, was elected to draft a new, more detailed bill of rights; after approval by the convention it was to be submitted to Smith for his opinion.

Discussion of the new bill, brought before the convention January 26, took several days. Riel attempted unsuccessfully to amend it by incorporating a demand that Rupert's Land be admitted to the Dominion as a Province, rather than as a Territory.

When another Riel motion was lost—that the Dominion's bargain with the Company be set aside and that sale of the territory be renegotiated with the people of Rupert's Land as a party to the proceeding—he flew into a rage.

"Devil take it!" he shouted. "We must win! The vote may go as it pleases, but the measure must be carried! It is a shame to have lost it, and a greater shame because it was lost by those traitors!" He jabbed his finger angrily at three French delegates, including his cousin Charles Nolin, who had voted with the English.

Nolin leaped up, sputtering French. "I was not sent here to vote at your dictation!"

For an instant Riel's better judgment warned him of his danger. He could not dictate to the convention as he had to his usually subservient council, and he could not afford to turn the convention against him.

"I do not wish to speak disrespectfully to the convention," he apologized. But his rage could not be contained; his voice rose again. "But I say it will be carried—at a subsequent stage! You must remember that there is a Provisional Government! Though this measure has been lost by the voice of the convention, I have friends enough who are determined to add it to the list on their own responsibility!"

He sat down, flushed and trembling, and glared at Nolin. They had never been friendly, and the bitterness born of this clash and others would have consequences undreamed of now.

Louis did subsequently succeed in obtaining from the Provisional Government the demand for Provincial status which the convention had rejected. But he was never able to carry through his attempt to repudiate the Dominion-Company contract; wiser heads even among the Métis knew this was infeasible.

Smith approved, in principle, the new bill of rights, but he could not guarantee its acceptance by Canada. With the assent of the other two commissioners he urged that the convention send delegates to Ottawa, expenses to be paid by the Dominion, and that they negotiate a final settlement there.

This the convention voted to do. Then Riel, by a masterly stroke of strategy, won full and unimpeachable legal status for the Provisional Government. Pointing out that the delegates had to have some official accreditation, he moved re-establishment of the Provisional Government by the convention. Some of the English, as usual, drew back; but after a committee had formally called upon the doomed Hudson's Bay governor, they yielded. Mactavish told them bluntly, "Form a Government, for God's sake; I have no power or authority!"

The Provisional Government and a legislative assembly or council were established on February 9. The assembly was to have twenty-four members, twelve French, twelve English. Louis Riel was elected President. Chief Justice was James Ross, an English barrister; Bannatyne was Postmaster General, and Thomas Bunn, the son of an English physician, was named Secretary of State. Louis Schmidt, Métis despite his name, was elected Assistant Secretary of State, and O'Donoghue was chosen Treasurer. Riel could command the votes of O'Donoghue and Schmidt and sometimes of Bannatyne, who was friendlier to him than any other member of the Scotch-English community.

It was a great triumph for the young Métis President, and he saw to it that Red River heard about it. It was almost midnight when the Government was completed, but he ordered salutes from the fort's cannon and fusillades from the riflemen while Métis ran through the streets to spread the news.

From the fort and from a few scattered houses, rockets sputtered in the cold, whistled and soared into the starlit sky. Firecrackers popped and Roman candles flung fiery trails across the snow. The fireworks had been laid in by some of the Canadians months before in anticipation of a celebration to welcome "Governor" McDougall. Most of their stock had been found and confiscated by the Métis. But some whose supply had been missed by the guards used it up on this night of Riel's victory. They were long overdue for a celebration, any government was better than none, and McDougall, after all, was far away.

Next day the convention elected three delegates to be sent to Ottawa, and adjourned. The delegates were Judge Black, Father Ritchot and Alfred H. Scott. Scott, a young Winnipeg store clerk, had been closely identified with the American faction although he insisted he was a British citizen. His election, supported by the Métis and bitterly protested by the English settlers, "weighted" the delegation for the

French; but he took little part in the subsequent. Ottawa negotiations.

THE PORTAGE REBELLION

Two days after the close of the convention Riel released sixteen prisoners, exacting a signed pledge that they would not take up arms against the Provisional Government. About twenty remained, refusing to sign the parole, probably because they did not yet realize the truly representative character of Riel's Government.

The President was in good humor and it was generally believed in Winnipeg that release of the remaining prisoners could be arranged within a few days.

But Riel's conciliatory gesture on February 11 was two days too late to forestall tragedy.

Boulton's men at Portage la Prairie had become restive and had been meeting, without their commander's knowledge, to plan a raid on the fort to free the prisoners. On February 9 about sixty of them told their dismayed leader that they were marching—though some were armed only with clubs.

Boulton, who realized that the force was hopelessly inadequate in numbers and equipment, exhausted himself trying to dissuade the mutinous hotheads. When that failed he felt impelled by duty to accompany them, though he attempted to resign the command. In this, also, he failed; the men reminded him that it was he, serving under Dennis, who had organized the movement in the first place.

By the time the force had reached Headingly, Boulton was somewhat heartened; it had grown to a hundred men. But here a blizzard overtook them and they were billeted in the homes of the settlers for several days. Meanwhile word had been sent to the hidden Schultz and the reinforcements recruited by him began to filter in.

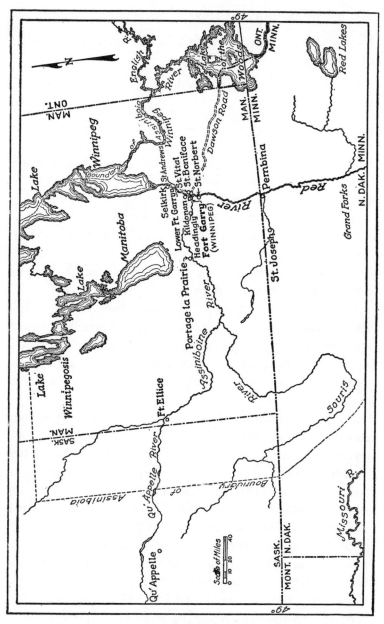

First Métis Uprising

At Headingly the settlers informed the rebel company that some of the prisoners had been freed and the others probably would soon follow them, and attempted to get them to call off the attack. Boulton also renewed his pleas; but on the night of the 14th the Canadians stubbornly resumed the march south.

Word of the expedition had long since reached Riel and well-armed Métis had been riding in from their outlying homes for days. Winnipeg was tense and fearful; stores closed and people stayed off the streets. When Boulton marched reluctantly out of Headingly at least six hundred skilled Métis riflemen were awaiting him in Winnipeg and Riel was having trouble restraining his impatient cavalry from an all-out charge which unquestionably would have annihilated the unmounted, poorly armed and even poorly fed Canadians. Riel insisted, however, that the Métis mobilization was solely for defense and not for aggression.

The "Portagers" came to the home of Henri Coutu, a French Canadian and distant relative of Riel whom the latter frequently visited. They surrounded the house. Boulton and Thomas Scott, the young Ontario Orangeman who had escaped from Riel's prison, forced their way into the house and searched it on the chance that the President might be there. At that moment, however, he was in Fort Garry pleading with his men to be patient.

When Riel was found, Scott boasted loudly, he himself would shoot the Métis scoundrel.

At Kildonan, Schultz and his main force—more than three hundred men—joined Boulton. The Canadians now numbered about five hundred but they still were poorly equipped and, because most of them were farmers, wholly untrained for combat. They had one small cannon, hauled by oxen from the Stone Fort; Riel had thirteen. They had few horses, whereas nearly every one of the six hundred Métis was mounted. For food they relied upon the meager winter stores of the settlers who were becoming more unfriendly as they encountered the Canadians' bullheaded determination to commit suicide. Riel's food supply—the great stocks of the Company—was more than adequate.

No more foolhardy military expedition was ever organized, and at Kildonan the Canadians were at last convinced of it. They were billeted in the Anglican church and school, and there the settlers came to plead for abandonment of the attack. A delegation of the older, wiser Englishmen told them the movement was futile and inopportune; the Provisional Government established by the convention would be the "most certain means of preserving peace until the Dominion, with whom the delegates from the convention are treating, takes the whole matter in hand."

The argument raged; and a feeble-minded Métis youth named Parisien wandered into Kildonan on his way home from Fort Garry, where he had been employed splitting firewood. He was seized by the Canadians as a "spy." The next morning he escaped, stole a rifle from a sled, and ran, hotly pursued by his guards.

Across the river, John Sutherland, a prominent Scotch settler, had just returned to his home from Fort Garry. He and others had pleaded with Riel, Bannatyne had persuaded the remaining prisoners to sign the pledge the President demanded, and all had been released. He had hurried back to Kildonan with the news; now he sent his son, John Hugh, on horseback to notify Major Boulton.

Riding hard, young Sutherland encountered the fleeing Parisien. The half-witted youth, beside himself with terror, mistook Sutherland for one of his pursuers. He raised his rifle, fired twice; Sutherland plunged from his horse fatally wounded.

Parisien's momentary pause to shoot the young Scot finished him as well as his innocent victim. The dying Sutherland pleaded for him: "The poor simple fellow was too frightened to know what he was doing!" But the Canadians struck him down with an axe which sliced open one side of his head, then bound him with two sashes. They dragged him head-first through the snow until Boulton met them, forced them to untie the blood-soaked, unconscious youth, and obtained medical aid. Parisien died a few days later.

These tragedies, the first violent deaths since Riel had seized the reins of government three months before, sobered the Canadians. They began to give more heed to the entreaties of Kildonan's peacemakers.

Then came a message to them from Riel. "For my part," the President wrote, "I understand that war, horrible civil war, is the destruction of this country; and Schultz will laugh at us if, after all, he escapes. We are ready to meet any party; but peace, our British rights, we want before all." The letter continued:

Gentlemen, the prisoners are out—they have sworn to keep peace. We have taken the responsibility of our past acts. Mr. William Mactavish has asked you, for the sake of God, to form and complete the Provisional Government. Your representatives have joined us on that ground. Who will now come and destroy the Red River settlement?

Though some of the Portage men still held out for attack, this took the heart out of the expedition. By the end of the day the men had begun to disperse.

Major Boulton urged them to go home singly or in small groups, but on the morning of February 17 one party of forty-eight—which, against his better judgment, Boulton himself accompanied—passed openly and armed within sight of Fort Garry, and by its somewhat furtive movements apparently gave the fort's lookouts the impression that it intended some hostile maneuver.

A large company of Métis cavalry commanded by O'Donog-

hue and Adjutant General Lépine sprinted from the gates of
the fort and raced across the snowy prairie on a dead run,
intercepting the Canadians. The people of Winnipeg watched
from windows and roofs, anticipating a battle, but the outnumbered Canadians, protesting their innocence of any
aggressive intent, offered no resistance and were escorted as
prisoners to the fort and to the cells from which twenty-four
prisoners had been released two days before. Among the
forty-eight now consigned to those cells were Major Boulton
and Thomas Scott.

A Métis court-martial promptly sentenced Boulton to be
shot. The movement he had originated, Riel argued with
some justice, had been responsible for two deaths and had
almost precipitated civil war just after peace had been made
possible by establishment of the Provisional Government.

Bannatyne and Miss MacVicar, a townswoman who accompanied him, found that this time Riel was deaf to their appeal, nor could any of the others who interceded for Boulton
make any headway, until Miss MacVicar thought of Mrs.
Sutherland. The mother of the youth slain by Parisien and
buried the day before left her bed and came to plead that no
more lives be sacrified.

"No, Mrs. Sutherland!" Riel said. "Boulton must die at
twelve o'clock! I hold him accountable for the death of your
son, the first bloodshed since the resistance to my Government began!"

Mrs. Sutherland dropped on her knees and renewed her
appeal. Riel, impressed always by the dramatic gesture, was
particularly moved now: no white woman had ever so hum-
bled herself before him, and she did it for the sake of a man
whose resistance, Riel knew, had been deplored by the Suth-
erlands. He stopped his restless pacing, leaned against a table
and covered his face with his hands. Finally he turned to her.

"That alone has saved him," he said. "I will give you Boulton's life."

News of the reprieve was rushed to Boulton and spread throughout the settlement within a few hours. The Canadian shrugged, said nothing. He had requested one thing before he faced the firing squad: a drink to warm him, lest shivering from the cold be mistaken for fear.

Riel went to Donald Smith. In return for the mercy he had shown Boulton, would Smith visit the English parishes and attempt to repair the damage the Portage party had done, persuade the English to keep the peace and support the Provisional Government? Smith would, and did.

The back of the Canadian opposition had been broken, but Riel could not be fully content while the worst enemy of all, the implacable Schultz, was still at large. The patrols went out again, and this time they rode as far as the Stone Fort. But Prince's Indians, left to guard that last Canadian stronghold, had deserted when they heard of the Portagers' fiasco; the Stone Fort was abandoned, and Schultz was not there.

It was some time before Riel discovered it, but the indomitable doctor had fled for his life on February 21. Still crippled and accompanied only by a guide, Joseph Monkman (the English half-breed whom Dennis had commissioned to recruit Indians), he had set out by dogsled and afoot for Ontario by way of Duluth, a trip requiring hundreds of miles of travel across open prairie in midwinter. He made it; and although the ordeal all but wrecked his health, he dragged himself bitterly from town to town in Ontario, addressing Orangemen, "patriots," loafers, credulous farmers; haranguing politicians; infecting the whole Province with his boundless, ungovernable rage. Soon his listeners in Ontario were contributing money, guns and even the family plate to finance his crusade against Riel and the Métis.

CHAPTER IX

Four Voted for Death

A RASH AND THOUGHTLESS MAN

THE capital of the Dominion was in Ontario. The death of an obscure young workman in a village of a few hundred people on a little-known frontier hundreds of miles away became the biggest political issue in years. It was so big that even Sir John A. Macdonald, expert dodger of issues and walker on eggs, stumbled and broke a few.

The obscure young man was Thomas Scott of Ontario and he cursed himself into eternity.

Young Louis Riel, who had spent his formative years in the company of priests, was in some ways a bit of a prig. Cursing, for instance, distressed him; he did not like to hear his Lord's name—or his own—taken in vain. He was, consequently, often distressed, because the West then as now was a cursing country.

First there was the time—it was months before Riel and his men turned back McDougall at the frontier—when they met on the street in Winnipeg and Scott, cursing, furiously attacked Riel with his fists. Louis, no fighter, was rescued by

182

onlookers. No one ever found out what caused this outburst. Even Riel apparently did not know.

Later, when Scott was first captured and imprisoned at Fort Garry, he screamed curses at his guards and beat upon his cell door. Then he escaped, and in the raid on Coutu's home he informed the indignant householder and anyone else within hearing that when he caught Riel he would kill the bastard.

Recaptured, he renewed his abuse of the guards. And one day when his cell door was opened as the President walked past he leaped into the corridor, flung himself upon Riel, and screamed: "You son of a bitch! If I'm ever free I'll kill you with my bare hands!"

Donald A. Smith said Scott was "a rash, thoughtless man whom none cared to have anything to do with." An English observer described him as "a hot-headed, irrepressible and irresponsible Orangeman." Montana's pioneer historian Nathaniel P. Langford, Federal revenue collector in that new Territory and brother-in-law of James Wickes Taylor, reported after a visit to Winnipeg, "I am inclined to believe he [Scott] was a bad man."

But of such stuff are martyrs often made. On March 4, 1870, Thomas Scott, adolescent show-off, was shot in the courtyard of Fort Garry by order of a Métis court-martial. And the Province of Ontario turned white with rage.

It started March 1, when the guards complained to Riel that Scott's obstreperous behavior was encouraging the other jail inmates to become insubordinate. Riel warned the prisoner, but Scott, he said, "sneered at and insulted" him. The guards, Scott jeered, were "a pack of cowards." He continued to make trouble.

On March 3 a court-martial was ordered and Scott was brought before it. Riel acted as translator (the defendant knew no French) and also as prosecutor, a hardly defensible expedient resorted to probably because he was the best Eng-

lish scholar among the Métis. Ambroise Lépine, Adjutant
General, was president of the court; other members were his
brother Baptiste, two uncles of Riel, Elzéar Lajimodière and
André Nault; Janvier Ritchot (a Métis, not the priest of the
same surname); Elzéar Goulet, and Joseph Delorme. Joseph
Nolin, brother of Charles and secretary of the court, and one
other witness offered defense testimony.

The culprit was condemned by a four-to-three verdict,
Lajimodière and the Lépine brothers voting to spare him.
Ambroise Lépine pronounced sentence: "Since the majority
is in favor of the motion, Scott will be executed."

The English-speaking community, alerted by the Methodist pastor whom Riel summoned to minister to the doomed
man, spent the night of March 3 and the next morning trying to save him. Smith anxiously interceded; so did Father
Lestanc, who represented the bishop. But Riel was immovable; the most he would grant was a two-hour stay.

Scott could not believe that the sentence would be carried
out, until the guard came to get him. Then he told his pastor,
the Rev. George Young, "This is cold-blooded murder!" He
asked and was granted an opportunity to say good-by to the
other prisoners.

At noon, his eyes bandaged and the Rev. Mr. Young beside
him, the young Canadian was led into the courtyard. He was
ordered to kneel in the snow. A firing squad of six Métis
lined up before him. Three of the rifles contained only powder and wads and no member of the squad knew which guns
held bullets. Some of the marksmen had been drinking to
still their misgivings; none had ever participated in an execution. Much was to be made in Ontario of the fact that the
firing squad was "drunk," but it is not uncommon today to
find drunken sheriffs officiating at hangings in rural county
seats.

The names of the members of the squad were never officially recorded by the Métis. It was evident even before the

fatal act took place that many, probably including Riel, regretted the decision; but they had gone too far to turn back now.

The signal to fire was given by André Nault, by dropping his handkerchief from one hand to the other. Three bullets struck Scott and he collapsed, moaning. Guilmette, a member of the squad, came forward and administered the coup de grâce, a pistol bullet in the head.

The Rev. Mr. Young's request for the body was rejected because Riel feared it might be used for hostile demonstrations. Immediately after the execution it was placed in a casket and lodged in a wall of Fort Garry, but it was removed that night by the Métis and secreted elsewhere and was never found. Most of the contemporary historians believed it was committed to the river, but Morice, the leading Métis apologist, claimed to have discovered that it was buried secretly in St. John's Protestant cemetery.

The Métis, like their Indian forebears, could be savage in a fight; but they could not justly be charged with an impulse to senseless cruelty. In the ten months they controlled Rupert's Land, Scott was the only person they killed—although they were armed, their acts had quasi-legal authority, they were sometimes drunk, and many of them, especially Riel, walked in daily danger of losing their lives. They lost their tempers, they took prisoners (at least once, when Boulton was captured, without adequate excuse), but they did not kill. With one exception.

"Consider the circumstances," Riel pleaded later. "Let the motives be weighed. If there was a single act of severity, one must not lose sight of the long course of moderate conduct which gives us the right to say that we sought to disarm, rather than fight, the lawless strangers who were making war against us."

But there was no placating the Province of Ontario, where

Scott's brother and the malevolent Schultz built high the fires of vengeance. A young Protestant citizen of Ontario, high-spirited perhaps but harmless, had been bestially done to death by bloodthirsty French Papists. Though it really was none of Ontario's business—the crime, if any, occurred not only outside its borders but even outside of the Dominion— nevertheless the Province offered $5,000 reward for capture of the "murderers" of its hero. (This, unlike the money it once had pledged for Red River relief, Ontario finally had to pay: ten claimants divided it in shares ranging from $290 to $2,000.)

Scott and Riel ceased to exist as men. They became symbols solely: Scott the Protestant, Riel the Catholic. As often happens, this was distortion. Scott, although he was a rabid Orangeman, was not noted as a churchgoer; Riel, who regarded himself as the most zealous of Catholics, was sufficiently insubordinate to put his bishop under house arrest and before his life ran out was to be branded Antichrist by a priest.

But for popular purposes that was the picture: young, progressive, dedicated Protestantism destroyed by entrenched, superstitious, corrupt Catholicism. It was a good sharp picture and it made for a foul and vulgar fight, whose repercussions echoed ominously throughout the next fifteen years.

A GUARD FOR THE UNION JACK

The shooting of Scott shocked Ontario more than it did Rupert's Land. There were mutterings in Winnipeg and the outlying English settlements, but the incident was soon almost forgotten on Red River. It did serve one purpose: the few remaining "militants" of the Canadian Party resigned themselves to submission or quit the country. Business was slowly resumed, though handicapped by shortage of money due to inactivity of the Hudson's Bay Company.

A few days after Scott's execution the Right Rev. Alexander Taché, Catholic Bishop of St. Boniface, arrived from Ottawa. With some difficulty in view of the rebuffs he had received when he warned the Canadian ministers months before of potential trouble on Red River, he had been induced to return from Rome and hurry west as a special representative of the Dominion. His reception by his erstwhile protégé Riel was surprisingly cool: for several days he was held under house arrest in the bishop's palace while Louis decided what to do about him. The President permitted the Fort Garry garrison to visit the bishop and receive his blessing, but he warned them, "It is not the Bishop of St. Boniface, it is Canada."

Within two or three days, however, Riel had made his decision. He summoned the new legislative council to meet and hear Taché, and he cordially received the prelate when the latter came to see him at the fort.

At long last Rupert's Land was tranquil. The council session was harmonious. Taché read a telegram from Howe which the latter had sent the bishop after learning the content of the convention's bill of rights: "Propositions in the main satisfactory, but let the delegation come here to settle the details." In Ottawa the bishop had been assured time and again that he could inform the people "the disposition of the Government is such that they may rely upon us with perfect security." That was all very well, the prelate had said, but the Métis had been guilty of some "blameworthy" acts and others might occur before his arrival at Fort Garry. "May I promise them an amnesty?" he had asked Sir John; and, he said, the Prime Minister answered, "Yes, you may promise it to them."

Incidentally, Sir John had added, he would like to have the bishop undertake a mission of great delicacy in the Government's behalf. He showed Taché a copy of Dennis's letter to the half-breed Monkman commissioning the latter to recruit Indians to fight for McDougall. Sir John would be most grateful if the bishop would hunt up Monkman, recover the original of this damning document, and "induce him if possible to abstain from taking any action in the matter, assuring him that he would be rewarded."

The prelate ultimately did recover the letter from Monkman and sent it to the Government, which presumably destroyed it. "The language of that commission was of such extraordinary character," Sir Georges Cartier later confessed, "that it was thought proper not to have it printed" in the official record.

Canada perhaps hoped that suppression of the letter and consequent falsification of the evidence would enable it to enter a demurrer to the anxious protests from the United States against fomenting an Indian uprising on the frontier. The theory was that if it didn't show it never happened. This, however, didn't work out. Too many, including probably the plaguy Stutsman, had actually seen the commission.

"I am proud to be a Canadian," Bishop Taché told the legislative council, and after his arrival the American faction steadily lost ground. The delegates left for Ottawa and the Americans made their last desperate effort to keep the Northwest out of the Dominion.

In April Oscar Malmros, the United States consul in Winnipeg, wrote the State Department to ask if he should now recognize the Provisional Government, and Special Agent Taylor followed up with a letter from Ottawa. The delegates were on their way, he reported; if they were received by the Dominion Government "it will be difficult to repudiate the Government at Red River which was installed by the action of the same Convention." The Riel regime already had obtained virtual recognition from the Hudson's Bay Company. And he concluded with some asperity: "Elsewhere than in an English colony, it would long ago have been recognized at Washington."

There was some truth in this, but now the opportunity had passed and Washington officials knew it, if the annexation bloc did not. Zachariah Chandler gave a belligerent speech in the Senate on his resolution demanding that Rupert's Land be recognized as an independent state and that negotiations be started with Riel looking toward annexation; but the State Department wrote Malmros: "Continue to maintain toward that Government the same attitude which you have hitherto borne." Whereupon Malmros, obtaining emergency leave, suddenly fled from Winnipeg. He got across the line (and was barely rescued from freezing to death in Dakota) just before the appearance of an anonymously published pamphlet containing his correspondence; it disclosed that his "attitude" had not been as circumspectly neutral as he had proclaimed it to be.

Washington did go as far as it dared. When the Dominion revealed that it was sending twelve hundred troops to Rupert's Land, the United States flatly refused to permit the soldiers or even their supplies to pass through its canal at Sault Ste Marie. This was a severe blow. London had been reluctant to permit the inclusion in this force of the four hundred British regulars demanded by Macdonald, and had consented only on his guarantee that the troops had no "coercive" mission and were only to guard against Indian attacks and to maintain order after amicable settlement of the controversy. The American action, though it was subsequently modified to permit transport of strictly nonmilitary materials, meant that the men and their equipment would have to be moved over the nightmare Dawson Road; many in America and England believed this to be impossible. Besides, Washington's decision showed lack of confidence in Macdonald's good faith and betrayed only too clearly where United States sympathies lay. Gravely concerned, the British Colonial Office sent Sir Clinton Murdoch to Canada to supervise the negotiations and help speed a settlement with Riel.

While the worried heads of statesmen bent over dispatches in the chancelleries, the drama of conflicting loyalties was being played out in simpler fashion in the courtyard of Fort Garry.

Riel issued a jubilant proclamation praising the convention and the legislative council. The latter, now become a deliberative body which took its responsibilities seriously, settled down and wrote a code of laws to replace the defunct statutes of the Company. Peace had been restored, Riel affirmed; highways were open and business could be resumed. He negotiated an agreement with the Hudson's Bay Company and it again set up shop. By dogsled, cart or canoe the "outfits" headed north and west for trade. The Métis began thinking about the hunt. Money was circulating, for the first time in months.

Then Louis raised the Union Jack of Great Britain on Fort Garry's tall flagstaff.

O'Donoghue, furious, took the hated ensign down. Riel restored it, stationed his uncle, André Nault, beneath it, handed him a rifle and instructed him to shoot the Treasurer of the Provisional Government if that irate Irishman again attempted to strike the Queen's colors.

O'Donoghue, thwarted, sulked for a day or two; then he got an idea. He went to "Fort Schultz," uprooted the flagpole there and brought it to Fort Garry, planted it and ran up the flag of the Provisional Government.

Riel let it go at that.

A PLACE OF GOD

Delegates Ritchot and Alfred Scott, who left for the East a few days before Judge Black, were met at the Ontario frontier by a magistrate who offered them an escort to Ottawa. They accepted with pleasure, whereupon they were escorted to jail.

They were arrested on an Ontario provincial warrant accusing them of complicity in the "murder" of Thomas Scott, with the latter's brother, Hugh, as complaining witness. Horrified, the Dominion Government intervened and they were released, but not before they had been summoned to "trial" before a local police magistrate who had to be convinced by a Dominion judge that he had no jurisdiction over an alleged capital crime eight hundred miles away.

Hands were wrung in London and a cablegram sped across the Atlantic, "Was arrest of delegates authorized by Canadian Government? Send full information by telegram." Harassed Ottawa responded that the Dominion had had nothing to do with it and that the delegates were being released.

Delegate Scott was amused by the incident but Father Ritchot was justifiably ruffled; he complained bitterly to the Governor General of Canada, Sir John Young, about Ontario's violation of diplomatic immunity. He was soon mollified, however, and negotiations began.

Though Canada subsequently attempted to deny it, the delegates unquestionably were "recognized" by the Dominion Government. The official record contains a letter dated April 26 from Joseph Howe to Ritchot, Black and Scott:

I have to acknowledge the receipt of your letter of the 22nd instant, stating that as delegates from the North-West to the Government of the Dominion of Canada, you are desirous of having an early audience with the government, and am to inform you in reply that the Hon. Sir John A. Macdonald and Sir Georges Et. Cartier have been authorized by the Government to confer with you on the subject of your mission and will be ready to receive you at eleven o'clock.

This document is indexed in the printed parliamentary record as "Recognizing them as delegates from the North-West." In the face of this official evidence, Sir John always blandly insisted that he had never "recognized" the Provisional Government of Rupert's Land.

Not only were the delegates recognized in fact, but the bill of rights they brought with them formed the basis of the Manitoba Act under which Rupert's Land and the Northwest entered the Dominion.

Even the name of the new Province was provided by the Provisional Government, and by Riel. After the delegates reached Ottawa they received a supplemental instruction from him: they were to press for formation of a small province in the heart of Rupert's Land to be named Manitoba, rather than Assiniboia as had been specified in the bill of rights.

An Indian word, *Manitoba* had been taken from the lake near Winnipeg. Several meanings have been attributed to it. In Saulteux or Cree it could mean "a place of God" or "the God that speaks"; or it could have been derived from a Sioux word, *Minnetoba,* meaning "water-prairie," a prairie lake. The official choice, which probably was the translation given by the delegates, was "the God that speaks." Addressing Parliament on the Manitoba Act, Sir George Cartier said: "The name of the new Province will be Manitoba, a very euphonious word meaning 'the God that speaks.' Well, let Canada's latest addition always speak to the inhabitants of the North-West the language of reason, truth and justice."

The Act created a small Province (twice enlarged later) and provided that the rest of the Northwest would be administered as a Territory under the jurisdiction of Manitoba's Lieutenant Governor. Most of the major provisions of the bill of rights were incorporated in it. A mutually satisfactory draft was completed May 3 after some fifteen conferences, nine of them attended by Sir John, and the Act was passed by the House of Commons June 12 on a vote of 120 to 11.

The nineteenth clause of the bill of rights had provided that an amnesty should be guaranteed. No member of the Provisional Government or anyone acting under its orders, this clause said, would be held liable for the resistance movement or any action occurring during the period prior to assumption of sovereignty by Canada. Ritchot insisted upon this as a *sine qua non* of any agreement, but since it was irrelevant to the actual process of forming a Province it was not included in the Manitoba Act. He was assured on several occasions, however, that the amnesty would be forthcoming—in interviews with Macdonald, Cartier, and the Governor General.

On May 23 Sir George Cartier wrote to Ritchot and Scott to confirm the conclusions about an amnesty the priest had drawn from an interview with Sir John Young:

> I wish to draw your attention to the interview you have had with His Excellency, on the 19th inst., in my presence, and in which it pleases His Excellency to express that the liberal policy which the Government intend to pursue, with regard to the persons in whom you are interested, is correct, and the one that ought to be adopted.

Cartier then added: "You may use this in any way you may think proper in all explanations you may have to give concerning the object for which you have been sent as delegates towards the Government of Canada." At this time Cartier was serving as head of the Government because Sir John had been incapacitated by illness.

In Rupert's Land Bishop Taché already had been proclaiming that an amnesty was assured, on the basis of statements made to him by Sir John Macdonald and the latter's instruction to him to use his best judgment in securing a peaceful settlement.

Reassured if not fully satisfied, Ritchot and Scott prepared to return to the West; Black had gone on to London. But who, Ritchot now asked Cartier, was to administer the Government of Rupert's Land until the Lieutenant Governor arrived to establish the Province?

Cartier wondered if Riel were sufficiently powerful to maintain order. The priest said he was.

Then, Cartier said, "let him continue until the Lieutenant Governor arrives."

The twenty-five-year-old President of the "New Nation," a novice in the tricky game of statecraft, had all but forced a checkmate in his opening gambit and had gone on to play a strong middle game. If he chose now to resign he could do so with the knowledge that he had won most of what he sought for his people and grudging respect for his own abilities from as arrogant an adversary as any young challenger ever faced.

PART THREE

Crackpot Crusade

CHAPTER X

The Jolly Boys

MISSION OF PEACE

THE delegates' return to Red River in June brought forth a salute of twenty-one guns to celebrate the success of their mission, and a special session of the legislative council was called by Riel to hear Father Ritchot's report. Thereupon a motion by Louis Schmidt was unanimously adopted: the Legislative Assembly of Rupert's Land, in the name of the people, accepted the Manitoba Act and entered the Dominion of Canada on the terms proposed.

It was all over, it seemed, but the shouting; yet the skeptics and the irreconcilables were not stilled. From Montana, Langford wrote to Taylor: "It is reported that the Red River people have ratified the acceptance of Canada; but I think that similar troubles will arise with reference to other parts of that country outside of Manitoba." The words were to be proved prophetic fifteen years later.

And the Provisional Government was uneasy. The new Lieutenant Governor, Adams G. Archibald, M.P., and twelve hundred Imperial and Canadian troops were on their way

west. Hudson's Bay officials and others had cautioned Ottawa
to make sure that Archibald reached Red River before the
armed force did, or at least at the same time; but the Government, as usual, fumbled. The civil executive's departure
was unhurried and Col. Garnet J. Wolseley's Red River Expedition got a big head start.

About eight hundred members of the expedition were
Canadian volunteers, most of them from Ontario; although
Quebec was represented there were fewer than fifty French
Canadians in the whole force. And the Ontario men promised
trouble. "The greatest danger," said Donald Smith, "lies in
the temper of many of the volunteers who are keen Orangemen and who enlisted merely with a desire to avenge themselves upon the French for the murder of Scott."

The American element in the settlements and the die-
hards led by O'Donoghue demanded that Riel prepare to
resist the troops at least until Archibald arrived to establish
civil government. A few score Métis marksmen, they pointed
out, could be stationed at strategic spots in the six hundred
miles of wilderness the expedition had to traverse and if
necessary could probably destroy Wolseley's floundering
force. It is likely that a guerrilla campaign of this sort would
have succeeded, especially since Wolseley was dependent
upon Métis guides.

Riel wavered, but—strongly supported by Taché and
Ritchot—he stood by his resolution to welcome the Canadians.
He wrote an elaborate address which he hoped to read to
Archibald in token of amicable submission; and he insisted
to Smith and others, "I only wish to retain power until I can
resign it to a proper government." His position was strengthened when a proclamation mailed by Wolseley as the expedition started reached the settlement; Riel ordered it printed
and scattered broadcast. "Our mission is one of peace," the
Colonel affirmed. "The force which I have the honor of commanding will enter your Province representing no party,

either in religion or politics, and will afford equal protection
to the lives and property of all races and of all creeds."

Wolseley told the Cabinet he could move his army from
Toronto to Fort Garry via the Dawson Road and Lake of
the Woods in seventy-two days. His estimate was too sanguine:
he needed ninety-six.

Nevertheless it was a remarkable feat. Two-thirds of the
force, the Canadian volunteers, were inexperienced, unac-
customed to hardship or to military discipline. The British
regulars were better men physically, but they too were ignorant of the exigencies of wilderness travel. None of the soldiers could handle boats, none knew anything about woods or
prairie trails; Wolseley therefore had to take along—and feed
—a company of Iroquois and French-Canadian *voyageurs* and
Métis guides.

Food was the major concern. Between Lake Superior and
Red River the expedition would not find a single settlement
nor even a farm, and wild game was so scarce in the bleak
"Laurentian Shield" that the small Indian bands which ventured into the region often perished of starvation. Moreover,
the supply at Red River probably would not stand the strain
of an additional twelve hundred hungry men. Rations for
the entire force for at least three months (the estimate was
deficient here, too) had to be taken along. Though food was
about the only thing the United States would consent to
move through its canal and on its railroads, it was the one
thing besides arms which the expedition had to have on the
march.

With experienced *voyageurs* as his advisers, Wolseley
bought or built the biggest boats the rivers could accommo-
date. Seventeen of them were required for just the vanguard
of the force—three hundred and fifty men of the Sixtieth
Royal Rifles and about fifty other British regulars. Almost
before the expedition was under way this brigade came to

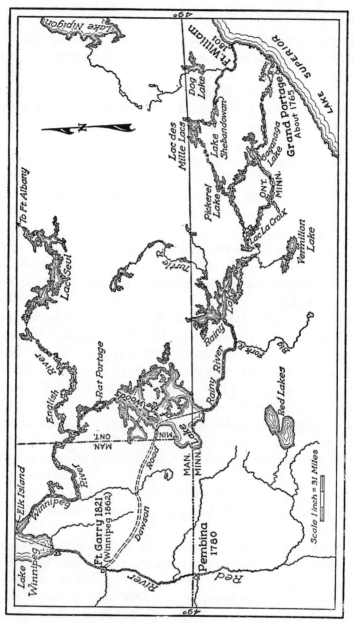

Canoe Route and Dawson Road

the first portage: uphill from Lake Superior to Lake Sheban-
dowan, forty-two miles. Fires and torrential rainstorms had
ruined the road; it took three weeks of dawn-to-dark labor
to clear the fallen timber.

The big boats were unloaded, set on rollers, and pushed;
and when the trail was too steep for that they were lifted to
shoulders and carried. The boats, and the cannon and ball,
the rifles and ammunition, the two-hundred-pound barrels
of salt pork, the sails and oars—all were carried on the backs
of men for hundreds of miles. Frequently more than one
trip was necessary to get everything across the longer portages.

Even after the boats were returned to the river it was often
necessary to "track" them upstream or through the rapids.
Part of their load was removed, towlines were tossed ashore,
and the men pulled them to quiet water, unloaded them and
sent them back for another cargo.

There were some glorious days, when a good breeze filled
the sails and the boats skimmed across the glittering lakes
and the *voyageurs* sang:

> *Trois beaux canards s'en vont baignant,*
> *Rouli, roulant, ma boule roulant,*
> *En roulant ma boule roulant,*
> *En roulant ma boule.*

But there were other days when the men sank to their
knees in the sodden black muskeg or were hauled half-
drowned from the icy rivers, and an hour later were drip-
ping with sweat under a blazing sun on a high rock "carry."
They shivered on the sunless trails deep in the woods, fought
colds and insects and dysentery, cried out at night from the
pain of knotted muscles and lamed backs. Yet they, too, could
sing. One of their favorites was "Tenting on the Old Camp
Ground," with a regional modification; their version made
it "cold damp ground." Then there was "Jolly Boys":

Come, boys, cheer up! We'll have a song in spite of our position
To help us in our labors on this glorious Expedition!
We'll keep our spirits up, my boys; and don't look sad or sober
Nor grumble at our hardships on our way to Manitoba!

   Jolly boys, jolly boys,
   Hurrah for the boats and the roads, jolly boys!

Some grumble, loudly exclaiming, " 'Tis not as I expected;
I did not know that great stockade would have to be erected;
It was only as a volunteer that I left my abode—
I never thought of coming here to work upon the road!

   .   .   .   .

We have talked about our going home, but now it don't appear
That we shall see our homes again in quite another year;
For if the girls of Manitoba are as kind as they are charming,
The half of us will stay behind, and settle down to farming!

On August 8 near Rat Portage the expedition met four
big boats filled with Métis from Red River who had come
to help guide the troops and clear the road to Winnipeg. The
next day the first brigade entered the Winnipeg River, last
stage of the long trek and with most of the forty-seven portages behind them.

Riel had sent the Métis boatmen and other half-breeds
were busy at the Winnipeg end of the Dawson Road—hired
by Canada, with his approval, to clear the tangled trail. They
had a secret assignment: to test the temper of the troops and
their commander and report back to Fort Garry.

Their reports were not encouraging. Wolseley was attempting to make a prisoner of everyone, friend or potential foe,
who approached his lines. The Métis could usually dodge his
sentries, but the atmosphere in the camps was ominous and
incompatible with the advertised aims of the expedition. The
soldiers, bored by the monotony of the trek and irked by
hardships, were spoiling for excitement: around the camp-

fires the Métis heard talk of bloody retribution to be visited upon the "rebels" who had started all this.

The united first brigade passed from the Winnipeg River into Lake Winnipeg and camped on Elk Island. A hundred campfires threw their light across the black water and bugle calls echoed in the woods. Fascinated Indians, as still as the wildlife which shared their shelter, watched the camp all night.

Next morning a fair wind filled the sails and the little armada, scattering over the southern end of the great lake, raced for the mouth of Red River like homing birds. Now the portages were over and the days were bonny and the job was all but done; they hoped there'd be a skirmish or two, then a carouse with the girls when the silly "war" was won.

But now, suddenly, the nights became hell. Gales drove rain in torrents through the camp, blew down the tents and left the men shelterless in ankle-deep mud. The last bivouac, on August 23, was the worst of all: the wind roared all night while solid sheets of water slapped at the helpless men huddled on their flattened tents. They were six miles from Fort Garry.

Reveille sounded at three but the rain was so troublesome that it took four hours to get the detachment ready and even then the men went without breakfast; it was impossible to start a fire. The boats took them to within two miles of Fort Garry, then everything had to be unloaded and packed into carts for the march across the prairie; and still it rained.

A grim gray ceiling of cloud rested on the roofs of Winnipeg's one-story cabins and below it a cold mist draped the waterlogged plain. The men stumbled ahead through mud now halfway to their knees; it sucked at their boots at every step or suddenly gave way and flung them on their faces in the water. Stops were required every few minutes to scrape the mud from the high wheels of the carts and to clean the carriages of the two brass cannon which became hopelessly mired every few yards.

A few English settlers along the banks of the river north of the village had come out to greet them, but here no one ventured into the downpour. The weary men looked from side to side, bewildered; they had expected flags and cheering crowds. They had spent ninety-six days on one of the most grueling military movements in history without the loss of a man; they had arrived to liberate these people from a blood-thirsty gang of rebels; where, then, was the welcome?

Redvers Buller, a member of Wolseley's staff and later a British Boer War general, wryly made a note for posterity. "We were enthusiastically greeted," he reported, "by a half-naked Indian, very drunk."

THE WAY THE WORLD ENDS

The Provisional Government of Rupert's Land and the New Nation of the Métis died the night of August 23 in angry bickering.

O'Donoghue, an Irish ally named H. F. O'Lone, and Delegate Alfred H. Scott had demanded that Riel send envoys to meet Wolseley at Lake Winnipeg, ask him if he had brought the promised amnesty, and if he had not, to warn him not to proceed to Fort Garry. Argument over this proposal raged in the council for six days. Riel countered with a suggestion that all available Métis troops (unfortunately he had released most of his one thousand potential soldiers and many of them were now far from Red River) be drawn up on the south shore of the Assiniboine to greet the Wolseley force with bonfires and salutes, and that a hundred picked cavalrymen be selected to meet the British at Fort Garry. But other members of the council vetoed this scheme.

On August 23 Riel saw Taché, just back from a hurried trip to Ottawa to see what had happened to the promised amnesty. The bishop said he had "all possible assurances, though none in writing." Louis was worried but polite. "What comforts us," he told the prelate, "is that you have done your utmost." He summoned the council; it was their duty, he insisted, to remain in Fort Garry until Wolseley occupied it.

They made up two scouting parties, one led by Riel and one by O'Donoghue, and rode near the British camp but learned nothing; at one o'clock on the morning of August 24 they returned to the fort. There was more futile argument, until the exhausted Riel retired for about forty-five minutes of sleep. When he awoke dawn was breaking and Wolseley's men were loading their stores for the last day's march.

At eight o'clock Riel breakfasted on cold meat. He received a visitor, started to tell him what he intended to do, broke off when he realized the man was paying no attention. Besides, he did not know what he intended to do. He had lost all initiative and there was no one to advise him sensibly; O'Donoghue, intelligent though most radical of his counselors, was unfriendly now, and Bishop Taché, who could have helped him most, rested in his dignity in the episcopal palace.

As the morning wore on reports drifted in from the troops' line of march. A Canadian whom Riel mistakenly assumed was a member of the expedition arrived with a friendly warning to the Métis leaders to flee for their lives. Others came with rumors: the murderers in Fort Garry were going to pay for all the discomfort, all the sickness and backache, the torn muscles and the bruises and the sore feet and the rain. . . . Members of the old Métis council began to lose courage and drift away; they wanted, they explained, to make sure everyone was safe at home.

Riel went down to the courtyard and dismissed the guards. He and O'Donoghue were alone in Fort Garry. The flags had been taken down because of the rain. That of the Provisional Government of Rupert's Land would never fly again and some member of the council had taken it away for safe-keeping.

Louis and the Fenian stood in a window and looked north across the drenched prairie. They talked a little; Louis even smiled as he recalled the offer which had come from an Indian chief at Rainy Lake. If Louis approved, the chief's messenger said, the tribe would destroy Wolseley's army in the Winnipeg River by releasing logs into the stream while the British boats were laboring in the rapids. It might have worked, but Riel had forbidden it. (Wolseley had feared some such maneuver. "I could not fail," he admitted, "to be impressed with the great embarrassments which a hostile feeling on the part of the Indians could have thrown in the way of the passage of our troops.")

Figures were emerging from the mist: B Company, the skirmish line—riflemen. They floundered in the mud, broke ranks, fell; the watchers could almost see them curse. The guns, only two, were far behind, the supply carts farther still. Four hundred men were exposed on an open prairie without so much as a tree for shelter, and because of the mud they could not even run.

Fort Garry had thirteen cannon, many rifles. The watchers, silent now, thought about what five hundred Métis sharpshooters on the walls could do to the exhausted Sixtieth Royal Rifles, lurching forward a few feet at a time through the glucy gumbo of Red River. They thought of lost chances: the ambushes on the wilderness road, the logs in the rapids, and four hundred men on an open plain in the rain.

But there were no sharpshooters. There were only two men in a window streaked with rain and dirt, men still in their twenties but aged in bitterness. They were Irishman and Métis, men of the oppressed minorities; they stood side by side but like many of their kind they now disliked even each other. Out of the mist the British, the superior race, were coming.

B Company was half a mile away now. Riel turned from the window, nodded to his companion. They began to gather up their gear. They walked down to the courtyard.

There was a bustle and clatter at the back gate. Someone tried it, but it was locked. B Company formed in ranks again to march around to the front. A bugle sounded.

It was time. Riel and O'Donoghue walked out of the front gate just before the first of the troops came around the corner of the wall. Louis had time for one backward glance at Government House, at the two flagpoles; the Fenian had been right, he could acknowledge now, to insist upon keeping their own banner flying. But it rained; no flags flew, no riflemen fired uneven salutes, the ardent band of St. Boniface College had put away its horns and was busy at its Latin.

The two men, carrying packs, walked unchallenged to the Assiniboine River and crossed on a raft they fashioned of fence posts lashed with their woven sashes. There was a ferry nearby; to prevent immediate pursuit Riel took a knife from his pocket and cut the cable. As he did so a salute of twenty-one guns boomed from Fort Garry and the Sixtieth Royal Rifles, at attention in the courtyard, gave three cheers for the Queen.

Riel, O'Donoghue and Ambroise Lépine had decided to go to Pembina until it could be determined whether they would be safe in Manitoba. Horses were the first need, and Riel wanted to see his mother in St. Vital. As the two men walked there a friendly but impoverished Métis farmer stopped them and offered them some food for the journey. He could spare very little but they accepted it gratefully, bade him good-by, and walked on.

As they opened the thin parcel of food another Métis came alongside and greeted Riel respectfully as "M'sieu le président." Perhaps Louis thought of the address he had prepared to read to Governor Archibald, of the ceremony he had planned so the Métis could relinquish their power with the dignity befitting a people who had created a new nation; perhaps he thought how a world can end with a whimper. There was savage bitterness in his voice when he responded to the greeting.

"Tell the people," he said, "that he who ruled in Fort Garry only yesterday is now a homeless wanderer with nothing to eat but two dried fish."

THE PRESIDENT IS UNCONVINCED

Colonel Wolseley paid off his troops and issued a proclamation praising their fortitude. In it, in direct violation of his orders, he denounced the Métis, whom the Dominion had authorized to govern the country until Archibald's arrival; his noble force, he said, had routed the "banditti."

The troops went wild. They began to loot Fort Garry and were stopped only when they could be convinced that its stores belonged to the Hudson's Bay Company and not to the erstwhile "rebel" Government. Then they descended upon the town of Winnipeg. Métis fled across the river to the French settlements, barricaded their houses and rarely ventured out except in groups. Members of the American faction hurriedly packed up and scuttled for Pembina.

Winnipeg's stock of whiskey lasted for three days. Soldiers brawled with Indians and half-breeds in the saloons, fought with knives in the streets and were dragged bleeding from gutter to guardhouse. The liquor was soon replenished by new shipments from the United States but in the interim the thirsty newcomers discovered the Ragged Edge and Robbers' Roost in Pembina. For months thereafter the Dakota town was the scene of pitched battles between Canadians and the Métis or their American sympathizers.

Archibald did not arrive until September 2 and consequently the settlements were without government for about ten days. Wolseley, remembering tardily that his was a mission of peace, was afraid to declare martial law. He forced

a reluctant Donald Smith to assume some civil functions and
to appoint what purported to be a police force, but the citizens selected for this hazardous service wisely decided to stay
out of sight.

The Ontario volunteers started to come in on August 27.
Some of them had been members of the Schultz faction imprisoned at one time or another by Riel; they had escaped or
been released and had fled to Canada; they were now determined to get revenge. But the British regulars had fulfilled
their mission, merely by making the trip. A few days after
their arrival, when they had recovered from their hangovers,
they started back east under Wolseley's command. The eight
hundred Canadians remained for a few months, then they too
were recalled, leaving Archibald a military garrison of fewer
than one hundred men.

Archibald was a barrister with some administrative experience and, in sharp contrast with McDougall, he was a
prudent, eminently fair and honorable executive. He went
to work swiftly at establishing responsible government and
in public statements and private conferences attempted to reassure the Métis. But he got little help from Schultz and his
partisans, who were soon back in Winnipeg and busy in the
Orange lodge which the first arrivals among the Ontario volunteers had established.

The first victim was Elzéar Goulet, a member of the court-
martial which sentenced Scott. Recognized in Winnipeg by
a man who had been a Métis prisoner, he was chased by this
civilian and two of the Ontario soldiers to the river. Goulet's
only hope was to swim to the French side, so he leaped into
the water. His pursuers stoned him until he sank and
drowned.

François Guilmette, who had administered the coup de
grâce to Scott, fled to the United States stalked by vengeful
Canadians. Within a week he was overtaken near Pembina

and murdered. H. F. O'Lone, O'Donoghue's friend, was also killed. Father Kavanaugh, a mission priest, was wounded by a trigger-happy rioter and another citizen was killed when rioters deliberately frightened his horse. André Nault, who had given the signal to the Scott firing squad, was pursued to Pembina, bayoneted and left for dead on the prairie; but he recovered and reached safety with other Métis leaders.

Disorders in the first few weeks of Canadian administration claimed many times more casualties than had occurred in ten months of Métis rule, and the trouble continued for months. Reporting to Sir John A. Macdonald a year later, Archibald told how his task had been complicated by "persistent ill-usage" of the Métis by Canadians. "Many of them," he wrote, "actually have been so beaten and outraged that they feel as if they were living in a state of slavery. They say that the bitter hatred of these people [Canadians] is a yoke so intolerable that they would gladly escape it by any sacrifice."

The Governor's problems grew as Ontario volunteers who elected to remain in the West were released from military service. These men were no longer subject to military discipline and many of them were anxious to finance their start in the new country with the $5,000 their Province had posted as reward for apprehension of the killers of Scott. They staged periodic armed raids upon Métis homes in search of members of the court-martial or firing squad. Ten of them burst into the Riel house, threatened Louis's mother and sister, and ransacked the little cottage; but they were unable to find a clue to the whereabouts of their quarry or to get it by terrorizing the women. In other instances unguarded Métis women and young girls were victims of more serious outrages.

A group of Canadians occupied a farming area previously staked out by Métis, armed themselves and defied the original claimants to recapture their property; then they named the

section the Boyne, for the battle in Ireland in 1690 by which
Protestantism conquered Britain, an event annually celebrated by Orangemen. Only the intervention of Bishop
Taché prevented a bloody battle, and the Métis never regained their land.

Dispatches from Pembina to the St. Paul newspapers reported "intense excitement" among the Métis who were said
to be gathering on American soil and arming themselves for
another showdown. Schultz and his faction, the St. Paul *Press*
said, "are carrying on with a high hand"; among other things
they had horsewhipped Thomas Spence, who had succeeded
to editorship of *The New Nation*.

Working in a corrosive fog of racial and religious hatred,
greed and hooliganism, Archibald battled for control. He got
no help from Ottawa; instead, when he acted swiftly to save
the Province from a smallpox epidemic he was rebuked for
exceeding his authority by cutting through governmental red
tape. But he made progress. Winnipeg and the French settlements were declared "out of bounds" for the troops. He
launched inquiries into the murder of Goulet; although these
did not result in prosecution they did deter other potential
assassins. He organized a well-armed mounted police detachment. And he resisted the demands of the Orangemen that he
order the arrest of Riel and others for the murder of Scott.
The Province of Manitoba, he explained patiently, had no
jurisdiction over an incident which occurred before Manitoba
existed.

Such legalistic considerations did not, however, discourage
the seekers of rewards. A justice of the peace from a distant
community was persuaded while visiting in Winnipeg to sign
a warrant; the complaining witness, perhaps significantly, was
a saloonkeeper. The warrant directed Captain Frank Villiers,
chief of the Provincial mounted police, to arrest Riel for
murder and if he resisted to bring in his corpse. Villiers took
the document to Archibald, who told him to ignore it.

Riel meanwhile was in St. Joseph, Dakota Territory, thirty miles west of Pembina. There he was joined by his mother for a time after the raid on her St. Vital home. St. Joseph, at the foot of a hill somewhat pretentiously named Pembina Mountain, had been established as a community when a priest erected a church there in 1851 and was a popular refuge from the floods which frequently inundated Pembina; but it had a longer history as an occasional trading center and rendezvous for prairie hunters: the North West Company had placed a post there in 1801.

O'Donoghue was in Pembina. The breach between the two leaders had widened to the point that they chose not to remain in the same town, and now the Fenian, scornful of his chief's melancholy and indecision, intrigued for command of the dissident Métis. Since Lépine was with him in Pembina and made frequent furtive trips north the Irishman had a temporary advantage; moreover O'Donoghue had "called the turn" on the conduct of the Canadian expedition and Riel's faith in a peaceful and dignified transition to Provincial status had been betrayed. Momentarily, therefore—at least when Riel was not on the scene—O'Donoghue's popularity equaled that of his young chief.

It was probably O'Donoghue and Lépine, rather than Riel, who sponsored the assembly of Métis leaders at St. Norbert— where the original resistance movement was born—on September 17, 1870, though Riel, as usual, presided. About forty attended, and they heard Louis and the Fenian engage in an argument so bitter that they almost came to blows. O'Donoghue, listing Métis grievances since arrival of the troops, demanded that the group invite the United States to annex Rupert's Land; Riel denounced the resolution and finally beat it down. It was the most serious challenge his leadership had ever faced.

Instead of acquiescing in American annexation the assembly roughed out the first draft of a petition to the President of the United States asking him to intervene with the Queen for an investigation of their grievances and reparation by Canada for the Dominion's "violated pledges." A committee (probably Riel, O'Donoghue and Lépine) was named to put this in final form; and the Fenian, probably over Riel's protest, was chosen to carry it to Washington and present it in person.

The "Memorial and Petition of the People of Rupert's Land" was a lengthy document which recited in detail the history of the resistance and described the negotiations by which Canadian sovereignty had been accepted. The United States was shrewdly brought into the controversy: Canada, it was alleged, had falsely represented to Washington that Wolseley's mission was peaceful, else the passage of his troops along the Dawson Road (much of it virtually on the American boundary) and movement of some nonmilitary supplies through American territory would not have been permitted.

The final draft of the petition was completed in a few days but Riel was still unwilling to release it, pleading that Archibald soon would establish order in Manitoba and that he had Taché's assurance that Canada would make good on its promises, especially the amnesty. This recalcitrance infuriated O'Donoghue and precipitated the final angry quarrel. Louis's rage was such that he cursed his former colleague and their relationship was never resumed; the two men, in fact, may never have seen each other after this clash. The Fenian, Louis told him, had been of no use at any time to the Métis movement "except for your God damned tongue."

O'Donoghue now went to work in earnest on his own conspiratorial designs, with the eager aid of Stutsman and other Americans in Pembina. Those among the Métis whom he still could influence were persuaded, without Riel's knowledge, to reaffirm the authorization for his trip to Washington;

then he and his fellow plotters "amended" the Métis petition. A few words were deleted and one long paragraph was added, and a document which had asked only for America's good offices to persuade the Dominion to adjust grievances now asked the President to help the Métis obtain "life, liberty, property and the pursuit of happiness under a government of our own choice, or in union with a people with whom we may think that we can enjoy these blessings."

The new junto acted swiftly; by mid-October O'Donoghue was in St. Paul giving interviews to the press and receiving a warm welcome. In December the annexation bloc in Washington was arranging conferences for him with important people, and the next month he saw President Grant and read him the petition. But Grant, though cordial, was unconvinced that the document represented the hopes of a majority of the people of Red River. He had, unknown to O'Donoghue, good grounds for his skepticism. Washington had received the whole history of the petition from the invaluable James Wickes Taylor; and Taylor, despite his own annexationist sentiments, had reported honestly that Riel could not be persuaded to abandon the Queen, and Riel was still "chief of the Métis."

Taylor, his secret assignment for the State Department capably concluded, had been appointed United States consul in Winnipeg in September, 1870. He was still in touch with the annexationists and still hopeful, but he would never encourage American intervention unless he could be certain that a majority of the people wanted it. Meanwhile he watched with admiration and helped all he could as Archibald slowly bound together the unruly elements of a new society. Manitoba's first election, the Governor announced, would take place in December. Captain Villiers and his mounted police would guard the polls.

Stutsman dashed off a note in Pembina and sent it north to Taylor. The election, he thought, would be rough. (It

was; the Métis and the police got the worst of it.) A bit of
advice:

... If, on Nomination Day, should Canuck, English and
Half-Breed blood flow to the saddle-skirt, I trust you will have
the prudence to seek protection beneath the ample folds of the
American flag.

But be very careful that Schultz and his "loyal" band do not
get down on you—for they are the Danites of Manitoba, the
veritable "Destroying Angels" in whose hands rests the question
of life or death.

CHAPTER XI

The Wardens of the Plains

FOUR HUNDRED SPRINGFIELDS

As Riel's resolution had flagged, William B. O'Donoghue's had strengthened. In 1871 he was twenty-eight years old and had had a taste of power as treasurer of the Provisional Government, as leader of the Irish-American annexationist coalition, and as self-appointed agent of the dread Fenians. It would take more than the skepticism of the President of the United States to convince him that Manitoba could not be wrested from the Queen and a painful blow administered incidentally to Ireland's oppressors.

O'Donoghue was born in 1843 in County Sligo. Before he was ten years old a million of his compatriots had perished by famine, and a desperate insurrection, with weapons fashioned on village forges, had dragged to its inevitable end. Thomas Francis Meagher, the silver-tongued rebel whom the tides of destiny were to carry to the Governorship of Montana Territory, was an exile in Van Dieman's Land; and the *caoiner,* the wind of mourning, sobbed ceaselessly over Ireland.

216

The lad escaped as soon as he could to the New World. In New York he completed his education and joined the Fenian Order, dedicating his life to the interminable struggle for Ireland's freedom. Then he headed west. At Port Huron, Michigan, in 1868 he met Bishop Grandin, who was en route to Red River, and offered his services in the Western missions. The bishop and his companion, Father Giroux, were favorably impressed; O'Donoghue, the priest concluded, was "a gentleman in the strict meaning of the word." They took him along, got him a job as professor of mathematics at the College of St. Boniface, and left him there. Soon he decided to study for the priesthood, but he abandoned this venture when he joined Riel at the start of the Métis resistance in 1869.

By any standard save that of the Canadians, who hated him even more than they did Riel, he was an unusually handsome man. He was tall and slim and, in contrast to most of the slouching Métis, erect of carriage. His thin face was sharply modeled, the cheeks somewhat hollow, and he had a brooding look; enemies regarded his aspect as "satanic" but friends could claim with equal accuracy that he resembled a disciple in an old religious painting. Though he was an excellent speaker he lacked the emotional power of Riel; on the other hand he was less subject to fits of despondency, less timid about bloodshed and less easily influenced by the priests. The priests had disowned him anyway after they learned of his Fenian affiliation, which was frowned on by the Church.

In April, 1871, O'Donoghue was in New York putting his case to the Council of the Fenian Brotherhood. The president, he claimed, really had been encouraging: if the people of Rupert's Land re-established an independent regime the United States would carefully consider the arguments for peaceful annexation. There had been a temporary setback, O'Donoghue acknowledged—because Riel had submitted; but now with Fenian guns and manpower a new "uprising" could succeed.

But the Fenian Council had wearied of Canadian adventures, which had been uniformly unsuccessful since they were started in 1866. Only the president of the Order, Gen. John O'Neill, supported the Westerner's appeal. And O'Neill was just out of prison, where he had spent six months for violating American neutrality in the 1870 raid from St. Albans, Vermont. That had been a terrible fiasco, even for Fenians, and O'Neill was not in very good standing at headquarters. So the council told O'Donoghue that all the help he could expect from the Irish Republican Army was its prayers.

This time he almost lost heart. He returned to the West. But in a month or two he was back in New York; Canadian outrages in Rupert's Land were continuing and he was convinced that invasion from Pembina would be popular with the Métis. All but a handful of the Canadian troops had gone home; if a sizable force crossed the border and was joined by dissident Métis en route north, the Winnipeg garrison of fewer than a hundred men counting police could offer no resistance. And there were two thousand men in Minnesota who were being laid off from railroad construction jobs; they would be ready for any interesting and profitable undertaking.

For the second time he appeared before the Fenian Council and begged for endorsement and military support. O'Neill again spoke for him, and offered his own services as leader of the Manitoba Fenian Expedition. But the council, through several stormy meetings, was immovable—and finally, in a towering rage, O'Neill resigned. He and whoever cared to join him would lead the movement independently; all he asked of the Fenian Order was that it refrain from denouncing the venture publicly. This the council agreed to do. Gen. J. J. Donnelly, who had been O'Neill's chief of staff, and

Colonel Curley, who also had served with him, quickly joined his cause.

The conspirators hurried west and attempted to find money and recruits. They already had arms—four hundred modern breech-loading Springfield rifles obtained by O'Neill from Maj. Henri LeCaron, a member of his staff who had secreted them after the collapse of the Vermont effort. (LeCaron, whose name actually was Thomas Beach, had been a Civil War companion-in-arms of O'Neill and was a trusted member of the Fenian inner circle for years; but he was a British spy who had kept Ottawa and London informed of every move of the Irish Republican Army in which he held a commission.)

The leaders stumped the cities of Minnesota and the grimy frontier villages of Dakota with fiery speeches and collection plates. But little money was forthcoming, nor were volunteers so eager to flock to the Fenians' green banner as O'Donoghue had promised. His colleagues taxed him particularly with the inexplicable failure of the Métis to rally to their cause, but he insisted they would sign up as soon as the "expeditionary force" crossed the frontier. Nevertheless, O'Donoghue was worried. It was September now, and only a few weeks remained for outdoor enterprises. Moreover, the inescapable publicity attending their campaign for men and subsidies had given Manitoba ample warning of what was in store for it. Word reached the Fenians that Archibald had anxiously wired Ottawa for return of some of the troops.

O'Donoghue did not know that his absence in the East had enabled Riel to regain full control over the Métis. On September 28 the leaders—Lépine, Lajimodière, Nault and others—met secretly at Louis's home in St. Vital to discuss their erstwhile colleague's grandiose scheme of conquest and to discover if they could, from informants brought from Pembina, just how many men he could command. In this latter inquiry the session was unsuccessful; there were too many rumors. But at the instance of Riel the Metis resolved "not to be prevailed upon by O'Donoghue whether he be strong or weak."

A few days before Riel had reassured Bishop Taché: "Be sure that there is not the least danger that I or any of my friends join with the Fenians. We detest the Fenians, for they are condemned by the Church, and we shall have nothing to do with them."

For a fortnight Archibald had been working with the French clergy to ascertain the mood of the Métis. If they chose to join O'Donoghue and the American rabble he was expected to recruit, the Governor acknowledged frankly, Manitoba would be lost to the Dominion.

Father Ritchot agreed. But, he pointed out, the amnesty had not come. Riel and his colleagues could hardly be expected to pledge loyalty to a Government which, if they ventured within its jurisdiction, might choose to hang them.

The Governor could see the justice of the complaint. Let the Métis come forward; he would guarantee the immunity of their leaders from prosecution for any past act while they were defending Manitoba from invasion; in the priest's language, *pour la circonstance actuelle*. He would even put that in writing. And he did.

On October 4, as Riel arrived at the home of Ambroise Lépine for another meeting of the old council, a messenger came from O'Donoghue. Would the leaders, including Riel, meet him immediately at Pointe à Michel, near Pembina? They would not; but Nault and Baptiste Lépine returned with the messenger in another effort to learn the Fenian's marching strength. André warned Louis that their people were getting excited and hard to control.

While they awaited the return of the two scouts with a

report—the mission would take at least two days—the Métis, like everyone else on Red River, discussed the rumors. Pembina heard that an army of two thousand had been recruited and was assembling in St. Joseph. As St. Joseph got it, the force was being mustered in at Pembina. By the time the story reached Winnipeg the army had grown to thirty-five hundred, but it had been organized in St. Paul.

James Wickes Taylor, American annexationist but no party to filibustering, had called upon Governor Archibald to inquire officially but discreetly what objection the latter would raise to the passage of American troops across Manitoba's frontier to quell a disturbance caused by American citizens. No objection at all, the Governor had responded; in fact he'd be delighted. Mr. Taylor said thank you, he had thought that was the way the Governor would feel about it, and withdrew.

When Manitoba actually was invaded, on the morning of October 5, the attacking force consisted of W. B. O'Donoghue, formerly of the Riel cabinet; Officers O'Neill, Donnelly and Curley of the Irish Republican Army, retired; and thirty-five men. The intrepid adventurers "captured" the undefended Hudson's Bay Company post just north of the line, where McDougall had read his forged proclamation to the wind nearly two years before. A few hours later the leaders and some of the followers were in jail in Pembina, where they had been escorted by Colonel Lloyd Wheaton and a bored company of United States infantry from the recently established garrison in that town.

O'Donoghue alone among the leaders escaped, but not for long. He was captured on the Canadian side of the line by a party of Métis, brought back to Pembina, and solemnly delivered to the United States Army.

FENIANS' FINISH

Fenians led the 1871 Manitoba Raid, but the order had officially washed its hands of the whole affair. Therefore the order was justifiably resentful when people—including historians who should have known better—insisted upon regarding this maddest of military ventures as one more item to be added to the long list of Fenian follies.

But the annoyance of the Fenians was nothing compared to that of the Province of Ontario when it discovered that the invasion scare had induced Manitoba's Governor to solicit, and receive, the help of "the murderers of Thomas Scott."

O'Donoghue's capture on October 5 by Manitoba Métis whom he had claimed as friends destroyed any hope the filibusters might have had of renewing their campaign. But Manitoba did not know that, and it heard that the absurd Pembina raid was a feint; the real one would come from St. Joseph.

On October 3 Governor Archibald, by proclamation, had requested the mobilization of all able-bodied citizens and had ordered out three militia companies, about two hundred men, to patrol the boundary. Before they reached their destination Colonel Wheaton and his American troops had jailed the raiders. Word of this did not reach Winnipeg until October 7, a day and a half after the event.

Meanwhile the Métis had met several times and reaffirmed their loyalty to the Canadian Government. At eleven on the morning of October 5, at the very hour Wheaton was rounding up the invaders in Pembina, Riel's council voted to organize an armed force to oppose the Fenians, and in another meeting the next day it decided to send couriers to outlying Métis settlements to order mobilization. A letter signed by Riel, Lépine and Parenteau went to Archibald. "As several trustworthy citizens have been requested to inform you," it said, "the answer of the Métis has been that of faithful subjects. Several companies have already been organized, and others are in process of formation. Your Excellency may rest assured that without being enthusiastic we have been devoted. So long as our services continue to be required, you may rely on us."

Archibald acknowledged the message with thanks, and on Sunday, October 8, he crossed the river to "review" the Métis force—more than two hundred well-armed "wardens of the plains," a name given them decades before by the Hudson's Bay Company when it organized patrols to apprehend smugglers and other offenders.

As the Governor rode up to their lines the Métis fired their customary salute and greeted him with cheers. He dismounted and was introduced to the leaders by a French-Canadian aide. "This man," the aide said, indicating Riel, "has been chosen by the Métis as their chief for this occasion." He did not speak Riel's name, but his identity was known to Archibald. Lépine and Parenteau, however, were introduced by name. The Governor shook hands with all three, thanked them for their loyal response to his appeal, and requested that some cavalrymen be sent at once to the boundary near St. Joseph; fifty were dispatched the next morning.

Word that Archibald had actually grasped the "bloody hands" of Riel and Lépine was not long in reaching Ontario and press and politicians heaped abuse upon him. The Métis had known, the Canadians sneered, that the Fenian danger was past before they volunteered; they had outsmarted Archibald and he had disgraced his office.

But the Métis had known nothing of the sort, and neither had the conscientious, worried Governor. At three-thirty A.M. on the day Archibald crossed the river to see the troops Riel had assembled, his militia commander, Maj. A. G. Irvine, penned a frantic dispatch in his tent near the border:

"There is no doubt the Fenians intend making a raid between this and tomorrow night. . . . I shall require reinforcement *at once; 150 men.*" Irvine sent along copies of notes from the Hudson's Bay Company agent and the Canadian collector of customs at the Company post three miles north of Pembina; both anticipated attack. The collector had learned from "the baker's boy" that "several hundred Fenians" in the Dakota town were awaiting the signal. "Hurry! Hurry!" the collector begged. "An attempt will be made on Fort Garry, and especially if successful here!"

In such a "war" it is not astonishing that military intelligence should have evolved from the gossip of a baker's boy, still less astonishing that the boy was wrong. There really were scores, and perhaps hundreds, of footloose adventurers in Pembina and nearby, waiting for something to turn up; but they were not Fenians and they had not been persuaded to participate in O'Donoghue's crackpot crusade. After noon on October 5, when Wheaton led the Irishmen back across the line to jail, Manitoba was safe.

The proof of Métis loyalty had not come tardily, as Ontario said, when Riel's cavalry formally reported for duty on October 8. It had come on the 4th and 5th, when the leaders had determined to stand by Canada and had sent mobilization orders to the outlying camps. Governor Archibald knew this and was grateful. "If among these people," he said, "there were—and I believe there were—some whose exceptional position might have led O'Donoghue to look for their support, it only adds to the value of the demonstration." What's more, he added, "if the half-breeds had taken a different course, I do not believe the Province would now be in our possession."

On October 13, about a week after the danger was over, Ottawa woke up and started two hundred Dominion troops again on the weary road to the West. This time the trip

took only about a month; but by the time the soldiers arrived
the Fenians had been almost forgotten.

O'Donoghue remained in custody only a few hours. On the
ground that the Americans had no actual evidence that he
had committed a crime (he had escaped before the troops
reached the Hudson's Bay post) and that he had been captured on Canadian soil, the civil court in Pembina turned
him loose. The following Monday, October 9, his colleagues
were freed on a similar convenient excuse: whatever they had
done had occurred outside United States jurisdiction. As
usual, American judges were unwilling to punish American
citizens for the innocent pastime of armed invasion of neighboring countries.

As Fenians the bunglers were through, and none of them
even attempted to regain a place in the councils of the Irish
Republic. The order was disintegrating anyway; by 1877,
when its American founder, John O'Mahony, died, it had
virtually ceased to function. But O'Neill had been its president and its commander-in-chief. He had lived for Fenian-
ism, and for fourteen years he had lived for war. He was an
Indian fighter in 1857, then a Civil War regimental commander, then a Fenian general. He had seen tough combat
and had been a capable officer; yet unaccountably he had
chosen to lead a comic opera "invasion" which made him
a laughingstock. His command had dwindled from two thousand well-trained Fenian troops, mostly Civil War veterans,
at Fort Erie in 1866 to thirty-five nondescript "border
banditti" at Pembina five years later.

O'Neill left Pembina and drifted sadly about the Middle
West. He visited LeCaron—still unaware that his former aide
was a traitor—and his ungracious host noted in a memoir
that he was a nuisance. Drink provided some surcease from
memories of lost causes; the brokenhearted man, LeCaron
wrote, "made my life a burthen." He was losing his proud

military bearing; the once distinctive features were eroded
and the sonorous voice was becoming husky; but the "great
egotism" which had always annoyed the boastful informer
LeCaron was still pitifully in evidence.

He got a job as agent for a land development company,
and LeCaron, who had clung to his coattails until he had
wormed his way into the Fenians' confidence, breathed a
sigh of relief and bade him good-by. For a few years O'Neill
was an important man again, bringing Irish settlers to Holt
County, Nebraska; it didn't pay as well as he had hoped, but
they did name the county seat after him, and he settled down
there with his wife and their three children. According to
LeCaron, Mrs. O'Neill had been a Sister of Mercy who had
nursed the handsome Irish officer when he was wounded in
the Civil War, had fallen in love with him and renounced
her vows to marry him in 1864. Another biographer, a
Catholic nun, said only that he had met his bride-to-be in
1859 when she was a student in a Sisters of Charity boarding
school in San Francisco and had married her five years later
in his home town, Elizabeth, New Jersey.

In 1878 he had a stroke. Mrs. O'Neill accompanied him
to the hospital in Omaha, but she had to hurry home to the
children and they were too poor to permit her to make frequent trips to see him. She was not able to get back in time
to be at his bedside when, three months later, he died.

General Donnelly had been an attorney with a lucrative
practice in Utica, New York, which he abandoned to become
a recruiting agent and Fenian agitator in Massachusetts and
Rhode Island prior to the Vermont campaign of 1870. He
left Pembina soon after his release from jail and set his course
for the West. His last stop was in Fort Benton, Montana;
there the destinies of this last of the Fenians, of the Métis,
and of Louis Riel were to be tragically joined once more, a
dozen years after the Pembina raid.

REQUIEM IN ROSEMOUNT

Jim Callan, an Irish farmer, found W. B. O'Donoghue on a country road in Minnesota, a few miles south of St. Paul, as the disconsolate ex-Treasurer of Rupert's Land walked from town to town hunting a job. Callan took him home and O'Donoghue promptly fell in love with his host's daughter, Mary.

The slim, handsome stranger might be down on his luck, but he was a distinguished figure in rural Dakota County. Mary had read about him in the St. Paul papers, and she learned much more as she sat with her father in the evenings and listened to his exciting stories of resistance and raid. He gave her his prayer book, the only thing he owned now except the clothes on his back; and she fondly cleaned and pressed his old military coat with the braid on the collar.

Callan soon got the interesting newcomer a job as a teacher in a country school in District 13. But Minnesota farm boys of this era were roughnecks, unimpressed by the scholarship and gentlemanly manner to which Mary had so swiftly succumbed; on his first day he had to fight the whole class. The stove was upset and a window was broken but the teacher won, and after that he had the respectful attention and even the affection of his pupils. He played shinny with the boys at recess; one day a carelessly handled stick smashed his collarbone but he finished the day's work.

For a time he boarded with the Niemeyers. Their seven-year-old son never forgot him because, in a household where bedtime pressed hard upon supper, the strange schoolmaster sat up half the night, writing interminably with a quill pen. Some said he was writing long letters to friends in Canada, others thought he was plotting another raid and the scribblings were marching orders for a great army of Fenians. But such nights did not help his health. His chest hurt a good deal lately, he had colds of which he could not rid himself, and the broken collarbone seemed never to have mended properly.

In 1877 the popular teacher, now well established in the village of Rosemount, ran for county superintendent of schools. He didn't win—his political experience in America was too limited for that—but he made new friends; and though his income was meager, his job was secure. Soon he and Mary could wed and settle down here in Rosemount, perhaps after this severe winter was over and they both felt better—for Mary, too, was "poorly."

Early in March O'Donoghue's friends became alarmed about his condition and took him to a hospital in St. Paul. There, on the 26th, he died of tuberculosis. He was thirty-five years old.

The body was brought back to Rosemount. Mary, looking very wan and ill, was at the funeral, clutching the prayer book in her wasted hands, too stunned to draw any comfort from the mass.

The grave was on a treeless mound three miles from Rosemount, then a part of the churchyard of St. Joseph's but later, after the church was gone, known as Highland cemetery. The farmers and villagers passed the hat and sent off to St. Paul to buy a proper stone for their schoolmaster. The inscription took a lot of study, and the Callans helped; but no one thought to have Mary edit the final copy, so her lover's name was misspelled:

In memory of W. B. O'Donohoe, died March 26, 1878, aged 35 years. Native of County Sligo, Ireland. May his soul rest in peace. He loved liberty and hated oppression, therefore he died in exile. Erected by his friends of Rosemount, Dakota County.

The error could not have mattered much to Mary, and probably she never saw the monument. On May 3 she died of tuberculosis.

Charlie Callan, Mary's kid brother, inherited the prayer

book and always treasured it. He had been fond of his strict but friendly teacher, he had thoroughly approved of the match, and he had been grateful: in his own circle a good deal of the handsome Fenian's aura of glamour had sort of sifted down on to Charlie. After all it was the Callans who had brought him here and he was a famous man with his name in the St. Paul papers and about as close to a hero as Dakota County had ever known.

There was another thing, too—the sort of thing a fellow never would forget. This O'Donoghue, this big Irishman who had once been with Riel and who had invaded Canada practically all by himself in '71—well, he had taught Charlie Callan how to smoke.

CHAPTER XII

The Politicians

NORTHWEST PASSAGE

THE men of French Canada and the Métis of Red River concerned themselves little about the affairs of Europe, but none could remain unmoved by the events of 1870 and the year that followed. . . . Yet perhaps only the priests and a few educated Métis leaders sensed the coincidence in the fact that a new nation, French in speech and tradition, had died ignominiously on a far frontier of North America in the same year that the Second Empire crumbled in France.

Next year the telegraph was extended to Winnipeg from the United States, and news that had required thirty days to reach Manitoba from the East now got there in twenty-four hours. "It has everywhere been an eventful year," noted *The Manitoban,* one of Winnipeg's two new weeklies. "What changes has it not wrought on the face of the globe!"

Changes not conducive to *la bonne humeur.* . . . The Franco-Prussian War was over; the Second Empire had fallen and Louis Napoleon had been a prisoner of the Germans. Bismarck's heavy-booted Prussians had marched arrogantly through a shamed and silent Paris. The provinces of Alsace and Lorraine and an appalling, unheard-of indemnity—a billion dollars—had been wrested from the newborn Third Republic of France by the newborn Empire of Germany. Paris had gone mad, and only after ten weeks of fire and blood had the Republic managed to smash the Commune and retake France's capital. Germany had supplanted France as the dominant power on the Continent.

In Britain the spirit of imperialism, all but extinguished by the coldly commercial, isolationist liberalism of Cobden and Gladstone, was reviving in the forges of the Industrial Revolution, with the dynamic Disraeli pumping the bellows. In 1853 Disraeli had regarded the North American colonies as "a millstone around our necks"; now he had changed his mind and under his leadership Britain's greatest era of national expansion was soon to begin.

So a few thousand people going quietly about their business on the prairies of British North America were suddenly, bewilderingly, caught up in Europe's political ferment. A colony which Britain a few years before had been quite willing to give away became, overnight, a jewel beyond price for the imperial crown. This was geopolitics, though no one had yet bothered to think up a word for it; it was enough to know that the dream of a transcontinental railroad, the Northwest Passage by land, had been born. It could carry British goods—and if necessary British troops—to and from the Orient.

British Columbia entered the Canadian Confederation in 1871, exacting a promise that the Dominion would build the railroad in ten years. But the vision was older than that. In 1865 two English explorers, Viscount Milton and Dr. Cheadle, published a book in London, *The North-West Passage by Land*, describing their journey across the North American continent. "Millions of money and hundreds of

lives have been lost," they wrote, "in the search for a North-
West Passage by sea. . . ."

. . . We have attempted to show that the original idea of the
French Canadians was the right one, and that the true North-
West Passage is by land, along the fertile belt of the Saskatchewan, leading through British Columbia to the splendid harbor
of Esquimalt, and the great coal fields of Vancouver Island,
which offer every advantage for the production and supply of a
merchant fleet thence to India, China and Japan.

The power that ruled the Northwest Passage would rule
the world.

"It seems to me," Governor Archibald wrote huffily to
Ottawa, "that the people here must be allowed to be judges
of how to manage their own affairs." If they were to be responsible to Ontario, he suggested, perhaps Ontario should
elect Manitoba's legislators.

But Manitoba's affairs were no longer strictly her own
concern. The people of Manitoba, and especially the French,
no longer mattered much. The clamant "patriots" and the
foaming Orangemen of Ontario were shouting now, like Mr.
Pickwick, with the largest crowd. Nobody paid any attention
to the Honorable Adams G. Archibald.

The Manitoba legislature, at its first meeting after the
Fenian scare, unanimously approved Governor Archibald's
handling of that incident, including his appeal for Métis
support and his recognition of Riel's response. But Ontario's
press and politicians raged and the Macdonald Government
quailed. There was to be a general election—Canada's second
under Confederation—in 1872; Sir John knew that if Riel
and Lépine were still at large in Manitoba then, his home
province would be mightily offended. On the other hand,
if they were jailed and tried for murder as Ontario demanded, all of Quebec—doubly touchy now since the French
reverse in Europe—would blaze with fury.

There was one solution. If Riel and Lépine could be persuaded to exile themselves Ontario might forget about them.

In December, 1871, Archbishop Taché (his see of St. Boniface was raised to an archbishopric that year) was in Ottawa to complain about the failure of the amnesty to materialize and about the Dominion's patronage policy in Manitoba: of eighty-five appointments made by Ottawa in the new Province, just five had gone to Métis. Sir John called the prelate into a conference and intimated that he might be able to speed up action on that amnesty if Riel and Lépine could be induced to leave the country for a year. Taché objected that they were penniless—evidence of their integrity, since they had had all the resources of the territory and of the Hudson's Bay Company at their disposal—and that they could not abandon their families. Sir John then produced one thousand dollars of public funds with which to buy their absence; he got the money from a "secret service fund" for which, obviously, he did not have to make strict accounting.

The archbishop returned to Red River and talked to the two Métis. At first they flatly refused to leave, but Taché insisted that their departure would aid their people's cause and their own. "If you command me as my Archbishop," Riel said finally, "and take on your shoulders the responsibility of my leaving my people at this crisis, I will go." Lépine reluctantly acquiesced in the decision. But they demanded adequate travel funds and a sizable sum for their families; Riel said he had noticed that Ottawa politicians did not stint themselves in their expense accounts.

Macdonald's one thousand dollars obviously was not enough. Taché called in Governor Archibald and Donald A. Smith. The latter, as representative of "the big money," found himself in the unhappy position of many a capitalist before and since; the combined powers of Church and State "persuaded" him to advance six hundred pounds of Hudson's Bay Company money on the assurance that some day the Dominion would pay it back. (It did, but the Company had a long wait.)

Riel and Lépine were given sixteen hundred dollars each in gold and the balance was retained by Taché for distribution to their families as it was needed. Riel had a struggle with his conscience, but he concluded that the Dominion owed the money, and more. By consent of Cartier, then head of the Government, he had administered the affairs of Rupert's Land for two months after the terms of transfer had been agreed upon; not only had he not been paid for this service, but he had been driven from office by a hostile armed force. Subsequently he had been libeled, chased from his home, left without protection while pursued by assassins, and his family terrorized. His Provisional Government had abdicated upon a promise of amnesty which had not been made good. He had rallied the remnants of his armed forces to serve as wardens of the plains during the Fenian alarm, and no one except Archibald had acknowledged a debt. Finally, nothing had been done about the distribution of 1,400,000 acres of land to the Métis as guaranteed in the Manitoba Act, and Riel and Lépine were entitled to their share of those acres.

Yes, Louis could make out a sound case. But he could not be happy about it. "My lord," he told Taché when the prelate handed him the money, "if the one who wants me to go away was here, this little sack of gold ought to be flung at his head!"

$5,000 FROM TORONTO

An incident occurred which helped to persuade Louis that abstract considerations of justice should not stand in the way of his departure. Better a live exile, he conceded, than a dead hero. Taché and others assured him that the hatred would be dissipated in time; but now his life was in danger.

Early in 1872 a newcomer from Ontario hatched a plot by which he hoped to become three thousand dollars richer. He hired four Winnipeg men, at five hundred dollars each, to bring him Louis Riel's head in a sack. He would deliver the head to "a man in Toronto" who already had promised five thousand dollars for it.

The conspirators were overheard on the night of the proposed murder by a Winnipeg citizen who hurried to Riel's home in St. Vital and, with some difficulty, persuaded him to flee with his mother to the home of Father Ritchot. Then the eavesdropper told his story to a police officer and returned with him to lie in wait near the Riel cottage.

The four hired gunmen appeared, searched the house, and, angered by their failure to find Riel, debated burning it but left without doing so. No arrests were made, even though a policeman had witnessed the "breaking and entering" and the informant was willing to testify to the murder plot and to name the culprits.

In February Riel and Lépine left St. Vital secretly, at night, with a police escort to see them safely across the frontier.

In September they were back—summoned, Riel said, by the archbishop. The prelate had been sharply criticized in the Métis community for arranging the banishment and was in danger of losing his influence over his flock. That is how it happened that Riel, instead of being safely out of the country when the general election approached in 1872, was triumphantly nominated as a Member of Parliament to represent the County of Provencher, Manitoba, in Ottawa; and since the county's electors were predominantly Métis, his victory was certain.

The American sojourn was not as tranquil as Riel had hoped it would be. The first intimation that Canadian enemies had pursued him even into foreign territory came in

St. Paul within a month, when two men he had known in Fort Garry disclosed that Dr. Schultz was in the city and, they swore, had attempted to bribe them to burglarize Riel's room and steal his Provisional Government records and personal correspondence.

W. Devlin and John Mager swore to the facts in an affidavit. Riel was living at the Montreal House, 79 Minnesota Street, a favorite rendezvous of the Métis "wagon men" of the Red River trails. On March 17, Devlin testified, Schultz came to him and offered fifty dollars cash and one thousand dollars "to be paid by the Government of Ontario" for Riel's papers. W. R. Bown, onetime editor of *The Nor'wester* whom Riel had driven from Fort Garry, joined the conference and offered another fifty dollars down payment. Devlin discussed the matter with his "partner," Mager, and they decided to warn Riel; meanwhile Bown approached them again, said that Schultz had left St. Paul so he would handle the affair, and promised them immunity from prosecution if they should be caught. The next day Devlin and Mager went to a justice of the peace, swore out their affidavit, and took it to Riel.

In April, while a crowd watched a fire near the Montreal House, two other men were overheard discussing a scheme to kidnap or kill Riel and Lépine. The intended victims were then urged by friends to leave St. Paul and did so, with a volunteer "bodyguard." Two days later in Breckenridge their protectors warned off four men who had been shadowing the Métis leaders and had been detected spending part of one night lurking in the door of their hotel.

There were other incidents, less overt. Louis and his lieutenant returned to St. Paul, convinced that they were safer where friends were more numerous. The strain began to tell on his physical and mental health; it became more difficult for him to distinguish between actual instances of threatened violence, supported by affidavits, and imagined persecution.

Finally they returned to the Northern frontier where their safety was assured, and Riel spent the last weeks of his exile in St. Joseph.

When the two men came back to St. Boniface in the fall the archbishop, now uneasily aware that the banishment had not been a good idea, was shocked to discover that Riel was obviously ill.

A SERVICE FOR SIR JOHN

It was madness, Governor Archibald felt, for Riel to stand for Parliament. If he won and went to Ottawa he would either be expelled or, more likely, shot. Yet the Governor acknowledged that the people wanted a representative man and "the general feeling in the Province" save for one district was favorable to Riel.

Henry J. Clarke, Attorney General in the Provincial Government, was the opposition candidate. Clarke did not have a ghost of a chance but could not be convinced of it. The Governor had hoped for a while that both men could be talked into withdrawing so a candidate less disturbing than Riel could be chosen; but Clarke was dazzled by visions of political glory and Archbishop Taché, once burned by reaching for Macdonald's chestnuts (he never fully regained his popularity among the Métis), refused flatly to ask Riel to quit.

Then the political fates played into Archibald's hands. Sir George Cartier was defeated in an astonishing upset in his district, Montreal East, where the election was held ten days before it was scheduled in Manitoba. This spelled disaster for Macdonald: Cartier had been his Deputy Prime Minister and he was spokesman for French Canada in the Conservative councils. A frantic telegram, in code, sped west to Archibald. "Get Sir George elected in your Province," Macdonald demanded. "Do not, however, allow late Provisional [President] resign in his favor."

That, Archibald thought ruefully, was going to take some doing. First he called in Clarke and bullied him into agreeing to retire from the race if Riel would do the same. Then he summoned Taché. The picture had changed; the archbishop, though he had refused to meddle before, could see the value of having the new Province represented by a renowned Cabinet minister, and a French Catholic, too. He agreed to intercede with Riel.

Taché approached the assignment with some reluctance, but he found Louis unexpectedly docile, probably because he was tired and sick. He was not so docile, however, that he could not make conditions. Sir George would have to make certain promises about Métis lands—promises already made in the Manitoba Act but not redeemed. That was all; he made no demand which could be construed to serve his own interests. He did not even mention the long-awaited amnesty.

The conditions were telegraphed to Macdonald, who replied querulously: the people of the French parishes should be delighted to be represented by a minister; it was ungracious to make demands. But Cartier made a gesture toward meeting the terms. Macdonald's dread lest he be put under obligation to Riel was allayed by a Machiavellian interpretation of the deal: Louis was not resigning in favor of Sir George; both candidates were retiring to win the Province a direct voice in the Cabinet.

On September 14 Sir George Cartier was elected. Riel, Lépine, Joseph Royal and Joseph Dubuc wired congratulations: "Your election in our county is by acclamation and [we] have reason to hope in the success of the cause trusted into your hands." Their new M.P. chose not to acknowledge this directly; instead he wired Taché to thank the "friends" who had assured his election.

Unprecedented violence occurred at the polls. The chief of the Provincial Police was wounded six times as he sought to protect Métis voters, some of whom were beaten. The offices of the newspapers, *The Manitoban* and *Le Métis*, both of which opposed the Orangemen, were wrecked.

THE HONOR OF THE HOUSE

On December 6, 1869, about a month after McDougall's expulsion from Rupert's Land but before the killing of Scott, the Governor General of Canada wrote a proclamation promising amnesty to everyone implicated in the Riel movement on condition of submission. In February, 1870—still before the Scott shooting—Sir John Macdonald, in his letter commissioning Taché as a negotiator at Red River, referred to the possibility of trouble over seized Hudson's Bay Company stores and said, "A general amnesty will be granted."

The archbishop was told to use these documents at his discretion. While he was en route to Red River, Scott was court-martialed and slain; but Taché, sensibly certain that Canada would not sacrifice a settlement because of a single act of violence, told the Métis the pledge of amnesty was still good. This was not disavowed by the Government, though Taché kept Ottawa fully informed; in fact he was congratulated on his efforts.

On July 5, 1870, after the death of Scott, Sir George Cartier, acting head of the Government, assured the archbishop in writing that Her Majesty "so to speak" had promised an amnesty. He told Father Ritchot in the presence of witnesses, "I guarantee you will get all that you have demanded." To Joseph Royal he said, "The amnesty has been settled upon," and to M. A. Girard, "Be sure that the amnesty will come before long."

Governor Archibald, though he acknowledged that he had never had specific instructions about it, said he had taken for granted that an amnesty was to be given, that it was implied as a condition of acceptance of the Manitoba Act by the people of Rupert's Land, and that it was necessary for the good of the Dominion.

But Ontario's howls for the blood of the "murderers" of Scott deafened Sir John to all appeals from the other side. He denied that he had ever promised an amnesty. The pledge in his letter concerned only confiscated Company goods; Taché had exceeded his authority; his deputy, Cartier, had been wrong. Why, Sir John protested, he had never even recognized the delegates who negotiated the settlement as representatives of Riel's Provisional Government—he had received them only as representatives of the (presumably stateless) "people of the North-West."

When Father Ritchot, who had headed that delegation, heard the remark he was furious. He confronted the Prime Minister. "Is that," he demanded, "what you told me at the time?"

"Oh, no!" replied Sir John, blandly. "I said that to my friends or the others!"

Archbishop Taché, in his letters and Ottawa interviews, became increasingly bitter, but there was nothing he could do in the face of Sir John's continual shifting about the ring. He no longer had any respect for the Prime Minister's word but he had to deal with him and to grasp at any opening which might restore his own status among the disillusioned Métis. That is how Macdonald won his help to persuade Riel to leave the country in 1872. "If you can succeed in keeping him out of the way," Sir John said, "I will make his case mine, and I will carry the point."

But after three years had passed and the Government still had not granted the amnesty, Taché decided that he had been "made sport of in a most disgraceful manner." To the horror of the Ottawa politicians, he announced that he intended to publish all the facts "in the game in which I have been the victim and the tool." Urgent pleas for his forbearance rained upon him; Sir John was going to London and would surely bring back the amnesty this time; his brother, Dr. J. C. Taché, Deputy Minister of Agriculture, busied himself arranging reassuring interviews with the Ministers—but succeeded only in estranging himself from the archbishop.

Then, on May 23, 1873, the ailing Sir George Cartier died. The County of Provencher was without representation in Ottawa and the specter of Louis Riel, M.P., rose again to haunt the harassed Sir John.

The Prime Minister called in Taché once more. Imperturbably he asked, Would the archbishop, while they were waiting for that amnesty, make it a point to see that Riel did not become a candidate again in Manitoba?

Taché contemptuously refused. And in October, although Riel was not in the Province, he was elected by acclamation. But the change of government in Ottawa which occurred in the following month forced a general election, the Dominion's third. This time—February, 1874—though another Métis ran in opposition to him, Riel won again, by a landslide. Sir John A. Macdonald and his Conservative Government were crushingly defeated in this election, but it sent Louis Riel to Ottawa at last as a member of the House of Commons.

That was the year of the Pacific Scandal. It was only one of the factors, however, which contributed to the repudiation of Sir John; according to some Canadian political analysts it was less responsible for his defeat than his equivocation on the Métis issue, which had alienated both Protestant Ontario and Catholic Quebec. This theory gains some support from the fact that he rode back into power four years later, after the Métis amnesty question had been settled by his more courageous successor, even though the revelations of the Pacific Scandal might well have eliminated him from public life forever.

It was disclosed that the new Canadian Pacific Railway Company, to which the Government had given the charter in 1873 to build the transcontinental railroad, had contrib-

uted large sums to the Macdonald party's campaign the previous year. The Premier and his ministers (especially the indiscreet Cartier) had repeatedly asked and received large
sums, totaling about $350,000. Though Sir John tried to de-
fend the contributions on the ground that he had given no
promises to get them (as he had not promised an amnesty to
win the submission of Riel!), the exposé drove him from office in November, 1873, and Alexander Mackenzie, Liberal,
formed a Government. Mackenzie appealed to the people in
a general election about two months later and was triumphantly returned. The incident not only wrecked the Conservative Government, it also smashed the first Canadian Pacific
company and forced its reorganization.

In Manitoba, despite Riel's election victory, the Métis
situation deteriorated. Archibald, whose diplomacy and mod-
eration had held all factions in a state of neutrality and who
had insisted that Manitoba could not prosecute for crimes
which occurred before the Province existed, was promoted
in October, 1872, to the Lieutenant Governorship of Nova
Scotia. His successor, Alexander Morris, was less sympathetic
to the Métis cause, though no more willing at first than his
predecessor had been to countenance legal persecution.
    In the summer of 1873 the attorney general, Clarke, still
resentful of Riel's Parliamentary candidacy against him the
year before, intimated secretly to Canadians that he would
favor the prosecution of Riel and others for murder if their
arrest could be contrived. To keep Louis within the jurisdiction he would prepare a spurious case against one of Riel's
alleged persecutors and subpoena the Métis to appear as a
witness.
    The plotters drew up four informations charging Riel and
Lépine with murder, sworn to by William A. Farmer of
Headingly, who had been a member of the Portage group
and had been imprisoned by Riel in Fort Garry for five

weeks. Farmer had visited Scott's brother in Ontario and had been urged by the latter to help bring the killers to justice; his role in the frame-up ultimately earned him two thousand dollars of the reward posted by the Province of Ontario.

Dr. John H. O'Donnell, who had traveled part way to Rupert's Land four years before with McDougall's party, was appealed to, as a justice of the peace, to sign the warrants. "Can't you find someone else?" he pleaded. "This will ruin me in my practice in St. Boniface!" But he signed (and the indiscretion cost him his commission) and the warrants were given to peace officers for service.

Lépine was arrested at his home the morning of September 17 by three men who had driven all night in the rain. The big Métis grumbled a bit and threatened to knock his captors' heads together, but after that he accompanied them without resistance and even dissuaded a party of Métis who caught up with them and offered to deliver him.

Riel escaped, though he had been seen in St. Boniface the day before. By the time his erstwhile adjutant general was safely lodged in jail Louis was across the border.

The following February a new indictment was brought against André Nault, Elzéar Lajimodière, Janvier Ritchot and Joseph Delorme, all of whom had been members of the Scott court-martial. Only Nault and Lajimodière were caught; Nault's arrest precipitated a terrific battle between his defenders and police in which he was severely beaten, and his captors had to lie flat in their wagon to dodge rifle fire as they raced to the Winnipeg jail with their quarry.

Lépine was tried in October, 1874, and convicted despite the fact that the Governor would not permit the vengeful attorney general to appear and the prosecution was handled by special counsel—while the Provincial Secretary, Joseph Royal, appeared for the defense. Royal was assisted by Joseph A. Chapleau, a prominent Quebec criminal lawyer. They produced evidence that Lépine had voted against Scott's execution and had not even been present in the Fort Garry courtyard when it occurred—an argument which threw all the blame upon Riel, whom the court declared a fugitive from justice. After the preliminary hearing, when the plea was overruled, no serious effort was made to challenge the jurisdiction of the court over a crime which occurred before the court was created.

This was the first involvement with the Métis cause for Chapleau. He could not have suspected that Louis Riel would haunt his subsequent political career as Provincial Secretary of Quebec and Cabinet Minister of the Dominion— or that because of Riel he would someday be branded a traitor to his race and to his faith.

A "hung jury" freed Nault and the case against Lajimodière was dropped; but—despite a jury recommendation for clemency—Ambroise Lépine was sentenced to hang. Appeals and petitions for commutation delayed his execution, however; and on January 15, 1875, the sentence was reduced to two years in prison by the Governor General of Canada, acting on his own responsibility with the consent of the imperial Government. Most of this time had already been served by the burly Métis and he was soon a free man again. Some years later he moved with other Métis to Saskatchewan, but he returned to Red River and died there in 1922.

Louis Riel, subsisting upon the remnant of the fund raised for his travels by Taché, set out to visit French-Canadian communities in the eastern United States but was soon struck down again by illness. In November, 1873, he was reported "very sick" in the establishment of the Oblate Fathers in Plattsburg, New York. Early in December he visited Keeseville, a lumbering village on the Ausable River south of Plattsburg, about eighty miles south of Montreal and predominantly populated by French Canadians. There he stayed with Father Fabien Barnabé, pastor of the little Immaculate Conception Church. "The curé," Louis wrote his mother, "has his good mother with him; they have been very attentive to me." This letter, first to disclose Louis's acquaintance with the Barnabé family, does not mention the priest's young sister Evelina, with whom then or later Riel fell violently in love.

He was soon back with the Oblate Fathers and on January 23 he left for Montreal. Henriette Pierrotte, a housekeeper in the priests' establishment, wrote his mother that his health was now restored but that friends thought it best for him to leave Plattsburg—why, she did not say. "He was very lonely," the letter added, "and I would go to see him in his room to cheer him up and pass away his time. He would always talk about his folks."

Early in March the Members of Parliament began to assemble in Ottawa for the opening of the session. A bumbling, task-ridden clerk of the House looked up from his desk when three men asked for his attention. Two Quebec Members, sponsoring a colleague, wanted him to swear in the new representative from Provencher, M. Louis Riel. The name sounded familiar to the clerk, but he was a busy man. He administered the oath, pushed forward the register. Louis Riel, M.P., signed his name.

When Parliament discovered that Riel had qualified to take his seat, the cries of rage from the Ontario delegation could be heard from Hudson's Bay to Halifax. Mackenzie Bowell, Member for North Hastings, a Grand Master of the Orange lodge, moved for his expulsion as an indicted criminal whose election had been an affront to the honor of the House. Fierce debate followed, but Riel did not hear it; his life was decidedly unsafe in Ottawa and he remained there only four days. Quebec's delegation supported him. One of the outstanding speeches was that of a young freshman Mem-

ber named Wilfrid Laurier; it was the first appearance on
the Parliamentary stage of the man who became, twenty-two
years later, the first French-Canadian Catholic Prime Minister of Canada and one of the greatest statesmen North
America has produced.

In February, 1875, in default of appearance for trial on
the Manitoba indictment, Riel was sentenced in that Province to five years' banishment from the Dominion of Canada
and forfeiture, for that period, of his political rights. He was
an exile but was no longer wanted for murder, and slowly
the tide was turning. Under the new administration—which,
if less able politically, was far more honest than its predecessor—a select committee of Parliament had investigated the
whole controversy and had concluded that despite the ambi-
guity of his statements and all his denials, Macdonald's
actions indicated that he had promised to obtain an amnesty.
There was, in particular, that matter of the one thousand
dollars given Riel and Lépine:

The fact remains that the First Minister of the Dominion has
used Civil Service money for the purpose of secreting from
justice and preventing the trial of one who was accused of treason
and murder. If this was not done in part fulfillment of an engagement on behalf of the Government to pardon the offense of
which Riel was accused, then it was a deliberate conspiracy to
bar the course of public justice. . . . The transaction . . . fur-
nishes another and perhaps stronger evidence than all the others
which have been adduced that the Government felt bound to
secure the amnesty to Riel and others, and that they sought, by
this means, to fulfill in spirit these engagements which later,
at a more convenient time, they expected to be able to carry to
their full extent.

On April 25, 1875, the general amnesty which Riel
thought he had been promised nearly five years before was
proclaimed—conditional, however, upon his exile for five

years as decreed by the Manitoba court. He who had once ruled Rupert's Land and the Northwest was again a homeless wanderer, pursued by real or fancied enemies, confused, resentful, often ill. He who had stationed an armed guard at the flagpole to protect the Union Jack had been deprived of his franchise and banished. A Member of Parliament, duly elected, sworn, and registered, he was a man without a country.

Well, at least he would not hang; and he had many friends in the United States. The new Government had compromised, to be sure; but it had shown more courage than Sir John, that man of bad faith and feeble spirit. It was good to know that at long last the people of Canada had caught up with Sir John. Conditions might improve now, and in 1880 Louis could go home. There would always be plenty for him to do for the Métis and he would always be welcome.

But in 1878 Sir John A. Macdonald again became Prime Minister of Canada.

PART FOUR

Decade of Death

CHAPTER XIII

The Dusk of Evening

SCALPS FOR A WAR PARTY

IF the Métis had won in 1870, their country would have become an organized native state. Such a state would have vastly changed the history of the West, Canadian and American. When Sitting Bull's Sioux—of the nation that in 1868 had dictated terms of peace to the United States after a victorious war—when Sitting Bull's Sioux crossed into Canada after massacring Custer's command in 1876, they would have found allies instead of a mere refuge. They might well have returned to Montana rested, re-equipped, and reinforced.

The Métis state might have been a nucleus and unifying force which would have united such native defenders of the West as the Cree and the Blackfeet. Such a native alliance would at least have postponed for many years the subjugation of the Western Indians, and it might have enabled some of them to establish semiprimitive but independent tribal societies capable of maintaining a finer way of life and developing in a better direction than in the actual outcome they

251

were permitted. The idea of uniting came to both Sitting
Bull and the Métis too late, but American and Canadian
military authorities had always feared that they might sometime have to deal with it.

That they never did have to deal with so formidable a
problem was due not only to the fact that neither Indians nor
Métis grasped the idea in time, but also to the crippling
effect on the Indians of disease, war, moral dissolution, and
famine. The fifteen years after 1870 were years when smallpox, whiskey, prostitution, and the slaughter of the buffalo
did more to win an empire for the whites than bullets could.
It may be that bullets could never have done it alone.

The Manito Stone was a large meteorite which rested on
the crest of a hill in the southern prairies in what is now
eastern Alberta. It was sacred to most of the Plains tribes, for
obviously it was no ordinary boulder: their legends said it
had come down from the sky. Indians passing anywhere in
its vicinity invariably turned aside to visit it and to leave
offerings—food, or totemic objects such as the wing-bones of
birds, or even money. Centuries of erosion and later reverent
rubbing by the hands of pilgrims had polished the stone's
metallic surface.

In 1869 white men removed the Manito Stone, carted it
off to Fort Victoria (Pakan, Alberta) and left it in the yard
of the Wesleyan Mission.

The missionary wrote friends that the Indian medicine
men were furious: they predicted that war, disease and famine would be visited upon the region by Manito in retalia-
tion for the vandalism. Fortunately, his letter concluded,
none of the promised evils had materialized.

A few months later the missionary sadly read graveside
services in his little churchyard for three members of his
family, dead of smallpox. Only the fact that he also had lost
loved ones saved him, his surviving children, and his mission
from destruction. Day after day the disease-crazed tribesmen

fled past the little fur trade post, shrieking in delirium or dully chanting their interminable death songs. As these sounds at last receded, the croaking of carrion crows and the breathless, eager bark of the prairie wolves caught up the dirge of a race; and for the second time in a generation even the wind-scoured grasses stank of death.

The Crees called it *omikē'win,* the scab—an old word, long used to designate a loathsome disease which occasionally afflicted the buffalo. Those beasts normally were healthier than domestic cattle, but sometimes huge sores appeared inexplicably on their bodies and they thrashed about madly in their wallows, the shallow circular pits in the prairie in which they rolled to shed their matted winter coats. At such times they were not hunted: the crazed creatures were too dangerous for one thing, and for another, close approach to them might infect the hunter's horse.

For as long as the tribal elders could remember the buffalo had contracted this disease, though infrequently; there had been rare instances of its transmission to horses—but never to men. Therefore even an Indian could reason that the disease which struck him down—and his band and sometimes his whole tribe—was something else. He gave it the same name because that name fit: *omikewin,* or *pekopuyewin,* an eruption, a rash; but he didn't blame the buffalo for it. He blamed, correctly, the white man.

Smallpox first reached the Plains from the Eastern seaboard before 1750, but the tribes were then widely scattered and there was little communication between them. Terror came with the great epidemic of 1837 and 1838, when the disease was introduced by infected articles from a Missouri River steamboat of the American Fur Company. The Mandans were the first victims: there had been sixteen hundred of them, and when the pestilence had run its course there were thirty-one left. Four thousand Assiniboines died, and

the spirit of that great tribe was broken forever. Five hundred Gros Ventres perished in a single month, and fourteen
hundred Blackfeet in six. That epidemic wiped out one-
third of the Plains Indian population.

A decade later the scourge appeared for the first time on
the Pacific slope; the Indians may have been right in suspect-
ing that the infection was imported in some supplies for the
Whitman Mission in the Walla Walla country. They retaliated by murdering Dr. Whitman and thirteen other whites.

In 1869 smallpox again booked passage on the Missouri,
and this time it disembarked at the head of navigation—Fort
Benton, Montana Territory. The pitiful remnant of the
Gros Ventres and the southern bands of the Blackfeet got it
first; warned in time, one segment of the Assiniboine tribe
fled the country and escaped infection. The plague rapidly
spread north; in midwinter it crossed the border and swept
along the Rockies through the camps of the Bloods, Piegans,
Northern Blackfeet and Sarcees.

Maj. Eugene M. Baker and a detachment of Second United
States Cavalry and Thirteenth Infantry totaling about three
hundred men found one of the Blackfeet camps in Montana
early on the morning of January 23, 1870. They were hunting Mountain Chief, a hostile Blackfoot accused of the murder of Malcolm Clark, retired fur trader; but the camp they
found was that of Heavy Runner, a friendly chief; and nearly
everyone in it was ill of smallpox.

Major Baker's orders from General Sheridan were fairly
explicit: "If you have to fight the Indians, hit them hard."
Few commanders ever enjoyed a better opportunity than
Baker did that morning on the Marias River, north of Fort
Benton. It was forty below zero and no one stirred in the
Indians' lodges. Few were able to, but Baker did not know
that at the time; what able-bodied braves remained in the
band were out on the prairie hunting something to eat.

Without warning, Baker ordered his men to fire on the unsuspecting camp. After an initial round at long range, the soldiers swarmed among the lodges, firing indiscriminately at men, women and children. One of the first victims was old Heavy Runner; the dying chief staggered from his tipi frantically waving the treasured papers which attested to his loyalty and friendship to the United States.

One hundred and seventy-three were killed, twenty wounded. Montana's first historian recorded the incident with satisfaction: "the first great lesson in good manners taught the savage of this Territory." In Canada, a shocked British traveler heard the story from a Montana prospector whose partner had been among the troops:

Baker just says, "Now boys," says he, "that's the devils, and just you go in and clear them out. No darned prisoners, you know; Uncle Sam ain't agoin' to keep prisoners, I guess. No darned squaws or young uns, but just kill 'em all, squaws and all; it's them squaws what breeds 'em, and them young uns will only be horse thieves or hair lifters when they grows up. . . ."

So the boys jist turned over the lodges and fixed them as they lay on the ground. Thar was up to 170 of them Pagans [Piegans] wiped out that mornin', and thar was only one of the boys sent under by a redskin firing out at him from inside a lodge. I say, mister, that Baker's a bell-ox among sodgers, you bet!

The War Department apparently shared the Montanan's view of Baker's military qualities. The incident was "investigated" and he was exonerated; historically the slaughter went into the records as "the Piegan War of 1870."

North of the boundary the whites were more squeamish. A few heroic but fruitless efforts were made to take medicines and food to the plague-ridden camps, and traders and missionaries earnestly warned the Crees to call off their habitual warfare with the Blackfeet and to shun their enemy's country.

But the Crees had had little experience with smallpox, and one band whose scouts reported they had found a deserted Blackfeet camp could not resist the temptation to see if there might be abandoned horses nearby. A war party of seventeen young Cree braves went to investigate.

One tipi still stood in the camp; over it hung the odor of corruption and another nauseating stench so heavy that even the wind could not dissipate it. The Cree warriors gagged and grimaced and joked about the *wechā'kun,* the foul smell, of their traditional foes; but childlike curiosity drove them inside the lodge. It contained several dead Blackfeet, their bodies black and swollen, partially decomposed, mutilated by animals and birds. The Crees fled outside and gasped for air while the magpies circled overhead and scolded. The warriors argued, like small boys confronted by a dare; then they laughed and went back into the tipi. This was an easy way to take scalps.

Bearing their trophies and some of the clothing of the Blackfeet, the young braves rejoined their band and rode happily eastward to a spring rendezvous of the Crees on the Saskatchewan River. There, encamped among hundreds of their people, fifteen of the venturesome seventeen died, and the two survivors learned to their horror that Crees dead of smallpox smelled just as bad as Blackfeet.

The terror-stricken tribe left the bodies of the victims unburied in their standing lodges and fled in all directions. They broke their bands up into small groups, hoping to minimize the danger, but someone in nearly every group already carried the disease.

The victim would feel a chill, pains in his back, a headache; these he could conceal for a while. But when he lurched from his horse and fell vomiting beside the trail his companions fled from him, screaming. He lay staring helplessly into the sun, and before the rest of the band was out of sight the ants and maggots were busy. Travelers who came along later, warned by smell, made one more wide detour in the trail.

The Indian dreaded smallpox more than anything he had ever known. The virulence of the form the disease took among aborigines was enough to justify his horror, but other factors contributed. The foul odor, the disfigurement, the delirium and helplessness destroyed his sense of human dignity, obliterated pride. The delirium was especially terrifying; the Indian had always feared insanity and in the rare instances of its occurrence in the tribe had ruthlessly stamped it out by killing or abandoning the lunatic.

The tribal medicine men were helpless because smallpox was a white man's importation and they had no myth to account for it, therefore no "medicine." (The whites were not much better off. Vaccination was still little understood, not universally accepted, and virtually impossible to explain to an Indian.) The only treatment the Indian could think of was a sweat bath followed by a plunge into an icy stream; usually all this accomplished was to speed the disease to its violent climax.

Indian victims often died within the first two or three days after infection, before the rash appeared. If they survived this stage the disease became confluent, the pustules merging under the flesh until the whole body swelled; this was fatal in ninety-five per cent of the cases. If there was time before they were reduced to helplessness, fathers of families frequently killed their wives, children and themselves to escape the final phases, the filth and ugliness and degradation they could not contemplate without going mad. Pregnant mothers sometimes contracted the disease and survived; when their babies were born pock-marked the Indians were convinced their race was accursed.

Sometimes the almost inevitable delirium would seize upon whole bands at the same time, and they would leap shrieking into rivers, rush suicidally upon enemy war parties, or fling themselves at the barred gates of the white men's forts, yelling taunts and shrilling their songs of death. Sleepless and out of their heads with fever, braves left their lodges on nightmare scouting expeditions and writhed on their bellies through the brush surrounding their own camps like blinded beetles, until they collapsed; if anyone bothered to look for them they were tracked by the hair snagged from their desiccated scalps.

Soon convinced that the wind could carry the pestilence, its demented victims dragged the bodies of their dead to the windward side of the white men's forts and stacked them there. They crawled to the walls, rubbed their suppurating sores on the gates, door frames, and windows; they fashioned "booby traps" of infected furs or other articles the white men might covet and left them temptingly within their sight. But the whites, shuddering within the barred stockades, submitted to quarantines and embargoes, sent to St. Louis or Winnipeg for more vaccine, and sought oblivion by gulping down their stocks of liquor.

The plague had indicated in 1837-38 that it could survive one western winter, but not two. It raged throughout 1870 and the plains were littered with the bodies of its victims. The toll, though much smaller than before, was a crippling blow to the tribes—probably about two thousand. The proud and indomitable Blackfeet, who had held the eastern slope of the Rockies against all comers for generations, never recovered sufficiently to challenge future invasions; and the Crees, demoralized and dispersed, could never again muster a coherent tribal front for warfare or even for negotiation with the whites. The Crees and Blackfeet fought their last battle in 1870; they made their first and only treaty of peace the following year.

If room in the West had been lacking before, there was plenty of it now: room for the Métis hunters of Red River, who escaped the plague by virtue of Governor Archibald's embargo and quarantine; room for the enterprising business-men of Montana, flogging their teams north with loads of "Injun whiskey" to finish the job of destroying a race which their pestilence had started.

WHOOP-UP TRAIL

In 1804, two years after President Jefferson had persuaded Congress to "prohibit" the use of alcohol in the Indian trade, Alexander Henry the Younger, trader at Pembina, made a note in his journal.

"Indians having asked for liquor and promised to decamp and hunt well all summer," he wrote, "I gave them some. Grand Gueule stabbed Capot Rouge, Le Boeuf stabbed his young wife in the arm, Little Shell almost beat his old mother's brains out with a club, and there was terrible fighting among them. I sowed garden seeds."

There is no biological reason why an Indian cannot handle alcohol as well as a white man. Many Indian tribes, though not those of the Northwest, had long used ceremonial in-toxicants concocted from herbs or vegetables, and had done themselves little harm; but the whites deliberately schooled the Indian to periodic, murderous debauch.

Once started, the habit was hard to break. Those indi-viduals or companies—such as, ultimately, the Hudson's Bay —whose conscience finally overmastered their greed, found themselves in competition with operators who had no scruples whatever, little investment to protect, and no in-terest in the fur business or the country beyond the "quick cleanup." These men, of whom the Fort Benton traders were typical, defied both United States and Canadian law and rarely balked at outright murder of Indians or each other.

The earliest French traders used liquor, and though the Hudson's Bay Company came to it slowly, it soon was distributing enormous quantities. One estimate put the amount used on the Plains annually in the early nineteenth century at 25,000 gallons, consumed by not more than 120,000 Indians. By the end of the second decade of that century, however, the practice was being seriously questioned in England, and by 1860 the Company had ceased almost entirely to use spirits in the trade.

But in that year the first steamboat reached Fort Benton on the Upper Missouri, and liquor was part of its cargo. From then until the commerce was summarily extinguished by the North West Mounted Police fifteen years later, a steady stream of "Injun whiskey"—unspeakably vile compared to the Hudson's Bay Company product—flowed north across the border. The profits of one season's operation of an illicit whiskey post could easily reach twenty thousand dollars; single wagonloads of alcohol (diluted with water after reaching the trading post) were worth two thousand dollars or more in trade. In one year two whiskey posts in the Blackfeet country, now southern Alberta, sent nine thousand robes, worth about five dollars each, to Fort Benton.

Liquor was the cheapest commodity which could be exchanged for robes and furs; a pint was standard payment for a robe. It was dispensed in quantity when the Indians had something to trade but rarely given at other times because to do so would impair its "market value"; the Indian therefore had no opportunity to become accustomed to it. Moreover the quality was bad and became steadily worse when it was discovered that an Indian literally would drink anything. Finally, since the trade was illegal, the consumers were impressed with the fact that they might never get the stuff again and must make the most of their present chance—a psychological factor which today, because of discriminatory though well-intended Federal law, probably contributes more than anything else to Indian drunkenness.

The most vicious liquor trade and the worst alcoholic

orgies occurred in the far Northwest, at altitudes which often
reduce the alcoholic tolerance even of habitual white drink-
ers; and the stuff the Indians consumed would speedily
incapacitate a white man accustomed to downing a quart of
bonded whiskey daily. Charles M. Russell, the Montana
cowboy artist, trenchantly described its effect:

> I never knowed what made an Injun so crazy when he drunk
> till I tried this booze. . . . With a few drinks of this trade
> whiskey the Missouri looked like a creek and we spur off in it
> with no fear. It sure was a brave-maker, and if a man had enough
> of this booze you couldn't drown him. You could even shoot a
> man through the brain or heart and he wouldn't die till he
> sobered up.
> When Injuns got their hides full of this they were bad and
> dangerous. I used to think this was because an Injun was a wild
> man, but at this place [on the Missouri] where we crossed the
> herds there's about ten lodges of Assiniboines, and we all get
> drunk together. The squaws, when we started, got mighty busy
> caching guns and knives. In an hour we're all, Injuns and whites,
> so disagreeable that a shepherd dog couldn't have got along
> with us. Some wise cowpuncher had persuaded all the cow-
> punchers to leave their guns in camp. . . . Without guns either
> cowpunchers or Injuns are harmless—they can't do nothing but
> pull hair. Of course the Injun, wearing his locks long, gets the
> worst of it. We were so disagreeable that the Injuns had to
> move camp.

"Trade" or "Injun" whiskey as distributed on the Northwestern frontier was made of one gallon of raw alcohol to
three gallons of water. For color and "flavor" the trader
added a pound of tea or a pound of rank black chewing tobacco, some Jamaica ginger and a handful of red peppers.
Northern tribes who still pined for Hudson's Bay Company
rum sometimes received a special brew containing, in addition to the other ingredients, a quart of black molasses.

Almost every tribe called liquor "fire water." The Cree

who named this foul concoction for his people was more precise, or more realistic: in that tongue it is *iskotawapoo,* "fire *liquid.*"

The most important of the illicit whiskey posts was Fort Whoop-Up, at the confluence of the St. Mary and Belly Rivers, eight miles from the present city of Lethbridge, Alberta, and two hundred and forty miles by wagon trail from Fort Benton. Its founders were John J. Healy, sheriff at Fort Benton ("a tough town," a stranger was once advised; "keep to the middle of the street and mind your own business"), and Al B. Hamilton. They built their first post on the site in 1867 and named it Fort Hamilton; it burned, and when rebuilt took the new name because a freighter dispatched to Fort Benton for more whiskey reported that business was "whoopin' 'em up."

The post cost about twenty thousand dollars. It was a hollow square stockade with walls of tightly joined logs, set vertically, about fourteen feet high; these uprights were sharpened on the ends so intoxicated customers could not climb over easily. There were bastions at the corners and the walls were loop-holed for rifles; the fort also boasted a small cannon and a mountain howitzer. A large log building against one inside wall of the stockade was partitioned off into rooms for dwellings, blacksmith shop and stores; doors, windows and even the chimney openings were barred with iron to prevent the entry of drunken Indians. The thick oaken gate contained a small wicket through which the traders received the Indians' offerings and passed out the liquor and other stock, usually guns and ammunition.

Life at Whoop-Up and the dozen other establishments of similar character was seldom peaceful. They were surrounded by degraded bands of Indians and were periodically attacked; their supply trains continually raced with United States marshals and Federal troops who had been ordered to stop the trade (and were singularly unsuccessful). Names of the posts, such as Slide-Out and Stand-Off, sometimes commemorated escapes from these American pursuers.

Men willing to engage in the brutal business or take employment at the posts were often unprincipled blackguards, but they had one virtue—they were almost without fear. Many were Civil War veterans or graduates of the bushwhacker or outlaw gangs of Missouri and Kansas. Their forts, on Canadian soil, flew the Stars and Stripes; the flag of the United States thus became identified in the Indian mind with drunken debauchery, fraud and cruelty. There was no law in the forts save that of self-preservation, and though the Indians flocked to get the liquor they recognized what was being done to them and shot whiskey traders on sight if they caught them alone on the plains. The isolation and the sinister environment told on the nerves of the men cooped up within the stockade and there was much violence. One member of the evil company at Whoop-Up wrote a friend in Fort Benton: "My partner, Will Geary, got to putting on airs and I shot him and he is dead. The potatoes is looking well."

Nor were Indians and United States marshals the only hazards. For a time the traders' most dangerous enemies were the wolfers, the frontier's toughest citizens.

Because the buffalo carcasses poisoned and left as bait by wolfers killed the Indians' dogs and sometimes the Indians, too, the tribesmen were continually at war with these hunters and their bodies often were found "so full of arrows they looked like porcupines." The wolfers, therefore, objected strenuously to the sale of magazine rifles and modern cartridges to Indians: not only did this speed up the killing of buffalo, making poisoned carcasses less inviting to wolves, but it also enabled the tribesmen to pick off wolfers more swiftly and at longer range.

A wolfers' camp on the Spitzee or Highwood River organized the "Spitzee Cavalry" to stop the sale of rifles and ammunition and plotted a series of raids on the whiskey traders' posts. Twenty-five of them, at gunpoint, ordered Hamilton in Fort Whoop-Up to surrender any weapons or munitions in his stock. Hamilton was unarmed at the moment, but he seized a red-hot poker, held it above a keg of gunpowder, and told the visitors that sooner than yield he would blow his fort, the wolfers and himself to hell. The "Cavalry" fled.

After the liquor trade was stopped, the Whoop-Up Trail became the supply route from Fort Benton to the Mounties' first post at nearby Fort Macleod, where legitimate American traders soon established themselves. For a short time around the turn of the century it was a channel for smuggling opium; in the 1920's it came into its own again as a liquor route—but traffic moved in the opposite direction to that taken by the whiskey traders of the preceding century.

Experience established a careful routine for the use of liquor in the Indian trade. When the Indians arrived with their robes, furs and pemmican (the posts were heavily dependent upon this buffalo-meat product to feed their own employees), they announced their readiness to trade by staging a dance before the gates of the post. Then, while their comrades capered with impatience, a favored few leaders were admitted to the stockade and treated to a drink. This was a solemn ceremony, accompanied by much mutual flattery and conducted with dignity befitting the toasts at a regimental reunion. After this first drink the Indians often politely asked for another; holding the searing liquid in their mouths they then dashed out of the gate and spat it into the eagerly opened mouths of their friends.

The "regale" was now sometimes ordered—a drink all around, for everybody. (This, under the Hudson's Bay Company's gentler system, followed instead of preceded the actual

trading, and as the Company tapered off the use of liquor
this was all the Indians got.) Squaws could get in on the
"regale" if they chose, but they frequently were too busy
hiding the weapons in anticipation of the inevitable bloody
brawl. This much of the party was free, but the traders soon
regained what it had cost them. After two or three gulps of
fire liquid, the braves fought for position in front of the
gate, which meanwhile had been closed and barred. They
pushed robes, furs and pemmican through the wicket; when
these were gone they traded their horses, their tipis, their
own food and sometimes their wives or daughters for more
liquor.

Within a few hours the traders had everything of value
the Indians had owned; or else—as occasionally happened—
they ran out of liquor. Then the trouble started.

Shrieking with drunken laughter or yowling with rage, the
crazed warriors staggered to the walls, helped each other to
scale them, and tried to force their bodies past the sharpened
stakes at the top. Inside the stockade the traders and their
men, using long poles, calmly poked them off. A little of
this, with its bone-cracking fall to the ground, convinced the
Indians that the fort could not be stormed that way, and they
started aimless shooting over the walls or—much worse—
launched an attack with fire arrows. This was stopped with
one or two shots from the cannon, or by coolly murderous
rifle fire from the loopholes in the stockade. If the squaws
were still able to do so, they now dragged their raving men
into the brush and got them to sleep; but many orgies were
recorded when every man and woman and every child big
enough to hold a cup was drunk.

Next morning, hung-over, sick and broke, the Indian
begged for liquor and food and often was given a little of the
latter to get him on his way. Almost invariably, despite his
bitterness, he paid his debts—such as horses which the trader
had not dared to open the gate to take during the riot. Desti-

tute and afoot, the band now dragged back to the prairies, subsisting on roots until it could make its first hunt.

Costly establishments like Whoop-Up, vicious as they were, were nevertheless superior to the furtive one-night stands in hidden coulees by still more unscrupulous traders. Their "posts" frequently consisted only of a tent or two from which they dispensed a single wagonload of spirits, counting on their customers' befuddlement to enable them to make a getaway. This was a risky business and required precise judgment of the right moment to pull stakes; usually it meant getting the Indians as drunk as possible in the shortest possible time and keeping them occupied with a keg in their own camp while the traders packed and fled. Any miscalculation, or weakness of will through which the traders themselves got drunk, could be fatal.

Some such slip-up occurred in May, 1873, at a shabby post on the eastern edge of the *Montagne de Cyprès*, the Cypress Hills, forty miles north of the Montana boundary. Forty lodges of Assiniboines were encamped there for trade with a party of sixteen white men from Fort Benton. After the Assiniboines had traded all of their robes and while they were helpless with drink, some of the whites—also drunk—suddenly became quarrelsome and accused their customers of stealing their horses. (Horses had been stolen, but by Crees.) Despite the efforts of one or two better-disposed whites and the frantic pleas of the Indians, some of the Montanans opened fire on the defenseless Assiniboines from concealed positions in the brush. They killed about forty, including women and children, and wounded others; the survivors fled into the hills. Though a few of the white murderers were subsequently apprehended the evidence against them was held to be inadequate and they escaped conviction.

TO MAINTAIN THE RIGHT

The Cypress Hills incident spurred a lackadaisical Government to act on an urgent recommendation made in 1871 by Capt. W. F. Butler, who had been sent by Governor Archibald to survey conditions in the Northwest Territories. Butler said the region desperately needed civil authority backed by a mobile enforcement agency, semi-military in discipline, unconnected with any political, economic or religious faction and established at key posts which would be supplied most easily, he suggested, from Fort Benton.

The proposal was endorsed by Col. Patrick Robertson Ross, Adjutant General of the Dominion, who prepared a plan for a mounted regiment of 550 men and specified that they should wear scarlet coats because in 1870 the Indians had looked askance at the green-coated Winnipeg garrison. "We know," they said, "that the soldiers of our Great White Mother wear red coats and are our friends." Later, when treaties were signed with the Plains tribes, the coat traditionally presented to the contracting chief was red.

In May, 1873, two years after Butler's report but immediately after news of the Cypress Hills massacre reached Ottawa, Parliament created the corps destined to become the most glamorous law enforcement agency in history. Originally it was to have been called the Canadian Mounted Rifles, but to avoid alarming the United States and to emphasize its civilian character, the designation North West Mounted Police was substituted. The crest of the corps—a buffalo head—and its motto, *"Maintiens le Droit,"* were probably selected by its first commissioner, Col. G. A. French. For more than thirty years the motto was misspelled on the corps' uniform insignia.

The original force, three divisions of fifty men each, was recruited largely in Ontario and mobilized at Fort Garry in October. The following spring three more divisions were mobilized and in July, 1874, the "Mounties," three hundred strong, left Manitoba on their epic march into the wilderness. Horseback and on foot the force trekked nearly a thousand miles west, carrying their supplies. One division, caught in an early blizzard, had to lift its horses out of the snow and rub them down continually to save them from freezing. The corps was well equipped and its horses were the best obtainable, all more than fifteen-and-a-half-hands high—still "Mountie" standard. Each man carried a pistol and cartridges in his belt and a Snider carbine in a boot on his saddle, which was the United States Army's McClellan, with high cantle and slotted tree. The uniform consisted of a tight red tunic, black breeches, a pillbox cap (the broad-brimmed stiff hat was a later development) and a white helmet for dress; high black-leather boots, and an overcoat with a cape.

The 300 men were the only law officers in an area of 2,300,-000 square miles. They were eight hundred miles from the closest Canadian authority, more than two hundred from the Americans, from whom little co-operation was expected anyway. (Actually, however, the "Mounties" and United States troops soon hit it off very well and worked closely together on Indian matters.) They were widely scattered because Ottawa had chosen four field posts; one division returned to the Manitoba boundary after a patrol totaling two thousand miles.

The most difficult and most dangerous assignment was that of Maj. James F. Macleod, the assistant commissioner, who with 150 men had to penetrate to the heart of the outlaws' country among the hostile Blackfeet, between the Cypress Hills and the Rockies, and there establish a fort. He reached his destination on October 13, three months after the start from Dufferin, Manitoba. The force had little time to prepare for the winter, so Macleod tried to buy Fort Whoop-Up. But the $25,000 price put on it by the American whiskey traders was $15,000 more than the Scot was willing to pay for an establishment which he intended to put out of business anyway. So he built his own post, Fort Macleod, twenty-eight miles west. By December, when the temperature was twenty below, he had his horses and enlisted men inside buildings, but some of his officers were still in tents.

Next spring another post was established—Fort Walsh, on Battle Creek in the Cypress Hills, two and a half miles from the scene of the Assiniboine massacre. Because that event had spurred organization of the force and because of this post's important role in history, Fort Walsh rather than Fort Macleod became known as "the Cradle of the Force."

The Fort Benton traders had talked freely in the Montana River town of their plans for armed resistance to the "Mounties," but Macleod found only one man at Fort Whoop-Up, and the onetime tough guys of the prairie surrendered without a fight when they discovered that the redcoats meant business. Even before Macleod had finished his fort he rounded up several whiskey runners, dumped their alcohol, confiscated their furs and robes, their horses, wagons and guns, and tossed them into an improvised jail. He then summoned them for "trial"—he and his officers were prosecutors, judges and jury—and sentenced them to pay two hundred dollars fine each or serve six months in jail. There was no appeal, and if the culprit dared to protest, Macleod doubled the sentence.

Bellows of rage came from the Fort Benton merchants who had "staked" the illicit operators. But American authorities could not be persuaded to intervene, even for the prominent citizen who insisted that the wagonload of alcohol which Macleod had wantonly poured into the snow was a "medicinal" shipment which had been ordered by the Blackfeet.

Within three months Macleod and his men wiped out a trade which had flourished under the noses of United States officials for nearly a decade. That was achievement enough to justify creation of the force, but its full significance did not become manifest for a few more years.

In 1876 and 1877 the United States fought two dismal, unnecessary and unjustified Indian wars in Montana. Fugitives from both of them fled across the line to seek refuge under the flag of the Great White Mother and her redcoated riders of the plains, protesting—with complete accuracy—that the United States did not honor its treaties, that the word of an American was as evanescent as an infant's cry: "He promises to give us what he has not given, to do what he knew he would never do." What is he, this white man? asked Charlot, chief of the Flatheads, after one of them—James Garfield, who subsequently became President of the United States—had forged Charlot's name to a treaty the chief had refused to sign. "Who sent him here? We were happy when he first came. . . . We first thought he came from the Light; but he comes like the dusk of the evening now, not like the dawn of the morning. He comes like a day that has passed, and night enters our future with him. . . . He comes as long as he lives, and takes more and more, and dirties what he leaves."

In September, 1877, the United States was fighting the Nez Percé tribe, a peaceful people who never before had raised a hand against the whites, in the last of these two Montana wars. In that same month, just across the boundary from the battlefields, Canada negotiated a treaty with the Blackfeet and associated tribes; these Indians had been the whites' implacable enemies for nearly a hundred years. The "Mounties" escorted the chiefs to the council and four thousand of their people came to watch.

Then said Button Chief, a minor leader of the Bloods:

"The Great Spirit sent the white man across the great waters to carry out His ends. The Great Spirit, and not the Great Mother, gave us this land. The Great Mother sent Stamixotokon [Macleod] and the Police to put an end to the traffic in firewater. I can sleep now safely. Before the arrival of the Police, when I laid my head down at night, every sound frightened me; my sleep was broken; now I can sleep sound and I am not afraid."

Said Eagle Tail, head chief of the North Piegans:

"The advice and help I received from the Police I shall never forget as long as the moon brightens the night, as long as water runs and the grass grows in the spring."

Said Red Crow, head chief of the South Bloods:

"Three years ago when the Police first came to this country I met and shook hands with Stamixotokon. Since that time he has made me many promises. He kept them all—not one of them was ever broken. Everything that the Police have done has been good. I trust Stamixotokon, and will leave everything to him."

Said Crowfoot, head chief of the South Blackfeet and immortal statesman of his tribe:

"The advice given me and my people has proved to be very good. If the Police had not come to the country, where would we all be now? Bad men and whiskey were killing us so fast that very few indeed would have been left today. The Police have protected us as the feathers of the bird protect it from the frosts of winter. I wish them all good, and trust that all our hearts will increase in goodness from this time forward. I am satisfied. I will sign the treaty."

With suitable ceremony the signatures were affixed and payments were distributed. Then the chiefs called at the council tent to pay their respects to the treaty commissioners and to say good-by. At their request, future payments would be distributed by the Police.

The last speaker was Macleod. The treaty promises would be kept, he assured the chiefs; "if they were broken I would be ashamed to look you in the face, but every promise will be solemnly fulfilled as certainly as the sun now shines down upon us from the heavens." He paused and thrust out his hands to the chiefs; their granite faces softened and they smiled at their friend. "I shall always remember," Macleod said, "the kind manner in which you have spoken of me."

The chiefs ceremoniously shook hands. Stamixotokon (Buffalo Bull's Head, from the uniform insignia bearing the Mounties' crest) stood rigidly at attention and watched them stalk grandly out of the council enclosure and across the field to their bands. He recalled what one of them had told him: "Before the Police came the Indian walked bent; now he walks erect." And so the Blackfeet walked—proudly erect, proudly bearing the presents which were the pledges of the Great White Mother's good faith: the treaty flags, the silver medals—and the red coats.

CHAPTER XIV

The Freedoms and the Fence

SELF-MADE MAN

TANTANKA YATANKA was intelligent, ambitious, and egotistical. He had been annoyed when soldiers and newspapermen carelessly mistranslated his name, but the damage was done now. White men greeted him with vast respect, even awe; they told him he was famous all over the world as the author of the most humiliating defeat ever suffered by United States arms. The battle had been so short that he had not taken it very seriously at the time, but he was soon convinced that his achievement was greater than he had realized.

That sort of reputation was worth keeping, Sitting Buffalo decided, even at the cost of being addressed forever afterward by the stupid whites as "Sitting Bull."

Much more exasperating was the insistence of Montana frontiersmen and the shamed military that he was only a medicine chief, not a warrior, and therefore could not have been the brain behind that catastrophe on the Little Big

Horn on June 25, 1876. The whites never did get anything straight and their confusion in this instance was particularly provoking: a man who starts out in a small way and works his way to the top likes to have his progress acknowledged. He had been a medicine chief, right enough—philosopher and hack story teller for his small band of followers—but that had been a long time ago. He had made the transition to warrior and captain of warriors. That was hard to do. A medicine chief, despite his important function, was not too highly regarded when the chips were down: like intellectuals before and since, he had to prove himself in battle to the satisfaction of his skeptical peers or be told to go mix a few metaphors.

He was a self-made man, almost. The fact that his uncle was Black Moon, hereditary chief of all the Sioux, helped considerably; but Sitting Bull was a shrewd tribal politician and an able leader in his own right, and knew it. In June, 1867, at a great convocation of the tribe, he was chosen captain of all warriors of the Hunkpapa Sioux. Nine years later, with Gall and Crazy Horse of the Sioux and their allies among the Northern Cheyennes, he set a trap, baited it with rag dolls and lined it with two thousand well-armed Indian marksmen. Into that trap, that fateful Sunday, rode George Armstrong Custer and 264 men of the Seventh U. S. Cavalry.

The meeting in 1867 at which Sitting Bull won his promotion was the most important the Sioux had ever held. They decided then that any Indian who showed the Black Hills goldfields to a white man, or betrayed the presence of gold there, must die; and any white man who discovered it would have to die, too. They approved a ban on the use of liquor—the West's first "Prohibition law" and just as unenforceable as its successors—and they adopted into the tribe, as a "brother" of Sitting Bull, an Oblate missionary, Jean Baptiste Marie Genin. This priest, whom the Pope had appointed missionary-at-large to the Indians of North America, had been wandering around the sub-Arctic and the prairies for three years and had become extremely popular with the Sioux.

Of course the white men found the gold. In 1874 an expedition led by Custer explored the territory and sent back the usual exaggerated reports—"gold in the grassroots." Thereupon the Americans first violated and then disavowed the solemn promises they had made to Sitting Bull's people in a treaty drawn in 1868. Into the Black Hills and beyond, into territory whose exclusive possession had been guaranteed to the Sioux, streamed thousands of prospectors, whiskey traders and other ruffians, and finally settlers. "It was very hard," said Sitting Bull, "to place any faith in the word of Americans."

But he had always distrusted them and despised the Indians who had meekly submitted to confinement. "God made me an Indian," he said, "but not a reservation Indian." He had gathered about him a growing company of irreconcilables, Sioux who valued their traditional way of life and had no intention of abandoning it. They were strongly attracted to the Dreamer religion of which he was an apostle; the Dreamers believed that someday all the dead warriors would arise and help the living to recapture their country.

When the showdown came in 1876 he was forty-two years old and at the peak of his career. Though short (five feet eight inches) he was muscular and sturdy; and he was a great talker, almost unbeatable in the tiresome debates of the council tipi. He had a massive head and—most unusual—brown hair. His face was pitted with smallpox and his expression was unrelievedly stern; the whites called it cruel.

In the opinion of Custer's widow Sitting Bull was a genius. Only a genius, of course, could have outthought and outfought her adored "Autie"—but the dazzled woman nevertheless may have been right.

Sitting Bull told his new "brother," Father Genin, all about the Battle of the Little Big Horn. The Indians had known for weeks that the troops were coming; but, he insisted, the Sioux did not want to fight if they could avoid it. The tribal assembly which the Army chose to attack was one of the periodic political and social get-togethers of the Sioux; its purposes had been to discuss plans to resist the whites and "to make our young men and maidens acquainted with each other so they could marry, as our fathers have done for many generations." Sitting Bull and his band were hosts; counting women and children there were ten thousand or more in the great encampment.

While the scouts watched the approach of the Seventh Cavalry the braves prepared themselves for battle and sent the women and children away. Sitting Bull piously assured the priest that the warriors had prayed for Divine protection; actually, as Father Genin well knew, few of the Sioux had been converted to Christianity despite his personal popularity among them. Subsequently the chief was inclined to give God all the credit—or blame—for the outcome, but as the hour of battle approached he took some precautions on his own. The Americans loved to descend in full cry upon unaroused camps, so he set the stage:

I sent my young men to light fires inside and outside the deserted tepees, placing conveniently at the door of each of the front tepees sticks dressed like men, and to put up stakes in the front streets of the village to which were tied pieces of blankets, so that when the fires were burning fiercely, and stirring the air, the pieces of cloth and old rags waved to and fro in the breeze and gave the appearance of a densely populated village. Then I marched behind the front row of hills with all my braves, and awaited the opening of the soldiers' fire upon my camp.

Everything worked as I had planned. True to their intentions, the United States soldiers killed my flag men whom I had sent to meet them and demand peace, and proceeding furiously forward opened fire upon my empty camp of old tepees and rag manikins. I then fell upon them from the rear, with all my forces, before they had time to recover from the shock of their furious charge and their surprise at finding the village deserted. My men destroyed the last of them in a very short time.

Now they accuse me of slaying them. Yet what did I do? Nothing. God saved our lives because we had called upon Him. They should then accuse God, for truly it was He who saved us. . . .

Let no man call it a massacre, Sitting Bull protested; it was merely an incident of war. "We did not go out of our own country to kill them; they came to kill us." He knew he was fighting Custer but did not recognize him during the battle, nor could he identify his body after it was over; Custer had cut his long hair, by which he was known to the Indians.

Sitting Bull knew he had won a battle but had lost a war. The Americans, he complained, never quit coming. His people, followed at a respectful distance by the Army, straggled north and in December started to cross the boundary. There was peace, they had heard, in the land of the Great White Mother; one Sioux band had been living in Manitoba since the early sixties. Besides, some of them still treasured medals which their forefathers had received from George IV when they fought for the British in 1812.

By the spring of 1877, when Sitting Bull himself crossed the line, there were about four thousand Sioux on the plains of southern Canada between Wood Mountain, Saskatchewan, and the Cypress Hills. This influx of American hostiles under the leadership of a renowned killer posed a tremendous problem for the 150 North West Mounted Police in the region. Macleod immediately visited Sitting Bull and urged him to return to the United States and accept the reservation offered him, but the chief flatly refused. Outright expulsion was not only contrary to Canadian tradition as regarded political refugees, but it was probably impossible. The Sioux were desperate and were well-armed: Father Genin reported that a four-horse team would be required to haul their ammunition and that they had many Springfields and even newer guns with telescope sights which they had taken from Custer's men. They had learned to fill and recap used cartridges, but Sitting Bull ordered all bullets saved for use on white men; bows and arrows were employed in the hunt.

Macleod, little as he relished their presence, had misgivings about assuring the Sioux that the Americans would treat them fairly. The Mountie had been shocked by practices across the line. "I was actually asked by an American who settled here," he reported to a superior, "if we had the same law as on the other side, and if he was justified in shooting any Indian who approached his camp after being warned not to advance. I am satisfied that such a rule is not necessary in dealing with the worst of Indians."

The newcomers took a heavy toll in the rapidly dwindling buffalo herds, and the Blackfeet and Crees complained bitterly. Only the fearsome reputation of the Sioux prevented attacks upon them. The refugees, however, were models of decorum, as they had promised Macleod they would be; during a stay of about five years they were not guilty of a single raid or even a serious disturbance.

In October, 1877, at Canada's request, the United States sent a commission headed by Gen. Alfred H. Terry across the line to attempt to persuade the Sioux to return. It was difficult to persuade Sitting Bull even to meet the Americans at the chosen place—Fort Walsh in the Cypress Hills. Major Walsh of the Mounties drew this assignment, and it was not made easier by the fact that the day he arrived in Sitting Bull's camp a large group of wounded, exhausted and starving Indians limped in from the south. They were refugees from the final battle between United States troops and Chief Joseph of the Nez Percé.

Major Walsh, with the help of two Métis, finally talked Sitting Bull and his councilors into coming to the parley, and escorted them to the Mountie post. General Terry and his associates were waiting, with Macleod and some police officers, in the orderly room. The Indians were induced to leave their rifles outside (though Sitting Bull objected that it would be quite in character for the treacherous Yankees to murder him) and then, led by Walsh, they stalked into the room. General Terry and the others courteously rose.

Sitting Bull strode across the room, shook hands heartily with Macleod and the other Mounties, grunted a few words of greeting to them, and sat down. The other chiefs took his cue: none greeted Terry or the other Americans.

Macleod spoke first, introducing the American commissioners and urging the Indians to give them a fair hearing. The Sioux, he said, could not expect assistance from the Queen; on the other hand they would not be forcibly expelled from Canada.

General Terry, though he had only been at Fort Walsh a few hours, had made a very favorable impression upon the police. Unlike some of the American officers they had met, he was a gentleman and he looked and acted like one. He was a huge man, six feet six inches tall; but he moved gracefully and spoke quietly. Now he did his best: the Sioux, he told them, were the only hostile Indians remaining in America and enough blood had been spilled; the United States would keep faith this time. They would have to surrender their horses and guns, but would not be otherwise punished. They would get a reservation—but it would not be in Sioux country; it would be in Indian territory, in the south.

Sitting Bull arose and started to speak. Still pointedly ignoring Terry, he looked past him as he began what obviously was to be a long recital of Indian grievances. Macleod risked the Indians' displeasure by an act usually considered a grave discourtesy: he interrupted. The Sioux must give their answer; this was not the time or place for recriminations. Sitting Bull accepted the rebuke without resentment and came quickly to the point. And now he addressed Terry directly.

"For sixty-four years," he said, "you have treated my people badly. Over there we could go nowhere. I shake hands with these people; you can go back home. The part of the country we came from belonged to us and you took it from us; now we live here."

The other chiefs gave brief speeches confirming his, as the will of the tribe, and the United States commissioners departed.

Meanwhile Father Genin had suggested to American authorities that they let him have a try at Sitting Bull, either with Terry or alone; he believed he could persuade his embittered "brother" to come home. The offer was ignored for several months and finally the priest was curtly ordered by the commanding officer at Fort Benton to "abstain from meddling." His popularity with the Sioux had made him suspect; he claimed, in fact, a unique distinction: he believed he was the only priest who had ever been regularly shadowed by American spies. There were two of them, he said, and they were on the Army's payroll at Fort Keough.

Father Genin had encountered the Nez Percé refugees in northern Montana a few days before they reached Sitting Bull, when they staggered into a camp of Métis hunters with whom he was staying. He had heard cannonfire from the Bear Paw battlefield two days before. Nearly all of the fugitives were wounded; while the priest tended to them the Métis hurried to prepare food.

One of the refugees had cut off one of his own hands and both feet to free himself from the chains with which he had been bound after capture. His action, which seemed likely to kill him, was attributed by the priest to the panic dread of hanging which all Indians manifested. Most of the leaders of the hostiles were convinced that the vengeful Americans would send them to the gallows.

TO FIGHT NO MORE, FOREVER

The battle which Father Genin heard was the end of the trail for the Nez Percé—a trail eighteen hundred miles long, from the Wallowa Valley of Oregon through Idaho and Montana and north almost to the Canadian line. Their thirty-seven-year-old leader, Chief Joseph, looked, as Sitting Bull had, for refuge with the Great White Mother. The Indians had been on the march for seventy-five days. With never more than three hundred and fifty fighters, Joseph had engaged a total of two thousand United States troops in eleven skirmishes and five battles; of the latter he had won three, drawn one, and lost the last. With defeat, as usual, came betrayal: the promise upon which he based his surrender was repudiated by the United States.

The Nez Percé War began June 13, 1877, at Slate Creek in Idaho, where three drunken Indian youths, one the son of a man murdered by a white, killed four settlers and wounded a fifth. They were members of White Bird's band, not Joseph's, but the outbreak was the climax of a long dispute involving several bands. These Nez Percé were "nontreaty," had refused to accept confinement to a reservation; at the time of the murders they had been peremptorily ordered to move to one which had been accepted by some other bands at Lapwai, Idaho. This meant, for Joseph's people, relinquishment of their claim to the Wallowa Valley of Oregon, long their home and sacred in the Dreamers' creed. Whites had moved in, had run off or stolen the Indians' cattle, and in at least one instance had murdered a Nez Percé herder.

In the first major encounter with the troops, at White Bird Creek, the Indians killed thirty-three and wounded many more. Their own loss was two wounded, none killed. They did not scalp or otherwise mutilate their dead enemies.

Gen. Oliver O. Howard, who had been sixth ranking general in the Civil War and now commanded the Army's Oregon Department, took the field after this battle with about four hundred troops. In his first engagement, on the Clearwater River, the opposing forces were about equal and so were the losses; the battle lasted two days and cost the lives of thirteen soldiers, fifteen Indians. Because the Nez Percé were able to continue their march in good order and outdistance the troops, this battle was a setback for the Army.

Joseph headed for Lolo Pass through the Bitterroot Mountains into Montana, nimbly side-stepped another force brought up to intercept him, and camped in the Big Hole Basin in southwestern Montana. There, although he was caught by surprise by Colonel Gibbon and 191 soldiers, he almost annihilated the command and would have if he had not had to withdraw before the reinforcements he knew were coming could reach the scene. Thirty-one soldiers were killed and thirty-eight wounded; many of the casualties were officers. The Indians lost eighty-nine, but only nineteen of them were fighting men; many women and children died in the troops' initial assault or in attempts to flee. Veterans of the Civil War said this was the most hotly contested battlefield they had ever seen; "few military commanders with good troops," General Howard said, "could better have recovered after so fearful a surprise."

A few days later Joseph retaliated with a night surprise attack, virtually unheard of in Indian warfare, on the vanguard of the troops. Only four soldiers were killed but the raid disorganized Howard's march because the Indians drove off the pack mules; Joseph gained nearly a week on his pursuers. He entered Yellowstone National Park, established the year before as the first "national playground," emerged and escaped north, eluding still another group of pursuers partly by virtue of a ruse: fast-riding braves wielding "brooms" of sagebrush stirred up a great dust cloud which drew off the major military force while Joseph and most of his band proceeded undetected in another direction.

A running battle, extending for nearly 150 miles, took a heavy toll of Joseph's fighting force before he reached the Missouri, but his enemies in this engagement were chiefly Crow Indians who were fighting for the whites. At the river he won two more skirmishes, and a few days later he halted his exhausted band at the northern edge of the Bear Paw Mountains, only a day's ride from the Canadian boundary.

Although the women, children, old people and the wounded had accompanied him every step of the way, Joseph had now far outdistanced his pursuers and could afford, he thought, a day or two for desperately needed rest. He did not know that Col. Nelson A. Miles and nearly four hundred men who had not previously been engaged were hurrying northwest from Fort Keough on the Yellowstone to intercept him.

Miles came upon the Bear Paw encampment on September 30 and immediately attacked. Despite Joseph's belief that he was safe, he had chosen a magnificent defensive position and had dug some trenches; as the attack started the squaws furiously went to work with knives and fragments of pots and pans to dig more trenches and rifle pits. Damming a stream, they not only provided a sizable cistern for their own water supply but drastically reduced that available to the troops.

Miles's command (it included the Seventh Cavalry, Custer's old troop, reconstituted largely with new recruits) suffered such heavy casualties in the initial charge that it was forced to withdraw. Of the Seventh, fifty-three were killed and wounded out of a hundred and fifteen engaged, and the

regiment had only one officer left. Two companies of the
Fifth Infantry lost every officer in the first assault; in the
second, thirty-five per cent of the men and a replacement
officer were disabled. That night Miles established a siege
line around the Indian camp. It began to snow, adding to
the suffering of the unsheltered wounded. Indians carried
water to some of the soldier casualties near their lines who
were suffering from thirst.

Joseph sent messengers to seek aid from Sitting Bull, but
they were intercepted by a band of Assiniboines and killed
for their horses and guns.

Miles brought up his artillery the next day and shelled the
camp, causing heavy losses; he then started negotiations to
persuade Joseph to surrender. Meanwhile Howard had
reached the Missouri and the main Army force was hurrying
to the scene. Joseph came to Miles's camp and was held overnight; the Indians retained, as hostage, one of Miles's officers. The surrender negotiations failed and both men were
released on October 2. The battle was resumed, though the
Indians knew it was hopeless; they were out of food and
almost out of ammunition.

Howard arrived the night of October 4 and the next day
sent his two Nez Percé scouts, both of whom had daughters
in Joseph's camp, to negotiate a surrender. Both Howard and
Miles promised Joseph that if he would yield he and his
band would be returned to Lapwai, Idaho, and that they
would be honorably treated.

Captain John, one of the scouts, brought Joseph's answer.
His lips shook and his eyes filled with tears as he stood before
General Howard and repeated the chief's words, carefully
committed to memory in Joseph's camp. The message was
taken down by the general's aide, Lieut. Charles Erskine
Scott Wood. Wood was to become a renowned poet and satir-
ist and dean of San Francisco's literary colony, but he would
never write lines as moving as those spoken by Joseph that

day. His simplicity, the tangibility of images and the brooding nobility of his expression of grief and defeat have won recognition not only as one of the finest examples of Indian oratory but as one of the great speeches of American history. "Tell General Howard," Joseph said, "I know his heart. What he told me before I have in my heart." He then dictated his surrender message:

". . . I am tired of fighting. Our chiefs are killed. Looking Glass is dead. Toohulhulsate is dead. The old men are all dead. It is the young men who say yes or no. He who led the young men is dead.

"It is cold and we have no blankets. The little children are freezing to death. My people, some of them, have run away to the hills and have no blankets, no food. No one knows where they are—perhaps freezing to death. I want to have time to look for my children and see how many of them I can find. Maybe I shall find them among the dead.

"Hear me, my chiefs. I am tired; my heart is sick and sad. From where the sun now stands I will fight no more, forever."

General Howard gave the ambitious Miles credit for the victory. When Joseph arrived, after a pathetic attempt to dress up for the occasion, and presented his rifle, Howard waved the gun aside to the other officer. In the Bear Paw battle the troops had lost twenty-six killed and forty-two wounded; the Indian death toll was eighteen and there were forty wounded in addition to the wounded among the hundred and four who escaped across the line. These refugees were led by White Bird, whose band had been responsible for starting the war; the chief, who feared he would be singled out for punishment on this account, spent the rest of his life in Canada. Total casualties of the campaign were 126 troops killed, 140 wounded. The Nez Percé lost 151 men of their fighting force and had 88 wounded; at least as many women and children also were casualties.

The Indians were escorted by Miles to his fort on the Yellowstone. From there, both commanders had said, they would be moved in the spring to Lapwai. But the Secretary of War and Gen. W. T. Sherman, head of the Army, countermanded the order and sent the Nez Percé south to hot, bleak Indian terrritory. There, for seven years, Joseph sadly watched his people die of malaria: the band dwindled from 450 to 280. Finally they were permitted to return to the Northwest but were split up and settled on two reservations.

Joseph died in 1904 at Nespilem, Washington, on the Colville Reservation; he was sixty-four. A few months before his death he welcomed as his guest, to spend five months with the tribe, Erskine Wood, the thirteen-year-old son of the lieutenant who had recorded his surrender speech. The boy wrote an account of his unique experience for *St. Nicholas.*

In the same document in which he insisted that Joseph, despite the promises, should be banished from the Northwest, General Sherman paid tribute to him. The war, he wrote, had been "one of the most extraordinary Indian wars of which there is any record." The Indians had displayed courage and skill, they did not scalp or mutilate the dead, they freed captive white women unharmed, did not indiscriminately murder noncombatants. "They fought with almost scientific skill, using advance and rear guards, skirmish lines, and field fortifications."

Howard and Miles both sharply protested the decision to move the Indians south, and both warmly praised Joseph. The Nez Percés, Miles wrote in an official report, were "the boldest men and best marksmen" he had ever encountered among Indians. As for their chief, "Joseph is a man of more sagacity and intelligence than any Indian I have ever met; he counseled against the war and against the usual cruelties practiced by Indians, and is far more humane than such Indians as Crazy Horse and Sitting Bull."

Joseph, showing more charity than his erstwhile enemies

deserved, eschewed bitterness. Indian and white alike, he said, faced a great problem of adjustment. In 1879 he gave a remarkable interview to the *North American Review.* "I know," he said, "that my race must change; we cannot hold our own with the white men as we are." But could not the same law apply to all men, regardless of race? And, with unfailing eloquence, he voiced the cry of his people:

"Let me be a free man—free to travel, free to stop, free to work, free to trade where I choose, free to choose my own teachers, free to follow the religion of my fathers, free to think and talk and act for myself. . . ."

Give me that freedom, Joseph said, "and I will obey every law, or submit to the penalty."

THE BOSOM OF THE MOTHER

Chief Joseph's War and the Sioux War a year earlier were the last major contests between "free" Indians and the whites. There were later battles, mostly arising from the Dreamer religion's great "ghost dance" agitation of 1890 (in which Sitting Bull was killed in South Dakota), but these were clashes between reservation Indians and whites whose mastery they had already acknowledged by treaty and thus were mutinies rather than wars. With Sitting Bull's flight and Joseph's pledge to "fight no more, forever," the West was won.

The scene of this last act of the Indian drama in the seventies was significant. The climactic battles, both in Montana, were fought within about three hundred miles of each other, in the heart of the great Western buffalo range. Though neither the Sioux nor the Nez Percé lived on this range, both visited it frequently on the hunt; without at least shared possession of it the Indian way of life could not survive.

When the fighting was over, portions of both tribes fled to

the Wood Mountain-Cypress Hills area of Canada, also a
part of the buffalo range. The free movement of aboriginal
peoples across national boundaries was countenanced in international law and the Anglo-Saxon precedent was to offer
sanctuary to political refugees, but movement on this scale
provided serious complications in Canadian-American relations. Canada did, somewhat reluctantly, provide a refuge—
at the cost of straining her good relations with her own
tribes. But sanctuary was a United States tradition, too, and,
ironically, within another decade that country, even more
reluctantly, became host to refugees from north of the line.
This time the fugitives were Métis and Crees.

Sitting Bull's victory and Joseph's defeat were important
chiefly as spectacular symbols: they dramatized the end of
an era. Actually neither war need have been fought and the
outcome of both was foreordained. Joseph knew before he
took up arms that final victory must rest with the whites and
that, while the conquerors might make a gesture of granting
him some of the freedoms he wanted, white civilization could
not grant the two upon which the whole Indian system
rested, and without these two the others were meaningless.
Joseph and his people, win or lose, never again could be
"free to travel, free to stop."

Freedom of movement is incompatible with private ownership of land. Without freedom of movement the Indian
tribal organization, Indian religion, and customary Indian
economic processes could not function; as for freedom to
think, talk, and act for oneself, there would be as much of
that as could be used by prisoners in a stockade.

Private ownership of land was a concept at first incomprehensible to the Indian; later, after it had been enforced with
guns, it was inexpressibly shocking, and especially so to the
Dreamers, among whom were both Sitting Bull and Joseph.
To them the earth was the mystic Mother; Smohalla, "the

Preacher," rebuked the whites who urged him to acquire a homestead and start farming:

"You ask us to plow the ground? Shall I take a knife and tear my mother's bosom? Then when I die she will not take me to her bosom to rest!

"You ask me to dig for stone? Shall I dig under her skin for her bones? Then when I die I cannot enter her body to be born again!

"You ask me to cut grass and make hay and sell it and be rich like white men! But how can I cut off my mother's hair?"

Even Indians with a generation of Christian training, who had forsaken most of their pagan beliefs, could not reconcile themselves to the idea that land could be bought and sold and fenced. Tribes might fight fiercely for buffalo-hunting privileges, but these were merely rights to *use* the land, won for a season through valor and perhaps the generous intervention of Manito; they never dreamed of challenging the equal right of any other tribe, if the other were strong enough to maintain it. And these conflicts were rare; most intertribal battles grew out of horse thefts, involved small bands and resulted in comparatively few casualties.

Years after the whites had negotiated treaties with Plains Indians on both sides of the boundary some chiefs protested, apparently in all sincerity, that they had not understood they were *selling* the land. They thought they had *rented* it; as first comers they were entitled to its use and they had yielded that right except on reserved portions; but the land was God's and no one could sell it. To this day it is difficult for an Indian to differentiate between his reservation, which his tribe owns, and the much larger areas on which the tribe once was granted hunting rights only.

As use of the land was permitted to all men, even whites, by the grace of God, so were all of life, all of life's appur-

tenances, a loan from God. It was not only inconceivable but
for an Indian it was impossible for one man to monopolize
life's privileges. The Plains tribe was a group of families, all
of them actually or theoretically linked in a kinship relation.
Economic and social functions were carried on communally.
The rearing of children was less a responsibility of the parents than of the band, and the child was taught very early
that his first obligation was to the group.

Horses were individually owned, partly because their ac-
quisition was a sign of manly prowess; but they were herded
together and were generously shared with the needy, as were
all other possessions. Most Plains Indians attached great significance to the "give-away" ceremonies, usually held to
honor a deceased relative, when a family would give away
not only everything possessed by the one whom they
mourned but all of their own chattels as well. "Poverty" thus
acquired was honorable and was soon relieved by gifts from
others. Today on the reservation an Indian who brings home
a load of groceries from the agency town may be cleaned out
overnight by hungry relatives who have traveled many miles
for the feast. He accepts this as a matter of course and goes
"visiting" in his turn.

"They were neither yelling demon nor Noble Savage,"
wrote Stephen Vincent Benét in *Western Star*. "They were a
people." Then, in some of the most perceptive stanzas ever
written about Indians, he continued:

A people not yet fused,
Made one into a whole nation, but beginning,
As the Gauls began, or the Britons that Caesar found,
As the Greeks began in their time.

    .   .   .   .

They were a people, beginning—
With beliefs,
Ornament, language, fables, love of children
(You will find that spoken of in all the books.)

And a scheme of life that worked.
                              We shall never know
What would have come of that scheme in the turn of time,
What cities or what nations or what fame.

A scheme of life that worked for the Indian was twice destroyed within a single century, sometimes within two or three generations. He was compelled, first, to hunt furs and robes for the white man's market instead of for his own food and covering. Though the whites had not yet encroached much upon his territory, his freedom of movement already was curtailed because trade, rather than functional considerations for the tribe, dictated where and when and how he must hunt.

Then, within two or three decades, the furs were gone or the market failed, as it did when felt replaced beaver in men's hats. Another decade or two finished off the buffalo; the Indian, who had made one adjustment with great difficulty, now confronted another and much more complex one. He could not go back: the game which Manito had put on the Plains to sustain him was gone. He could see no way to go ahead: the whites had taken the land, subtly robbed him of his age-old skills, weakened him with alcohol and disease and new, less nourishing foods, and destroyed his self-respect. The face of Nature had been transformed, the balance of Nature had been upset; by these he had lived. The white man had knifed the mother in the breast and the spirit had fled from the child.

Desperately the Dreamers prayed and Smohalla exhorted them: "All the dead men will come to life again; their spirits will come to their bodies again. We must wait here in the homes of our fathers and be ready to meet them in the bosom of our mother."

But the spirits of the dead men were sluggish and cold and slow to respond, and meanwhile the knife of the white man rose and fell, again and again.

CHAPTER XV

The Prince of the Prairies

PEACE RIVER TO NEW MEXICO

IT seemed to be the intent of General Miles, Canada complained to Washington, to prevent the buffalo from completing their annual northern migration. Lord Lorne, the Governor General of the Dominion, suggested to the Secretary of State that nothing should be done to impede the free movement of the herds.

Miles, who had advanced in rank after defeating Chief Joseph two years before, was patrolling the Montana-Dakota frontier with the ostensible purpose of preventing an influx of Canadian Indians to hunt. This was bad enough, Ottawa felt; but by interposing his troops between the boundary and the southern winter range he was holding the buffalo in Montana for slaughter. The herds, scenting man ahead, retreated and reversed their course.

Nor was that all of the story. That same year a disastrous series of prairie fires swept the grasslands just north of the

line, and the few buffalo which did get that far found no
forage and turned back. The Governor of Manitoba could
not regard this as coincidence; "the fires were started," he
said, "at different points almost simultaneously, as if by some
preconstructed arrangement." They extended from Wood
Mountain, midway in the present Province of Saskatchewan,
to the Rockies and north as much as a hundred miles. Americans, their dismayed neighbors were convinced, had set the
fires deliberately to keep the herds south of the line; and it
is probably true that some were started by American Indians
with the encouragement of Montana's white buffalo hunters.

On the other hand, buffalo were whimsical beasts, given
to inexplicable shifts in their range. There had been other
years when they had vanished temporarily from their usual
feeding grounds and the Red River hunters had fasted in
consequence. But this time they did not come back. After
1879 there were virtually no buffalo north of the boundary,
whereas in Montana they held out for four more years.

The number of buffalo on the Western range before the
white man came can never be known, but a popular guess,
made before the great herds were gone, was sixty million.
Some support for this estimate may be found in the tales of
awe-struck travelers. (The first to see them in the wild state
on the plains was probably Cabeza de Vaca, Spanish explorer,
in 1528, though Cortés had seen captive animals in Mexico.)
Even allowing for exaggeration and assuming that sometimes
the observers must have witnessed the beginning of great
annual migrations, before the herds broke up into smaller
groups on the open plains, the fact remains that they could
have seen only a fraction of the number in existence; their
reports, therefore, make the sixty million figure seem conservative.

There was, for instance, the Canadian party which camped
in the Qu'Appelle Valley of Saskatchewan, heard the buffalo
coming, fled into the brush to get out of the way, and

watched for twenty-four hours as the animals waded into a ford, clocking them at several hundred a minute. These spellbound witnesses insisted there were nearly one million animals in that herd.

Traveling south from the Cypress Hills in 1873 another party spent seven days, riding twenty to thirty miles a day, passing through one placidly grazing herd. In the fall of the following year the Mounties shot their first buffalo there, and one of their officers, en route to Fort Benton, saw eighty thousand animals in one group. In the same area the secretary of the American Boundary Commission climbed eighteen hundred feet above the prairie to view a herd and reported he could not see its end in any direction.

When these vast herds were seen the Indians and Métis had been hunting for generations. But systematic extermination by white men or at their instigation had been under way only ten or fifteen years, since the railroads had been pushed into the West and the policy of "starve the Indian out" adopted in the United States. By 1890 there were fewer than one thousand buffalo left on the continent, most of them in captivity; today there are about thirty thousand, all on government or private range.

Nevertheless some native methods of killing buffalo were wasteful. Such were the *piskuns* and pounds, use of which, however, was generally abandoned by the Indians some time before the herds disappeared. The *piskuns* were cliffs over which the buffalo were driven, and the pounds were giant log corrals or cul-de-sacs in the hills into which a herd was hazed and there destroyed while milling about in frantic fear.

These methods took a heavy toll of calves, which were of little use to the Indian, and also damaged the bones, sinews and robes—all essential in Indian housekeeping. Above all, the *piskun* and pound were not much fun, whereas the chase on horseback was the most important element of Indian life.

The hunt was a gauge of manhood and of women's skills; its excitement and its mystic significance were recorded in song and dance; it produced food, clothing and shelter.

In the sixties the medicine men told their tribes they had been warned in dreams that such brutal processes as the *piskun* offended the buffalo and Manito, who had stocked the Plains for His people. If the killing continued on this scale the buffalo would go away. Obediently the braves returned to the hunt; but skeptical whites said it was not the vision but the general availability of firearms and the flourishing market for robes which inspired the change. The *piskun* was a communal enterprise and the buffalo thus slain were distributed equally; but with a good horse, a good gun, and the liquor habit, an Indian could almost be converted into a businessman. He would never quite understand unrestricted free enterprise, but he could be taught that skill and daring would pay off in whiskey and other blessings of white civilization at the trading post.

Skill and daring he had always needed. If he were without either, though the tribe would support him, he would be put to humble jobs and his voice would not be raised in the council tipi. But if he possessed these qualities they would win him honor, one or several wives, and a place in the front row of the medicine lodge where he could sing of his prowess. They would win election to a select secret society, the right to participate in the buffalo dance, and perhaps even the greatest reward—custodianship of a sacred bundle. And his name would live forever in the tribe.

The great hunter deserved these things. In every chase he and his fellows risked their lives scores of times. A day's hunt might not last more than an hour, but in that time they would make five to ten "runs" through a stampeding herd, on ground honeycombed with badger or gopher holes, loading and firing while their horses nimbly side-stepped animals weighing more than a thousand pounds which crashed in their path.

An Indian scout with his ear to a gopher hole could detect a moving herd of buffalo thirty miles away. Once on their way they moved in a straight line from point to point, scorning any obstacles except mountains; and their trails from the Peace River of northwestern Canada to New Mexico, worn deep in the prairie sod, led many a lost white adventurer to water or shelter from a storm. The sound of a running herd—most common in the rutting season in July, when the bulls fought each other and pursued the cows—thundered in the earth and at a distance was heard as a deep, continuous hum. Observers of buffalo sexual practices were amazed to discover that the young bulls, after these battles had been won, chose the older cows, leaving the young ones to the defeated veterans of the herd. This singular behavior was incorporated in the buffalo dance of some Plains tribes, during which the young braves chose old squaws and escorted them to their lodges; but there the mimicry ended—the braves left them at the door.

A running herd was difficult to overtake or intercept, but there frequently was a grazing herd nearby. The Indian hunters would attempt to get within a distance of two gunshots of such a herd before they were discovered by it; they were aided in this by the fact that the buffalo's only keen sense was smell, and his vision, none too good, was better to the side than in front. But in the approach the hunters were handicapped by the wild excitement of their horses, often stallions, which had to be curbed so that all might make the first killing run together; otherwise the herd would be started too soon and only those with the best mounts would get within range. The trained buffalo horse, regarded by frontiersmen as the most intelligent animal that ever lived on the Plains, was high-strung, "spooky," and impossible to hold once the killing run started; he knew his own job and expected his rider to take care of himself.

When the hunters were detected by the herd the bulls snorted, pawed the ground, then drew together into a bunch and started running. The fleeter cows, which always grazed ahead of the bulls, then bunched and fled. Because the meat of bulls was tough and unpalatable, the hunters sought the cows—and to reach them had to plunge through an almost solid phalanx of racing bulls while dust rose in choking, blinding clouds.

If the hunter was thrown during this passage through the bull herd his chances for survival were slim because of the milling mass behind him; on the other hand an unwounded buffalo would not deliberately trample him, and, because of the shape of the horns, was unable to gore him if he lay flat on the ground. However, if the hunter was scraped off onto the head of a bull, as frequently happened, the animal would toss and retoss him in the air, without slackening its pace, until the mangled body would no longer catch on the horns.

Stray bullets were another hazard. Guns were loaded and fired swiftly, the aim was usually from the hip, and the dust and uneven ground caused many misses. The big-bore muzzle-loading muskets used before introduction of the magazine rifle could blow a man apart at close range. Frequently a ball lodged halfway down the barrel and the gun exploded; loss of fingers or a hand was the most common casualty of the hunt. Only the first ball was wadded down; others were carried in the hunter's mouth and after the first shot he jerked a charge of powder into the barrel from his flask, spat the ball into the muzzle, pounded the butt on his saddle to lodge the ball in the breech where the saliva held it momentarily in the powder, and, lest the ball roll out, held the gun erect until he was ready to fire.

The gun was brought down swiftly, aimed at a point behind and below the left shoulder where the bullet would penetrate to the heart, and fired at a range of five to ten feet; a new cap was fitted or priming put in the pan, the gun was reloaded, and the hunter raced on through the dust, usually keeping to his own row. The horse as well as the hunter sought out openings in the stampeding mass ahead; if the rider needed to change direction he had only to swing to one side or the other to let his mount know what the course was to be.

After the run—a mile or two—the hunter returned along his row, identifying animals he had shot by characteristic features of the carcasses or of the wounds; there were few disputes over this. Sometimes a hunter dropped a bit of cloth or other identifying fragment near his kill as the horse sped on. The return ride was as dangerous as the original run because of the buffalo practice of playing possum; and recumbent buffalo, unlike domestic cattle, could spring up on all four feet at once. Animals only slightly wounded would lie as if dead until hunter and horse were almost upon them, then leap up and charge.

The bow and arrow, though slower, were safer and more deadly than the gun. The saskatoon or chokecherry-wood arrow was often driven clear through the body of the buffalo. Many Plains Indian hunters used bows and arrows by choice as long as the herds lasted.

Such hunts gave the buffalo a chance, and despite the use of *piskuns* or pounds when the tribe was in immediate need of food or when an unusually good opportunity appeared (it was not easy to get a herd into position for such a drive) there is good reason to believe that Indians and Métis caused little reduction of the herds until commercial killing for robes and pot-hunting were introduced. Pot-hunting was killing for the sake of the tidbits especially sought by the white gourmet: the tongue, the thirty-pound *grosse bosse* or hump, and the *dépouilles,* two layers of tender flesh along the ribs. A skilled Indian or Métis horseman might kill eight or ten buffalo in a day but it usually was many days before he encountered the herd again; white hunters often killed more than a hundred a day per man. One of the greatest white assaults on the herds occurred in the Cypress Hills in 1874-75, in the winter, a season in which Indians did little hunting. The pot-hunters, armed with repeating rifles and concealed in brush or behind snowdrifts, ambushed and totally destroyed a huge herd.

The whites were usually poor horsemen, trailed a herd on foot, and if there were enough hunters, surrounded it. When they opened fire from several sides, the bewildered beasts, unable to determine the origin of the attack, huddled together helplessly until all were destroyed.

Despite such methods some whites shared the astonishment of the Indians and Métis when the herds "suddenly" vanished. The Indians could not be convinced for a generation that the great beasts had not simply abandoned the Plains and retreated into a hole in the ground; even today the elders of the tribes can point out the pits into which, their fathers told them, the buffalo disappeared. But in the mid-seventies, at the time of the Cypress Hills slaughter, it was confidently asserted in Fort Benton that the buffalo were increasing, because the wolfers were taking such a heavy toll among the predators which were the beasts' worst enemies.

BIG BUSINESS ON THE PLAINS

The Indian hunt was a breath-taking spectacle, full of color and sound and furious movement. That of the Métis was all this and more: it was a military campaign under rigorous discipline, a social and political convocation, and, for its time, a monumental business enterprise requiring the services of a thousand people, as many vehicles, and an investment of a hundred thousand dollars.

There were two Métis or "Red River" hunts annually, in

June and in September or October. The system of mass hunts started in 1820 and continued as long as the buffalo lasted, but was at its peak in the decade of 1840 to 1850. Until the seventies the only major assembly points for the annual expeditions were Pembina and nearby St. Joseph; later, as the herds moved west, hunts also started from new Métis settlements on the South Saskatchewan, in the Cypress Hills, at Fort Victoria near the present city of Edmonton, Alberta, and on Milk River and Spring Creek in Montana—the last now the site of the city of Lewistown.

About June 1 the "Plains mania" seized the Red River Métis. The tasks on the home place were assigned to the elderly and infirm, the hunters tinkered with their gear and dickered with the Company for credit with which to buy supplies, the wives worked into the night repairing utensils and tents and making clothing. Leaders of the expedition waited upon the Bishop of St. Boniface and respectfully requested that he assign a priest to accompany the people. Meanwhile the Anglo-Saxon farmers watched primly, deplored "casting off the habits of industry to go to the prairies," blind to the fact that in the week of preparation for this mass movement and two months on the Plains the Métis did more work than the farmers did in a year, and braved more hardship than the farmers did in a lifetime.

On June 15 the great procession started south. Horses, carts, dogs, people horseback and afoot emerged from every settlement and spread out for miles on the trail to Pembina. There, three days later, the rendezvous was made with the Métis of Dakota and the great camp was established. It was a circular city bounded by hundreds of carts enclosing triple rows of tents. On the plains outside the circle the boys herded the horses and oxen; in the "common" in the center the people met to choose their leaders and approve the regulations of the hunt, to listen to the priest, to gossip and play and make love and get married.

Organization of the hunt at the rendezvous took three or four days. Finally the big day arrived and the camp was awake at dawn. At about five o'clock the priest said mass and an hour later the flag was raised on the cart of the day's leader. In half an hour more the expedition was under way —a six-mile-long procession, in staggered rows a mile wide to cut down the dust, a stately march but clamorous with the cries of children and the commands of drivers, the barking of the dogs, the snorting of the horses, and under and over all the incessant shriek from the wheels of the carts.

The Métis Plains hunter was partial to buckskin shirts with bright beaded designs, usually in the floral figures of the Cree, and black woolen trousers bound below the knee with beaded garters or ornamented leggings of wool or buckskin. The "Assomption" sash, taking its name from L'Assomption, Quebec, whose hand weavers first produced it for the fur trade, was bound around his waist or looped over one shoulder; tobacco pouch, powder bag and other articles were tied to the sash or stuffed under it. His headgear originally was a handmade pillbox cap of wool bordered with an ornamental design in beads or porcupine quills; later he adopted a round-crown felt of the Stetson type, usually black, with a bright feather cockade or beaded band. He was invariably shod in moccasins. The standard garb for women was a loose dress of rough black woolen stuff and head scarf of black silk, varied on special occasions by the addition of colorful embroidered shawls or aprons. They wore "squaw boots"— moccasins with attached tops of soft buckskin, usually intricately beaded; men and women wore out several sets of footwear on every hunt and much of the wives' time was spent making moccasins.

The June hunt of 1840 was typical of these Métis mass expeditions. It engaged 620 hunters, 650 women and 360 children for two months, required 1,210 carts, about the same number of draught animals, and 403 hunting horses. A con-

temporary reporter, Alexander Ross, itemized the investment in this hunt and estimated the total, in values of the
time (he put the hunters' labor at a shilling a day each, and
the women's at ninepence), at approximately 24,000 pounds
sterling. The biggest problem, of course, was transport, because room had to be left for the meat and robes which
would be brought home. In addition to tipis and housekeeping equipment, the expedition carried 740 guns, 150 gallons
of gunpowder, 1,300 pounds of balls, 6,240 flints and hundreds of knives, axes, and harness sets. Much of the ammunition would be expended on the hunt but a sizable reserve
had to be retained for the return journey as a safety factor:
they might encounter the hostile Sioux.

The most expensive single item in Ross's compilation was
the hunting horse, valued then at fifteen pounds, nearly fifteen times as much as the sturdy, handmade Red River cart.
The price of a good buffalo runner never fell below this
figure in forty years and was sometimes as much as $250.
The fact that a good horse was the most valuable thing on
the Plains goes far to explain the incessant horse-raiding by
Indian bands and the flourishing industry of "rustling" created by whites.

The first act of business during the rendezvous at Pembina
or St. Joseph was the election of officers at a general council.
Ten captains were chosen by vote of the men of the camp
and one of these was named chief of the hunt, or governor.
Each captain commanded ten "soldiers" who assisted him in
maintaining order and enforcing the regulations. The captains took their responsibility seriously and, though the
Métis were normally a cheerful and friendly people, dis-
ciplinary action, when necessary, was sudden and severe. Ten
guides took turns directing the expedition's course, and the
camp flag was affixed each day to the cart of the captain
whose guide led the march. Raising the flag in the morning
was the signal to start, and while it was up the guide was

chief; even the captains were subject to his orders. When the flag was lowered as the signal to camp, the captains and soldiers took over, under the chief; they pointed out the order of the camp and sent every cart to its appointed place. Much of this organization had been planned and effected during the day's march, so the camping maneuver, performed like clockwork after long practice, could be completed in half an hour.

After the election of officers, regulations were drawn; like all other public announcements they were communicated to the camp by the crier. Under orders of the chief he circulated among the lodges every day to announce the discovery of lost articles, changes in the route, penalties for transgressions, or anything else concerning the company. Much of the hunt's procedure was dictated by custom and few "laws" were necessary; the standard rules varied little from year to year. The regulations in 1840 as recorded by Ross were:

1. No buffalo run on Sabbath Day.
2. No party to fork off, lag, or go before without permission.
3. No person or party to run buffalo before the general order.
4. Every captain with his men in turn to patrol camp and keep guard.
5. For first trespass against these laws, offender to have saddle and bridle cut up.
6. For second offense, coat to be taken off offender's back and be cut up.
7. For third offense, offender to be flogged.
8. Any person convicted of theft, even to the value of a sinew, to be brought to the middle of the camp, and the crier to call out his or her name three times, adding the word "Thief!" each time.

At the end of each day's march the chief and his captains assembled in council outside of the camp, squatting on the grass with their guns beside them and pipes in their mouths. The events of the day were discussed, offenses were judged, and the next day's route selected. Few "crimes" came before this group because the Métis, impatient of laws and other restraints of civilization, accepted the individual responsibility which such an attitude required if their society was to survive. "They cherish freedom," commented Ross, "as they cherish life." He was struck by their unselfishness and general regard for the welfare of the group.

Difficulty in discovering a buffalo herd or delays caused by straying of animals or accidents on the trail were numerous and often serious. The 1840 hunt took nine days to make one hundred and fifty miles and by the time the buffalo were located the adults were weak and the children crying from hunger.

When the herd was found at last the hunt was marshaled with great speed and efficiency. The captains assembled the hunters—in the first 1840 chase there were four hundred of them—the priest blessed the venture, and the women emptied the carts and prepared to follow for the meat. The chief surveyed the herd, a mile and a half away, through a telescope, carefully examined the intervening ground, and at last, with a cry of "Ho! Ho!" and a sweep of his arm, gave the signal. He was an old man on a gentle horse, and custom forbade any rider to pass him until the buffalo took flight and the actual killing run started. The horses were held at first to a slow trot; as they fought for their heads they were permitted to canter, and when the herd broke they started on a dead run; now it was every man for himself.

The ground trembled as with an earthquake and a canopy of dust darkened the sky. The Métis plunged into the herd. The women and children, hurrying on with the carts, could see nothing, but they listened impatiently for gunfire and cried with joy as they heard it continue for a long time and fade into the distance—a big herd, food for everyone.

The ground was bad and Ross counted twenty-three horses

and riders sprawled on the plain. There were no serious casualties this time, however; three hunters were wounded, one
horse was killed by a buffalo bull and two others disabled.
That night the women brought 1,375 buffalo tongues into
camp. For the benefit of the needy, families which had no
hunter, the riders made "free runs" through the herd.

Butchering was swift and skillful. Back in camp with the
meat, the women cut it into slabs a quarter-inch thick, two
feet wide and four feet long, and hung the strips on racks of
poles. In a couple of days, given good sun, the meat was
dried. It was then baled and tied with buffalo sinew. When
pemmican was to be made some of the strips of dried meat
were placed on a hide or canvas cart cover, flailed with
sticks until shredded, and thoroughly mixed with hot tallow
or buffalo fat in large kettles. Marrow fat and berries, if
available, were sometimes added, and the mixture was
poured hot into bags of buffalo hide holding a hundred
pounds, compressed as it cooled, and the bags sewn shut.
After cooling completely the pemmican was so hard that a
sharp blow was necessary to break off a fragment. It was
eaten cold or used with vegetables or roots in a stew.

Properly cared for in a cool, airy place, pemmican kept
for years. With berries it was a tasty dish; without them it
was dull in flavor and unappetizing in appearance, but nutritious—a pound of it was equal in food value to four pounds
of fresh meat. It was the staple food not only for the Plains
hunters and the men of the cart brigades but also for the
trappers of the North, who were supplied by the annual "outfits" sent from Fort Garry; a modern product much like it
was used by Arctic troops in World War II.

By August the hunters were back at Red River, with less
than a month to rest up, celebrate, and prepare for the second expedition. The 1840 hunt described by Ross started
badly but ended triumphantly: the adventurers had eaten

well after the herds were once found, had kept their equipment in repair, had obtained all the hides and other products they needed for their households, and still had brought
back a full load—nine hundred pounds—for every cart, a
total of 1,089,000 pounds of meat. This was two hundred
pounds for every man, woman and child then living in the
Red River settlement and there was dancing and feasting
when the carts came home. Sales of meat and robes to the
Hudson's Bay Company brought 1,200 pounds sterling—considerably more than all of the properly industrious farmers
got that season for all of their produce. And everybody had
had a wonderful time.

A PLACE CALLED BATOCHE

One day in the spring of 1870 thirty or forty Métis families
set out from Red River on a hunt from which they did not
intend to return. The Provisional Government still ruled at
Fort Garry, but it had submitted to Canada; as surely as the
wolf pack trailed the wounded buffalo, the whites would take
over Manitoba and the Métis way of life there was finished.
But there were other grassy, well-watered valleys in the West.

A few of the wanderers settled on Milk River in Montana,
a few on Spring Creek; but most of them chose a spot on
the South Saskatchewan River between the present cities of
Saskatoon and Prince Albert. This portion of the valley had
many groves of aspen and poplar and had long been a favorite shelter for buffalo; some even wintered there. Métis
hunters had established semipermanent camps in the area in
1868 and their leader, Gabriel Dumont, sang the praises of
the region when he visited Red River the following year.

Father Julien Moulin, an Oblate priest, came to minister
to the newcomers in 1870, but since no permanent mission
had been established he left the next spring. A few months
later Father Alexis André, who had served in Pembina and

St. Joseph and was well known to the Métis, joined them for the hunt. In 1873 he persuaded the bishop, with some difficulty, to establish a mission, and in 1874 it was built. Father André named it St. Laurent.

The Métis community straggled untidily along the shores of the South Saskatchewan for several miles. At first it bore the name of the mission at its northern limit, St. Laurent. When another church was built six miles south, the village of St. Antoine de Padua was born, but finally the district took the name—actually the nickname—of the builder of its most pretentious establishment. He was Xavier Letendre, "called Batoche," a prosperous trader. His big store and his two-and-a-half-story gabled house with columned veranda were the marvel of the prairies. Soon the village huddled on the riverbank below the Church of St. Anthony became known as Batoche.

When Batoche came into being in 1870 its leading citizen, Gabriel Dumont, was only thirty-two, but his word was law throughout the Saskatchewan country. Even his father, Isidore, and his uncle, who were nominally the elders of the community, deferred to his judgment.

Gabriel was a man of medium height, with heavy shoulders and head but the trim torso of a horseman, and with an open and kindly, almost childishly innocent face. Leadership came naturally to him: his father and uncle had negotiated a Métis peace pact with the Sioux, something no one had been able to do before. And he was the sort of man about whom legends grew. Before he was ten he had his first gun, a gift from his uncle as reward for a display of courage. Gabriel and his brother, busy at an assigned task of building a smudge fire to discourage mosquitoes, heard a roar which Gabriel took to be the sound of an approaching band of Sioux. He ran to his father and demanded a gun with which he could help defend the camp. The noise was that of a buffalo herd but Gabriel got the gun. Already a skilled bowman, he soon became one of the best marksmen in the camp and in his maturity was for a short time a professional sharpshooter.

At twenty-five he was chief of the hunt, with about three hundred followers from two or three consolidated camps. He had acquired—no one knew how, because few even among the Indians could still do it—the age-old trick of "calling" buffalo, and could lure as many as a dozen into a trap. His ingenuity on the trail, his skills (he was the camp "doctor," an expert horsebreaker, and, unlike most Métis, a swimmer), but above all his generosity, made him the "prince of the prairies." He spoke several Indian tongues and French, but he could not read or write, could not speak English and understood it very little.

When a member of his gang on a road job for which Gabriel had contracted became a father, Gabriel gave him a horse and cart and filled the cart with meat. When this job was finished, Gabriel bought from his own pay two sacks of food and gave them to the priest for distribution to the elderly and needy of the parish. On the hunt he habitually made a "free run" and donated eight or ten buffalo to the poorer families in his camp.

But as a chief he was a severe disciplinarian who brooked no violation of the code and frowned even on mischief. The tongue-lashing he gave some youths for interfering with a herd became famous among his people, and he once administered a bad beating to an Indian and Métis who had "gone before" on the hunt. On another occasion, by fining and seizing the equipment of a Hudson's Bay Company hunter who had tried to get a head start on the Batoche brigade, he precipitated an incident which brought the Mounties hurrying to the scene and inspired scareheads about "rebellion" in the Canadian press.

The trouble began when Lawrence Clarke, the company

factor at Fort Carlton, complained to the Governor of Manitoba and the Northwest in July, 1875, that Gabriel and his Métis had enacted laws "of a most tyrannical nature" and were punishing violators of these laws "with criminal severity." But he omitted the background. Nearly two years before Father André had inspired the organization of local government and the Métis had adopted a simple code of laws, fixing penalties for theft, slander, seduction and starting prairie fires, establishing free ferry service for churchgoers, and making a few other regulations. Gabriel was chosen "president," and the group expressly said it had no intention of setting itself up as an independent state.

In 1875, during Gabriel's second term of leadership, a small tax was levied to support a school and a new code written for the hunt. In June Gabriel arrested, with forty "soldiers," a group of hunters who had violated this code and confiscated their horses and carts. The property he later returned but the leader of the party, who had been supplied by the Hudson's Bay Company, he fined twenty-five dollars. This man's complaint, relayed by Clarke, brought fifty Mounties.

The police reported that the trouble had been grossly exaggerated by Clarke, that Gabriel and his people were loyal and law-abiding, and that regulations such as those drawn by the Métis "are absolutely necessary on the prairie." And the Secretary of State for Colonies in London approved. "It would be difficult," he said, "to take strong exception to the acts of a community which appears to have honestly endeavoured to maintain order by the best means in its power."

This incident was the first occurrence to call official attention to the fact that there was an important new Métis community, then called St. Laurent, on the South Saskatchewan. The Chief, Gabriel Dumont, was said to have met Louis Riel for the first time at Fort Garry in 1869; Gabriel had shown little interest in the Red River troubles but had told

Riel that it would be a mistake to let the Canadians enter the country.

At the place called Batoche, a tiny village which still exists but is accessible only over a primitive prairie trail, the Nation of the Métis which Louis Riel created on Red River established its new capital; and here it made its last stand.

PART FIVE

Path of Providence

CHAPTER XVI

The Psalms of David

THE HEART IS READY

BUT for the pusillanimity of Catholic liberalism, said the implacable Ultramontanes of Montreal, Manitoba could have been saved for French Catholicism and Riel and his colleagues would have been speedily amnestied. The time had come for militant propagation of the faith, for revival of the seventeenth-century Jesuit dream of a Roman Catholic continent. Catholic liberalism had plunged into a stinking pit and now floundered in the muck of heresy: it acknowledged the temporal authority of a Protestant state; it even accepted freedom of choice in religion.

Modern ultramontanism—literally "beyond the mountains to Rome"—developed in Europe early in the nineteenth century under Jesuit auspices. It aimed at restoration of the medieval Catholic spirit and union of Church and State, with the political power subordinate. Protestantism, it held, was not a religion and had no rights; a true Catholic could not forsake the dogma of intolerance. The laws of the Church were universal, binding even upon heretics. No one, Catho-

lic, Protestant or unbeliever, had the right to read a pro-
scribed book. No judge or Parliament could annul a marriage, and children of a second union were illegitimate regardless of the religion of their parents. Priests had the right
and duty to designate favored political candidates in pre-
election sermons, and to determine subsequently in the confessional if Catholic voters had obeyed their orders.

This authoritarian movement, aimed frankly at the sup-
pression of all freedom of thought, made little headway in
Canada until about 1870. In 1872 Bishop Ignace Bourget of
Montreal committed himself to leadership of the "New
School"—ultramontanism—by incorporating its principles in
a *Circulaire* distributed to his clergy. In this he acted in flat
defiance of the "Liberal" Archbishop of Quebec, and in
opposition to the well-established Sulpician Society and the
Recollets (Franciscans); but he was strongly supported by the
Jesuit Order and the Congregation of Oblates, the most pow-
erful missionary groups.

Le Nouveau Monde, a Montreal newspaper, became the
leading ultramontane organ, and its proprietor, Senator Al-
phonse Desjardins, soon was recognized as the movement's
political spokesman.

Through Desjardins, long a loyal friend, Louis Riel of the
Métis was caught up in the ultramontane crusade. It was
based upon esoteric political and theological concepts which
he never clearly understood, and his involvement may have
helped to upset the precarious balance of his mind and to
encourage his fantastic religious ventures, a decade later, in
the little church of Batoche, two thousand miles from Montreal. About all Louis Riel got out of ultramontanism was
hero-worship for its leader, Bishop (later Archbishop)
Bourget, and there was a fine irony in the fact that he ultimately attempted to set up this prelate, who preached sub-
servience to the Vatican in all things, as superior to the Pope.

Senator Desjardins lived in Terrebonne, which also was

the home of Mme. Joseph Masson, whose generosity had made possible Riel's education, and whose son, L. F. R. Masson, may also have helped to draw Riel into the ultramontane orbit. Masson was educated in Jesuit centers of the movement before he became a lawyer, politician and writer; he was eleven years older than Louis and may have had considerable influence on him. Riel visited these friends on his return to Canada from Plattsburg in January, 1874. He was then a fugitive from Manitoba's murder warrant; before he slipped away to Ottawa to sign the register of the House he was hidden in Desjardins's home.

The decree of expulsion from Parliament in the spring of 1874 launched the embittered young leader of the Métis on two years of distracted wandering across half of the continent.

First he headed west, despite the risk he ran of being kidnaped and brought within the jurisdiction of Manitoba's vengeful court. While the Parliamentary inquiry into Métis grievances and the amnesty was under way in Ottawa, Riel was hidden in St. Paul and St. Joseph, where he remained for several months. His countrymen came secretly to report on developments at Red River, most of them bad. Lépine was in jail, awaiting trial for the "murder" of Scott; Nault and others had been indicted. The City of Winnipeg had been incorporated; it boasted two thousand people and a mayor—Francis Evans Cornish, an Ontario barrister, bitter enemy of Riel and originator of the plot which had resulted in his indictment with Lépine. Though grasshoppers had ruined two years' crops, Anglo-Saxon immigrants were crowding into Manitoba. The buffalo had disappeared and more Métis had left to seek new homes on the Saskatchewan or Montana prairies.

In September Riel returned sadly to Montreal, where he remained until midwinter. The ultramontane struggle was at its height and hands schooled for the gentle gesture of bene-

diction were now clenched fists. Bishop Bourget's faction had
launched a "reign of terror" against freedom of discussion
and had beaten most of the press of the province to its knees.
Some organs of Catholic liberalism had been destroyed.
L'Institut Canadien, a scientific and literary society, was
being methodically wrecked because it had admitted Protestants to membership and had countenanced "heretical" discussion. Joseph Guibord, a Catholic member of this group,
was denied burial in consecrated ground; when the *Institut*
had this decree set aside by court action later, the funeral
cortège was stoned by a mob and the vindictive Bourget
"deconsecrated" Guibord's grave by personal interdict. The
confessional was freely used to "convert" or suppress journals
hostile to the movement; wives of their readers were refused
absolution until they persuaded their husbands to cancel
their subscriptions. On the other hand *Le Nouveau Monde*
was praised from the pulpit and priests became virtually its
circulation agents. Dominated by Bourget, its writers did
not hesitate to attack even the archbishop.

Riel, convinced, reasonably enough, that the persecution
he had suffered had been inspired by his religion and his
political principles, was strongly attracted to the new "holy
war," and some of the Ultramontanes probably saw him as
a valuable ally. He now began to dream of a new French
Catholic state in the West. His friend, Father Barnabé of
Keeseville, appears to have shared much of Louis's enthusiasm; he was an Oblate, probably sympathetic to the
"New School." The Saskatchewan country, where Catholic
Métis and Indians were in the majority, was a possibility,
Riel thought; or perhaps even Dakota or Montana Territories, where the Métis if skillfully organized might hold the
balance of political power. And he had not yet lost hope of
freeing his beloved Manitoba from political domination by
the Canadian element. So, financed by Montreal friends and
sympathizers, he took to the road again.

Louis was in his element now, for he loved political intrigue and religious discourse above anything in life. Considering his exalted mood, it is not surprising that a vision was forthcoming, an experience which changed his life and in which he believed implicitly to the end of his days. The miracle occurred on December 18, on a hilltop. Later on, he described it:

. . . The same spirit who showed himself to Moses in the midst of fire and cloud appeared to me in the same manner. I was stupefied; I was confused. He said to me, "Rise up, Louis *David* Riel. You have a mission to fulfill." Stretching out my arms and bending my head, I received this heavenly messenger.

From this day he identified himself with the King of Jerusalem and ever afterward signed his name Louis David Riel. His Métis intimates said that to the usual prayers with which their priests had familiarized them Louis added others they had never heard; but the Métis had had no opportunity to study the psalms of David. It is not surprising that in the mind of the God-intoxicated Riel the words of the great poet of Israel rang like bells:

He delivered me from my most mighty enemy, and from them that hated me; for they were too strong for me. . . .
He teacheth my hands to war: and maketh my arms like a bow of brass. . . .
I will pursue after my enemies and crush them: and will not return again till I consume them.
I will consume them and break them in pieces, so that they shall not rise: they shall fall under my feet.
Thou hast girded me with strength to battle: thou hast made them that resisted me to bow under me. . . .
Thou wilt save me from the contradictions of my people: thou wilt keep me to be the head of the Gentiles: the people which I know not, shall serve me.

"My heart is ready, O God, my heart is ready," Louis sang with David. And to his subsequent written record of the

vision he added a few words which betrayed the development
of Messianic delusions. A lifetime might not suffice to complete his mission. Some had suspected for a long time that
he had supernatural powers; "Bishop Bourget was the first
to inform me of this favor of the Savior; this learned prelate
wrote to me that I had a mission to fulfill. At first I was
inclined to doubt it, but later on [after the vision] I recognized my error. . . ."

I have worked for men, and with what success the world
already knows. Events are not finished in a few days or a few
hours. A century is but a spoke in the wheel of eternity. I have
obtained practical results, but much more still remains to do.

His education among the Sulpicians had ended just when
he was starting his philosophy course; unfortunately he had
needed its disciplines. Strongly drawn to mysticism, his approach was wholly pietistic and even in this he failed; he
could not submit with serenity to God's will although he
identified it, as invariably he did, with his own interests.

"The keynote of Catholic mysticism," a Church scholar
has said, "is certainly joy; however hard the life, it is always
lived in a joyful spirit." But for Louis there never would be
joy, or even—until the last days of his life—resignation. His
occasional transports were flights from reality, from indecision or fear, not ecstatic communion with the purpose of
learning, and surrendering to, the dictates of God. The
morose young Métis knew just enough about the saints and
martyrs to confuse their self-immolation with his own self-
hypnosis, and rarely has a little learning proved more dangerous.

His "mysticism" was also strongly tinged with magic, with
the "medicine" of generations of Indians and Métis. He believed in signs and portents: a nervous tic, a rumbling in his
stomach, natural phenomena such as an unusual flight of
birds, a new and strange sound—these had significance, and

on them he built "prophecies." In the Indian or Métis mind such things could justly be called manifestations of superstition, though they honored such dreamers, who had "heard the coyote bark"; Riel was uneasily conscious of this and justified his own credulity on the ground that there actually were signs his people could read, sounds they could hear, which were too slight for detection by the senses of white men —and this was true.

To some extent, too, certain phenomena had valid meanings for the Indian or Métis hunter, instinct-keen as a prairie wolf, which the white man would never learn. But they were simple meanings, having to do with tomorrow's weather, or where a herd was grazing, or the fact that a war party had taken to the trail. Louis tried to read into them the divine auguries he had now come to expect, and never realized that though the Métis might be closer to Nature than the white man he was no closer to God.

In this as in everything else his thinking epitomized the struggle which went on constantly within him and in the souls of his people. He sought to be half medicine man, half Christian mystic, turning to God without ever wholly losing sight of Manito. He failed—but not in the worshipful eyes of the Métis.

Louis hurried to Keeseville to describe his supernatural experience to Father Barnabé. He wrote in January, 1875, to the Archbishop of Quebec, to thank him and his clergy for the sympathy they had shown in "my religious and national struggles." Then he went to Woonsocket, Rhode Island, to visit an aunt and address the French population. This was in February, and in his speech Louis anticipated the amnesty which was granted him two months later; it would come, he said, as a result of the efforts of French Canadians in Quebec, in the United States, and above all those of the Hon. J. A. Chapleau, the Quebec politician. (A decade later this same

Chapleau would help to send Riel to the gallows and his brother, the sheriff in a remote prairie capital, would supervise the execution!)

Woonsocket was predominantly French, peopled by natives of Quebec and Three Rivers who had been drawn into its textile industry. Wherever there were French colonies, old school friends, sympathetic priests or anyone at all who would listen, Riel took his message: freedom for the persecuted Métis, westward extension of French culture and the French faith. Manitoba had been all but lost, but if the people of Quebec who since 1850 had streamed by the thousands to the textile towns of the United States would repatriate themselves, the Northwest still could be saved. And unless a bulwark of French Catholicism could be erected somewhere soon (said the Ultramontanes) its adherents would be doomed forever to the status of a neglected and oppressed minority.

Come home, Louis pleaded; come West. He went from Woonsocket to Suncook, New Hampshire, and Nashua; on to Worcester, Massachusetts, and to Albany. Late in October he arrived in Washington to see a compatriot, Edmond Mallet, who may have been the best friend he ever had.

THE MANIA OF AMBITION

Maj. Edmond Mallet, born in Montreal, had come to the United States with his parents when he was four. He had won a commission, and a citation for bravery, in the Civil War. When Riel first visited him in Washington he was employed as a Treasury clerk; later he was to become an agent and inspector for the Indian Bureau. He was a prominent Catholic layman, associated with the Oblate priests in welfare work among French Canadians. His zeal and effectiveness in laboring for his compatriots had already established him as their "unofficial ambassador" and some years later he was elected president of their national organization.

Mallet welcomed the hero of the Métis. They were almost

the same age—Louis thirty-one, Mallet about a year older—
and Riel's romantic story appealed to the young soldier,
bored in his Government job. He knew the ropes in Washington and arranged interviews for his guest with people
who could help the Métis cause. Riel met President Grant;
he would have liked an appointment to the Indian Bureau
but didn't get it. He had a talk with Senator Oliver P. Morton, the Indiana statesman and a powerful force in the Republican Party, to whom he presented a plan for taking
Manitoba away from the Dominion. But Louis was nervous
and incoherent and Morton did not react favorably. A day
or so later the disappointed crusader wrote to apologize
because his difficulty with English had handicapped his
presentation.

After a month or so Mallet realized that his visitor's ideas
and actions were becoming irrational. Louis would vanish
for days and return in a state of exaltation, which would
yield suddenly to fits of depression. He talked incessantly of
his mission and flew into violent rages if its feasibility were
challenged. Normally gentle and considerate, he would brook
no argument when he expounded his religious and political
notions, and Mallet found them to be fantastic.

When Louis arrived in Washington he had brought about
a thousand dollars—the gift, Mallet understood, of "a wealthy
Canadian." His friend discovered to his dismay that Riel had
given almost all of the money, bit by bit, to a blind Italian
beggar.

At last Mallet was convinced that Louis was out of his
mind. There had been signs and sounds, divinely inspired,
Louis said: he now knew that he was to die for the Métis. He
was ready for martyrdom, but—another sudden savage change
of mood—before it occurred he would destroy the enemies of
God. David had foretold their fate: "I shall beat them as
small as the dust of the earth: I shall crush them and spread
them abroad like the mire of the streets."

On December 8 Louis interrupted mass in St. Patrick's Cathedral in the capital by bursting into hysterical laughter which he vainly attempted to smother with his handkerchief, and he was hastily removed by friends to Mallet's home. His host, who was married and the father of small children, could no longer undertake his care. He took counsel with the clergy, borrowed some money from a priest, and accompanied Riel to Worcester. There he was placed in the charge of a mutual friend of Mallet and Riel, Father Jean Baptiste Primeau, the rector of the Catholic church.

After only eight days Father Primeau found the task also beyond his capacities and, with a guard, took Louis to Suncook. He wrote to Mallet that he had left Riel there with a friend, a M. Picher, whom Louis had known in Manitoba; alas, he said, Louis's "fixed ideas" had taken root to such an extent that he now believed Mallet and Primeau had failed him. In Primeau's opinion only a miracle could now restore him to normality; "very likely his role is finished."

In January, 1876, Louis was taken to Keeseville, but there was no improvement in his condition and late that month Father Barnabé sent for his uncle, John Lee of Montreal, who took him back to Canada in February. On March 6 Louis was decoyed into St. Jean de Dieu asylum at Longue Pointe and kept there by force until he could be committed, under the name "Louis David." In May he was moved again, apparently because of crowded conditions at Longue Pointe, to Beauport asylum near Quebec. There he was to remain, save for one or two unexplained "paroles" for very brief periods, until January, 1878.

At Beauport he was registered under the name of La-Rochelle. The aliases probably were employed because he was technically violating the decree of banishment from Canada for five years which accompanied the amnesty proclamation of 1875.

Controversy over Louis Riel's sanity has plagued historians for fifty years. Riel himself and the more articulate and far-seeing among his Métis followers were determined that the stain of lunacy should not dim the luster of his achievements or the pride of his "New Nation," but more realistic friends in French Canada, to save his life, sought to prove him insane. Sir John A. Macdonald and his Government, whose fate was to hang upon the issue, had to insist that the Messiah of the Métis—whom they heartily despised—was not only mentally sound but virtually a genius. And the experts, as usual, disagreed.

Riel's commitment to Longue Pointe was signed by Chapleau, then Quebec Provincial Secretary. Years later, when he was Secretary of State in the Dominion cabinet and fighting for the life of the regime in some of the most acrimonious Parliamentary debates on record, he said he had known when he signed the commitment order that Riel was shamming insanity. He had consented to the incarceration, Chapleau claimed, to prevent Riel's assassination by his enemies. This implausible tale was supported to a degree by statements from two doctors, one of whom visited Longue Pointe regularly as a staff consultant and the other a Montreal friend of Riel: they had observed him frequently and believed him to be sane.

But the two best-qualified alienists drawn into the case, Dr. François Roy and Dr. Daniel Clark, both subsequently testified that Riel had lost his mind.

A modern psychiatrist, studying the case record and Riel's own writings (unfortunately only Clark among his contemporary examiners seems to have read them), would probably find him insane. He showed symptoms of paranoid schizophrenia: grandiose illusions, bound together to form a sometimes plausible, sometimes incredible, delusional pattern; an egocentric attitude and spells of morbid introspec-

tion; excitability when the fixed idea was challenged; a
sense of persecution, and the conviction that since so many
enemies pursued him he had a divine mission. The com-
pulsions which had plagued the Métis for generations, which
had made potential schizophrenics of a whole race, ripped
his mind apart.

Dr. Roy and Dr. Clark called it "megalomania, the mania
of ambition." Its onset is slow and it is subject to occasional
remission, but its victims rarely recover completely; on the
other hand they rarely suffer complete mental disintegration.
Riel appeared to be normal most of the time he was confined,
and visitors, even physicians, who did not draw him into
discussions of religion or politics went away convinced he
was hiding out or faking. But there were other times when
he was so violent as to require physical restraint.

Most of his days were spent brooding upon religion and
the "liberation" of the Métis. He had written several times
in 1875 to Bishop Bourget and had received replies to which
he attached great significance. His use of these letters among
the credulous Métis, who construed the episcopal signature
and seal as virtually holy symbols in themselves, subsequently
bolstered his position as a prophet among them.

Bourget had written him in July that a letter recently
received from Louis was "proof to me that you are motivated
by excellent sentiments and at the same time tormented
internally by an impulse or I do not know what, which
causes you to find duty in the allegiance in which you
walk. . . ."

I have the intimate conviction that you will receive here below
and sooner than you expect the recompense for those interior
sacrifices, which are a thousand times more difficult than the
sacrifice of material and visible things.

But God, who has always directed and assisted you to the
present hour, will not abandon you in the strength of your

prayers, because He has given you a mission which you must accomplish in all points.

Only God's grace could preserve Louis in the course mapped out for him, Bourget continued. The bishop had prayed that God would help him persevere to the end; "may your faith be more and more alive and animated in order that you may never yield before difficulties which the present life necessarily offers in whatever situation one finds oneself."

The letter closed with a caution:

Take care of your health and commit yourself to the direction of your doctor. Confide in Divine Providence and believe that nothing happens in this lower sphere without God's order or permission. Keep yourself ready for all eventualities by preserving unalterable calm.

In January Bourget had written again, to acknowledge letters Riel had written from Washington and Suncook. The prelate thanked him for "the good sentiments which, on all occasions, you do not fail to express profusely." He was praying that God would not abandon Riel and would "direct you in all your undertakings so that you may not depart from the way marked out for you by Divine Providence, for your own greater good and that of your land and your people. . . . May you be blessed by God and men, and may you be patient in your troubles."

The references to his mission and to his life path as mapped out by Providence, and the blessing at the end of the letters—standard practice with the clergy—were seized upon by Louis as evidence of episcopal endorsement of his religious and political pretensions. The letters became his most treasured possessions, carried on his person for the rest of his life; they were some of the most unfortunate pieces of correspondence ever to figure in North America's history.

EVELINA

Riel was released from Beauport, certified as cured, in January, 1878. He hurried to Keeseville, and there he spent much of the next year. His interest in the quiet little sawmill town on the Ausable River was easily explained. There, and in the home of his loyal friend the priest, for the first time in his life Louis Riel had fallen in love.

The girl was Evelina, the young sister of Father Barnabé. She was in her late twenties—pious, affectionate, a tall quiet girl, blonde and blue-eyed. She played the organ in her brother's church. For a short time the tortured soul of the wanderer found peace with her. They strolled through the streets and surrounding woods, or sat in the priest's little garden. Louis told her of his mission. "Enemies" had induced his friends to put him in the hospital, but the course mapped out by God still lay before him. Still, he now knew he must exercise more restraint in his speech; and perhaps the mission was not, after all, the only important thing in life.

Correspondence of this period seems to provide evidence of a somewhat pathetic attempt by Louis to establish himself economically so he could settle down like other men and, presumably, marry Evelina. It is significant, and consonant with a diagnosis of paranoid schizophrenia, that he had never before loved a woman, much less considered marriage; withdrawn, narcissistic, he had been sufficient unto himself. Now, immediately after his release from the asylum, he sped to her and for a short time sought fruitlessly to change the pattern of his life, to turn aside from the "path of Providence" which he suspected led to martyrdom.

He wrote to Archbishop Taché at St. Boniface, seeking to sell any property he might have acquired under the Métis grant—forgetting, apparently, that he had conveyed his rights to his mother. He wanted, he said, to go to Nebraska and settle down.

But it became apparent that he had no talents which would enable him to fit into the urban economy of the East. No one had a job for him. Barnabé arranged to accompany him to New York, where a friend in the clergy would help him to get work, the priest said, "in the best offices in the city." But the trip was postponed several times and may never have been made at all. Riel was reduced to "visiting" again; wherever he stopped there would be a letter from Barnabé or some other friend assuring him that something would turn up.

In October Barnabé reported to Mallet that their friend, though physically rather unwell due to fatigue, was perfectly sound again mentally; one would never know his mind had failed. Yet there was no work, and Louis finally decided that he would have to go back where he belonged, back to the frontier. Barnabé, generous friend though he was, perhaps was not unrelieved to be rid of the burden. He was sure, he told Louis, and all those to whom he had talked were sure, "there will be a place for you in the West." But Riel could not go, as had so many others, as a penniless, purposeless fortune-seeker. There was, after all, the mission. Louis's interest in it now revived, and he was encouraged by Barnabé and others.

John Ireland, coadjutor bishop of St. Paul and one of the outstanding Catholic prelates of American history, was organizing his Catholic Colonization Bureau to provide homes in the West for European immigrants whose distress in the crowded industrial centers had disturbed him. Gen. Thomas Francis Meagher, en route in 1865 to Montana to become the Territory's acting governor, had urged Ireland to make Montana Catholic, and had given a speech in St. Paul about it. Meagher had now been dead for more than ten years but the idea survived. Father Barnabé wrote to Bishop Ireland, commending Riel as ideally suited by experience and ambition to become a leader in this movement.

In February, 1879, Louis was in St. Paul. The bishop received him cordially, but nothing came of it. The prelate, thoroughly familiar with Red River history, may have had misgivings about sponsoring the mercurial hero of the Métis even before he heard Riel expound the ideas which a priest in Nashua had found "so extravagant I interrupted his dissertation by proposing for him a game of draughts."

"I have many occasions to think about you," Evelina wrote, after receiving three letters in rapid succession from her lover. "Last spring I so often saw you working around the house, either helping M. Content or alone; and this year you are very far away from us. . . ."

. . . But in thought we are always near you. M. Content has finished the seeding; today he is planting trees in the flower garden.

The air smells sweetly of spring. Beautiful Nature, which quickens to life at first breath, fills me with joy and revives me. I often go and sit under the lilacs, which are about to bloom. I hasten to gather a few blossoms to give you. I am carried back to that time when we were so happy, both of us seated on the same bench.

So you are pursuing your plan of going to spend the summer on the prairies. That is good; go, and good luck! I don't want it to rain pins and needles, but indeed rather a dew of heavenly blessings which will guide you surely to your goal and make the Indians willing to agree to all your plans. I am pleased that your dear friend M. Lépine is going with you.

Dear Louis, you tell me in your letter that you are arranging everything to come and get me soon, but I suppose that would not be before your advance, if God wills that you should succeed. I tell you plainly that if you came to get me I should only be a hindrance to you; however, it's no good telling you so and I am sure of it, too; you will come for me so that we may have a home of our own; that is what you mean in saying that.

I am much afraid that you will be sorry for your choice. It

seems to me that I do not possess the qualities that you expect to find in a wife. I am a humble and not very brave woman, and I shall not be suited to the greatness of position that I should have to occupy if you are successful. Pray that God will put into my heart all the virtues I need in order to be a perfect Christian and a worthy helpmate!

I have just come from praying at Mary's altar in the church. Her altar is nicely decorated; we have surrounded it with our house bouquets. She is beautiful, Mary amidst all that foliage. . . .

Evelina enclosed a pressed blossom of lilac, asked Louis to write often, and signed the letter "your affectionate little sister, Evelina."

Evelina's humility was probably genuine, but there must have been other misgivings about following her starstruck lover into the wilderness. The French girl had been lovingly, decorously reared where spring was soft and sweet-smelling, amid lilacs and organ music and quiet altars on which Mary rested serene and snug in a bower of blooms. But there had been nothing for Louis in that gentle place. He had re-dedicated himself to struggle in the dry and lonely and bitter land where spring was short-lived and often savage, so flowers dared not thrust their heads far above the thin tough sod; where the smells were rank with blood and sweat, whiskey and buckskin tipi-tanned; where an apprehensive Virgin drew her robes more tightly about her as the blizzard and the displaced gods beat at the whitewashed logs of her bleak chapel.

At the time Evelina wrote, though obviously she had not yet learned of it, fate already had intervened in the romance. Her brother was fatally infected with tuberculosis.

Louis was barely able to survive in the West and could not have sent for Evelina, or paid his way back to her; and she probably would not have left her dying brother and aged mother. They never met again.

In 1883 Father Barnabé died. Evelina and her mother took
the body to their old home, L'Assomption, Quebec, and remained in Canada. There evidently was some further correspondence, for Louis learned promptly of the priest's
death. He was then in Montana, and he wrote a little com-
memorative poem. Fabien's charity, the poem said, blazed
like candles on his bier, and his great soul would live forever; Louis asked God to reward the faithful curé for his
goodness to an unhappy wanderer.

CHAPTER XVII

John Brown of
the Half-Breeds

HIGHWAY OF EMPIRE

WHEN returning east to report on his successful mission to the Métis in 1870—a mission accomplished on the snow-packed field of Fort Garry—Donald Smith had met James J. Hill of St. Paul on the Dakota prairie in a blizzard. They talked of Smith's triumph and of the future of Red River: fortunes awaited men with initiative, daring and stamina.

Eight years later they teamed up to buy, from Dutch bondholders, a somewhat ambitiously named railroad, the St. Paul & Pacific, whose tracks at the time reached all the way from St. Paul to Minneapolis. And in 1880 they became associated, with others, in the development of the Canadian Pacific, the world's greatest transportation system.

Jim Hill, the dynamic little St. Paul promoter, had boosted himself from a minor clerkship to wealth and influence as the Red River country's leading freighter, warehouseman and agent. He now promptly renamed his railroad the St. Paul, Minneapolis & Manitoba, and started to build a branch north to the Canadian boundary. This was a venture first suggested years before to St. Paul businessmen by James Wickes Taylor as one means of acquiring British North America for the United States.

Meanwhile Donald Smith busied himself as a lobbyist in Ottawa, and the first track laid on the Canadian system was the Pembina branch, south from Winnipeg to connect with Hill's road. Since the latter ultimately became the Great Northern, two of the major transcontinentals may be said to have started in the Red River Valley.

In 1877 a Red River stern-wheeler owned by Hill, the *Selkirk*, brought the Canadian Pacific Railway's first locomotive, the *Countess of Dufferin*, to Winnipeg from St. Paul, which it had reached by Mississippi steamer. This locomotive still stands in the Manitoba capital as a historical relic.

In December, 1878, the Canadian Pacific and Hill's line were joined at the boundary. As the promoters of the scheme had anticipated, the money rolled in. There had been steamboats on the river since 1859 (the first had been put there, as might have been expected, by the unfailingly enterprising St. Paul Chamber of Commerce), but low water had sometimes laid them up for several seasons, they were slow, and their rates were very high.

Hill's financial associates in the St. Paul railroad company were George Stephen and R. B. Angus of the Bank of Montreal; Hill had met Stephen through the latter's cousin, Donald Smith. In 1880 Stephen, who was personally wealthy in addition to controlling the bank's resources, was persuaded by Sir John A. Macdonald to bring into his group Duncan McIntyre, who controlled some eastern Canadian lines, and to form a syndicate which would undertake to build the Canadian Pacific as a private enterprise.

Hill was born near Guelph, Ontario, in 1838, but he had

become an American citizen. His new loyalties may have been partially responsible for the brevity of his association with the Canadians, but his withdrawal from the syndicate in 1883 was chiefly due to the fact that he did not stand to get the profits he had expected. He was determined that Winnipeg should be the eastern terminus of Canada's new transcontinental; traffic would there be diverted to his line and proceed east from St. Paul over existing American or Canadian roads. This was the proposal James Wickes Taylor had made to the St. Paul Chamber in 1859.

Economically, Hill's (or Taylor's) argument was sound: the bleak Laurentian Plateau north of Lake Superior never could produce enough to support a railroad, and construction there would be ruinously expensive. But the Canadian Pacific was to be the new Northwest Passage, the lifeline of Britain; Macdonald and its other political sponsors insisted that it must be "an Imperial highway across the continent of America entirely on British soil." They had not forgotten that the real motivation of Taylor's proposal, which Hill now sought to sell to Ottawa, had been annexationist: by making western Canada dependent upon St. Paul for transportation, the Americans figured, that vast undeveloped section of the Dominion sooner or later would be forced to join the United States.

When it became apparent that the Lake Superior line was going to be built despite all he could do to prevent it, Hill quit the Canadian Pacific and channeled his great energies into creation of a rival transcontinental, the Great Northern Railroad, using his St. Paul, Minneapolis & Manitoba as a nucleus. The border country, and especially the rich agricultural area of Red River and the mining districts of British Columbia, became the battleground in a railroad war in which no quarter was given or asked. The two lines raced west, pausing only for thrust and counterthrust of branches to the international boundary to tap the resources of the narrow strip separating their main routes.

Damning Hill's northward-reaching spur lines as "hungry hounds ready to jump," the Canadian Pacific's great engineer, William C. Van Horne (an American whom Hill had hired for the C.P.R.), built his railroad as close to the boundary as he could. This was fortunate for Canada, for when Louis Riel and his people once more challenged the Dominion the still unfinished steel lifeline of empire stabbed straight into the heart of the Métis nation and won for Canada the War for the West.

When Louis returned in 1879 to live in the West he found that much had changed on Red River. The steamboats were through, with the coming of steel; and so, of course, were the Red River carts. The prosperous freight business which had supported many Métis families for three decades died overnight. The buffalo were gone, making their last stand in Saskatchewan or Montana. The meager supply of timber was exhausted. The railroad might be bringing prosperity to Red River, but not for Métis.

Many of his people had given up hope of survival in competitive and discriminatory white society and had "reverted," slipping away to Turtle Mountain or other Indian settlements. Some were pushing farther west, driven by desperate instinct; actually they had little hope that the feeble Métis could withstand white numbers and military power which had wiped out, in the last three years, the much stronger nations of their Indian cousins.

Louis stopped for a time at his old headquarters, St. Joseph, Dakota Territory. White encroachment or Métis whim had caused his people to move, six years before, to a new site nine miles east of the original one. It was not as pretty as the first, which rested at the foot of Pembina Mountain. Nor was it as busy. Few hunts began at St. Joe now, and there were not many hunters. (The first St. Joe, one of North Dakota's oldest settlements, is now the flourishing farmers' town of Walhalla; the second is a tiny hamlet called Leroy, with a few Métis families still in residence.)

But it was good to get back. Even if one's friends were poor, in a Métis village one was always welcome, and as in an Indian camp, the visitor would always be housed and fed. There was still "Red River salmon"—catfish—and bread and strong black tea; there were delicious berry puddings and pies. The bread wasn't very good—a coarse, dirty, blackish loaf baked from local flour; but one could fall back on *galettes*, flat fried dough cakes which the whites called bannocks. When the host could afford it there was the pleasant custom, shared by Métis and white, of drinking port after dinner until bedtime; it helped to keep one warm. Unfortunately the prized *boueau*—literally "slop" or "filth"— was now hard to get. It was a stew of buffalo pemmican and potatoes, and probably got its name from the fact that careless cooks often left some buffalo hair in the pot.

And there still were parties, best of all the weddings. After the priest had finished the ceremony, everyone kissed the bride; failure to do so was a grave insult to her and to her fortunate spouse. A feast followed at her home. The bride, enthroned in a chair (a rare object in St. Joe), crossed her feet primly and attempted to prevent the theft of one of her moccasins by the rowdy young bachelors; if she lost one the bridegroom had to pay a forfeit to recover it and the money thus acquired was promptly spent on liquor for the party, just in case the host had failed to provide enough.

The feast table at parties was reserved for men; women sat on the floor around the walls or in chattering clusters in the corners. The food was prepared in the fireplace, which was built of logs set erect and plastered with mud. (The Métis fire was built tipi-fashion, the long sticks of firewood interlaced in a cone—a faster, hotter blaze than the white man's "laid" fire, with its logs flat on the andirons.) A pan of tallow on the hearth, with a cotton rag for wick, often served as the only light.

After some of the feast had been consumed the dancing began, with a Métis fiddler supplying the music—the Red River jig, the "Pair o' Fours," the "Reel o' Cats," and traditional French steps centuries old. Save for intervals for more eating and drinking the dancing continued all night and sometimes all of the following day.

As in Indian dancing it was difficult for a white observer to determine when one dance stopped and another began, or on what signal the dancers left the floor. New groups were continually streaming into the dance area to replace exhausted friends. The youngest and most enthusiastic leaped high into the air and executed intricate figures; the Métis braves pounded their heels on the floor and shouted "Ho! Ho!", signal for the ride through the buffalo herd, or "Hiah! Hiah!", the universal *alerte* of the Plains Indians. Through all the clamor the mad cry of the fiddle knifed, stepping up the tempo of the dance. The solemn-faced Métis babies, silent and unafraid, gazed at the huge shifting shadows on the walls which chased each other faster and faster as the maniac fiddle sobbed and shrieked.

Everyone dressed in his best. For Louis, the distinguished visitor, this meant the black trousers, frock coat, white shirt and black tie which he affected; but the other men ran more to color. They favored buff buckskin trousers, elaborately decorated with Métis designs adapted from the Cree: the five-pointed star and floral patterns—stems, leaves and blossoms, all formed of tiny beads sewn individually on the garment. The older women wore bright shawls, retaining their dull dark dresses, but the girls liked colorful calico; and all the women had beaded ornaments and lavishly embroidered "squaw boots," moccasins with high soft tops.

Louis did not especially enjoy the parties, and probably he

fretted because a people apparently so near their doom could forget their troubles in spasms of heedless hilarity. In fact there were more parties than ever before because there was not much else to do. But Louis was more white than red, and consequently he was a worrier. No Indian, and few Red River Métis, any longer worried about anything until it happened and sometimes not then; it was too late, so what was the use? Louis had managed to excite his people once about their future, in 1869-70; there had been a great fracas and some of it had been fun, especially the horseback patrols. But it had served no purpose and they were worse off than they had been before. To be sure there were rumblings from Saskatchewan, but that was still Métis country, with few whites; this was white country, and what was there to do about it?

While Louis had worried himself into asylums his people had eaten and drunk and danced. This careless enjoyment of life while it lasted did not endear them to their Messiah, and in the next few years he could not restrain himself from making occasional petulant reference to such weaknesses. The problems he had foreseen were developing now to plague the Saskatchewan colonies, but white civilization had already conquered the Red River country and his people there were spiritless and indifferent.

He still had a mission, and he still wanted Evelina. There was nothing for him in the dying village of St. Joe; the vigorous elements had already pushed west. He paid some furtive visits to family and friends across the line and prepared to move on.

An estimate by an American official in that year of 1879 put the number of Métis in the United States and Canadian Northwest at 33,000, a figure which was far from adequate. Half of these, he said, were in Michigan, which he included in the region. He assigned "more than a thousand" to Montana; but Montana had only 53,000 people and 32,000 of them were Indians or Métis. Approximately 1,300 half-breeds lived in Dakota. The large Michigan group, descendants of the first of their race, had lost their Métis identity though they retained some of their French tradition; they had never heard of Riel's "New Nation." Nor had 1,450 in Wisconsin, several thousand in Missouri and Illinois, and two dozen who had unaccountably strayed into Iowa. There were at least 6,500 left in Manitoba and about the same number in Canada's Northwest Territories; these, remembering Red River and 1870, still bitterly resented the advance of white civilization.

This was the Métis world, scattered from Michigan to Montana's Rockies, from St. Louis to Great Slave Lake. Louis Riel chose Montana, which, together with Saskatchewan just over its northern boundary, represented his people's last frontier.

PARVULI PETIERUNT PANEM

Riel went to Carroll, a settlement in the heart of the badlands or "breaks" of the Upper Missouri, about two hundred miles by river below Fort Benton. A squalid collection of mud and log huts, too small and too dirty even to be called cabins, it was nevertheless one of the most important landings on the river because steamers unloaded there when water was too low to permit passage to Fort Benton. A year after Riel arrived the Army established Fort Maginnis in the Judiths south of Carroll and from the river town an important freight trail led south to Diamond City, Last Chance (Helena) and other gold camps.

Frontier civilization, such as it was, had passed Carroll by. Louis, who had become accustomed to frock coats, salons and dignified halls of statecraft, here stepped back into an ugly, brawling, lawless community worse than Pembina had been a few years before. The country north of the river was Indian reservation. Carroll and neighboring Rocky Point were the last stands of the freebooters, the "border banditti" whose presence in Dakota had so alarmed McDougall. A sizable portion of the ever-shifting population was made up of horse thieves and illicit whiskey traders; the rest, comparatively honest, were hunters, wolfers, or woodchoppers who supplied fuel for the steamers. Not to mention the Indians. It was the kind of town which could only exist in a transitional society.

The Missouri "breaks" extend, river distance (and the river was then and is still the only way they can be traversed), for about four hundred miles. They were christened *mauvaises terres* by the Métis, but the English word is better because much of the area is timbered and—though the 130-mile-long reservoir of Fort Peck Dam has flooded some of the best land—there still are thousands of acres of rich grass. But there are badlands, too—mile after mile of sandstone towers, knobs, ridges; gullies gray and white and red; rock platforms stark against the sky, looking as if they had been erected for sacrifices to the ancient gods. As the sun descends the hot wind dies and then comes the miracle of color, purple and yellow and flame and unnamed mutations, merging at last in a golden haze over the muddy Missouri, suddenly transformed into a ribbon of silver.

The roughness of the terrain, which made cultivation infeasible, made the "breaks" a paradise for game for several years, and it was this which attracted the Métis—food (though it was soon exhausted) and freedom. In hundreds of miles of canyons and coulees, many of them with hidden entrances, the hunters, the men who trapped wolves for bounty, the woodchoppers and the outlaws scattered their one-room log-and-adobe hovels, or dug caves in the hillsides. The tiny cabins were usually windowless, though those of the rustlers had portholes for rifles. Here if men chose they could laugh at law. No Montana peace officer and no military detachment ever entered the region except for brief visits at such settlements as Carroll. But in 1884 vengeful white cattlemen formed a vigilante company (known as "Stuart's Stranglers" after their leader, Granville Stuart) and staged a whirlwind clean-up of rustlers, with free use of gun, torch and rope. In one instance the hideout of eleven outlaws was besieged for a full day and ultimately nearly all were killed.

Riel became a woodchopper, a subagent for a trading company, and an unofficial "fixer"—business interpreter and mediator between Indians or Métis and whites. He also occasionally accompanied the half-breeds on a buffalo hunt, acting as their purchasing agent for such enterprises, and handled their relations with the Army and the civil authorities.

He did not forget his mission. And though he always insisted that he would "free" the Métis by peaceful means, a curious Montana incident which went unreported until 1950 indicated that his protestations were not wholly sincere.

According to an old-timer's story, Frank P. Eckley, a freighter, and his partner encountered a long train of Red River carts led by Louis Riel soon after the latter's arrival in Montana. The carts were loaded with furs and buffalo robes; the freighters were carrying supplies to Fort Ellis in southern Montana territory. Included in the supplies were ten cases of guns and a large stock of ammunition.

Riel, said Eckley, offered to pay the amount of the freighters' bond, double the sum they would get for carrying the cargo to the fort from the mouth of the Musselshell, where they received it from a river steamer, and a thousand-dollar cash bonus, "if you have a broken axle and find it necessary to leave the arms and ammunition behind for a time."

The freighters refused, and Riel promptly doubled his offer. When they still declined to betray their trust, he appealed to their love of liberty, Eckley said, and Eckley weakened. "Let's sleep on this," he suggested to his partner, "and let General Riel know in the morning."

"Done," the partner agreed. "But the answer will still be 'no' by me."

The Métis chief then warned them that his men could seize the wagons and their precious cargo and set the freighters afoot on the prairie, but he acknowledged that he was reluctant to treat in this way citizens of a country which had given him refuge; and while the freighters slept the Métis took turns guarding their load.

In the morning the freighters still refused to make a deal, and Riel, undoubtedly realizing that theft of the guns and munitions would precipitate a search by United States troops whom he could not hope to elude, sadly let them go.

In business Louis favored T. C. Power & Company, one of the two big outfits which battled for the Territory's prairie trade, probably because Power and his agent at Carroll, Thomas O'Hanlon, were Catholic. O'Hanlon, unusually devout for a frontiersman, was the most generous friend the Jesuit missionaries had in the region. Riel warred constantly with Power's competitor, C. A. Broadwater, whose local agent he accused of selling whiskey to the Indians though he absolved Broadwater of any personal guilt.

The moral deterioration of the Indians and half-breeds became virtually an obsession with Louis and he wrote to the newspapers and railed at military and civil officers because they did nothing about it. So far as Indians were concerned he had a case, since sale of liquor to them was clearly prohibited. But with the half-breeds the matter was not so simple. Some traders were forbidden by army officers to sell to Métis, but this order could only be justified on the ground that through the Métis the liquor would reach the Indians: the Métis themselves were not wards of the Government, not registered members of any tribe. Therefore under strict interpretation of the law they were free to drink all they chose, and despite Riel's fussing most of them did.

One post near Carroll, he complained, sold two thousand gallons of trade whiskey in one winter. Another dealer catered to the cocktail-lounge set; Louis described a scene in his place:

. . . the half-breed women of that camp used to go in number and get drunk in his saloon. On one occasion ten or twelve of these miserable and degraded females were seen paying treats at the counter and striking the bar with their fists. They were boasting of having money to pay. At the same time, pieces of silver, precious and necessary to buy the bread and clothes for their poor children, rolled and rang on the shop table. When they left the saloon they could hardly walk; they were crying, clamoring and falling on the road. . . .

His concern was justified and was echoed in the comments of other observers who were well-disposed toward the natives; but such observers were few. One was a Jesuit priest, Father Frederick Eberschweiler, who found that liquor and starvation had driven the Indians to large-scale prostitution. The Indian Agent officially reported that venereal disease was the major cause of death among the tribes in his charge.

Conditions were particularly bad at Fort Assiniboine, an Army post northwest of Carroll, near the present town of Havre. Though the commanding officer posted special guards to keep the Indians away, prostitution flourished unchecked. Soldiers slipped out of the fort to find the Indian women waiting in nearby coulees, usually accompanied by their husbands or fathers, who collected the standard fee—twenty-five cents. Especially prized were the Indian virgins, the priest said, "maidens scarcely over twelve years old"; their favors also sold for the frontier's smallest coin—"two bits."

Truly the Métis and Indians had been abandoned, Father Eberschweiler wrote his superior. "The lamentation 'Parvuli petierunt panem et nemo dabat illis' [the little ones sought bread and there was none to give it them] holds good for these tribes."

MARGUERITE

O'Hanlon leaned heavily upon Riel and recommended him to his employers as a reliable man and, because he was agent for the Métis, a good customer. The trader consulted Louis when he had cattle to move through Indian country, employed him as go-between to recover horses stolen by the Nez Percé, and, with army support, encouraged him to go among the drifting bands of Sioux to dissuade them from raiding the ranches and trading posts.

In August, 1880, Riel wrote General Miles at Fort Keough on behalf of the Métis, asking him to forward their appeal to Washington. They requested that a special reservation be set aside for them in Montana (today, seventy years later, they are still asking it) and that financial aid be given for the purchase of implements, seed and livestock. In return they would require all Métis to obtain valid title to their land, would exclude liquor from the area, and serve the Government in other ways. Riel explained:

We ask the Government to kindly consider that as Half-Breeds we stand between the civilized world and uncivilized man and are closely related with the several tribes of the Northwest, owing to which fact we indirectly exercise some influence and from the Indian blood in our veins we are inclined to believe that Indians will listen to us more favorably than to the majority of those who are not connected by family ties with them.

If the Government would wish to use our influence, such as it is, among the Indians we freely offer it. . . .

The Métis were ready, he concluded, to undertake any peaceful mission and would even, if called upon, act as scouts.

To organize support for this appeal and to encourage his

people to vote for candidates who promised to help them, Riel toured the major half-breed settlements—Milk River, Fort Benton, Helena, and Spring Creek, now Lewistown. His efforts came to the attention of Montana newspapers and he was dubbed "the John Brown of the Half-Breeds"; the frontier press, anti-British on general principles, was friendly to him until one faction was alienated by his partisan political activities.

The largest and by far the best Métis community was that on Spring Creek. The hunters who founded it had chosen one of Montana's most beautiful locations, midway in the green, well-watered Judith Basin, surrounded by three mountain ranges, and a favorite resort of the buffalo. Twenty-five families came in Red River carts in 1879 and thereafter the colony grew steadily; before any appreciable white migration occurred it had 150 Métis families.

This was an orderly, busy, God-fearing community which had little in common with such places as Carroll. Early arrivals declared their citizenship intention and took up homesteads, and though they had come penniless and almost without tools they soon built substantial log homes, one of them extra large so it could be used as a church. Jesuit missionaries made periodic visits; when there was no priest the people assembled on Sunday mornings to recite the rosary. Daily prayers were customary in the homes and the children went to Alexander Wilkie, builder of the big house, for regular religious instruction. Wilkie, member of a family whose men had been leaders among the *Bois-Brulés* from earliest times of the race, was a musician, too—a singer and violinist. From the youngsters of the colony he built a choir and trained it in liturgical music he had learned at St. Boniface and Pembina. So on sparkling Sunday mornings in the heart of a mountain basin in the Western wilderness, the voices of half-breed children rose in plain chant which was centuries old, or in hymns in French and Cree for low mass. Visiting priests were astonished and delighted to find this oasis of gracious worship in what they regarded as a desert of dissent and apostasy, and it lightened somewhat their despair over the fact that most Montana communities of the time were firmly under the control of licentious atheists, Protestants, or—worst of all—Freemasons.

The educational level at Spring Creek was unusually high. Most of the elders could speak and read French and Cree, and many could even write those languages; few, of course, knew any English. French and Cree books which a missionary had given them at Red River were their most prized possessions and were used for instruction of the children.

Had Riel come first to this settlement and established himself his future might have been very different. Evelina, perhaps, could have been happy here. These peaceful Métis adjusted themselves better than most to the coming of the whites and some of them became pioneers of Lewistown.

But Louis had business and political connections at Carroll, and he had come to regard the latter, especially, as essential to his career. And so, though he undoubtedly visited Spring Creek, he did not choose to remain.

And there was now another attraction at Carroll.

During one of the hunting expeditions Louis met the family of Jean Monette *dit* Bellehumeur ("called Good-tempered"), who had followed the buffalo south from his old home at Fort Ellice, on the western boundary of Manitoba. He had settled between Carroll and the Little Rockies, twenty-five miles north, and Louis became a frequent visitor because Monette had a daughter, Marguerite.

Aside from the clue given by his nickname, almost nothing is known of Monette Bellehumeur. Both he and his wife were Métis; the few who knew his daughter reported she was "very dark." She was timid, silent, self-effacing; and she wor-

shiped Louis Riel. She was a loyal companion and became
a painstaking, affectionate mother; friends said she showed
real happiness only when she was with her own or others'
children. She may have been a very pretty girl, as so many
of the Métisse were. But so slight was the imprint of her
personality upon her contemporaries that almost nothing was
ever written about her—even by Louis Riel. And no picture
of her has been found.

The romance of the exiled President of Rupert's Land and
this dark daughter of a wandering prairie hunter was a
strange and pathetic and ultimately tragic affair. She could
not read or write; she spoke Cree, of which Riel also had a
passable knowledge, but at this time she knew little French
or English. Still, there was no question of her love for Louis,
and he was desperately lonely.

He tried to make her over in the image of the lost Evelina,
and though he never succeeded in this he did become genu-
inely attached. His manner toward her throughout their brief
life together—within six years after their meeting both were
dead—was unfailingly considerate and even (absurdly, in the
eyes of the frontier) somewhat courtly. He wrote poems to
her; a draft of one, in English, is among his papers. But it
was not a love poem. It was, as usual with Louis, a religious
admonition. It began:

> Margaret! Be fair and good,
> Consider the sacred wood
> On which the perfect Jesus
> Died willingly to save us . . .

and continued in that strain for several stanzas. Aside from
a reference to her "dear soul," there was little in it that could
be construed as having been prompted by love for the one
to whom it was dedicated.

Their marriage was "blessed" on March 9, 1882, at Carroll
by Father Damiani, Jesuit missionary from St. Peter's, 150

miles west. Marguerite was twenty-one years old. Louis's letters home and other biographical material supplied by him indicate that the "marriage"—prairie style, without benefit of clergy—occurred April 28, 1881, and Father Damiani's record of the March ceremony says he "blessed the marriage previously contracted."

The "prairie marriage," a simple verbal contract to be solemnized later when the priest appeared, at that time was a legitimate marriage under Catholic Church law when it occurred in an area which could be visited only infrequently by priests, providing it was subsequently affirmed by the religious ceremony.

The Riels' first child, a son whom they christened Jean, was born May 9, 1882, probably at Carroll.

Louis was a family man now, and it was more than ever essential that he establish himself, find a career, make some money. First he tried politics, and like many another Montanan promptly got into trouble.

CHAPTER XVIII

Leader of a Sedition

THE PERILS OF POLITICS

RIEL's letters to the papers had now made him well known, especially in the Territorial capital, Helena, whose Republican *Weekly Herald* had been generous with its space. Democrats were in control of the Territorial administration and Louis blamed that party, and its newspaper satellites, for the plight of his people. Democratic officials, he complained, "pillage them [the Métis] year after year in the most open and scandalous manner."

In the fall of 1882 he set out to deliver the Montana half-breed vote to the Republicans. Though today this vote would be infinitesimal, it was important then in the sparsely settled prairies, where a handful of electors could choose a delegate to the Territorial Assembly. Riel was acting dangerously and perhaps not too scrupulously since he was not himself a citizen or voter; but as a Métis he undoubtedly still had a sense of "dual citizenship."

News traveled slowly even within the Territory, and though there were rumors about his political activity nothing came of them that fall. He resumed his campaigning next year; but first he took the precaution of becoming a citizen of the United States.

Judge D. S. Wade of the United States District Court granted Riel citizenship in Helena on March 16, 1883—an act which was to have far-reaching consequences. Louis said he had waited until the Canadian decree of banishment and suspension of civil rights had expired so it would be clear that he was transferring his allegiance in good faith.

Two months later he was indicted by a county grand jury in Fort Benton, charged with inducing Métis who were not citizens to vote, at Carroll. Louis angrily denied it. The Métis were fully qualified, he said, and had taken an oath to that effect before three white election judges who had supervised the poll. He acknowledged that earlier in the day the same Métis had been refused the right to vote at Rocky Point, but attributed that to hostile and discriminatory election officials.

The Fort Benton *Record,* Democratic, denounced him as an illicit whiskey trader, as an unscrupulous fixer of elections, as a "low scoundrel of foxlike cunning," and, to top it off, "about as much a gentleman as Sitting Bull." This outburst had been inspired by the Helena *Herald,* Republican, which called him "the Honorable Louis Riel," and said no one who talked with him for half an hour could fail to see that he was "a gentleman and scholar, a worthy and desirable friend." What's more, the *Herald* said, his enemies in Chouteau County were "miserable and contemptible" men who were "prostituting public positions and power to partisan malice." There was more "honest, noble manhood" in Louis than in "the whole batch of his persecutors."

Probably Riel was not wholly guiltless, but considering Montana electoral practice of the time the furor sounded silly to everyone and the indictment was soon dismissed for lack of evidence. Later a prominent Fort Benton citizen revealed that there was conclusive documentary evidence that the two Métis mentioned in the true bill as having voted illegally were actually citizens, so it may have been that Louis was just lucky.

He was at least as articulate as most of the whites then in public life and he had hit back at his tormentors effectively in the press. But the publicity caused grave concern among his best friends, the Jesuit missionaries, and they now began to urge him to abstain from such dangerous doings.

Riel may well have been bewildered by this counsel. The Jesuits he had hitherto known, in Montreal, were the backbone of the ultramontane movement, fanatically devoted to Catholic political action. For years he had been told that it was the duty of every Catholic to fight for the Church and his coreligionists at the polls.

But the Jesuits of the far Western missions probably had never heard of ultramontanism. And if they had, they would not have touched it with a tipi pole. This was particularly true in Montana, where Masonry was so firmly entrenched for the first few decades that the Jesuits believed themselves lucky to survive at all and maintain their missions. Louis had moved from a Catholic province and Catholic cities in the East to a Territory whose judges, public officials, businessmen and even ranchers and miners were predominantly Protestant and members of the Masonic order. Even the famed Vigilantes of Virginia City, gold camp and second Territorial capital, were of Masonic origin.

He would have understood it all better had he known of the afflictions of Father Eberschweiler, who was assigned in 1883 to the Fort Benton parish.

The German Jesuit was moved suddenly from tranquil Burlington, Iowa, to "the seaport of the Northwest," the head of navigation on the turbulent Missouri, a "city" of 2,500 populated by Indians, half-breeds, Americans (many of whom preferred not to tell, when asked, "What was your name in the States?"), Negroes and Chinese. When he reached St. Peter's, other missionaries, veterans of the prairie, warned him gently that he must expect disappointment; he would accomplish nothing in that sagebrush Sodom. But he was young and confident and when he found a substantial church and a comfortable cabin awaiting him in the river town he was sure his informants had just been tired.

He soon changed his mind. "All are alike," he remarked sadly of the people of Fort Benton, "in the 'auri sacra fames' [sacred love for gold]." Virtually everyone, including the hopelessly "indolent" members of his own flock, was abandoned to vice. Promiscuity and drunkenness were so common that those few who did not practice them were looked upon as a little odd. Called to minister to a dying child, the priest found the cabin full of drunken men, one of them the boy's father, who cursed and threatened him until a relative summoned by the mother got him out of the place.

Some of the children in his Sunday school were illegitimate; several were sadly neglected at home. He discovered to his horror that one of the "church trustees" who had invited him to come was "a rich Protestant," another an apostate Catholic who was now head of the local Masonic lodge, and a third—religion, if any, undetermined—was an insurance man who had insured all the church property with himself without asking anyone's permission.

The curé had a good attendance for his first mass but he soon realized that had been inspired by curiosity; after that almost nobody came. Finally, in despair, he summoned the "trustees" and asked why he had been invited. "Well," said one of them (perhaps the insurance man), "we all came here to make money and we care very little for religion, but we like to have a priest here for marriages and deaths, and also for improvement of the city. We receive many letters from the States inquiring if there is a Father here; if one is here more new people will come and settle in this town."

This Chamber of Commerce evaluation of the faith was too much for Father Eberschweiler; he abandoned Fort Benton to its sins and moved out on the prairies. The Irish troopers at Fort Assiniboine were the best Catholics he found, "though far from being overpious." He formed a temperance society among them after some "unaware Catholics" had carelessly joined one initiated by the plaguy Masons. He dropped this new venture after the chairman of his group was lodged in the guardhouse for drunkenness.

Missionaries were certainly needed, he wrote his superior, but they had to be armed with "strong zeal." He had often had to console himself with St. Ignatius's sentence: "To have prevented but one sin is a sufficiently great remuneration for all labors and cares of one's whole life." Under the circumstances, political action was probably the last thing he would have been interested in, and his colleagues felt the same way.

Yet it was a priest who gave Louis Riel the first job he had ever had for which he was reasonably well equipped.

In the summer of 1883 Father Damiani, in charge of St. Peter's Mission in the Sun River country, hired him to teach Indian boys at the mission school and to take charge of the whole educational program next year, when a girls' school was to be established. The post would provide no more than bare subsistence, but Louis jumped at it. Marguerite, too, was pleased; there was another baby coming and she would be safe and well tended at the mission.

The uncomplaining Marguerite by this time may have had reason to be concerned about the family's future. Louis was no good as a hunter, and he had spent too much time away from home to support his family adequately by woodchopping. He had made one unfortunate venture into sheepherding and had been fired; his employer said the flock strayed while Louis was "being blessed with visions." Marguerite had been hired at that time, too, for housework, and their son had been farmed out with her parents. The rancher's wife said she was a good worker and was devoted to the ranch couple's baby boy, for whom she crocheted wristlets of yarn in the soft powder blue dear to the heart of Indian women. Her hands were never still, she rarely spoke, and she sat on the floor "like a squaw."

En route to the mission to take up his new work, Louis stopped in Fort Benton to call upon an old admirer whom he had met by chance there during his political travels.

This friend was J. J. Donnelly, General of the Army of the Fenian Republic, retired. After the collapse of the 1871 raid at Pembina led by his old chief, General O'Neill, Donnelly had dropped out of Fenian history; he had "moved west." Actually he had gone straight to Fort Benton and re-entered his old profession, law. When Riel met him about ten years later he was well launched in politics: he had been county clerk and probate judge and a member of the Territorial legislature.

Donnelly was six years older than Louis. He was born in Rhode Island and finished law school shortly before the Civil War, from which he emerged a lieutenant colonel, twice wounded. His wife died in 1866, and, grief-stricken, he abandoned law practice and flung himself into the preposterous Fenian movement. He participated in the major attacks upon Canada and was wounded again in one of them.

The Irishman was delighted to see Riel. Did Louis still dream of freeing his people and the Northwest from the galling yoke of Ottawa and the damnable Orangemen?

Louis confessed that he did.

And a splendid dream it was, said Donnelly. Come back again; a lawyer could help—not to mention a veteran of several skirmishes on Canadian soil.

Riel did confer several times with the Fort Benton man

on his plans for the Métis. Donnelly advised him on the
wording of petitions and—just in case it should come to that—
on military strategy. The Canadians, under British command, would fight in the "British square," the Fenian
thought (they did try it), and would be sitting ducks for the
expert prairie marksmen if they established positions like
this. . . . And he drew charts and maps.

Louis was right, of course, to insist that his objectives were
peaceful and constitutional. Nevertheless, if war should come
—well, perhaps he could get some help. The order might be
dead, but there was fire in some Fenians still.

There were rumors. London newspapers reported that
Alfred Aylward had led a group of former Fenians, thirty-
six armed men, westward through Dakota en route to help
Riel; and there was a story in Fort Benton that a relief caravan, several wagonloads of food and ammunition, started
from there for Saskatchewan. But if such expeditions ever
existed they lost heart or were "dry-gulched" by Indians or
outlaws before they reached their destination; the Métis
never saw them.

Valiant, headstrong O'Neill died penniless and broken-
hearted in an Omaha hospital in 1878. O'Donoghue, the
Dakota country schoolmaster, went that same year. In September, 1899, the last of the Pembina plotters, last of the
irreconcilables, perhaps last of the Fenian fighting men,
joined his comrades. General Donnelly walked down to the
Fort Benton levee, filled his pockets with fourteen pounds of
rocks, slit his throat from ear to ear, and marched unfalter-
ingly into the Missouri River.

STARVATION WINTER

The Riels' daughter and second child, Marie Angélique,
was born at St. Peter's Mission in September, 1883.

This mission, established to minister to the Blackfeet on
the buffalo plains before they had a reservation, had been

moved several times and closed for long periods because of the hostility of the tribe. Now on its fourth site, it apparently was firmly lodged, and its school for boys, with about a score enrolled, was becoming popular among the Indians and Métis.

The staff when Louis arrived consisted of Father Damiani, two other priests (but all three spent much time on the prairie) and a couple of lay brothers. Next year Father Damiani hoped to bring in Ursulines for a girls' school. The boys were taught to read and write French and English, to do rudimentary arithmetic, to handle domestic animals and do other farm work, carpentry and shoemaking. The girls would learn the languages and be taught to sew, keep house, to handle milk and care for poultry.

There was no cabin available for the Riels and they moved in with the James Swan family. "We have to ourselves one corner of his little house," Louis wrote his brother Joseph at Red River. If it should be the will of God, he hoped soon to be able to put his family in a house or lodging of its own, but he was very poor.

He began teaching at once. Apparently he liked the work and did it satisfactorily; the only criticism Father Damiani ever made of his protégé was that he was far too interested in politics. In the evenings he wrote endlessly—poems, religious dissertations, plans for the Métis. A dozen of the poems appeared after his death, published in Montreal at the instance of friends in a thin paper-bound pamphlet with the title *Poésies religieuses et politiques*. Included are an invocation to the Christ, other religious pieces, and verses praising Archbishop Taché, Father Damiani and other clerics; but the longest poem, fourteen pages, is an envenomed denunciation of Sir John A. Macdonald. Riel's verse style was uneven, the word selection and images were naive; but some lines were filled with such intensity of feeling that they still can move a reader.

The winter of 1883 was late and when it came the cold was deadly, a tangible horror. It was the "white cold" of the high country, a shimmering mist in which a lantern ten feet away looked to be half a mile, which diffused the sun's rays and created eerie twilight at noon.

The mission suspended classes and everyone huddled about the fireplaces. The cold pushed through the walls and the logs cracked like bull whips. It was a solid icy mass, creeping a little farther into the room each day, pressing toward the hearth and the frail flame of half-frozen fuel. Most of the time the fire was the only light, for oil and tallow had to be sparingly used, and day after day there was no sun.

The people sat cramped before the fires and gazed into them and slept. The air in the crowded rooms was dank and sour, but there was nothing to be done about that; open doors could mean death. Even if the sun gave some feeble light it was now almost due south, behind the mountains, so here there were weeks when it seemed there was no day or night, just dingy interminable time.

Outside the snow fell thinly and incessantly. When a door was opened to admit Father Damiani, checking on his flock, the white sandy stuff scuttled in on the floor and twisted and danced about the room.

Sixty below zero, Father Damiani said. It would be well to pray for all the poor souls on the prairie, for Father Prando, snowbound in his cabin on Birch Creek, his mission station among the Blackfeet—a secret and illegal establishment because the Government had arbitrarily divided up the reservations among religious sects and the Blackfeet were supposed to be Christianized by Protestants.

But Marguerite prayed for Marie Angélique, only four months old when the cold came. The baby was croupy and undernourished, much of the time barely alive. Somehow her mother brought her through that dreadful winter.

It was the Starvation Winter of the Blackfeet. They were

deserted by their agent on their reservation 150 miles north of the mission and they had almost no rations because, to make a record for himself, he had falsely reported them "almost self-supporting" from farming. When the rations gave out the Indians ate their horses, their dogs, rats they dug from nests in the rocks, scraps of bark, and finally *babiche*— the rawhide thongs of their snowshoes.

Father Prando somehow got word of the disaster to St. Peter's and the nearby Army post, Fort Shaw. Freighters floundered through the drifts with wagons and sleds loaded with food.

Louis had been in touch with the Blackfeet chiefs since he came to Montana and he hoped that when a Métis crisis came he could count on their support. Surely this experience could only strengthen their bitterness against the whites and link them more closely to his cause.

But it was some time before he learned what the relief expedition had found.

Six hundred Blackfeet, one-fourth of the tribe in the United States, were dead of starvation. Some had gone mad from hunger and grief while wolves prowled among their unburied dead in the silent tipis. Scores, though living, were crippled by diet-deficiency diseases. And the spirit of a warrior race was broken for all time. No matter how bitter the Blackfeet might become, they never again would be able to do anything about it.

GALLOWS ON A HILL

Louis arose early on Sunday, June 4, 1884, and looked out upon one of the typically gemlike, immaculate mornings of a mountain spring. He stepped outside to savor the cool air, and walked up the trail to watch the rose glow filter into the deep fissures of Bird Tail Rock and light the eastern faces of the seven giant monoliths, interlaced in a fan, from which the landmark peak a few miles away took its name.

The little creek in the mission grounds was bank-full and muddy. All about him patterns of cólor sprang suddenly from the sod, as if they had been evoked by the viewer: the velvety rose and blue of yarrow in mossy clumps; the creamy sweet pea blossoms of mountain loco; the first glacier lilies, slim and regally yellow. He could smell the sap-filled willow and currant bushes and the moist earth, moist here so briefly and so gratefully.

Louis looked about him for a few moments at the land of the Métis, then turned back to the cabin. Soon it would be time to accompany Marguerite to mass.

During mass he was called from the church. There was someone to see him and it was important. This was unprecedented, and Louis was annoyed. He strode into the mission yard to find a cluster of excited youngsters surrounding four mounted men.

The visitors dismounted, hurried to Louis and presented themselves: Gabriel Dumont, "prince of the prairies," already known to him; two other Métis from St. Laurent, Moise Ouellette and Michel Dumas; and an English half-breed from Prince Albert, James Isbister. They had ridden 680 miles from the Saskatchewan settlements to ask Riel to come back with them and take charge of their campaign for redress of their grievances against Canada.

Louis's heart leaped; but it would not do to show his emotion. He directed the visitors to his cabin, excused himself, and hurried back into the little church. He knelt and offered thanks; his mission had been confirmed. The enslaved people had sent again for David.

He welcomed the four men as his guests but asked for a day to give his answer. Probably his decision had been made instantly, but he was not one to slight the historic event. He would prepare a written reply. He invested the occasion with all the pseudo-mystical significance he could manage on the spur of the moment: since there were four delegates and they had arrived on the fourth day of the month seeking a fifth, himself, he must have until the fifth day to reply. Yet the written answer, delivered to Gabriel the following morning, was straightforward and practical. The invitation honored Louis particularly, he wrote, because both French and British half-breeds had extended it, with the sympathy of white settlers. "I record it as one of the gratifications of my life."

He doubted whether his help, now that he was an American citizen, would be as valuable as the Saskatchewan people believed, but he was willing to try. He admitted ("to be frank is the shortest") that he had a personal interest: Canada owed him a two-hundred-and-forty-acre Métis land grant, it owed him five lots in the Red River settlement, "and something else." The "something else" probably referred to compensation he believed due him for maintaining a government in Manitoba for two months after agreement was reached in 1870, and for the distress and persecution he suffered during the early years of his exile.

"Considering then your interest and mine," he continued, "I accept your kind invitation. But my intention is to come back early this fall." Montana had a large and potentially important half-breed population with which he was just getting acquainted; "I would like to unite and direct its vote so as to make it profitable to themselves and useful to their friends." Moreover he had made friends in this Territory amongst whom he liked to live. "I start with you," he concluded, "but to come back here sometime in September."

The Riels needed a few days to prepare for the move, and the schoolmaster wanted to finish his term. The four visitors lazed around the mission, resting from their long ride. They were somewhat shocked to discover their hero's poverty. "The humble condition of Riel's home," they said on their return, "reminded us of the opportunities he had for several years to become rich, and even to make an ex-

ceptional fortune, and how at all risks he stood firm by the
confidence of his people. We know how much he wrought
for Manitoba and how much he struggled for the whole
North-West, and seeing how little he worked for himself,
we came back with twice as much confidence in him as we
had on leaving."

Marguerite packed their few household effects and
Louis's documents, some of which he entrusted to a Spring
Creek Métis to save for him. There was a trunkful of papers
to be carried along, meaningless to her but important because Louis said they were. Many people came to tell them
good-by, and most of them urged them not to go. Louis was
admired, despite his aloofness and melancholy; and the
patient Marguerite, always ready to help with anyone's
children, was popular with the mission people and their
neighbors.

On June 10 the long trek north began, with a cart added
to the caravan for Marguerite, the children and their possessions. No one, probably not even Louis, knew what Marguerite thought about it; but Gabriel could see that she
was unhappy. Well, he thought, probably she is just worry-
ing about Marie Angélique, who was ill again. But she may
have had other reasons to brood. Life at St. Peter's had been
hard, but she had always been poor anyway, and there had
been security there and even a little prestige. Now she was
on the prairie again in a shrieking Red River cart, bound
for God only knew what mad venture.

About twenty miles from the mission was the town of
Sun River, with a weekly paper, the *Sun*. Publicity-wise,
Louis insisted on a stop there to call upon the editor. The
latter was impressed, and he knew a good story when he saw
it. On June 12 he described the little expedition, reported
that the members of the Saskatchewan delegation had been
"wealthy and educated" men, touched on Riel's plans. Louis
was an American now, and "only goes to assist his people

as much as lays in his power, and after which—be it much
or little—he will return to Montana."

That was the news, but the editor had a somewhat surprising personal note to add to the story:

Meeting Louis Riel today recalls another day some fifteen
years ago when, led by the now famous Colonel Wolseley, we
with some five hundred others marched in close formation over
the ground where the city of Winnipeg now stands, and up to
the walls of Fort Garry, then occupied by Mr. Riel and his rebel
army. We remember how the massive gates were battered down
by the excited soldiers, how we rushed in over the fallen timbers
expecting a hand to hand conflict, but to find the birds flown,
the fort empty.

It was queer to sit and talk to this man, and remember how
as a drummer boy of fifteen we longed to spill his blood (or see
someone else do it) as ardently as any vet. We recalled the opening of Scott's supposed grave, in the courtyard of the fort; the
coffin pulled from it, opened, its contents: bricks and shavings.
We remembered that Scott's grave was never found, but we did
not ask Mr. R. to tell us where those bones await the final
trumpet call, because we don't believe he knows. . . .

Well, concluded the editor of the Sun River *Sun,* David
B. Hall, "all the same Mr. Riel has our best wishes for the
success of his mission."

In Fort Benton the little company found Father Eberschweiler and asked for his blessing. He gave it before the
altar and permitted Louis to speak a prayer he had made
up: "Father, bless me according to the views of Thy Providence which are beautiful and without measure." But when
the priest heard the purpose of their trip he tried earnestly
to persuade them to turn back. Louis assured him that the
mission was peaceful, but the Jesuit was not convinced. The
Métis could not win a war, he warned; "supposing you win

every battle but in each engagement you lose fifty men, you will ultimately be defeated."

"Father," Riel said quietly, "you are a good man, but you have not been obliged to endure the many injustices. . . . I tell you finally I intend to go through with it."

Eberschweiler, still protesting, accompanied them for a short distance. Describing the experience some years later, he attributed to Louis one last, suspiciously prescient remark; and yet it is possible to credit seeming clairvoyance in this instance because Riel had been virtually under sentence of death for years and had long been obsessed with the idea that he would be martyred. The priest said he left Louis staring at the crest of a hill near the trail, and the Métis called to him as he turned to go.

"Father," Louis said, "I see a gallows on top of that hill, and I am swinging from it."

PART SIX

Prophet on Horseback

CHAPTER XIX

The Right of People

IN THE RANKS OF PUBLIC MEN

TEN miles from Batoche, as the Riel party crossed the plain and approached the broad valley of the South Saskatchewan River, seventy Métis streamed out to meet them, cheering and firing salutes. They escorted Louis to the settlements where hundreds more awaited him.

Batoche, or St. Antoine de Padua (the post office was in the parish house adjoining the Catholic Church), was a typical Métis village about forty miles southwest of the fast-growing English community of Prince Albert. The Métis cabins, many of them well-built, clean and comfortable, straggled along the riverbank for a mile or two; there were no streets, but a trail led from the prairie where the church stood down to the river and the ferry, "Batoche's Crossing." Stores, homes and farms were on both sides of the river, which at this point was about a hundred yards wide. Another ferry, maintained by Gabriel Dumont, was located about six miles upstream (south) at "Gabriel's Crossing." The church and parish house for Batoche, almost alone on the crest of the coulee, were a mile from the houses on the river.

Louis and his family were taken to the home of his cousin, Charles Nolin, with whom Louis had clashed during the Rupert's Land troubles but who had joined in urging that he be invited to return from Montana to lead the Métis again. The Riels were to be guests at this home for about three months. Nolin was a prosperous, cautious and ostentatiously pious man whom a Mountie who had kept him under surveillance regarded as "the most intelligent and most dangerous" of the malcontents. Unlike other leaders of the Red River movement in 1870 he had quickly made his peace with the Manitoba government and had been briefly a member of the Provincial Cabinet, but he had then moved west and become a justice of the peace at Batoche.

In the early stages of the Saskatchewan agitation Nolin had been especially valuable to the Métis because of his education, his skill in drafting communications to Ottawa, and his political prestige; but Riel had good reason to distrust him and did not like being his guest. As soon as the movement was well under way the Métis provided him with a home of his own.

There was nothing in Louis's conduct during the first few months to justify the fears of the Fort Benton priest or his own misgivings. He was so circumspect and so obviously capable of the task set for him that even those who had opposed his coming, including the priest Alexis André, were won over. André was the oblate superior for the district and had previously served the half-breeds as a missionary in Pembina and St. Joe. "He upbraids, threatens and even strikes us," a Métis once reported to the bishop; "but he does well; that is what we need, for we are very wicked." Now André wrote the Governor of the Territories, "I do not entertain the least suspicion about Riel causing any trouble."

Louis's first public meeting was held in front of Nolin's

house on July 8. Three days later, with a large Métis group accompanying him, he addressed a nearby English settlement. Here, with the aid of W. H. Jackson of Prince Albert, secretary of the radical agrarian Settlers' Union, he began to bring together the complaints of the whites and his own people for presentation of a united front to the Canadian Government.

He was next invited to address a mass meeting in Prince Albert, whose seven hundred people were predominantly Anglo-Saxon. Mindful of the danger from sympathizers of Thomas Scott, he politely declined; but after receiving a petition signed chiefly by whites and after being strongly urged by Father André, he consented to make the appearance. The meeting was a resounding success. The priest, reporting again to the Governor, said Louis had "acted and spoken in a quiet and sensible way" and that it had been an event "such as Prince Albert has never seen." Some people still thought he was plotting a disturbance, "but I tell you the country is quiet and as far as I can see Riel has no other purpose than to help the people in their difficulties. I have not heard a hard word fall from his mouth."

The Prince Albert speech was shrewdly planned and the program Riel urged was moderate. He asked that the Métis be given free title to the lands they then occupied (most of them unsurveyed), that the three Territorial districts of Saskatchewan, Assiniboia and Alberta be raised to Provincial status or at least be given representation in Parliament, and that the land laws be changed to eliminate the confusion which had delayed immigration and which kept the original settlers in a continual state of alarm lest they lose their holdings.

Riel's coming might allay, rather than augment, the discontent, Father André felt. "We wanted something to occupy us for a while, talking about him," the priest said, "and put an end to the talk about the crops and the poor prospect before us." (It was a drought year.) Riel's influence was great among all classes and the Government should refrain from interfering "as long as he remains quiet." Specifically, André warned against accepting the counsel which might have come from Riel's enemies—the arrest of the visitor or dispatch of an extra detachment of Mounted Police. "For God's sake," he implored, "never commit such an act before you have good motives!"

Meanwhile Louis was in his glory. "It is not long since I was a humble schoolmaster on the distant banks of the Missouri," he wrote to relatives at Red River; "and today here I find myself in the ranks of public men, the most popular in the Saskatchewan. . . ."

. . . Last year no one wished to see me in influential political circles in Manitoba; this year the people follow my words in the heart of the Northwest. The banqueters invite me to their table, and their enthusiasm makes them clap their hands to signify their approbation. The rich who in the past regarded me with an air of pity are disturbed at present. They open their eyes in astonishment; they are alarmed; they are vexed. What is it that causes all this? . . . You know that it is God. I humble my soul nearly to the ground. The Lord has prepared me for some great things.

Most remarkable, the letter continued, was the fact that the English had befriended him. He claimed "several of our old prisoners [at Fort Garry] have invited me to their homes; they say they have wronged me and thank me for defending their interests in spite of themselves."

There is no doubt that whites, self-seeking or sincere, were in the forefront of the agitation both before and after Riel's arrival in Saskatchewan. In many instances they had legitimate grievances similar to those of the Métis—inability to obtain from a dilatory Government any promise of security on their lands. But some of the professed allies of Riel were speculators who hoped to launch a real estate boom as soon as the Métis received land scrip, which they expected to buy, as had their colleagues at Red River, for a fraction of its value. After the collapse of the Métis movement some correspondence which incriminated well-known Prince Albert citizens was recovered from the files of Will Jackson and burned.

Jackson, a brother of the druggist in Prince Albert, was an intelligent, enthusiastic but perhaps somewhat unbalanced crusader. (It was testified at Riel's trial that he lost his mind at the height of the Métis crisis.) He was a college graduate and politically a liberal, like most of the white participants in the movement, for whom the chance of discrediting Macdonald's conservative regime was an important motive.

Jackson took charge of the agitation in the English settlements and threw the support of the Settlers' Union behind it. Within a month of Louis's arrival the young Canadian had ardently embraced his chief's Messianic concept of his mission—before André or other associates realized that this concept existed. Writing to Louis to report success in organizing meetings and raising funds, Jackson said: "We will not get much respite until after the petition, but we can rest calm and peaceful as to the result, while the enemies of our God are tossing on their beds devising evil things against themselves." A few months later Riel persuaded him to become a convert to Catholicism.

A list of Hudson's Bay Company prices came into Jackson's hands, and he rightly regarded it as "a valuable document." Though official records and historians virtually ignored this phase of the trouble, resentment among the Métis over the low prices paid trappers was one of the major causes of unrest and remained longer than almost any other grievance in the minds of those who participated in the Sas-

katchewan uprising; veterans of the rebellion were still
grumbling about it in recent years. At that time the Métis
got only twenty-five cents for a skunk or three muskrats, a
dollar for a mink and one or two dollars for a fox; but the
goods they bought from the Company or from American
traders were steadily mounting in price.

During the fall Riel's movement was strengthened daily
by the adherence of Indians and whites. Big Bear, a restless
Cree chief who headed a band of about five hundred and
had been the leader of the most recalcitrant element in that
tribe, conferred with Louis at Jackson's home in Prince Albert and was assured that the Métis and their white allies
would insist upon adjustment of his grievances, too.

The new petition, drafted under the guidance of Riel,
was sent to Ottawa in December; an accompanying letter
signed by Jackson remarked that "our previous petitions
would appear to have gone astray." On the whole the appeal
was moderate. In addition to urging settlement of the Indians' claims, it asked that land scrip be given to the Métis
and patents to their present holdings in river front farms,
that representation be provided in Parliament, that a responsible local government with jurisdiction over natural
resources be established, and—a favorite Riel idea—that a
railroad be built to Hudson's Bay to give the region access
to European markets for its produce.

Meanwhile Louis wrote to an old sympathizer, James
Wickes Taylor, the United States consul in Winnipeg. The
treaty between Canada and the Provisional Government of
Rupert's Land in 1870 had not been carried out in good
faith, he said; the Métis of Manitoba had been discriminated
against politically and had not received what had been promised them. He himself had never been given his land at Red
River. (Actually most of the Métis in Manitoba did receive
land scrip a few years after the troubles, but Riel, under
criminal charges in the Province, did not; nor did those

who had moved west into the Territories before scrip was distributed. And many of those who were induced to sell their scrip immediately to speculators never fully realized what it was and forgot that they had ever received it.)

As an American citizen, Riel told Taylor, he felt that he would not have had any right to come north to help the Métis were it not for the fact that he had a personal interest equal to theirs in obtaining indemnity from Canada for lands they had never received. But the worst grievance of the Métis, he continued, was economic and political discrimination:

The people of the Northwest are poor. They are not happy under the Canadian rule, not only because their public affairs are improperly administered by the federal government, but because they are practically denied by that government *the enjoyment of the right of people*. That is principally what is ruining them.

The emphasis was Riel's. With his letter he enclosed a copy, four pages in English, in his own handwriting, of the demands of the Saskatchewan people.

Ottawa acknowledged receipt of the new petition but said nothing about what it intended to do. Subsequently Sir John A. Macdonald denied, in the face of the official record, that any such list of demands had ever been transmitted to his Government.

DEPARTMENT OF DELAY

Actually, as Sir John well knew, the Métis of the Territories had been appealing since 1873 for security on their lands, land grants or cash subsidies for schools, loans for seed and implements. In the Manitoba Act of 1870 the Government had recognized a Métis title similar to the "aboriginal title" of the Indians; in May, 1873, the first petition for land grants under this precedent had been forwarded to the Governor of the Territories and sent on by him to Ottawa.

Thereafter petitions and letters from half-breed and white settlers and from the French priests went to Ottawa every few months. By 1878 the Government's own representatives were urgently appealing for action, but nothing happened. The Ministry of Interior, a politician later noted, was "a department of delay, a department of circumlocution, a department in which people could not get business done, a department which tired men to death who undertook to get any business transacted with it."

Among those begging for adjustment of the Métis difficulties was Col. John Stoughton Dennis, whom Riel's cavalry had driven from Rupert's Land in 1870. As Deputy Minister of the Interior, he visited the region and suggested various ways of placating the people. Another pleader was Charles Mair, the poet and journalist whose indiscretions had contributed to the Red River outbreak; he was in Prince Albert when Riel arrived from Montana, and he went east to urge pacification. Though these men knew the Métis and had firsthand experience of what they would do when they felt themselves wronged, the Government did not heed their warnings.

Some surveys were started at Prince Albert, and river front lots on the French pattern were permitted there; but elsewhere, to the dismay of the Métis, the American rectangular system was imposed. Moved by their bitter protests, the Dominion land agent appealed in 1882 for a resurvey of the French villages on the river front plan, since no entries had been made under the other survey anyway. His letter went unanswered for six months while angry Métis besieged him. Finally the Minister of the Interior replied curtly, "It is not the intention of the Government to cause any resurveys to be made." The Minister at that time was Sir John himself. He had assumed the Interior portfolio in addition to the

Premiership—a bad move because he had little time to give the department, was poorly informed about the Northwest, and appeared to be wholly uninterested in its people.

In September, 1882, the people of St. Antoine de Padua again petitioned Sir John to let them keep their river front lots; the plea was written by Nolin, and Dumont's name led those of forty-seven signers. The Minister of the Interior replied: "When the proper time arrives the case of each *bona fide* settler will be dealt with on its own merits; but as regards the surveying of the land in question . . . all lands in the Northwest Territories will be surveyed according to the system now in force."

Father André added an indignant voice to the clamor. His own mission's two-hundred-acre claim at Duck Lake, which had been in his possession for seven years and which he had laboriously fenced himself, was "jumped" by a newcomer named Kelly.

But response from Ottawa, if it came at all, was evasive or arrogant and the conclusion is inescapable that deliberate racial discrimination as well as bureaucratic stupidity contributed to the swiftly developing crisis.

In April, 1884, Louis Schmidt, a prominent and prosperous Métis, wrote to Ottawa to complain that the people "during the last four years have sent petitions upon petitions. . . . I feel bound to say that such a state of things is almost intolerable."

The next month, their patience gone, the people sent for Louis Riel.

A month after Louis's arrival Sir John sent a couple of observers to Saskatchewan and informed the Governor General of Canada that he was "watching the situation." They could count upon Father André to keep them informed of developments, he said; meanwhile he was thinking about what should be done. The mistake made at Red River must be

avoided. There the Métis had been given negotiable land
scrip and had promptly sold it and squandered the proceeds
on whiskey. He did not regard the problem as urgent yet in
the Northwest; if the troublemakers got cold enough they
would shut up.

I think the true policy is rather to encourage them to specify
their grievances in memorials and send them with or without
delegations to Ottawa. This will allow time for the present
effervescence to subside, and on the approach of winter the
climate will keep things quiet until next spring.

But just to be safe he would "anticipate" the wishes of
Parliament and would increase immediately the strength of
the Mounted Police. Superintendent L. N. F. Crozier, in
charge of the northern detachment at Battleford, had warned
that unless the Métis were placated soon more police would
be needed.

This was precisely what Sir John had been warned by
Father André not to do, but obviously it held much more
appeal for him than the wearisome sifting of petitions and
a genuine effort to meet the terms of the distant colonists.
So in September he shoved aside the letters from the Northwest and wrote a confidential note to Donald A. Smith of
the Hudson's Bay Company.

Would the Company lend the Government its buildings
at Fort Carlton, about twenty miles west of Batoche, to be
used as emergency quarters for additional Mounties? "I
write you privately," Sir John said, "because it is not well
that any intelligence should go to the Northwest of our intention to increase the force, in advance. If the Company
could lend or rent us the buildings, which I am informed
are not much used just now, possession could be taken without previous notice to anyone."

Thus Sir John again resorted to an expedient he had
adopted before—an armed force to which would go "the

chance of glory and the risk of a scalping knife." And again
he sadly misjudged the temper, the intelligence and the
courage of Louis Riel and his people.

Only a fraction of the population of Canada's Northwest
Territories actually became involved in the final catas-
trophic phase of the Métis movement. This was partially
due to the fact that Riel, and not the much more militant
Gabriel Dumont, was the supreme leader. It was partially
due to the decimation of the Blackfeet by starvation and
disease, and the great influence among them of a famous
missionary, Father Lacombe, who undertook a Government
mission to the camps along the Rockies and persuaded the
powerful Canadian tribe to keep the peace. But in view of
what could have happened and almost did, one can conclude
that the Dominion of Canada was far luckier than it deserved to be. If Riel had not frightened the Anglo-Saxon
settlers, alienated the priests, and, above all, if he had not
interfered with Dumont's aggressive military program, the
War for the West might have ended differently and certainly
would have been much bloodier than it was.

The French villages along the South Saskatchewan, in
which the trouble centered, contained about two thousand
people. A few hundred in the Battleford district to the west
and several Indian bands which included perhaps a thousand men, women and children, also were drawn into the
conflict. But those whites in Prince Albert who had helped
to promote the struggle did not stick to see it through.

"Benefit" meetings brought in some revenue for the campaign, and small sums with which Riel maintained his
family in the house provided for them by a Métis friend.
But gradually the Anglo-Saxon element, including the speculators, began to lose their nerve. The Saskatchewan *Herald*,
Battleford's newspaper, was hostile. "Riel," it said, "has gone
as far as he ought to be allowed to go." He was "an alien

demagogue" who set class against class, and the people of Prince Albert who had joined in inviting him north had made a mistake.

The priests, too, became alarmed as the winter wore on and they became aware of Riel's religious and political obsessions. They met to discuss his eccentricities and to determine whether he should be permitted to continue in his religious duties as a practicing Catholic, in view of his state of mind when religion was mentioned. When it came to the faith and politics, they agreed, he did not seem quite sane; but they did not reach any decision about excluding him from the rites of the Church.

The secrecy of his operations among the people also was condemned by the clergy. But Louis promptly retorted (and with justification, since André was regularly reporting to the Governor) that this was necessary because the priests had become informers.

Father André now sent an urgent appeal to the Governor to get Louis out of the country. It could be done, he thought, by paying him $5,000 as indemnity for his Red River claims and years of exile, though Riel's demands ranged from $35,000 to $100,000. D. H. McDowall, a member of the Territorial Council, also interviewed Riel about leaving the country and he seconded André's recommendation.

In February, 1885, with no answer yet to the petition, Louis proposed at a meeting of the Métis in Batoche that he return to the United States. Angry protest filled the room and he consented to remain. Nolin, who presided at the meeting, testified subsequently that Riel had arranged in advance for this demonstration, but Nolin's testimony was not entirely unbiased; he had split with his cousin and was desperately trying to extricate himself from the movement. Considering the temper of the people they probably needed no urging to ask Louis to stay.

Crozier sent another anxious appeal to Ottawa. "I have

the honor to request," he wrote, "that matters concerning the half-breeds be settled without delay—could not a surveyor be sent *now* if it is intended to allow the half-breeds their land as they wish to have it laid out?"

If this plea had been answered promptly by appearance of a surveyor to draw the lines of the river front lots, the Northwest Rebellion probably would not have occurred. Instead the Government sent word to André that it had decided—*eleven years* after the first Métis petition—to "appoint a commission" to look into the complaints. The priest passed the word along to his flock. But a commission was not enough. It only meant a drawn-out inquiry; and the people no longer had any faith in Sir John, to whom they now applied the derisive nickname first given him by the Indians—"Old Tomorrow." Moreover, with characteristic sluggishness, though the decision to name the commission was reached in January, the Government did not get around to appointing its members until March and did not give them their orders in Ottawa until the 30th of that month.

That was four days too late.

Police Superintendent Crozier was guessing at the state of the Métis mind from the excitement which his men observed in the settlements and the secrecy which now veiled the movements of Riel and his associates. Louis's public speeches were still above reproach so far as their content was concerned, but his manner was becoming more and more violent.

Actually, though none but a few intimates knew it, Riel had now decided upon a dangerous gamble—establishment of a Provisional Government under the protection of Métis cavalry, as he had done in Rupert's Land. He looked upon this as a demonstration rather than as an act of war, and it had worked on Red River; he was convinced it was the only way to bring Ottawa to terms. But he was not thinking as clearly as he had fifteen years before; his judgment had been impaired by mental lapses, by years of brooding exile, and perhaps most of all by his emotional response to the enthusiasm with which his people had received him in Saskatchewan.

Riel forgot that the country over which he now proposed to set up a government was indisputably Canadian, not stateless as Rupert's Land had been in 1870. What then had been reluctantly countenanced by the new and weak Dominion largely because of fear of the United States, and what had been perhaps *ex necessitate* under international law, was now riot, rebellion, or even treason. Though the Government's neglect, which looked like deliberate provocation, might seem to provide some moral justification, it did not constitute a legal defense for insurrection.

On March 2 Louis confronted Father André and demanded that he, as superior of the priests of the district, give his approval to formation by the Métis of a Provisional Government. André sharply refused, and Riel upbraided him as a traitor and announced to the people that they had been abandoned by their priests.

IT HAS COMMENCED

Charles Nolin, working frantically with the clergy to forestall rebellion, now thought up an excuse for delay. Let the Métis engage in a ten-day period of prayer, and decide after that what they should do.

Riel objected, but he put Nolin's proposal, and his own, to a vote of the leaders at his own house near Batoche on March 6. Nolin's idea appealed to the pious Métis and was approved. The novena started March 10, and was scheduled to conclude March 19, the feast day of St. Joseph, patron saint of the half-breeds.

Louis did not appear in the church at Batoche until Sunday, March 15. The little chapel was filled and Father Vital

Fourmond took advantage of this to review what he had been saying all week about the unwisdom of revolt. He harshly rebuked those who might lead the Métis to destruction, and then he delivered what the clergy hoped would be the decisive blow. All who took up arms against established authority would be refused the sacraments.

The people were stunned, but while they milled around in the churchyard after the service, Riel called the priest out and angrily denounced him. "You have turned the pulpit of truth into one of politics, falsehood and discord," he said, "in daring to refuse the sacraments to those who would take up arms in defense of their most sacred rights!"

The priest stood his ground, and Louis produced his precious letters from Bourget, calling upon Fourmond to admit that his mission had episcopal sanction.

The letters were old, the priest retorted; and besides they did not mean what Riel said they meant.

Fourmond left the scene as Louis harangued the people. The Spirit of God had left the Church of Rome and the Pope, he declared, and had taken up its abode in the person of Bishop Bourget who had endorsed the cause of the Métis. If their priests would not sustain them the people would go forward without their priests; they would be their own priests. He would administer the sacraments himself.

But the Métis were bewildered and fearful. It was not to be doubted that Louis was a prophet, and the papers from Bishop Bourget were most impressive. But was Louis a priest? It had not been anticipated that one might be risking his immortal soul by joining the Métis crusade.

For three days the clergy's ultimatum was worriedly debated in the cabins and around prairie campfires. Attendance for the novena picked up, and Father André and his colleagues happily looked forward to big crowds on St. Joseph's Day. The crisis had almost passed, they were convinced; Riel and the militants were losing ground every hour.

In contemporary Métis accounts, in the stories of survivors, and in Riel's own testimony, responsibility for touching off the Northwest Rebellion is put upon Lawrence Clarke, the Hudson's Bay factor at Fort Carlton and a member of the Northwest Territorial Council. Clarke denied it, but there is some indirect evidence to support the Métis story.

Sir John Macdonald had appealed to the Company for permission to use buildings at Clarke's post for housing police reinforcements. Obviously Clarke had to be informed when this request was granted. The need for secrecy may not have been impressed upon him; but he knew, of course, that Macdonald's idea that he could send more Mounties into the country without the knowledge of the inhabitants was absurd.

On March 18, the day before the period of prayer was to end, the French settlements were electrified by a rumor: Clarke had told some freighters whom he met on the trail that five hundred more police were en route to Saskatchewan and Riel and other leaders soon would be under arrest.

Louis called a mass meeting and a council of twelve men was formed. The cry, "To arms!" echoed through the villages. For miles up and down the South Saskatchewan the Métis hunters seized their guns, mounted and rode to Batoche to protect their chief. Within a few hours the old Red River cavalry, the wardens of the plains, again took form. The council, which at Riel's urging promptly proclaimed itself a "Provisional Government," chose as its adjutant general the popular Gabriel Dumont, the best marksman in the Northwest and, as it developed, a brilliant military strategist.

Riel led a group of his men to the Church of St. Antoine,

the people trotting along behind. He summoned the only priest then present, Father Moulin, from the parish house.

"The die has been cast for war," he said. "There is no use opposing it. I am going to take possession of the church."

The priest, standing in the church door, tried to address the people, but Louis and his soldiers shouted him down.

Finally Moulin made himself heard for a moment. "You are a heretic," he shouted to Louis. "I protest against your touching the church!"

Riel turned to the crowd, laughing. "Look at him! He is a Protestant!"

The Métis obediently laughed, too, though somewhat un-easily. Louis shouldered the priest aside, but Moulin stum-bled ahead of him into the church, removed the monstrance, the vessel for the Host, and fled with it into the parish house.

Riel led the people into the church and spoke to them briefly. "Rome has fallen!" he said. He asked what should be done with Father Moulin—should he be imprisoned? The others were unwilling to go so far; leave him be, they sug-gested, and watch him.

"In answer to our petition, the Government sends police," Louis cried. He gestured proudly to the armed Métis. "These are my police!"

He led his little army back to the village. While fifty armed men swarmed outside, he and a few others entered the store of Kerr Brothers, on the east side of the river, and told George Kerr they wanted his stock of guns and ammu-nition. Kerr wisely did not resist. When some of the men swarmed behind the counter Riel rebuked them and urged Kerr to hand down the articles wanted, keep an account, and "charge it."

The group now moved across the river on the ice to the other store, operated by Walters and Baker. Walters refused to accede to Riel's demand that he hand over all guns and ammunition, and he was gently thrust aside while they helped themselves.

"What is this all about?" the storekeeper demanded.

Riel smiled. "Well, Mr. Walters," he said, "it has commenced."

That night Métis horsemen rode out on the prairies and cut the telegraph wire in several places. Two men who came out to repair it were taken prisoner, along with Walters, his clerk, some freighters and one or two others suspected of being in league with the police, ten or a dozen in all. The Northwest Rebellion, the last stand of the New Nation of Louis Riel, had begun.

CHAPTER XX

"Marchons, Mes Braves!"

EXOVEDE

On March 19 Charles Nolin was arrested, "court-martialed" by the Métis council, and condemned to death as a traitor because he refused to take up arms. The people were again summoned to the church and Nolin was taken there under guard; no one, apparently, protested against the severity of the council's action. The election of the council was announced, Riel proclaimed the creation of the Provisional Government of the Saskatchewan, and Dumont called for popular support.

Louis closed the meeting. "What is [Fort] Carlton?" he asked. "What is Prince Albert? Nothing! We march, my braves!"

That night the wily but thoroughly scared Nolin told the council that Riel had been willing to leave Batoche and abandon his people if he could get the indemnity he demanded from Ottawa. This revelation upset the group sufficiently to win him revocation of the death sentence and release from custody, though he continued under close surveillance. A few days later he managed to escape and find sanctuary in Prince Albert.

Carlton, twenty miles west of Batoche, consisted only of the Hudson's Bay post, a few buildings including a storehouse which had been borrowed as barracks for the Mounted Police. Major Crozier, the superintendent of the northern police district, had been there for about ten days with seventy-five men. As soon as he learned of the Batoche incidents he sent to Prince Albert for Thomas McKay, a Scotch half-breed and Hudson's Bay Company agent, to be his go-between in negotiations for release of the prisoners and goods taken by the Métis. Crozier asked McKay to assure Riel that he would meet him personally to discuss a settlement; he was unwilling to precipitate an armed clash on his own responsibility because his superior, Lieut. Col. A. G. Irvine, Commissioner of the Police, was en route from Regina with about a hundred men to reinforce the northern garrisons.

Riel reorganized and enlarged the council and the new group served notice on Crozier that he must abandon Carlton and his headquarters at Battleford; if he did so the police would be given safe passage out of the country. The ultimatum, dated March 21, concluded:

. . . In case of non-acceptance, we intend to attack you when tomorrow, the Lord's Day, is over; and to commence without delay a war of extermination upon all those who have shown themselves hostile to our rights. . . .

Major, we respect you. Let the cause of humanity be a consolation to you for the reverses which the governmental misconduct has brought upon you.

At Crozier's urgent request Prince Albert reluctantly contributed about seventy civilian volunteers to bolster the police garrison at Carlton. The English community, approaching panic, suggested that the outlying post be abandoned and that all available men be concentrated in Prince Albert for the protection of that much larger settlement, but Crozier insisted and after a few days he got the men he wanted.

McKay went to Batoche in a courageous but fruitless effort to dissuade the Métis from open rebellion. Riel refused to meet Crozier, but consented to send envoys; he then denounced McKay in the council chamber as a traitor to his own people. The would-be mediator was lucky to escape with his life; nor were his subsequent negotiations, accompanied by other emissaries of Crozier, any more successful. Maxime Lépine and Nolin, the latter an unwilling tool of Riel's council, met McKay's party halfway between Batoche and Carlton, but all agreed that Riel's terms could not be compromised with those of Crozier, who now demanded that the Métis surrender their leaders to him and disperse to their homes. Nevertheless these maneuvers delayed matters a few days and the threatened attack on the police Monday, March 23, did not develop.

The note to Crozier was the first "official" document of "The Councillors of the Provisional Government of Saskatchewan." It was signed by "Louis 'David' Riel, *Exovede*," and sixteen others. The term *"Exovede"* puzzled all recipients of Riel's communications for months—until, after his arrest, he explained it himself. He had taken it from Latin, he said: *ex,* from; *ovede,* flock. It was intended to designate him as "one of the flock," as were all members of the council, which he called the *"Exovidat,"* and was a specific disavowal of personal leadership.

Despite this gesture Riel wholly dominated the council and no other member ever used the term which he, proud of his classical scholarship, had devised. His council at Red River had sometimes been recalcitrant, but he had no such troubles in Saskatchewan. Nolin alone had challenged him and Nolin was now thoroughly cowed. Dumont had the standing among his fellows to curb Louis if he chose to do so, but sincerely loved him and rarely disputed his decisions—never in public. Even after Louis began to interfere in military matters, Gabriel acquiesced with good grace for several weeks, though Louis's strategical judgment was invariably bad and Gabriel knew it.

Overnight, the idol of the Métis became their dictator. Much more sure of himself than he had been in 1870 and sustained by his faith in his mission, Louis accepted the role as his due, yet he cannot be said to have sought it. Up to a fortnight before the first overt acts, the raids on the stores, he could have been persuaded to return to Montana; later, a more independent council could have controlled the movement if it had wished to do so, because Louis sincerely believed that he was an instrument of the people and of his God and subordinate to the will of both. On one occasion, asking the *Exovidat* to weigh his reasons for a certain course, he nevertheless assured it that he was its agent, not its master:

. . . Be convinced, dear Sirs, that when you have examined what I now submit to you, if you adopt a course contrary to my views I shall look upon it as an expression of the permission of God, and I will help you with all my strength to carry out your views as though they were my own, to the greater glory of God.

But with one or two exceptions the French leaders were wholly in accord with Riel. So far as the fatal decision to fight was concerned, Dumont undoubtedly exerted much influence, and he was far more bloodthirsty (or realistic) than his chief. Yet both men knew that if it came to full-scale war the Métis could not win.

It was not to be war; it was to be a demonstration, a show of strength. The people would not even go that far, Louis knew, without some religious impetus; so he harangued them constantly and moved with speed and daring to supplant the unco-operative priests. The first hint of his plans came on Wednesday, March 25, the feast of the Ascension, when he again called the people to the little chapel of the Church of St. Antoine to hear him renounce the Roman Catholic faith on behalf of the council and himself. Soon, he said, there would be a new religion in the Northwest.

He then hunted up Father Moulin and demanded that he renounce the Pope and become the first priest of the new Church.

"You can kill me," the priest told him, "but I will never abandon my religion."

"Then I will drive you from the country!" Riel threatened.

"My country is the universe; I am not afraid," Moulin said.

Louis angrily sought out another priest, Father Végreville, and insisted that he become "chaplain" of the Métis cavalry. He refused.

But there had to be a chaplain; the Métis had decided to march the next day. Very well, *mes braves,* said Riel, I will be your priest.

DUCK LAKE

Sir John acknowledged, in response to nervous inquiries in the House, that there was a little trouble on the frontier, confirming fragmentary reports in Ontario newspapers of an "uprising," the plundering of stores and imprisonment of citizens. But it was a minor disturbance, he said, and there was no cause for concern. That was March 23.

Mounted Police reinforcements had reached the scene and a hundred men of the Ninetieth Battalion of Canadian militia had been sent to help. The Government was appointing a commission to look into Métis discontent. But those people were always complaining; "If you wait for a half-breed or an Indian to become contented," the Prime Minister joked, "you may wait till the millennium." That was March 26.

On March 27 frantic wires from Minister of Defense A. P. Caron to militia commanders throughout the Dominion fixed their quotas for twenty-four-hour mobilization. The West was aflame.

At a place called Duck Lake, or maybe it was Stobart because that was the name of its post office, and anyway nobody had ever heard of it, the unthinkable had happened. Sir John's "miserable half-breeds" had thrashed and put to ignominious flight a detachment of Mounted Police and civilian volunteers, killing or wounding twenty-five per cent of the loyal force. The rebel loss, if any (dispatches were unclear on this point), was certainly under five per cent. The Métis adjutant general, Gabriel Dumont, had outsmarted and outfought Major Crozier, a veteran officer of the Mounties; now, despite the arrival of their reinforcements, the police were abandoning outposts like Carlton without a fight.

The Indians were rising. Panic-stricken Prince Albert had lodged all the women and children in the Presbyterian Church and manse and surrounded them with a cordwood stockade. Anglo-Saxon settlers, their isolated farms in flames, were fleeing for their lives over snow-choked trails or in frail boats on rivers full of drifting ice.

An emergency corps of volunteers, a couple of hundred men, was being armed and mounted and rushed south to the Montana line, beyond which lived thirty-two thousand Indians and Métis, potential allies of Riel. The Dominion was appealing to the commanders of 1,680 United States troops in Dakota and Montana to help guard the boundary.

At Edmonton, 350 miles west of Batoche, a squaw man told the newspaper editor everything would be all right "so long as you can hear the drum in the Indian camp." Next morning the drum was silent, the camp gone.

The War for the West, begun fifteen years before on Red River, had entered its final desperate phase.

The night of Riel's meeting in the St. Antoine Church, March 25, Gabriel Dumont led a small force to Duck Lake, a Métis community about midway between Batoche and Carlton and on the edge of a small Cree Indian reserve. The Stobart & Eden store there was one of the largest in the district and at this time, in addition to its own stock, contained a large shipment of Government supplies destined for Indian agencies and police posts.

Dumont's men partially looted the place; more were coming next day to finish the job. At two o'clock in the morning of the 26th the Métis captured two scouts sent out by Crozier and imprisoned them in the store, along with the clerk. A few hours later, unaware of what had happened, because his scouts had not returned, Crozier sent Thomas McKay with an escort to bring the police supplies from Duck Lake to Carlton. This party was met by Dumont and his men and turned back after an argument.

When the rebuff was reported at Carlton, Crozier set out for Duck Lake with a force of fifty-six Mounties and forty-three Prince Albert volunteers, most of them mounted. They took Crozier's only cannon, a little seven-pounder, and sleighs to bring back the supplies. This advance was a grave error in judgment because Colonel Irvine was then less than fifty miles away, riding from Prince Albert with the reinforcements. But the supplies at Duck Lake were important, and Crozier was under pressure from the outraged civilian volunteers; the latter had more spunk than good sense and demanded that the rebels be promptly put in their place. The police superintendent was persuaded that continued inactivity would reflect upon the honor of "the Force."

Two miles from the Duck Lake trading post, Crozier's advance scouts spotted the Métis on a low hill about two hundred yards away. Most of the rebels were lying prone on blankets, shielded by brush or hummocks of sod; some, including Gabriel Dumont, were on horseback in a small coulee. It was snowing and visibility was poor.

Crozier halted and had the twenty sleighs drawn into a line across the road, ordering his men to dismount and take shelter behind them. At the right end of his line, commanding that flank at murderously close range, stood a log cabin, seemingly deserted. If Crozier noticed it he did nothing about it.

Isidore Dumont, Gabriel's brother, came forward with an Indian from the Métis line on the hill, apparently for a parley. Major Crozier and his interpreter, an English half-breed named John Dougall Mackay, advanced to meet them. All four men were on horseback.

Crozier extended his hand to the Indian, who was unarmed, but the latter made a grab for the interpreter's rifle. The interpreter fired, and Isidore Dumont plunged from his horse, dead.

Major Crozier glanced quickly at the rebel line; it was in motion, spreading around his left flank. He spurred his horse back to the sleighs and shouted a command to fire. The Indian was mortally wounded in the first volley.

With the first answering fire from the Métis, Crozier realized to his dismay that he had been outmaneuvered and that his force had ridden into a carefully prepared ambush. Dumont did not appear to have many men (he subsequently claimed to have had only twenty-five when the fight started) but they were distributed in a wide semicircle and most of them were invisible to the troops; moreover Crozier now discovered that the cabin to his right contained sharpshooters who could pick off men on that end of his line almost at will.

Now, about a hundred and fifty Métis fighters swarmed to

the battlefield from the settlement beyond the hill—at their head Louis Riel, mounted, unarmed, holding at arm's length a crucifix a foot and a half long which he had taken from the church in Duck Lake. The police fired at him, but he was out of range. "In the name of God the Father who created us," he cried, "reply to that!" The Métis cheered and fired. Bullets kicked up dirt and snow in their faces but could not touch their chief; had he not told them himself that he was invulnerable in battle? He continued to exhort them, in the name of Jesus and the Holy Ghost, and with each shout from him his hunters sent another volley into the doomed company on the field below.

The cannon held the Métis in their positions for a few minutes, but after it had been fired three times to check envelopment of the left flank and was swung around at last to shell the cabin, a rattled gunner inserted a shell before the charge of powder was placed and put the piece out of action.

The movement around the left flank began again and Crozier started to pull in his men for a retreat. He would be lucky, he now knew, if he escaped a massacre.

Gabriel Dumont, mounted again, rode recklessly to within sixty yards of the troops. A bullet plowed a deep gash through his scalp and he fell, almost senseless; his horse, also wounded, jumped over him and fled. He struggled to his feet but dropped again, and a nearby Métis, Joseph Delorme, cried out that their general had been killed. "Courage!" Gabriel yelled. "As long as I haven't lost my head I'm not dead!" Another brother, Edouard Dumont, ran forward to drag him out of the line of fire but Gabriel sent him back to take command.

By order of their own officer and without Crozier's approval, the volunteers, maddened by the sniping from the cabin, made a foolhardy charge upon it in which they lost heavily. Crozier was now hopelessly outnumbered and he ordered a headlong retreat from the field. The dead and wounded who could be reached (most of the volunteers' casualties were too close to the cabin) were loaded on the sleighs and the surviving horses were harnessed under fire. Then the loyal troops fled, without even rear-guard fire to restrain the Métis.

But in the rebel line an argument raged. Gabriel, blood streaming over his face, and his brother Edouard shouted to their men to follow the fleeing enemy and annihilate the entire detachment. Riel countermanded the order. "In the name of God," he pleaded, "let them go; there has been too much bloodshed already!"

As he nearly always did, Gabriel bowed to the decision of his chief and there was no pursuit. The wounded Dumont was tied on a horse and the victorious war party rode back to the village, the men shouting with joy and Louis, still waving the crucifix, singing praises to God and the saints. They took with them a wounded Prince Albert volunteer who had been left on the field by his mates; he was put under the care of the Canadian prisoners and when he had sufficiently recovered from his leg wound was released.

In Duck Lake, Louis summoned the people and lined up the troops for review. He offered a prayer of thanksgiving and ordered a special prayer and three rousing cheers for Gabriel Dumont, weaving wearily on his horse. "Give thanks to God," Louis commanded, "who gave you so valiant a leader!" He then ordered the bodies of the rebel dead laid out in a nearby house and for the rest of the day led the people in prayer for their souls.

The skirmish had lasted half an hour. It had cost the loyal force twelve dead and eleven wounded out of ninety-nine engaged. Nine of the dead and four of the wounded were volunteers, most of them victims of the attack on the cabin. Among the volunteers killed were some bearing notable names: a son of Sir Charles Napier; a nephew of the Nova Scotia statesman, Joseph Howe; a cousin of the leader of the opposition in Parliament; and a nephew of Sir Francis Hincks, Governor of the Windward Islands.

Five rebels, four Métis and one Indian, had been killed and three, including Gabriel Dumont, slightly wounded; their effective force had numbered about two hundred.

Among the rebels on the battlefield was a boy of fourteen, a distant relative of Gabriel Dumont whom the latter, without children of his own, often treated as a son. More than fifty years after the Duck Lake battle his memory of it was still vivid. "You be scared like I was scared that day," he said, "you never forget either."

The boy, whose name was Alex, lay shivering for hours in the snow on top of the hill while the Métis awaited the police. He heard Uncle Gabriel cursing because his force was inadequate; Riel was not yet there with reinforcements and scouts had warned that Crozier was bringing about a hundred men.

"Nobody move!" Gabriel had ordered, going among his men, forcing them to lie still and flat and far apart behind the clumps of brush.

Then the police came—slow-moving, erect little shadows in the gray light and the snow, seeming to ride toward them in the sky because in this sunless void there was no horizon. Alex had no gun; he had tagged along uninvited and now his assignment was to run down the hill and snatch cartridge belts from police casualties when and if Crozier's men were repulsed. Even if the enemy did not fall back, Alex boasted, that job would have been easy: "any boy who couldn't outrun a bullet was no good." Footracing was the chief recreation of Métis youngsters.

He heard the word passed along the line: *"A la garde!"* He saw the abortive parley in the field, ducked as the first police volley thudded into the hillside—far too low. He was a better marksman than these redcoats and volunteers and it was too bad he had not been given a gun. He had asked Gabriel, who had slain Blackfeet, what it was like to kill a man, and Gabriel had said it was not much different from killing game. Alex had done that, but he could see a great deal of difference now: the game was stalking the hunter over this snow-covered field. He remembered, too, that when overconfident Métis had remarked that the police were only fair shots and the volunteers no good at all, Gabriel had answered grimly that men could very quickly learn to shoot well.

At one time early in the fight Gabriel flung himself prone near Alex, wormed forward to the crest of the hill and fired a dozen shots from his beloved Winchester carbine, aiming at the gun crew; he hated cannon, against which his Métis had no defense. He inched his way back, reloaded, and mounted his horse to hurry to the left flank after the gun was silenced. Meanwhile Louis had arrived and the boy watched, fascinated, as their chaplain-chief rode back and forth waving the big crucifix.

Alex did not see Gabriel shot from his horse, but he saw him stanching the flow of blood from his forehead with hand-fuls of snow, saw him crawl to his cousin, Auguste Laframboise, who was dying, and weakly attempt to make the sign of the cross over him.

When the boy looked back at the enemy they were milling around the sleighs, trying to hitch up under fire. One wounded volunteer, unable to rise, was pushing himself with one bent leg toward the sleighs. His booted foot would scrabble in the snow, trying to dig a hold, then there would be a little push and he would move a few inches. Alex thought the snow curled aside from his head like sod from a plow. He watched the man's jerky, painful progress for a long time, while the teams were hitched and the other wounded loaded into the sleighs. The boy felt as if he wanted to call out to the police to wait. They didn't, and the wounded man was left still plowing blindly toward the road.

Alex woke up then to his duty and joined the triumphant warriors who were stripping the dead volunteers of guns and cartridge belts and carrying the bodies into the cabin where they would be safe from marauding animals. (Riel sent word to Prince Albert that no harm would befall anyone coming to recover the dead and men were sent to do this a couple of days later; the Métis helped them place the bodies in their wagons.)

The rebels got a dozen good rifles, some ammunition, eight horses, and five sleighs or wagons. But Gabriel scolded because they had not captured Crozier's wretched little seven-pounder popgun.

That night, although Colonel Irvine and the reinforcements had arrived, the police decided that Carlton was indefensible; moreover the volunteers, whose opinion of the rebels' intelligence and military resolution had undergone a sudden change, clamored to return to Prince Albert to defend their homes and families.

The next day, Friday, Carlton's stores were hurriedly packed for the retreat. During the night fire broke out and they let it burn; when the detachment left for Prince Albert Saturday morning the warehouse had been destroyed. Métis scouts watched the evacuation, moved into the post and checked the fire before it spread to other buildings, then raced off to report to Dumont.

Gabriel went eagerly to Riel. There was, he said wheedlingly, a certain place he knew on that trail, a lovely place, where Crozier's whole force would have to pass through a narrow gap in a thick grove of trees. Perfect for an ambush . . .

No, said Louis Riel.

A few years later, in a sworn account of the incident, the

hard-headed, single-minded, forthright Gabriel sighed for this lost opportunity:

"We could have killed a lot of them, but Riel, who was always restraining us, formally opposed the idea."

BET YOUR BOOTS

Maj. Gen. Frederick D. Middleton, commander-in-chief of Canadian militia, detrained the first detachment of Winnipeg's Ninetieth at Qu'Appelle, Saskatchewan, established a base camp a few miles north, and sat back to wait for reinforcements. He was nearly two hundred miles southeast of Batoche.

He reflected that he had seen few Indians in his lifetime and no prairie Métis at all. But he had fought the upstart Maoris in New Zealand when he was barely out of his teens and the Royal Military College at Sandhurst; rebels were rebels anywhere. He should have had the Victoria Cross for that business in the Sepoy Mutiny, too; never got it—damned technicality: C.O. wouldn't recommend him for it because he happened to be on the staff. Other chap who figured in the same incident got it, of course.

Now he was in the field again, at sixty. Rotten luck, but he would have been retired on a lieutenant colonel's pay after his stint as commandant at Sandhurst except for the lucky break of Luard's retirement. That had opened this spot in Canada, with promotion, last November.

Yes, rebels were rebels anywhere. One thing they had taught him, however: never underestimate the enemy. Especially savages. Astonishingly difficult sometimes to determine how the aboriginal mind worked!

Better to underestimate your own, especially when they were militia, all volunteers. Bank clerks, college students, shoe clerks, farmers, lawyers, blacksmiths, teachers, artisans. Never fired a shot in combat. Most of the officers the same, save for a few who had popped off at the ridiculous Fenians at Ridgeway or Pigeon Hill and thought they had seen war. Poor lot on the whole, and their mothers and wives and sweethearts—and the politicians—would kick up a beastly row if any of them got hurt. Thought it was all a lark, most of these chaps. Good idea to play it safe, keep losses down.

Asked that company commander in Ontario what sort of men he had in his lot; damned fool boasted about their score on the rifle range. Took him down a peg: suggested he keep in mind that this time the target would be shooting back!

In Ottawa, Van Horne of the Canadian Pacific told the Government that he would get the troops over the gaps in his unfinished railroad in eleven days if he could have two days' notice and a free hand. He got them. Van Horne had moved troops on the Chicago & Alton during the Civil War and he knew what was required; but that had been a railroad, and the C.P.R., the potential corridor of empire, was hardly a railroad yet. Technically it now reached to the foot of the Rockies, but 250 miles along the north shore of Lake Superior were under construction, with temporary track or no track at all.

In British Columbia three hundred armed strikers were being held at bay in a C.P.R. camp by eight Mounties, and there was trouble elsewhere because the company was broke and the men were unpaid. Stephen and Smith had sold or pledged everything they owned. "Donald," Stephen said, "when they come they must not find us with a dollar." They were ruined and the railroad was doomed unless a Dominion loan could be obtained. There had been bickering over this for four months; Sir John was holding out, as usual, for a political deal. But if Van Horne could get the troops west in time to save the Territories, the Cabinet would have to come around.

So Van Horne moved about five thousand men, most of them eighteen hundred miles and some twenty-five hundred, into the land of the Métis. It took nine days to get one bunch over that unfinished section but others made it in four, and none needed the eleven he had given himself as a safe limit. He put rails down on ice and snow, ran trains over frozen rivers, used construction trains and work engines, imported Chinese coolies from the United States to lay track. Sometimes his locomotives could move only six miles an hour; for ninety miles there were no locomotives because there was no track; the men rode in sleighs if they were available and if not they walked. But they moved, and by April 10 most of the expeditionary force was in the Northwest, marching on the Métis. And on April 30 the C.P.R. got its loan.

Between Dog Lake, seven hundred and fifty miles west of Toronto near the present town of White River, Ontario, and Nipigon, halfway around the north shore of Lake Superior, there were four trackless gaps ranging in length from seven miles to forty-five. At the start of each of these the men, supplies and equipment had to be unloaded and loaded again, and at the end of the gap the process had to be repeated—sixteen operations in all. There were more than a hundred miles with only construction tracks, work engines and flat cars. Van Horne had four-foot walls nailed to these cars to provide some protection from the wind and had hay thrown in on the floors; but there were no roofs and no stoves and about all that could be said for this transport was that it was better than walking. After a night of it the men often had to be lifted out of the cars.

It is conceivable that no troops anywhere, with the exception of Russia or Siberia, have undergone an ordeal worse than that of the raw Canadian volunteers who headed west in March and April of 1885. Wolseley's famous march of 1870, terrible as it was, was less so than this trek because it was made in the summer and there was not so much urgency about it. The heroic Northwest Field Force of 1885 set out

at the worst time of the year and slogged over some of the
roughest terrain in North America, knee-deep in snow one
day and in icy water the next, whipped by rainstorm, blizzard and prairie wind, blistered by sun and ice-glare, and
much of the time hungry and poorly clad.

Commissariat and supply were scandalously inadequate.
The first detachment to entrain was instructed to bring its
own lunches. Many had to provide their own boots, socks,
shirts and underwear—without the foggiest idea of what
would be required. To add to the confusion there were three
kinds of rifles—Snider, Winchester and Martini-Henry—and
much of the ammunition was bad. Saddles, harness and pack
outfits were of poor quality. Hospital equipment was un-
available in Canada and had to be bought sight unseen and
hastily imported from New York. Hay for the expedition's
horses was bought at Qu'Appelle for $20 a ton but freighters
got $10 a day for their services and their teams, which ate
about half of each load en route to Middleton's last headquarters near Batoche; the result was that half a ton of hay
sometimes cost $220 and the force used five hundred tons a
month. The militia private's pay was fifty cents a day.

Canada had never fought a war, not even an Indian war.
There was no Western military base; one had to be established at Winnipeg almost overnight by telegraph. There
had never been any integration of field command and supply
and the problems of military transport were undreamed of.
Serious mistakes were made, and had Dumont rather than
Riel been the supreme authority among the Métis they could
have caused disaster. Supply lines were extended and absurdly vulnerable: Middleton left some of his stores on the
line of march under guard of one man. Morale was better
among the men than in the command; the General did not
trust militia officers and they resented his caution.

Men and money were wasted, but the job was done. In
twelve days the troops and their equipment were moved to

the Saskatchewan, and reserve supplies including six thousand rifles, a million cartridges, additional cannon, some fifteen hundred extra kits for infantrymen, and a quarter-mil-
lion pounds of canned rations. Still, if it had not been for
Van Horne and his superintendents and stationmasters, including one who baked fresh rolls daily for the boys, the
Northwest Field Force of 1885 would have starved to death.

General Middleton would not have been amused, but one
Toronto contingent found it funny that one of their outfit
had forgotten to leave the combination of his office safe with
his employees, another had left the gas burning in his home,
and a third was paying three cents a day fine on an overdue
library book.

They received telegrams about such matters at the bivouac
at Dog Lake, end of track, after a comfortable ride in over-
heated railroad cars and nourishing, if not fancy, meals at
designated C.P.R. stations. It was chilly, but fairly comfortable in the tents; tomorrow they would climb into sleighs
for the trip over that first gap in the line, forty-five miles.

But in the morning it was discovered that there were not
enough sleighs to carry men and equipment, too, so most of
the men walked. It was twenty-five below zero.

They walked the second gap, too—seventeen miles; and
the third, twenty miles; and the fourth, seven miles. Some
of them collapsed, delirious, and were picked up by the
sleighs following with their supplies. The lucky ones who
had been assigned to ride as guards were pitched into snow-
banks time after time as the sleighs overturned on the rough
trail or the horses plunged into potholes sometimes three
feet deep.

The men stumbled across the cruel blue ice of Lake Superior and reflected sun glare beat on their faces like whips,
leaving the flesh hanging in strips and their lips gashed and
bloody. Some had been issued snow goggles but some had
not, or had lost them; for these last, who included Colonel

Otter, the brigade commander, there was the agony of snowblindness with its stabbing, maddening pain.

At night stops they waited as long as an hour and a half in
line, shivering in cold rain or snow, for tea and hardtack.
The tents were not large enough to house all of them and
some slept outside in wet clothing; they were beaten or
kicked awake at intervals to go to the fires and dry out, lest
they freeze to death. Standing at the fires, they had to be
watched because they would be overcome by the deadly sleep
of exhaustion and cold and topple forward into the blaze.

When it was all over and the surgeon general submitted
his report, it was noted that rheumatism, bronchitis, pleurisy,
tonsillitis and pneumonia had put more men out of action
than the enemy had.

But, like Wolseley's "Jolly Boys," the Canadians still could
sing. Given a fire, a rock-hard army biscuit and a fast-freezing
cup of tea, they would swing into a favorite:

The volunteers are all fine boys and full of lots of fun,
But it's mighty little pay they get for carrying a gun;
The Government have grown so lean and the C.P.R. so fat
Our extra pay we did not get—
You can bet your boots on that!

They will not even give a shed that's fitting for our drill,
For Ridgeway now forgotten is, and also Pigeon Hill;
But now they've wanted us again, they've called us out—that's
    flat—
And the boys have got to board themselves;
You can bet your boots on that!

To annexate us some folks would, or independent be,
And our Sir John would federate the colonies, I see;
But let them blow till they are blue and I'll throw up my hat
And give my life for England's flag—
You can bet your boots on that!
The flag that's waved a thousand years,
You can bet your boots on that!

CHAPTER XXI

Justice Commands

"STIR UP THE INDIANS!"

WHILE the half-frozen militia sloshed wearily westward, the *Exovidat* of the Provisional Government of Saskatchewan met daily, opening its sessions with a prayer written for it by Louis Riel:

> O Lord, our God, who art the Father of mercy and consolation, we are several French-Canadian Métis gathered together in council, who put our confidence in Thee; grant that we may not be covered with confusion, ever defend us from this, enlighten us in our darkness of doubt, encourage us in our trials, strengthen us in our weakness, and succour us in the time of pressing need.

Gabriel Dumont chafed at such pious pastimes. He should be in the field. His scouts had intercepted telegrams reporting the Canadians' movements and one of his shrewdest agents was with the troops; he knew every step the enemy took. Now he could launch a guerrilla campaign, he told Riel, which would hold up the advance for weeks or months.

His scheme was thoroughly sound. He wanted to disrupt the Canadians' transport and supply arrangements by dynamiting the C.P.R. tracks and making sudden descents upon the inadequately protected prairie outposts where food for the men and hay for the horses was being stored in preparation for Middleton's northern march. He also planned to demoralize the troops by subjecting them to nightly raids on the foolishly exposed position north of Qu'Appelle which Middleton had selected for his base camp. The Canadians were exhausted, Dumont knew; later he commented that if he had been permitted to carry out his plan, "I could have made them so edgy that at the end of three nights they would have been at each other's throats." And he proved the effectiveness of this night terrorism before the campaign ended.

But Riel refused to assent to guerrilla warfare when Gabriel first proposed it, even though it had been urged on him before—by the Fenian Donnelly in Fort Benton. His arguments now indicated that he still hoped the Métis outburst would be regarded as a demonstration and a threat, and that all avenues to peace were not closed. The Métis had friends among the advancing Canadians, he insisted.

Gabriel scoffed. "I wouldn't consider as our friends those who would join the English to kill and plunder us!"

"If you knew them," Louis retorted, "you wouldn't try to treat them that way." Besides, Gabriel's tactics were "too much like those of the Indians."

The adjutant general yielded, but this time he grumbled. "I was convinced," he said, "that from a humane standpoint mine was the better plan. But I had confidence in his faith and his prayers and that God would listen to him."

Dumont's suggestions never were submitted to the council. Instead Louis insisted upon taking up the time of that body with religious matters. The new Church he had promised to give the Métis must be immediately established.

Though Riel's maneuvers in the council at this time (im-

mediately before and after the Duck Lake fight) were primarily motivated by his own obsessive concern with religion,
they also reflected sound judgment of the psychological needs
of his people. Still, as Gabriel told him, he could have pursued his religious objectives among the older men of the
council while Dumont and the young hunters were in the
field hounding the approaching enemy. The truth was that
Riel was afraid to let his peerless military leader out of his
sight. Though he had not hesitated to veto Gabriel's campaign plans, he actually had so little confidence in his own
military abilities that he dreaded being left to direct the
defense of Batoche if some surprise maneuver by the Canadians made it necessary.

Louis also was showing at this time, probably uncon-
sciously, some sense of history. In effect he was attempting
to recreate, on a minute scale in the Western wilderness, the
Jesuit-dominated seventeenth-century state of New France,
in all but its orthodoxy as to faith. His new Saskatchewan,
like New France, was to be a consecrated state, its chief char-
acteristics piety and dedication to militant propagation of
the faith.

The faith itself, however, was to be somewhat modified.
The council proclaimed the establishment of "the Living
Catholic Apostolic and Vital Church of the New World,"
and designated Archbishop Bourget of Montreal as its Pope.
The right of Louis Riel to direct the priests was "recognized." "We adopt for the line of our conduct," the Métis
announced, "the three admirable letters from the Archbishop Ignace Bourget written to Louis David Riel."

But the warnings of their furious priests had had some
effect. While an army marched on its headquarters, the council took note of the fact that its members had been refused
the sacraments, and thereupon cut the ground out from
under the Roman fathers by a neat, if somewhat naive, theological ruse: it abolished eternal punishment. "The *Exovidat*

of the French Canadian Métis believes firmly," the declaration said, "that hell will not last forever," and continued:

. . . that the doctrine of everlasting future punishment is contrary to Divine mercy as well as to the charity of Our Savior Jesus Christ; consequently the *Exovidat* of the French Canadian Métis establishes the truth that however long hell may last, prolonged though it be for millions on millions of years, it will come to an end one day by the goodness of God through the merits of Jesus Christ.

After testimony had been solemnly entered upon the record that Father Végreville had refused to administer the last sacrament to Métis under arms and had warned that they would be held responsible for any Indian offenses, too, the *Exovidat* ordered him imprisoned in the parish house of St. Antoine and announced that it was taking over his functions: "If God so wills, if He has decided in His eternal designs, we desire nothing better than to be His priests and to constitute . . . the new religious ministry of Jesus Christ."

By vote of nine of the ten members present, Louis Riel was proclaimed a prophet; the one skeptic asked for more time to make up his mind. At Louis's suggestion the days of the week were renamed so that each might have some religious significance, and Saturday was chosen as the Sabbath. It was decreed that the body and blood of Christ were only symbolically, not substantially, present in the Host; Riel, ready enough to credit the supernatural in his own visions, balked at the miracle of the mass.

He had no vote in the *Exovidat,* but all of the religious ideas were his and he wrote all of the proclamations. In a few days he turned out thousands of words of such material, but much of it was copied from documents he had brought with him from Montana. When his thirst for religious rhetoric was finally satisfied, he yielded to Gabriel's demand that

they get down to business and send appeals to Métis and Indians throughout the district to join in the resistance. Dumont already had sent some messages of this sort, but Louis
was unaware of it.

"Justice commands us to take up arms!" Louis wrote—a
slogan repeated in many of his appeals to their "relatives."

. . . Be ready for everything. Take the Indians with you.
Gather them from every side. Take all the ammunition you can,
whatsoever storehouses it may be in. Murmur, growl and
threaten. Stir up the Indians. Render the Police of Fort Pitt and
Battleford powerless. . . .

Most of the messages, even those to pagan Indians, ended
with religious admonitions, calling upon the recipients to
pray; "Be certain that faith works wonders."

A group of whites, formerly supporters of the movement
in Prince Albert, sent a cautious resolution expressing sympathy for the Métis but asserting their own neutrality. Riel's
answer was uncharacteristically mild. He acknowledged that
"situated as you are it is difficult for you to approve immediately of our bold and just uprising," but he went on to
plead: "Gentlemen, please do not remain neutral. For the
love of God help us to save Saskatchewan!"

About two thousand Indians lived on reserves around
Battleford, a hundred miles west of Batoche. The first to
respond to Riel's appeal were the Crees of Poundmaker's
band. Poundmaker was one of the foremost chiefs of the
tribe, intelligent, a renowned orator, and handsome—more
than six feet tall, slender, with a thin sensitive face and an
air of dignity and repose. His mother was a half-sister of the
great Blackfoot chief Crowfoot, who adopted Poundmaker
as a "son"; by virtue of this connection the Cree negotiated
a treaty with his tribe's traditional enemies and became
known as "The Peacemaker."

Poundmaker was respected by the whites, but his tribe had been troublesome at times and now was ripe for rebellion. It resented the new restraints of reservation life and the Government decree that rations, which had been insufficient anyway, were to be issued only to those who did farm work. In 1884 the Indians had angrily done the work, only to see their crops wither in drought. Said the pagan Poundmaker, "Of old the Indian trusted in his God, and his faith was not in vain. He was fed, clothed and free from sickness. Along came the white man and persuaded the Indian that this God was not able to keep up the care; the Indian took the white man's word and deserted to the new God. Hunger followed, and disease and death. Now we return to the God we know; the buffalo will come back and the Indian will live the life that God intended him to live!"

Poundmaker's hungry Crees learned of the Duck Lake battle from Métis messengers two or three days after it occurred and determined at once to move on Battleford and loot its stores, despite their chief's counsels of caution. On March 30 they came within sight of the town. On that same day and the next the first Indian outrage of the Northwest Rebellion was committed by a nearby band of Assiniboines. This group murdered their farm instructor and a bachelor farmer, then took the trail to Battleford to join the Crees.

The people of the village and settlers in the vicinity had ample warning of the Indians' approach and fled to the fort. Five hundred and twelve persons, about three hundred of them women and children, were brought inside the stockade. The town was some distance away, beyond the range of the fort's cannon, and could not be defended; on the other hand the hilltop stockade was invulnerable to Indian attack.

The night of their arrival the Indians began sacking the village and continued this for days, until every house and store, including the large Hudson's Bay post, had been emptied and destroyed. Weeping, the gently reared Canadian and English women watched from the fort as the Indians, hysterical with delight, danced into the neat little houses and out again, ripping off their own blankets and donning the precious silk gowns and party bonnets, shattering the heirloom china on the ground like destructive children, pounding the silver to bits with their war axes, ripping the linens and bedding into streamers with which they ran about the prairie. Mattresses were torn up and the feathers scattered over the field; unfamiliar foods were poured out on the grass. One woman watched as her piano, which had been freighted across the plains by ox-drawn wagon, was kicked to fragments in front of her house. Every room was looted, even attics; the Indians discovered with joy the purpose of ladders. When nothing remained indoors, the floors were torn up, windows hacked out, and usually the house was set on fire. One home which was burned to the ground was that of a judge; it was worth, counting its furnishings, about $75,000. Battleford's total loss was nearly half a million dollars.

The Crees then ranged beyond the town to the farms and burned everything that would ignite. For weeks fleeing homesteaders reported that their way was lighted at night by the flames from buildings and haystacks. A few farmers, unable to get away in time, were murdered.

The fun over, the Indians returned to Battleford and calmly sat down to wait until hunger should drive the whites from the fort. They were unaware that the Canadians had three months' food supply in the stockade and a herd of cattle behind it, across the river from the besiegers. The people of Battleford had enough to eat, but crowded quarters, illness and exposure caused much distress before the siege was lifted after almost a month.

Meanwhile the flight of settlers and agency employees continued. One agency farm instructor, warned by the fate of his colleague among the Assiniboines, loaded his family into a wagon and raced nearly two hundred miles to a railroad point through snow three feet deep. The family was pursued several times by Indians whom they managed to outdistance; they had only an axe for defense. Friendly Indians helped another farm instructor to escape; he put his wife and two small daughters in a rowboat and set out on the ice-filled North Saskatchewan River for Prince Albert. They traveled only at night, hiding during the day in brushy backwaters, and spread their food supply, normally enough for three days, over twelve.

L'ESPRIT ERRANT

April 2 was Maundy Thursday and in the little church at Frog Lake, on an Indian reserve between Battleford and Edmonton, Father François Xavier Fafard celebrated mass and administered communion. He was a veteran of ten years in prairie missions. Today he had an assistant, Father Félix Marchand, visiting from his own nearby mission station at Onion Lake. Marchand had been in the country only a couple of months. Both were Oblates.

The church door was open. Indians traipsed in and out, disturbing the mass. Father Marchand moved to close the door, but the older priest quickly drew him back and continued the service in fluent Cree, carefully appearing not to notice the whispers, the shuffling feet. Big Bear, the chief of the band, stood stonily beside the door and frowned on his people.

Pére Fafard prayed. "May the Body of Our Lord Jesus Christ keep my soul unto life everlasting. . . ."

The eyes of the priests flicked briefly to the aisle of the church as another Indian entered, strode almost to the altar rail, lowered himself slowly to one knee, and stared at them unblinkingly.

Father Marchand gasped and reddened with anger. The newcomer was *L'Esprit Errant,* Wandering Spirit, war chief of the Crees, and he was in full war regalia. He wore his lynx-skin bonnet with five eagle plumes—one for each slain enemy —and decorated buckskin shirt and leggings. His eyelids, lips and chin were painted a hideous yellow. He carried a Winchester rifle which he set butt-down on the floor and used to brace himself in his kneeling position.

The mass droned on. After the first glance Father Fafard paid no attention to the pagan war chief kneeling mockingly before the altar, his implacable eyes following every movement of the priests.

The church was filled now. Father Fafard noticed that virtually all of the whites of the community were present, though several of them were Protestants. One more sign that something was wrong. . . . Either they sought sanctuary here, and clung together for safety, or they had been compelled to come. (The second guess was right; Wandering Spirit had ordered everyone in town to go to mass.)

The congregation was fascinated by the immobile figure of the war chief in the aisle and the responses gradually grew fainter and died.

If Wandering Spirit sensed the tension developing in the room behind him, he gave no sign. He had not changed his position since he entered the church.

The war chief and Big Bear's son, Imasees, shared leadership of the recalcitrant young men of the band. Wandering Spirit was a tall, lithe, nervous man with a deceptively gentle voice but a thin cruel mouth. His heavy black hair was curly —most unusual among Indians—and there were ringlets in his braids. He was vain, ambitious, and brutal, and he made no secret of his undying hatred of whites; he was feared by everyone, including Big Bear.

Word of the police defeat at Duck Lake had reached Wandering Spirit a day or two before this Thursday of Holy Week. Since then, at his instigation, the Indians had been dancing. Before mass that morning they had looted one

store, had obtained some articles from the Hudson's Bay
post, and had threatened the Indian agent, Thomas Quinn.
Then the war chief had herded all the whites into the
church.

Father Fafard concluded the mass, blessed the congregation and stepped forward to the altar rail. Speaking hurriedly
now, he admonished the Indians against acts of violence.

Wandering Spirit rose and swung around to face the
people. *"Neá!"* he commanded. "Go!"

The Indians obediently trooped out, the more devout
among them—with a backward glance for the war chief—
pausing to dip their fingers in the holy water font and cross
themselves. The whites followed; as they emerged from the
church a group of armed braves fell into step beside them
and escorted them to the Indian agency buildings.

The tribesmen milled about on the road which cut
through the little settlement. Wandering Spirit was arguing
with Quinn, the Indian agent.

"Go to our camp!" the war chief ordered.

Quinn refused. His place was in the village, he said, and
he had not been invited to the camp by Big Bear.

"I tell you go!" Wandering Spirit shouted. Quinn shook
his head.

The Indian jerked his rifle up and fired at point-blank
range in Quinn's face. The agent dropped dead at the war
chief's feet.

Huddled under guard in the home of John Delaney, the
farm instructor, the whites heard the shot, heard the war
chant of the Crees burst instantly from scores of throats:
"Nipuhao, nipuhao! [Kill! Kill!]"

Big Bear clawed his way into the center of the mob of
young braves. *"Chasqwa!"* he screamed. "Stop!"

But Wandering Spirit had control of the band now. He
danced in the road, swinging his Winchester over his head,
singing a new war song. "I have killed Sioux Speaker. . . .

Kill! Kill!" (Quinn, part Indian himself, had been an accomplished linguist and was known to the Crees as *Kapwatamut*, Sioux Speaker.) The young men caught up the cry, danced frenziedly about their leader.

A group of braves went to Delaney's house and herded the whites out onto the road. The captives had taken only a few steps when the Indians opened fire.

Charles Gouin, a half-breed carpenter, and John Williscraft, a mechanic, fell first. John C. Gowanlock, who had come to Frog Lake only a few months before to erect a gristmill, gasped as the bullet struck, stumbled against his wife and carried her to the ground with him. Delaney fell dying with two bullets in him. His wife flung herself on his body and screamed for the priests, who had been fruitlessly attempting to quiet the maddened Indians. Father Fafard ran to Delaney and knelt beside him, making the sign of the cross.

Wandering Spirit stepped over to the little group and, as Mrs. Delaney attempted to shield her husband's body with her own, coolly shot the priest in the back of the neck.

Father Fafard fell across Delaney's body, moaning. Round-the-Sky, a young Cree "convert" whom Fafard had fed and clothed, danced forward and shot his benefactor in the head.

Young Father Marchand, hurrying across the road to join his colleague, plunged face down in the dirt, killed with a single shot.

George Dill, a trader, and William C. Gilchrist, an employee of Gowanlock, ran for cover. The Indians let them get far enough to be worth chasing, then rode them down on horseback and fired bullet after bullet into their bodies.

Only three whites present in the village at the time of the massacre survived. They were the widows of Gowanlock and Delaney, and William B. Cameron, a young Hudson's Bay clerk who was temporarily in charge of the local post in the absence of the trader. Henry Quinn, the Indian agent's nephew, escaped fifteen minutes before the shooting began, heard the gunfire and carried news of an outbreak to Fort Pitt, the nearest police post.

The bodies of the nine victims were thrown into the cellars of one of the houses and the church, and all buildings in the village were set afire.

Young Cameron's friends among the Indians wrung a reluctant promise from Wandering Spirit to spare his life. The two women were bought from the Indians by friendly half-breeds for thirty dollars and four horses. All three became captives of the band, but one of the half-breeds, John Prichard, the agency interpreter, maintained a constant guard over the women, provided a place in his wagon for them to ride, and saved them from being forced to become "wives" of the young braves. When the Hudson's Bay trader, James K. Simpson, returned he was added to the group of prisoners; he was in a favored position, however, because his wife was a Cree half-breed and he was an old friend of Big Bear. John Fitzpatrick, another farm instructor—the Indians particularly disliked the luckless men who were assigned to teach them domestic agriculture!—was next brought in; his life was spared because he was an American and the Crees knew about Riel's hopes for help from across the line. That brought the total number of white captives to five, in addition to a few half-breeds suspected of white loyalties, but the list was soon to grow.

DIARY BY DICKENS

The prose style of Inspector Francis Jeffrey Dickens, commanding the Mounted Police detachment at Fort Pitt, had little in common with that of his famous father. But the third son of Charles Dickens was not like his purposeful, somewhat flamboyant parent in any respect. He was born in January, 1844, about a month after publication of *A Christmas Carol,* and there was a phrase in that book which his colleagues thought fitted him—"secret, and self-contained, and solitary as an oyster."

The novelist thought his son "a good, steady fellow," though he was sorely tried by Frank's indecision about a career after his education was completed. He had been sure enough of himself when he was fifteen and in school in Germany. "Dear papa," he had written, "I have given up all thoughts of being a doctor. My conviction that I shall never get over my stammering is the cause; all professions are barred against me." So he had decided to become a gentleman farmer and all his father had to do was send on money for his passage to Canada or Africa, fifteen pounds more to acquire his establishment, a horse, and a rifle. Charles Dickens replied that Frank probably would be robbed of the fifteen pounds, would be thrown by the horse and would blow his own head off with the gun, so he felt it necessary to oppose the project at that time.

Finally Frank elected to become a district superintendent of the Bengal Police. The novelist's death in 1870 brought him home from India; he had then come out to Canada and, in 1874, joined the Mounties.

He was a small man, red-bearded, precise; his manner was humorless, even gloomy. He had always been shy and now he withdrew more and more from human contacts, for another affliction had succeeded the stammering: he was becoming deaf. The fact that he had not risen above the rank of inspector although he had been in "the Force" since the year it was organized indicated that he was not blessed with outstanding leadership qualities, and the deafness would prevent any promotion now. He was looked upon as efficient but unimaginative; no one would have guessed that his father once fondly nicknamed him "Chickenstalker" in recognition of make-believe hunting adventures around the home place.

Inspector Dickens's Fort Pitt diary was as colorless and

concise as his speech. On April 2, day of the Frog Lake massacre, his entry read: "Fine morning. Const. Roby left for Onion Lake with team for lumber, returning in afternoon. He reports Indians very excited on reserve."

The big news arrived late that night, but the next day's notation in the journal was still undramatic:

Fine weather. Mr. Mann [a farm instructor], wife and family arrived from Onion Lake at 1 a.m., he reports that Indians at Frog Lake massacred all the whites. Fatigue all night barricading Fort. Extra guards posted, etc. Henry Quinn arrived from Frog Lake having escaped the massacre, confirms reports of Indians risen. Mr. Quinney [a Protestant missionary] and wife arrived from Onion Lake escorted by Chief Saskatchewan. Guide Josie Alexander left for B'frd with despatch.

Nevertheless this item reflected some of Dickens's dismay. His force consisted of twenty-two men. He knew that a night spent barricading Fort Pitt was wasted but for its effect on the morale of the police and the twenty-eight civilians whom he had brought into the establishment. Actually the place was indefensible. It consisted of half a dozen police and Hudson's Bay buildings, grouped in a hollow square on a level flat, surrounded by cultivated fields. There was no stockade. A hill commanded the position, and from its crest an attacking force could send bullets or incendiary arrows into the compound. Sacks of flour and oats were piled in the windows, carts and cordwood stacked in the gaps between buildings, but these would be of little help. The worst problem was water: there was no well and the river was four hundred yards away.

Everyone, including the teen-age daughters of the Hudson's Bay trader, W. J. McLean, took turns at sentry duty. One of the girls learned with delight how to prepare her rifle for night duty: moisten the sights with saliva and rub a sulphur match on them so they would glow in the dark.

On April 4 Dickens's diary noted two false alarms and the scares came frequently after that. The work of improvising a stockade and erecting bastions continued, but there was no sign of Indians. They were feasting at Frog Lake on the food taken from the stores and on stolen cattle which, child-like, they pretended were buffalo and hunted down on the prairie.

On April 11 the inspector ordered work begun on a scow— tacit admission that a retreat downriver might be necessary. The next day was Sunday; the journal noted that much ice was drifting in the river, that divine service was held, and that fire signals had been seen by a sentry.

Early Monday morning Dickens sent out three scouts— Constables Cowan and Loasby and the civilian, Henry Quinn. Taking a circuitous route to Frog Lake, they just missed encountering two hundred and fifty Crees. The Indians arrived an hour or so later and encamped near the fort.

Big Bear sent a prisoner with a letter demanding tribute of tea, tobacco and other items from the Hudson's Bay store and proposing a parley with McLean. The trader agreed, hoping he could persuade the Indians to withdraw. The goods were sent out and he met the Cree councilors on the field in front of the fort, but the Indians insisted upon another conference the next day and sent him back.

Tuesday McLean went out again. He was persuaded to go to the Indian camp and was there taken prisoner. While he wrangled with the chiefs, the three scouts returning from Frog Lake rode almost into the midst of the camp. Indian sentries screamed that the band was being attacked and a fusillade was opened on the redcoat riders. Cowan was killed and Loasby wounded; Quinn, of the charmed life at Frog Lake, again escaped. (He was captured next morning but his remarkable luck held; a friendly Woods Cree chief insisted that his life be spared.) Loasby had made his way close to the fort before he was shot from his horse, and Stanley Simpson, a young Company clerk, went out and helped him into the enclosure.

The Indians now ordered McLean to write a note to his wife instructing her to lead their family, the Company employees under his protection and all other civilians to the Cree camp to surrender themselves as prisoners. If this were done, Big Bear promised, they would be treated fairly and the police would be permitted to withdraw without bloodshed. The alternative was annihilation.

McLean, acknowledging in his letter that "I was too confiding in the Indians" by going to their camp, told his wife he could see no course open to the besieged whites except submission on the Crees' terms.

The ultimatum galled Dickens but common sense dictated surrender. He now had only twenty able-bodied men in uniform and perhaps a half-dozen among the civilians, most of whom were women and children. But the humiliation for "the Force" would be even greater than that at Duck Lake. This would be another Carlton, retreat without a fight. At forty-one Dickens was nearing the end of his career and this would be a shameful wind-up.

The decision rested with the civilians and they voted to follow McLean's advice. Guided by a hint in her husband's letter, Mrs. McLean stalled their departure as long as she dared to give the police time to pack their guns, ammunition and food in the scow. Finally the civilians trooped out as the Indians watched, and the police scrambled into their crude vessel and started across the river.

It was a rough trip. Huge blocks of ice crashed continually into the sides of the scow and it began to fill with water as the wind whipped waves over the gunwales. The river was three hundred yards wide and the current was swift. Some of the more playful Indians could not resist loosing a few rifle shots at the laboring boat and all hands were too busy keeping afloat to answer the fire.

Constable Loasby, the wounded scout, required considerable attention because of the cold and wind. The craft was nearly swamped several times, but the crossing was finally effected and a miserable camp for the night was established while it rained. Dickens made an entry in his diary:

Tuesday, April 14—Very windy weather. Mr. McLean still parleying with Indians. During parley the three scouts out yesterday rode through the camp. Const. Cowan was shot dead and Loasby wounded in two places. Quinn got away. McLean and Dufresne [interpreter] taken prisoners. Indians threatened to burn fort tonight unless police left. After a great deal of danger got to the other side of the river. All the white people and halfbreeds in Pitt went to the Indian camp as prisoners.

For six days the Mounties fought ice, current and gale, bailing furiously, as they pushed the leaky scow downstream to Battleford. Their soaked clothing froze to their bodies and the water ruined some of their food and ammunition. Finally they stumbled ashore before the stockade of the headquarters of the northern district, which was still under siege, but safe. A Mountie band played them into the enclosure, they were warmed and fed and told that they had done all that could have been expected of them.

Inspector Francis Jeffrey Dickens was not so easily reassured. He leafed through his diary, wondered what he could have done to prevent this ignominious end of his command. Somewhere in these pages there had been a time for glory. . . . There was no longer any purpose in keeping a journal; probably there would be no more commands for "Chickenstalker." He reread his final entry, made the second night out:

"Wednesday, April 15—Very cold weather. Travelled."

Well, as Sam Weller had put it, "it's over, and can't be

helped, and that's one consolation." In the spring of 1886, after the Northwest's troubles had ended, Dickens resigned from "the Force." On June 11, while visiting a friend in Moline, Illinois, he died of a heart attack. He was buried in Moline, with the consent of the Dickens family; it was a long and lonely way from the cluttered Victorian house at Gads Hill. "Take ye heed," says the inscription on the simple stone marker over his grave; "watch and pray, for ye know not when the time is."

Big Bear received Mrs. McLean with courtesy and his braves helped to erect the big tent she had had brought from the fort. It was well that it was big, for that first night it sheltered the McLean and Mann families and the Rev. Mr. Quinney and his wife. The McLeans had eight children and the Manns five; there were nineteen persons in the tent and no room for anyone to lie down.

The Crees now had nearly forty white captives in addition to half-breeds and Indians who had been living among the whites or serving them and were therefore suspect.

Big Bear had agreed to let McLean supervise "distribution" of goods in Fort Pitt the next day, so as to safeguard the post's twenty-thousand-dollar stock of furs, but his uncontrollable young braves started the looting that night and the ultimate loss to the Company was about seventy thousand dollars. For days the Indians feasted and at first they were generous with food for the prisoners, but after the first couple of weeks the problem of supply began to worry them. The whites were dragged along as the band ranged over a wide area seeking game or loot. They went to Frog Lake, then back to Fort Pitt. On this second visit the last of the fort's supplies were taken and the buildings were burned. A third move took them to Frenchman's Butte, twelve miles farther east.

There was dissension in the camp between the Plains

Crees, who wanted to join Poundmaker at Battleford, and the Woods Crees, who did not and who were rapidly tiring of the whole affair. As food became scarcer, some of the Plains Crees proposed slaughtering the white captives, but the Woods Crees refused to permit it. Meanwhile McLean's eldest daughters, in almost nightly danger of abduction by young braves, were saved by friendly squaws who hid them in their own lodges.

To restore harmony, the tribe's leaders decided, a dance was needed. So they stopped at Frenchman's Butte for a thirst dance which would require several days of preparation, three days for the ceremony itself and two or three days for recovery. This would propitiate the gods, welcome the spring season, and make everyone feel better. By this time it was May and the tribe and its prisoners had been moving aimlessly about the prairies for nearly two months.

At Frenchman's Butte the Canadian troops finally caught up with Big Bear's band. The diversion permitted a few of his prisoners to escape, but most of them, including the McLeans, were held for another fortnight—until the Woods Crees finally broke with their cousins, slipped out of the line of march, and turned the captives loose with food and horses to make their way to Battleford.

The rift in the Indians' ranks was fortunate for the prisoners, because the Canadian force which encountered them fired only a few shots. With three of his three hundred well-armed men slightly wounded, the commanding officer, mindful of what had happened to Custer, Crozier and others who had blundered into Indian ambushes, suddenly decided the Indians had the better position and ordered a retreat which did not end until his command was back at Fort Pitt.

Actually the Canadians had had the battle virtually won when they turned and fled. Prisoner McLean, noting the effect of the cannon and the developing panic among the Crees, happily assembled his brood from their favorite nooks and crannies of the Indian camp (some of the younger ones had found their captivity to be quite a lark) and had everyone all packed and ready for the anticipated rescue. He was hopping mad when the shooting stopped and he went out to meet the rescuers and found them vanished.

CHAPTER XXII

Malbrouck Has Gone A-Fighting

A TOAST TO THE DOCTOR

"I HAVE seen a flock of dark geese," Riel brooded in the journal he kept at Batoche. "They had the appearance of wandering away, but in truth they were hovering in the air. I saw them disperse into two groups. . . ." One group had flown east—"though they were in the sunshine, they did not reflect the light; they were covered with darkness."

The Métis must not disperse like geese. They must remain at Batoche and listen to the prophecies of the new David, which were revealed each morning to the *Exovidat* and announced to the people.

But Gabriel Dumont had reached the end of his patience.

Canada's Northwest Field Force was on the move. The first division, nearly nine hundred men, had started the two-hundred-and-thirty-mile march north to Batoche from Qu'Appelle, led by General Middleton. The second division, five hundred men and two hundred teamsters, was moving swiftly to the relief of besieged Battleford from the railroad point of Swift Current, two hundred miles south. It was led by Lieut. Col. W. D. Otter. Still farther west, Maj. Gen. T. Bland Strange was marching through Alberta toward Edmonton with six hundred men to make sure the Blackfeet did not go back on their promise to remain neutral. Some fifteen hundred more militiamen were rapidly garrisoning the key railroad towns, river crossings and rail junctions.

The Métis had already lost their best opportunities to throw the Government's war machine out of gear. It was too late now to dynamite the railroad, too late to attack the detraining depots; largely because of the squeamishness of Louis Riel, more than three thousand men had reached the Northwest safely and now were marching against the rebels. Dumont could be certain of fewer than five hundred soldiers for defense.

His major concern was the first division, aimed at Batoche. It still might be possible to sack Middleton's supply depots on the prairie and to harass his troops and transport. The Canadians were floundering north on crude prairie trails; one day their horses slipped and stumbled to their knees on hard-packed snow or ice in the ruts, the next they plunged to their bellies in quicksand or in mud which had the consistency and color of porridge. Their wagons, carts and guns were continually mired in the marshy creek bottoms. Alkali bubbled out of the sod to poison their drinking water, burn the horses' hooves like acid, eat into the cheap leather of the troopers' boots. Moisture and cold seeped through the shoddy uniforms which had been ripped and almost worn out on the trek around Lake Superior.

The first night out of Qu'Appelle the temperature was twenty-three below. Next morning the tent pegs had to be chopped out of the ground with axes.

Jerome Henry, a teamster with Middleton and a Métis spy,

made it clear that transport was the vulnerable phase of the campaign. Four hundred horses were required to move the column's supplies, and it was impossible to guard four hundred horses on the open prairie. But even these were not enough, and Middleton had ordered additional supplies, including feed for the horses, brought down the South Saskatchewan from railroad points in the West on river steamers. One of these, the *Northcote,* had started from Saskatchewan Landing near Swift Current, Otter's base, and Middleton hoped to meet it at Clarke's Crossing, forty-five miles south of Batoche.

But the *Northcote,* slowly butting its way through drifting ice, grounding on sand bars and fending off snags, was late for the rendezvous. Middleton waited impatiently for several days, finally made up his mind to press on. At the same time he decided unwisely to split his force in order to launch a two-pronged attack on Batoche. He formed two columns of approximately equal strength and started them north along both banks of the river.

A map of the Canadian position at Clarke's Crossing and information about the plan of march quickly reached Dumont through his alert spies, and the Métis general knew he had been given his last chance to wreck the offensive. He had enough men and ammunition to engage half of Middleton's division, but if he waited he would be compelled to defend a fixed position against overwhelming odds. The Métis and their Indian allies were cavalrymen and guerrillas, temperamentally unsuited to withstand a siege; nor could they assemble food and munitions for such an ordeal.

On April 23 Gabriel had it out with Riel. He could no longer accept Louis's "strategy," he declared, and his men backed him up; they must attack Middleton at once.

The worried Riel yielded without an argument. "All right," he said wearily, "do as you wish!"

The adjutant general lost no time. That same night all the

armed men he could muster immediately, except thirty whom he left for the defense of Batoche, started south by horseback. His force totaled just 200; the Canadian "right column," which he would encounter on the east bank of the river, numbered 440. The "left column," strength 373, was only a few miles behind, but it was on the west bank and had only a scow with which to cross the stream.

Riel went along with the Métis detachment and led the men in prayer at the first rest stop, eight miles south. While they ate a late supper there, they were overtaken by couriers from Batoche reporting the appearance of police scouts from Prince Albert; an attack was feared and the thirty men left in the village thought they might need reinforcements. Reluctantly, Gabriel sent fifty of his two hundred men back, led by Riel.

At daybreak of the 24th the Métis scouts located Middleton's column in camp on a farm twenty-two miles south of Batoche. Gabriel halted his men five miles farther north on a stream called Fish Creek which cut across the prairie in a ravine forty feet deep. Here he prepared an ambush. He hid the major portion of his force, 130 men, in the ravine, where they quickly improvised rifle pits in old game trails, facing up the slope so the enemy troops would be silhouetted against the skyline as they came over the brink of the coulee. The remaining twenty men, still mounted, he led to coulees farther south where he hoped to hide them so they could fall upon the rear of the Canadian force after it had stumbled into the trap in the ravine.

"I wanted to treat them as we would buffalo," Gabriel explained, and in fact he had reproduced a buffalo "pound" from which few of the whites would have escaped if all had gone as he planned; but the great character flaw of Métis and Indians, lack of discipline, upset the masterly battle plan of their leader.

Dumont had given strict orders that all movement was to

occur off the road, that his men should disperse and ride through the grass so as to leave no trail. But he could not watch them all, and some of the irresponsible young warriors could not resist the fun of a chase on horseback after a few stray cattle, up and down and across the main road.

Early the next morning, as Middleton's column broke camp, its English half-breed scouts found the sign of the Métis horses and raced back to report.

When the battle of Fish Creek began at seven-twenty A.M. on April 24, 1885, the advantage of surprise for which Dumont had worked so carefully rested with the Canadians. Gabriel and his little company of mounted men, en route to their hiding places in the coulees, unaware that they had been betrayed by carelessness, rode straight into a deadly silent Canadian advance guard with rifles at ready, and had to run for their lives.

One or two of the Métis horsemen were felled with the first Canadian volley and others fled the field of battle in sudden panic. Gabriel rallied the fifteen riders who remained, had them dismount, and made a stand in a thicket which held the Canadians off long enough to prevent complete demoralization of his command. As it was, when he finally got back to the ravine in which the main force had been stationed, he found only forty-seven of the hundred and thirty men he had left there. This gave him sixty-two on the battlefield, with a few more engaged in isolated sniping on the flanks of the Canadian column. At this stage he was outnumbered six to one; when the fight ended nearly twelve hours later the odds against him were ten to one.

A horseman started on a dead run for Batoche to bring back the men who had been permitted to return with Riel, and to attempt to round up the deserters and persuade them to get back into the fight. Gabriel was determined to make a stand, though loss of the element of surprise upon which he

had counted so heavily had almost brought disaster. He still
had the advantage of position, however; and he had made a
shrewd guess as to the mettle of the green troops and the
temper of their overcautious commander.

Meanwhile, four miles upstream and across the river, the
"left column" heard the first cannon fire and hurried north,
soon to encounter a messenger from Middleton ordering it
to cross and come to his aid. But this was a clumsy operation
with only a scow and rafts in a swift-running river full of ice,
and it took several hours to get part of the column to the
east bank.

Dumont's preparations in the ravine soon paid off in Canadian blood. Bypassing the thicket from which his fifteen
stalwarts directed a slow but appallingly accurate fire, and
attempting to surround it, the leading elements of the Canadian force promenaded in orderly ranks over the crest of the
coulee—then broke and fell back in dismay as they were met
by a decimating volley from riflemen they could not see. Two
cannon were rushed forward but it was soon found that they
could not be placed on the lip of the ravine because their
crews were outlined against the sky. The guns could not be
aimed accurately and the shrapnel shells fell harmlessly far
beyond the rifle pits, most of which were less than a hundred
yards below the hilltop.

Middleton's distrust of his raw recruits appeared to be
justified in the early phases of the battle. When a popular
officer fell while urging his men into a charge, there was a
moment of panic; but the young militiamen soon settled
down and began to fight for their lives. The aging general
rode into the front line, and a bullet tore through his fur
cap. He saw the shot fired and swore that the marksman was
Dumont. That might have been true, Gabriel acknowledged
casually in a subsequent account of the fight, "but he can
congratulate himself I didn't recognize him." Gabriel didn't
know how many Canadians his Winchester accounted for be-

cause he took cover after each shot; but, he said, "I couldn't
have missed often."

Hours passed. The sixty-two Métis and Indians dwindled
to fifty-four through casualties, desertions or the dispatch of
messengers; but still they held more than four hundred white
troops back of the hilltop. Middleton had no idea of the invisible enemy's strength; he estimated it all the way from
one hundred and twenty-five to three hundred.

It began to rain. The Métis were fairly snug in their
brushy shelters in the game trails and draws, and anyway they
were used to discomfort; but the Canadians were miserable.
One detachment, after a daring charge on the rebel line
failed, was pinned down for three hours in six inches of water
in a marshy hollow.

It was the Canadians' first battle of the campaign and for
most of them the first combat anywhere. The young account-
ants and shop clerks and "sparrow legs" or "remittance men"
—inept or troublesome younger sons banished to the colonies
by their English families—saw the dead dragged back from
the line and left carelessly uncovered beside the hospital
tents. They gagged as they saw the rain drip red from torn
bodies, forming pools churned by the boots of the hurrying
stretcher bearers into a stinking swill of blood. They stared
horror-struck at jagged ugly wounds in bellies and heads; not
all of the Métis had rifles and some were using muzzle-loading shotguns into which they poured irregularly shaped
scraps of lead or broken horseshoe nails.

(The American rebels at Breed's Hill had used similar
missiles in their rusty duck guns and the British had complained that it was shockingly bad form, but 110 years after
the so-called "Battle of Bunker Hill" British commanders
still were shoving their men in a solid, meaty phalanx into
the close-range, murderous fire of eagle-eyed and ungentle-
manly colonials.)

About noon the Canadians tried a general advance and

failed again. After that the scrap settled down to dreary hours of sniping, at which the Métis excelled. Some of their stragglers returned, entering the ravine far above the battle scene and worming their way to the pits and trenches. Morale was high. Isidore Dumas began to sing "Malbrouck," the derisive dirge which eighteenth-century France had chanted for Winston Churchill's renowned ancestor, the Duke of Marlborough, and everyone came in on the roaring chorus: *"Mironton, mironton, mirontaine!"* Someone else started "Falcon's Song," and from somewhere, incredibly, came an instrumental accompaniment; one of the rebel warriors had brought along his flute. The sun came out briefly and some of the Métis delightedly called the attention of their fellows to the first yellow and purple blooms of the spring wildflowers.

Gabriel joked. "Don't be afraid of bullets," he said, "they won't hurt you." Then he nonchalantly picked off a foolish young Canadian officer who had come to the crest of the hill to see what he could see. The Métis laughed as they heard the dying youngster sobbing like a child.

The Canadians threw hundreds of rounds of ammunition and scores of cannon shells into the coulee without aiming; the Métis never wasted a shot. Nevertheless the whites' massed charges, half-hearted as they were, worried Dumont because they caused a drain on the rebels' limited stock of ammunition. In midafternoon he learned that Middleton's reinforcements had begun to arrive, and at that time he had only seven cartridges left for his Winchester.

Eighty more Métis were riding hard from Batoche, but if the Canadians chose to attack now the rebels could not hold. Gabriel tested the wind and decided on a daring gamble. As a new line formed on the enemy's right flank he ordered the prairie grass and brush fired, and told the Métis to charge under cover of the smoke.

The heavy atmosphere after the day's first rain held the

smoke close to the ground as they swarmed, screaming savagely, out of their pits. Crouching like Indian raiders they raced to within a few yards of the Canadians, dropped prone and fired point-blank into the faces of the milling whites, then raced back to their ravine. The Canadians, choking in the smoke, gathered up their casualties and re-formed their lines; they did not break and run as Dumont had hoped they would—but on the other hand they did not launch the all-out attack they had been organizing.

It began to rain again and to grow dark. The Canadians chafed with impatience and some of their officers begged Middleton to order an attack by the whole force. This would quickly have won the battle, but the Englishman was unwilling to accept responsibility for the losses it would entail. Instead he tried half-measures again, splitting off a part of the force for a flanking movement up the ravine while the others maintained a cursory fire from the front. The Métis contemptuously ignored the harmless shooting from the hilltop, swung their sights on the flanking column and quickly drove it back.

The eighty men from Batoche, led by Gabriel's brother Edouard, arrived; their comrades, some of whom had been lying cramped in the same position for ten hours, cheered wildly.

Desultory firing continued for another hour, by which time it was too dark for either side to see the enemy. The Canadians began to withdraw from the field and the Métis rose to their feet and jeered. But they had had a narrow escape and they lost no time getting to what horses they had left; more than fifty of their mounts had been killed. One wildly jubilant party of about thirty warriors rode almost into the Canadians' lines to shriek insults. A medical officer had abandoned his kit in the retreat; it contained two bottles of brandy in which the Métis solemnly drank his health, with the grinning Gabriel proposing the toast.

Neither "army" had eaten since dawn. Now, at a respectful distance from each other, they grabbed for rations and tried to thaw aching limbs before the campfires. Gabriel debated the wisdom of a night attack, but the weather was too bad and his men too tired; it was decided to return to Batoche.

The Métis had won the first encounter of the Canadian Army and the rebels. They had abandoned their position, but of their own volition and only as the attackers withdrew; they had fought the troops to a standstill and their resistance so thoroughly frightened Middleton that he kept his force immobilized at this spot for two weeks, waiting for more ammunition and more men, and arranging for removal of his wounded. This last was an important aspect of war the Canadian command had forgotten, and a makeshift ambulance service had to be created in the field.

Casualty figures told the story. The rebels lost only six men —four dead (two of them were Sioux Indians) and two wounded. But the Canadian casualties totaled fifty, more than ten per cent of the number engaged on their side. Ten of these, including an officer, were killed and forty, four of them officers, were wounded.

The day of the Fish Creek Battle the siege of Battleford was lifted by Otter's Second Division. The Indians who had surrounded the fort fled before the troops arrived, and the ordeal ended for five hundred people penned for nearly a month in an enclosure less than two hundred yards square.

The next day at Batoche Dumont learned that Riel had led the women of the village in prayer from dawn to dusk on the 24th. The adjutant general was grateful; undoubtedly, he told Louis, the prayers had brought victory to Métis arms. Gabriel was one of the most modest men (except about his marksmanship) ever to administer a sound licking to a British general, so he really believed it.

A LESSON FOR POUNDMAKER

Some of the militiamen, like soldiers anywhere and any time, began to wonder what they were doing here.

The Métis, it appeared, were not "ignorant savages." They were tough and intelligent fighters. Moreover, such of their home life as the Canadians had seen indicated that they had something to fight for. Perhaps they were not the idle troublemakers, incurable malcontents and bloodthirsty Papists they had been pictured by Sir John Macdonald and the Orangemen of Ontario.

"The feeling that the half-breeds have been wronged, that the Government has been criminally negligent, and that the politicians should be held accountable for the whole trouble" was growing among the troops, a newspaper correspondent wrote home. He continued:

The sight of these comfortable homes and the coupled knowledge that the men who reared them, suffered the rigors of frontier life and fostered a love for the very soil itself, cannot get sufficient title to raise $10 by mortgage on one thousand acres, bring home to every man the reality of the residents' grievances. No one defends the alliance with the Indians, nor do any deny the folly of the insurrection or counsel compromise at this stage of the proceedings, but feelings nearly akin to sympathy find lodgment in many of the bravest breasts. Hostility against Riel is outspoken, because it is believed his have been the unwise and demagogic counsels and measures which have led to hardship and bloodshed. . . .

But the home front need have no fear, the writer concluded: the militia would not fight any the worse because of its sympathy for the enemy. He was right; nor did these faint stirrings of doubt about the justice of their cause deter the troops from looting and burning the "comfortable homes," driving off the Métis stock and destroying the meager crops and robbing even loyal traders who were unlucky enough to have mixed blood. One of these traders, who proved that he had been a helpless prisoner of rebel Indians, subsequently won a judgment from the Government for furs "confiscated" by General Middleton, the choicest of them shipped east and consigned to the distinguished soldier himself. Middleton testified at an inquiry that he did not receive this particular parcel, but that he did not think he had done wrong "in allowing some of my staff to take some of the furs as mementoes of the campaign, or even taking some of them myself." He had bought a lot of furs while in the West, the general said, and quite a few had been "given" to him.

After the *Northcote* had finally caught up with Middleton's column and the troops were marching north again, the first place they came to was Gabriel's Crossing, home of the Métis general, six miles from Batoche. They burned Gabriel's house and tore down his stables, using the timber from the latter to strengthen the thin walls of the steamer and build bullet-proof shelters on its deck—for Middleton had decided to put a "battleship" into action on the South Saskatchewan. Gabriel didn't give the loss of his house and farm buildings a second thought; that was what one could anticipate in war. But he was somewhat annoyed because the troops swiped his billiard table and his wife's foot-powered washing machine.

The extent of Chief Poundmaker's personal guilt in the sacking of Battleford was far from clear, but there unquestionably was danger that the Indians on his reserve, delighted with their success in looting every white establishment for fifty miles around that town, soon would join Riel's forces at Batoche. Therefore Colonel Otter decided that as soon as his Second Division had rested from its long hike he would teach Poundmaker's Crees a lesson.

Like every decision made so far in the Canadians' campaign (and every one made in Ottawa before the troops were

sent west), Otter's was thoroughly unwise. But for the forbearance of Poundmaker it could have cost him his whole
command; fortunately the soft-spoken, dignified Cree chief,
like Riel, had no taste for slaughter.

Otter started from Battleford in the afternoon of May 1
with three hundred and twenty-five men, including a detachment of about seventy-five Mounted Police. "Artillery" consisted of two seven-pounder cannon and a Gatling gun, one
of the three machine guns being tried out by the Northwest
Field Force. The column marched until seven o'clock,
camped for four hours, and pressed on again in moonlight.
The plan was to surprise Poundmaker's camp at daybreak.
Otter's scouts had reported that Poundmaker had three hundred and fifty braves; actually only a couple of hundred of
them had firearms.

The Indians had been anticipating an attack. One of them
told a white friend that he had been eating very lightly because Indian braves had learned that filled intestines increased the chance of fatal abdominal wounds from bullet
or arrow. However, Otter's night march did bring his force
into contact with the Indians before the latter expected it
and for a few moments (the battle started at about five A.M.)
he had the advantage of surprise.

The Crees had been camped in the valley of Cut Knife
Creek, named for a famous victory over a Sarcee chief, thirty-
eight miles south of Battleford. Just before the troops arrived the Indians had moved to a nearby plateau which was
crowned by Cut Knife Hill, and a sentry on the hill was the
first to see the approaching troops and warn the camp. An
Indian camp, though never wholly asleep, is not given to
early rising, and the first alarm found only about fifty braves
ready for action. They raced up the hill and took positions
in the brush.

Otter's men immediately cut loose with the Gatling gun
and the seven-pounders and did considerable damage in the

swiftly emptying tipis; but the Canadians made the fatal mistake of waiting on the hilltop until their full force was assembled instead of taking immediate advantage of their initial gains. Within a few moments the tipis were empty, the squaws and children out of range in the brush, and the braves had taken up their positions—as swift, as deadly and as invisible as rattlesnakes. Twenty minutes after the first shot had been fired the Canadians were surrounded on three sides and their front rank was being methodically cut to pieces by hidden sharpshooters. It was apparent that the Indians had planned it all and that the whites once more had stupidly strutted into a trap.

The Gatling, though it fired several thousand cartridges, was ineffective because its two-man crew couldn't see what they were shooting at. The two seven-pounders were all that saved Otter from disaster, and after a hundred-odd shells had been fired both guns collapsed because their wooden carriages, rotten with age, fell to pieces. At one time a shell from one of these guns narrowly missed annihilating a company of the Canadians who had been sent into an exposed position.

The Indians used an age-old trick, raising their war bonnets or scraps of clothing on sticks and picking off the Canadians when they rose from a prone position to fire. Hand-to-hand conflict developed for the first time in the rebellion when a group of Crees, yelling insanely, rushed the gun crews. This attack was beaten off with the aid of the Gatling and the Indians were forced into a headlong retreat which could have become a rout if the Canadians had dared to leave their guns for the pursuit.

The fight continued for more than seven hours. The Crees slowly closed the gap on the fourth side of the hill, and shortly after noon, with his force virtually surrounded, one cannon useless and the other nearly so, Colonel Otter acknowledged defeat and ordered an escape route cleared. This was difficult and caused the heaviest losses of the day, but with the aid of the remaining gun, lashed to a wagon tongue with ropes, the Indians were held off long enough for the whites to get off the hill.

The Crees and their half-dozen Métis helpers had hardly been hurt and they now clamored for permission to pursue the beaten Canadians and cut them down on the prairie, but Poundmaker would not assent. At ten that night the column was back in Battleford, beaten; eight had been killed and fifteen wounded and nothing at all had been gained. The Indians, outnumbered, partially surprised and poorly armed, had lost six dead; no authentic record of their wounded was ever made. The Canadians had gone into battle with two cannon, a machine gun and rifles with a range of eight hundred to a thousand yards; the Indians had axes, clubs, bows and arrows and obsolete guns with a maximum range of two hundred yards. The third battle of the rebellion and the first against an army composed almost wholly of Indians was a third mortifying defeat for the forces of white civilization. Poundmaker's Crees, whom Otter had marched forth to overawe, staged dances of celebration, checked their weapons, and prepared to move to Batoche to join the Métis.

THINGS THAT ARE CAESAR'S

But in Batoche fear had come like a laggard winter wind and the old men and the women and children huddled in their huts and came out reluctantly when they were summoned by Riel to hear the news or his hopeful prophecies.

The news was good: three battles, three victories. But Riel and Dumont looked into the faces of the people, stiff with fear, and into eyes in which they read dumb reproach; and they knew the people were not deceived. These were the simple ones; they had not meant to have war, but it had come—and they would not survive it. It might be that a death-wish had overpowered their prophet-dictator, and that it would impel him to carry his people to destruction with him. It no longer mattered; they were already dead.

Louis harangued them. If he should be killed, he said, they need not mourn; he would return from the grave and prove his divine mission. But the mothers with the shriveled faces looked at him dully. They did not doubt him, but they knew well enough that their children, their reckless men and they themselves were mortal; and what purpose would be served if Louis were resurrected in a charnel house?

"Look!" Louis cried desperately. "Look at those devils murdering your whole nation, see your wives and daughters ravished before your streaming eyes, your children tortured, dishonored, disemboweled by the savage soldiers paid to destroy the half-breed nation! To arms! Or will you crouch and submit? God tells you to follow me; the Holy Ghost is with you in my person. Courage; we will conquer!"

But the faces of the people were frozen and their voices stilled. They obeyed orders mutely, went about the business assigned to them by Gabriel and his captains, and their look told their chiefs that the war was lost. When the warriors came home for their meals they found the women secretly weeping and rebuked them, but the women said there soon would be no food for the children because the gardens had been neglected and there had been no hunting. It was as it had always been, the women said: the men riding here and there and shooting off guns and boasting, and not knowing or caring that their children were hungry.

Well, the men retorted angrily, if there was so little food why did some of the women slink off up the hill to take bread or eggs to the five nuns and four priests imprisoned in the parish house beside the Church of St. Antoine? Were they then robbing their children to feed those fat priests, those traitors who had refused absolution to their own husbands?

But the women said that Riel and Dumont, hating the

religious, had forbidden the farmers who usually supplied their wants to deliver any produce to them and they were living meagerly on some stores they had managed to smuggle in from the closed mission of St. Laurent. When they took things to the parish house, the women said, the priests and nuns comforted them and blessed them in the little chapel they had set up to replace the church Riel had occupied. There for a little while they could forget the war and their fears. If the men would go also, perhaps the priests would relent and lift the awful threat of excommunication. . . .

Gradually a few men began to follow their women up the hill. Riel and Dumont raged but could not stop them—unless they murdered the priests, which they did not dare to do. The fathers were summoned frequently to inquisitions before the *Exovidat,* cajoled and threatened; Indians in war paint and angry Métis invaded their quarters and talked of killing; but still the masses were said, and the women and children and more and more of the men met on the paths leading up the hill, looking shamefaced and bewildered, not greeting one another because if one spoke he might betray his fear.

The struggle for the soul of the Métis reached its climax on May 4. A few who had been losing their faith in Riel's religious pretensions summoned up enough courage to demand that his new Church prove itself in debate, in a test of strength, with the Church he now called sneeringly "the old Roman," and they nominated Father Vital Fourmond to uphold the ancient cause. Fourmond had been rector at St. Laurent until Riel closed that mission and imprisoned him with the others, and he had been a prairie priest for seventeen years. His hair and beard were prematurely white and he had the face of a benign St. Nicholas, but he was fearless and fierce in his faith. He accepted the challenge and was escorted down into the village to confront the prophet of the new dispensation.

Walters and Baker's store on the west bank of the river was chosen for the big council. It was filled, and people were crowded about the door, as the priest stalked in, greeting former parishioners; some turned their faces away and others mumbled timid responses. He came up beside Riel and stared coolly into his eyes. Those eyes looked "maniacal," the priest thought, and the face was wax-pale; but Fourmond could not know that fear, not hate, lay behind the fixed and bitter glare.

Louis launched the attack at once.

"How can these poor people," he cried, "whom you try to deceive and mislead as to the truth of my divine mission, for one moment believe you when they have the proof that you are a traitor to them, unworthy of their confidence?"

Father Fourmond's deep voice was slow and calm. "Yes, I have said often before, and I repeat it here to your face and in the face of these poor misguided people whom you are leading to their destruction, to despair and death: it is a crime to take up arms against the constituted authorities!"

Louis attempted to interrupt but the priest's voice rolled on. "It is a crime to raise the standard of rebellion! God proclaims it the duty of all Christians 'to render to Caesar the things that are Caesar's, and to God the things that are God's.' "

Riel's hands swept up angrily and his wild eyes transfixed the crowd. "Yes!" he shouted. "Render to God glory, honor, and adoration! But to the tyrants of the world render that which is due them: fling back into their teeth the authority they have usurped; tumble them down from power! That is what God orders!"

At last there was a stirring in the audience. Louis sensed it at once and leaned forward, tense, his face working.

"Listen to this priest who dares to tell you that it is a crime you are committing, under my direction, in fulfillment of my sacred mission! Listen to him who dares to call it rebel-

lion when you take up arms in a sacred cause, a cause ordained and directed by God! The cause of your native land
which is bleeding and prostrated at the feet of tyrants! The
sacred cause of the rights, liberties and lives of your wives
and children for all time to come!"

Father Fourmond gazed at the hypnotized people, and
looked into the face of Riel. This man, he thought, is Antichrist, and he is mad. The priest prayed, then turned his eyes
despairingly upon the people. Can't you see, he pleaded silently, that your Louis is mad? He willed them to see it; but
the Métis gazed with adoration upon their leader, who could
outtalk a priest, whose words surged and sang with passion
and gave them pride in their blood and their cause. For the
moment they had courage again; for the moment the hungry
children were forgotten.

Father Fourmond's white head was bowed and his lips
moved silently. But he could not believe that all reason had
fled, that there could be no awakening from this nightmare
of Batoche, that one madman could make, and destroy, a
little world. He spoke again, reasonably and quietly, as if to
children:

"Now one calls our Holy Mother Church 'the old Roman,'
thinking by that to humiliate us and humiliate the Church!

"Indeed the Church is old, and will be old as the world is
old! Let us be proud of our glorious Mother Church and of
our forefathers; let us cry together, 'Long live the old Roman!' "

But no response came from the people. His words struck
against the icy wall of their indifference and were lost, unheard. The eyes of all were fixed still upon Louis Riel.

There was no more to say. The priest waited. Riel's face
was stony now, his glacial stare willing the people to silence.

Father Fourmond walked sadly out through the voiceless
mob. A woman, the wife of a Métis who had been a mission
servant, plucked timidly at his gown as he passed the place

where she squatted on the floor, and he looked down at her and smiled.

He walked down to the river where a boat waited to take him back to the eastern shore. As he put out a foot to get into the craft he stumbled on the skirts of his gown. His arm was quickly seized and a voice said, "Look out, Father! Let me help you!"

The priest looked up, startled and pleased. What man, in all that hostile or distrustful or intimidated company, had followed and befriended him and was now gently assisting him into the boat?

The man was Riel. The wildness had gone from his eyes, the priest noted; they were somber now, almost as if they were about to fill with tears; but Louis smiled warmly as he released the priest's arm and nodded good-by.

The boat swung out into the current of the muddy river, its taciturn oarsman impatient to get this chore done. Father Fourmond bent low in his place, shaking his head. He would never understand that man Riel, that lunatic, that Antichrist!

PART SEVEN

Cardboard Shrine

CHAPTER XXIII

The Ignorant Armies

LET'S GET ON WITH IT!

At Fish Creek the Northwest Field Force waited, waited—and grumbled. Morale was lower than it had been at any time since the troops started west.

The humiliating check given the expedition by an enemy force now known to have been vastly outnumbered contributed to the discontent, but it was by no means all that did. There was the growing realization, already noted, that there was much to be said for the Métis cause; more important, there was growing doubt that these people actually were, as the militia had been told, an organized and irreconcilable revolutionary element determined to destroy the Dominion and the Crown.

On the one hand there was the propaganda of the Government; on the other there was the evidence in the field. The simplest soldier wondered when he saw those ugly wounds, made by scrap metal or even pebbles fired from outmoded, short-range, smooth-bore "fowling pieces." Surely a people

445

with hearts evilly set upon rebellion would have seen to it that their army was better equipped?

Then there were the homes and farms, vacated by the score as their Métis tenants trooped into Batoche at the call of Riel. Some of the livestock had been taken along, but much of it had been left in pastures or on the prairie. Stored crops, farm equipment, furniture and prized personal possessions— "holy" pictures or musical instruments or the children's homemade dolls and toys—remained untouched; sometimes unfinished meals still rested on the tables. Bewildered, the Canadians helped themselves to souvenirs. But didn't these strange people know what war was, and that they were engaged in it?

Riel and Dumont knew what they were about, no question of that. But as for the rest, the Canadians wondered. They fought off their sense of guilt and relieved their inner tensions by impatient outbursts. Let's get on with it! Let's hang Riel and Dumont and go home!

Despite the looting, which every invader (sometimes including commanding generals) has justified to himself, this was the most righteous army to take the field in modern times, and the most ingenuous. Its young volunteers had responded to the summons out of sincere patriotism, and most of them, only two months ago, had stepped out of the doors of good middle-class homes where they had been reared in the strictest nine-teenth-century Protestant tradition. Without some drive as strong as patriotism, which was now being weakened by inaction, few of them would willingly have hurt even a stray dog.

They were race-conscious, but unrealistic about it; they had none of the cold, cynical resolution of the American regulars just to the south of them. The Yankees, to start with, were a wholly different type of men; moreover they had learned from horrible experience how well "savages" could defend themselves. There were some vindictive Orangemen in the Northwest Field Force, preachers of religious hatred, and as usual they made themselves heard; but they were few and ineffective in comparison to the number which accompanied Wolseley west fifteen years before. These well-meaning young militiamen for the most part had no grudge. And they would have been utterly astonished, then outraged, had they heard Riel's tirade accusing them of plotting to rape, disembowel and finally annihilate the Métis.

They were punctilious about church attendance, even while on the march on the prairie. They had virtually no liquor and no women; of five thousand men only one required hospital treatment for alcoholism and there were no recorded hospital cases of venereal disease. That further set them apart from the hard-bitten United States cavalry, whose camp followers, Indian and white, were quickly ensconced in "whiskey gulch" slums on the outskirts of whatever military reservations the tough American regulars chanced to occupy. True, liquor and women were hard to get on the Canadian frontier, but what is significant is that it rarely occurred to the conscientious young men who made up this army to complain about it. They complained about the waiting. There was nothing for them to do but fight, and General Middleton wouldn't let them do that.

If the morale of the men was bad, that of the officers was worse. The commanding general, many of them felt, was a pompous ass, a chucklehead, and a coward. There had been no excuse for the setback at Fish Creek; there was no excuse that they could see, despite the difficulties with the wounded, for the long delay before the advance on Batoche.

Few commanding generals have had worse relations with their staffs. Middleton curtly rejected advice and isolated himself not only from the rank and file but from his officers. And some of the latter he infuriated, especially Major General Strange, the Alberta rancher retired from the Army who had donned his uniform again to lead the westernmost division, and the only officer in the campaign who held rank

equal to Middleton's. Strange several times suggested a joint
movement of his division and Middleton's against Big Bear;
Middleton did not even reply to him, but instead wrote the
Cree chief a letter urging him to surrender. Strange snorted.
"General Middleton's letter addressed to Big Bear," he said,
"for various reasons—among others the deficiency of pillar
post boxes—failed to reach that gentleman."

Against the advice of men familiar with the terrain and
the enemy's likely tactics, Middleton left most of his cavalry
behind to guard the railroad and the rear of his division,
when it should have been in the van. An offer was made to
him by settlers, all experienced riders and marksmen, to
form a volunteer force to patrol the railroad and boundary,
which would have released many of his men; he ignored it,
but they organized anyway. His most serious error was one
which gave rise to unjustified charges, spread across Canada
by the newspaper correspondents and returning militiamen,
that the Mounted Police were cowards who had shirked a
fair share of combat.

Colonel Irvine, the Commissioner of the Force, was bot-
tled up in Prince Albert with about a third of the five hundred Mounties who were nominally under his command in
the Northwest; actually, as soon as Middleton entered the
country, Irvine came under his orders. At least twice the
Mountie officer sent word to the general that he was awaiting
his command to take the field; once he suggested, when he
heard indirectly of Middleton's march north, that a con-
certed attack be made upon Batoche by militia from the
south and police from the north. For weeks Middleton did
not even report his whereabouts to Irvine, and when he received the latter's wise proposal for a joint attack he merely
ordered him to remain where he was. When Irvine one day
led a police party on a "reconnaissance in force" from Prince
Albert, he was met fourteen miles out by a messenger from

the commanding general and peremptorily ordered to return to his post.

The troops with Middleton and the newspaper correspondents were unaware of all this, and the derisive nickname "gophers" was soon applied to the helpless Mounties, chafing in the enforced confinement. Nothing could have been more unjust to the most courageous and most intelligent group of white men in the country. In the few engagements in which they were permitted to participate, Mountie losses were heaviest in proportion to their number. Their patrols ceaselessly guarded the obscure Indian and Métis trails across the border, near the Cypress Hills, Wood Mountain, Fort Macleod and Medicine Hat; and their Maj. Sam Steele and a small detachment, at great risk to their lives, wrested a Métis spy and negotiator from the camp of Chief Crowfoot, head of the Blackfeet, and jailed him, thereby helping to persuade that most dangerous warrior in the West to keep out of the troubles.

Middleton's senseless disregard of the quality as well as of the legitimate interests of the Mounted Police reflected seriously upon his ability to command. The effect upon the reputation of the Force back East, where the Mounties at that time did not function, was important only when Parliamentary appropriations were at stake; but it was calamitous in the West, where the Mounties had to take over after the militia left and knit together a badly raveled social fabric. It took the redcoats years to regain the respect of the Indians (they never did regain that of the Métis) and they were gravely handicapped in their task of restoring tranquillity to a country which would never have lost it if Ottawa had listened to their continued warnings.

The militia's officers and men were all the more willing to make scapegoats of the police because of their resentful realization that their commander felt they too were of little account as soldiers. After Fish Creek, rumors continually swept the camp that Middleton intended to appeal to London for British regulars, and bitterness grew among the "colonials" who had not been given a chance to show what they could do.

Nevertheless there were points to be made in Middleton's defense. He had never commanded volunteer militia—and few militiamen anywhere were as green as these. The politicians he now served had never fought a war and would look upon losses in terms not of strategy but of votes lost among indignant families and friends in Ontario precincts. He had never seen the country in which he had to fight and he was unacquainted with his enemy.

Middleton was physically courageous, even foolhardy, but like many a commander before and after him he lacked moral courage. His plight, oddly enough, recalled that of another commander of great physical bravery who rode to his doom nine years before, George Armstrong Custer. Both faced determinative contests against wily native enemies, and on similar terrain; Batoche, slighted as it may still be in the texts, was at least as consequential historically as the Little Big Horn. Both were renowned professional soldiers whose reputations, though for different reasons, were at stake. And the specter of the luckless Custer rode always before the eyes of Middleton, Strange, and one or two others among the better-trained members of the Canadian command.

Custer had needed a spectacular victory, and by very reason of his dreadful failure to gain it, Middleton needed a bloodless one. So, bored and angry, Canada's Northwest Field Force mended its pants and stood guard and formed a square for divine service on Sunday, and waited. What in hell, its men asked their friendly home-town officers, was it waiting for?

FRIEND OF THE GUN

Well, for one thing, the officers said, we're waiting for the Gatling.

Otter had one of the new machine guns at Battleford; it hadn't helped him much at Cut Knife, but Middleton didn't know that. The other two were on the *Northcote*, feebly struggling downriver to Fish Creek. Also on the *Northcote* was their demonstrator, their master and their lover, Lieut. Arthur L. Howard of New Haven, Connecticut, U.S.A., commander of the Second Regiment's machine gun platoon, Connecticut National Guard, on leave and currently attached—somewhat informally—to the Canadian Northwest Field Force.

The venturesome Howard was farther from home than any other member of the expedition. He had left a wife and four children in New Haven to involve himself in a quarrel which certainly did not concern him in the least—because he loved a gun. Dr. R. J. Gatling, who had invented in 1862 the first successful machine gun ever devised, made it clear that Howard was not an employee of his firm; he had gone to Canada, Gatling said, merely as "a friend of the gun."

There was no question about that. Howard had chivied and coaxed and cursed until the Connecticut National Guard had authorized the organization of machine gun platoons; then, in thirty days, he had the first one ready, fully equipped and splendidly trained.

He was no dewy socialite Guardsman, addicted to crisp uniform and show-off drill and soirees. He had had five years of Indian fighting with the United States cavalry as a private and noncom before he went back to Connecticut to settle down. There, because he was an expert machinist, within a few years he built a carriage manufacturing business which was netting him fifteen thousand dollars a year. He sold it and devoted his full time to inventions, most of them connected with firearms or munitions. He had used the Gatling in his American service and he knew as much about it as any man alive; when he learned that Canada was going to try it out against the rebellious Métis he hastened to offer his services.

He had a comfortable, happy home in sedate New Haven and he loved his family, but he also loved that gun. He thus joined the company of implausible characters who strode across the stage during the climactic scenes of the Northwestern historical drama. He had traveled more than twenty-five hundred miles into a foreign country to kill men against whom he had no feeling whatever; yet he was not a grubby soldier of fortune and he was not a killer—he was a mechanic. His interest in the mass murder of Métis was wholly scientific, cold as mercury in a tube. Batoche was to be his laboratory.

There had been too few opportunities to test the beloved gun on human flesh and bone. It had been used briefly in the closing years of the Civil War, and even less extensively in the Franco-Prussian War of 1870. During the nationalist revolt in Egypt in 1881 the British had fired it over the heads of rioters in Alexandria, and had made such an impression that Ahmed Arabi's nine thousand rebels were afraid to attack the city's British garrison of only four hundred. It had been used a few times against American Indians. But that was about all, and now it had been improved.

Howard had fired it, time after time, into two-inch spruce planks, had meticulously measured the penetration and checked the spiral scratches on the bullets, changed the elevation by a degree and fired it again, computed range. But it was not the same; the Gatling had been made to kill men, not to drill spruce planks. He had drilled and splintered and shattered a good many, building up his speed at the handle which he had to revolve to fire the gun. Theoretically the weapon could discharge twelve hundred bullets a minute (which is faster than any "automatic" machine gun today) but few men could turn the handle that swiftly, or keep at it for long. Well, if it was humanly possible, Howard would do it; in so far as a man could make himself a mechanical unit, build himself into a machine, he had done that.

The Métis and their French-Canadian sympathizers, understandably, hated the cool man from Connecticut above anyone they had ever known, except Sir John A. Macdonald. Their bitter outcry against his "brutal" intervention in an affair which was none of his business roused their coreligionists everywhere, caused a stir in the newspapers, and brought the disavowal from Gatling and later ones from the Connecticut National Guard and the United States Government. Therefore Lieutenant Howard, "friend of the gun," was on his own. He was not perturbed about any of this; he was blissfully happy; and he was not in the least "brutal." He was merely scientific.

He was also effective. The newspaper correspondents in the field, the troops in their letters home, and even the austere command sang the praises of "Gatling Howard." And the prosperous New England mechanic who fell in love with a machine and followed it into the wilderness was astonished when he found that he had been immortalized in campaign doggerel:

Full many a line of expressions fine
  And of sentiments sweet and grand
Have been penned of "our boys" who from home's dear joys
  Set out for the North-West land.
We've been told how they fought for the glory sought,
  We've heard of the deeds they've done;
But it's quite high time for some praise in rhyme
  For the man with the Gatling gun.

Music hath charms even midst war's alarms,
  To soothe the savage breast;
None can hold a candle to that music "by Handle"
  That lulled Riel's "breeds" to rest.
And they sleep that sleep profound, so deep,
  From which shall awaken none;

And the lullabies that closed their eyes
  Were sung by the Gatling gun.

All honour's due—and they have it, too—
  To the Grens. and the Q.O.R.
They knew no fear, but with British cheer,
  They charged and dispersed afar
The rebel crew; but 'twixt me and you
  When all is said and done,
A different scene there might have been
  But for Howard and his Gatling gun!

MAN O' WAR IN THE MUD

The stern-wheeler *Northcote* had two hundred troops
aboard or on the two barges it was tugging downstream, and
about three hundred tons of supplies and ammunition. The
hundred-and-sixty-foot steamer drew thirty-four inches of
water, and unfortunately there were a good many places in
the South Saskatchewan Channel at this time, before the full
spring run-off, in which there were only thirty inches. Therefore the *Northcote* "crutched" its way along, grounding on
sand bars about every ten miles and hauling itself off by
"sparring."

This operation, used in all river steamboating, consisted of
setting the vessel's spars—tall, heavy timbers like telegraph
poles—in the channel, one on each side of the boat, with
their tops inclined toward the bow. High on each spar was a
tackle block over which a Manila cable was threaded. One
end of each cable was attached to the gunwale of the steamer
and the other wound around a steam-powered winch. As the
winches turned and the paddle wheel revolved, the boat was
lifted and thrust forward a few feet; the spars were then reset
farther ahead and the operation repeated until the steamer
was clear of the bar. The grotesque appearance of the boat
during "sparring" gave this operation the nickname of "grass-
hoppering."

On May 3 the impatient men at Fish Creek finally had news: the vessel they awaited was stuck, as usual, near Saskatoon, where it was found by some of Middleton's mounted scouts. The scouts watched while the creaking spars wearily lifted the boat into deeper water once more, then they galloped back to camp to report. The Northwest Field Force took on new life; the long wait was nearly ended.

At Saskatoon the *Northcote* unloaded medical officers and base hospital supplies, and on May 5 it arrived at Fish Creek. The rest of the supplies and ammunition were quickly removed and Lieutenant Howard and one of his Gatlings joined the artillery.

The other machine gun stayed aboard. To the astonishment of everybody, especially the *Northcote*'s long-suffering civilian crew, General Middleton had dreamed himself up a navy. The *Northcote* was it: the first "gunboat" ever to navigate on the Canadian (or any other) prairie. And of all the fantastic expedients resorted to by either side in the Northwest Rebellion of 1885, this attempt to convert the *Northcote* into a war vessel was undoubtedly the most ludicrous. It was little more than a barge with two decks, an exposed engine and boiler on the lower and a cabin and pilothouse above. Its top speed under then existing river conditions was not much more than five miles an hour. On its trip from Saskatchewan Landing it had averaged only about fifteen miles a day; a doctor who had been left behind embarked alone in a canoe six days after the *Northcote* departed and easily overtook it.

Middleton put the vessel in charge of S. L. Bedson, chief of transport for the Northwest Field Force. In civilian life Bedson was warden of the Manitoba penitentiary and thus probably was the first and only penologist in history to command a warship. Thirty-five soldiers were put aboard; with the crew and other able-bodied passengers this provided a complement of about fifty armed men. Three, however, were sick. One of these, a victim of erysipelas, was Lieut. Hugh J. Macdonald, the son of Prime Minister Sir John A. Macdonald.

With the aid of timbers brought from Dumont's stables at nearby Gabriel's Crossing, the lower deck was encased with a double wall of two-inch planks. Oats and other sacked or boxed matériel were packed on the upper deck and around the vulnerable pilothouse. Armament consisted of one small cannon, the remaining Gatling and the rifles of the troops; Middleton couldn't spare any more guns and in view of the probable effectiveness of his man o' war, that was just as well. Civilian Captains Seager and Sheets and Purser Talbot, who knew their boat, took a dim view of the whole project; but they were in the Army now. The *Northcote,* dragging its clumsy barges, was to proceed downriver to Batoche, await the arrival of the overland force, then open fire upon the rebel stronghold from the river simultaneously with the attack which would be launched by Middleton on land.

This, if the Métis stood still for it, would trap them between two broadsides and the war would be over in short order. It was unlikely, however, that the enemy would cooperate, in view of the fact that its scouts, securely hidden in the brush, had watched the whole operation of "armor-plating" the boat (directed by Captain Haig of the Royal Engineers) and had gleefully reported all details to Gabriel Dumont. The fact that there were Métis scouts about was no secret; Middleton's patrols almost caught three of them and came back, somewhat staggered, to report that the enemy trio had been tranquilly playing cards.

A complicated system of signals was worked out by which the steamer, using its whistle, would communicate with the land force and the latter would reply with bugle calls.

At last all was ready. The *Northcote,* built in 1873 and since then prosaically engaged in supplying Hudson's Bay posts along the river, was—outwardly at least—transformed.

Captains Seager and Sheets, who doubled as pilots, still had grave misgivings: only the lower part of the pilothouse could be shielded, lest vision be obstructed. Whoever occupied that position was going to do a lot of dodging, and Seager and Sheets knew all too well who that would be. But now—it was early on the morning of May 7—they manfully tooted the whistle. A bugle answered from the neat ranks on shore, and the joint land-and-water expedition set forth from Fish Creek.

Eyes right, the Northwest Field Force marched past a stone cairn topped by a tall white cross of peeled poplar which marked the resting place of the victims of the Canadian Army's first clash with the Métis, and swung into stride on the trail which led north alongside the river. The first spring blooms, the purple wild crocus or Pasque flower, nodded gently in the breeze. It was a glorious day, sunny and warm. The column contained about nine hundred men in uniform; teamsters and other civilian employees raised the total to more than a thousand, and there were six hundred horses.

Awaiting them in Batoche were two hundred Métis fighting men, haphazardly armed, and their families and noncombatant friends, probably in all about seven hundred people. Moving slowly to join them—but too slowly to get there in time—were an unknown number of Métis reinforcements, probably not more than fifty, and Poundmaker's Crees.

In the afternoon of the 7th the Canadians halted at Gabriel's Crossing and camped, and the *Northcote* tied up. From that point to Batoche, six miles north, the river road was unsafe: it led through dense brush and small timber in which the Métis could station snipers or even establish an ambush. Therefore when the march was resumed the next morning the troops were led out of the ravine on a wide detour over a prairie trail which would take them several miles from the river and bring them back to Batoche from the east. The *Northcote*'s commander was instructed to remain where

he was for the day and to proceed cautiously the next morning.

The steamer and the troops were to meet at Batoche at
nine o'clock the morning of May 9. General Middleton, than
whom a more cautious commander never lived, had done
everything he could think of to build an overwhelming offensive except the one thing that would have helped the most—
calling out the experienced Mounties at Prince Albert.

If everything developed as planned, the last stronghold of
the New Nation of the West, the log-cabin capital of an upstart colored race, would be reduced in at most a few hours.

In Batoche, meanwhile, the most indomitable man that
New Nation had produced went quietly about his business.
Gabriel Dumont was confronted now with the battle of position he had desperately tried to avoid, and would have
avoided had not Riel, after Fish Creek, again overborne his
pleas for a guerrilla campaign. But Gabriel shrugged. *N'im-
porte!* He would do what he had to do. Although, as an
"illiterate," he could not have known it, he was not the first
commander to have his strategy upset by the political arm
of the state, but he took it with better grace than most.

He checked Métis assets and liabilities. Two hundred
fighters, every one a sharpshooter; but some of them, like
their Indian forebears, had never fully comprehended the
idea of collective and organized fighting. The cowards who
had fled at Fish Creek had been weeded out, but there still
were some whose resolution had been weakened by their
wives and the priests. Miscellaneous armament—Springfield,
Winchester and Martini-Henry rifles; many shotguns and
ancient muzzle-loaders: that was bad, but couldn't be helped.
Terrain—Gabriel and his warriors knew every inch. Holes in
the ground, and brush and logs. Dirt and fire. And a psychological factor: a prophet, Louis David Riel, with a wonder-

working voice, some letters from a bishop, and a crucifix a foot and a half long.

Well, it was not enough to win. But, *sacre bleu!*, he had always known they couldn't win. It would serve; it would upset the English apple cart.

CHAPTER XXIV

The Darkling Plain

SATURDAY

DAWN came at four o'clock. At five-thirty the Northwest Field Force was on the march from its overnight bivouac nine miles east of Batoche. In the lead were seventy-five mounted scouts under the command of Major Boulton, who had headed the "Portage party" in 1870 and once was under sentence of death in Fort Garry.

Next came the Gatling on its wheeled carriage, and other guns.

At seven o'clock the *Northcote* cast off its lines and started slowly downriver from Gabriel's Crossing.

The sun was bright and a soft spring breeze stirred the bunch grass, green and tall and tangled now that there were no buffalo to feed upon it. The crocuses turned their cupped, gossamer heads to the light and bowed, and their purple petals opened like the arms of Cree dancers worshiping the sun. Nine hundred army boots crushed millions of tiny blossoms hidden in the clumps of grass, in the gravelly ruts of the trail, under rocks.

460

Along the riverbank the willows, sap-red and tumescent, quivered in the wind but seemed to shake with the surging life and lust of spring. The air was scented by them, and the men on the *Northcote* stood on the deck and breathed deeply. A wonderful day, never to be forgotten; a day to tell about back home where spring was slow-winged and long-lived and did not just suddenly happen, all at once.

Boulton's horses and the guns raised some dust but the breeze carried it off, and most of the time the marchers could see for miles. There were no houses, no people, no creatures. The birds, few in prairie country, cowered in their nests scooped in the sod. Nothing moved, nothing lived but the grass and brush and flowers. One of the marchers noted mentally, for his letter home, that it was almost as if they were the first men. Truly a great lone land, he would write, but lovely; one could understand that men might be willing to die for it.

This war didn't make sense; damn the politicians, on both sides. But it would soon be over, and it was good to be alive today. He must remember to write what spring was like. . . .

There was little talk and few commands were needed. But sounds carried a long way. The rattle of the horses' gear, the creak and thump of the gun carriages on the uneven trail, could be heard to the end of the long column.

So could the sudden rattle of gunfire, and the frantic, futile squeals of the *Northcote*'s little whistle.

The steamer had been under way for less than an hour. It was approaching a long sand bar which jutted into the river from the eastern shore, at the southern limits of the straggling Batoche settlement. The channel was very narrow at this point and the pilot was feeling his way, hugging the brushy bank opposite the bar.

Suddenly, on an unseen and unheard signal, rifle and shotgun fire from both banks of the river raked the vessel's deck.

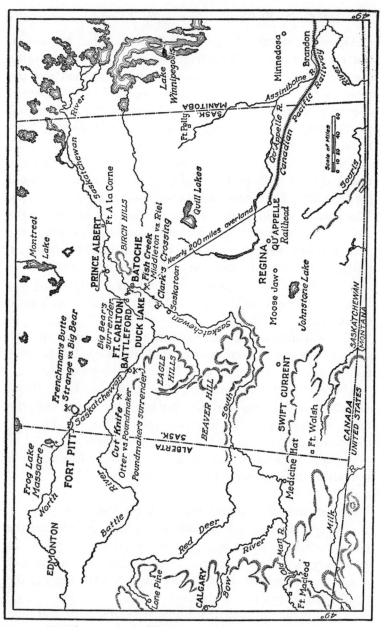

Northwest Rebellion (Second Métis Uprising)

Bullets thudded harmlessly into the thick timbers behind which the troopers promptly flung themselves prone, but they pierced the unshielded hull and the flimsy walls of the cabin on the upper deck. The sick men rolled out of their bunks in the cabin, grappled frenziedly with their mattresses, thrust them against the walls. Lieutenant Macdonald, the Prime Minister's son, his face swollen and aflame from his malady, seized a rifle and crawled out on deck.

A horse with Gabriel Dumont standing in the stirrups danced out on the bank. Gabriel shouted to the Métis marksmen and the line of fire moved up. Bullets riddled the pilot-house. The helmsman, splinters of wood flying about him and a bullet hole in his jacket, let go of the wheel and dropped to the floor. The *Northcote,* out of control, careened into the sand bar, caught in the current, scraped the other side of the channel. Dumont shouted again and a few Métis broke from cover, running to board the lurching vessel, but the Gatling started up then and they raced back. Gabriel watched for a moment, heedless of the bullets flying about him; then as he saw that the current would keep the boat from grounding he spurred his horse and set off on a run for the center of the settlement.

It was eight o'clock, an hour before General Middleton had "scheduled" the start of the Battle of Batoche, and the troops were nearly four miles away.

Purser Talbot, a rifle in his hand, crawled into the pilot-house to "cover" the helmsman, Captain Seager, who had taken the wheel again and now had the steamer straightened out. Co-captain Sheets and the engine crew were building the steam pressure to the limit; Seager swung the boat into the middle of the river and the *Northcote* ran for its life. Only one or two shells were fired from its cannon; the gun was too slow. But the Gatling raked the banks behind the boat and the Métis kept their distance.

The steamer reached the center of the settlement and

chugged on toward the ferry landing. Too late, Captain Seager saw Dumont and a group of men working feverishly with the two ferry cables. He tried to stop the boat, but its momentum carried it on as the Métis dropped one of the cables to the river's surface, just behind the vessel. The other cable, a few feet ahead, was coming down, too. Seager signaled frantically for full speed ahead, plowed into the cable just as it scraped the top of the pilothouse. The *Northcote*'s two stacks, its mast, its two tall spars and its whistle were yanked off and flung on the upper deck. The deck immediately began to burn.

While a bucket brigade doused the deck under fire, the vessel slid around the big bend in the river. The Métis bombardment dropped off; the steamer was out of range now and almost safe. Captain Seager went on another mile or two and dropped anchor in mid-channel. All hands went to work to repair the torn and charred deck and reset the stacks, spars and mast. Restoring the whistle to its high perch on a stack was the worst job and no one would undertake it until Private C. Coombes of the Toronto Infantry School Corps, promised a fifty-dollar bonus, volunteered. Just as he finished, a Métis sniper spotted him and opened fire, too late.

Bedson and others tried to induce the ship's civilian captain and crew to swing about and go back to Batoche, but they refused. Anyone ought to be able to see by now, they argued, that the *Northcote* was not a gunboat. Three men had been wounded while the rickety little craft ran the gantlet for five miles; the vessel, if it returned, could not get past the lowered ferry cables and its passengers would be sitting ducks for the Métis.

The military men had to admit that the captains were right. So the first and only warship ever seen on the prairie "sat out" the war three or four miles from the major battlefield, plaintively tootling its little whistle in the hope that somebody would come and find it and tell its military complement what to do. But nobody heard the whistle, and the Métis were between the vessel and the marching troops, and soon everyone was too busy to worry about the *Northcote*. A few days later, accompanied by another steamer which had come up from Prince Albert, it got back to Batoche. The war was over, but the *Northcote* got there in time to blow its whistle for the victory celebration.

The last scattered shots were being fired at the *Northcote* when, promptly at nine o'clock, the advance guard of Middleton's column came within sight of the Church of St. Antoine and the parish house. Unpainted and already shabby, the clapboarded buildings looked ugly and out of place on the flowering prairie. Behind them, and stretching for some distance to the north, there was a dense thicket of willow brush and small poplar trees.

Batoche lay in the ravine below, not yet visible to the approaching troops. Across the road from the church and on a little promontory of its own above the river valley was the cemetery. Near it were two or three small cabins, typical Métis homes.

There were no preliminaries to conflict; Middleton was in no mood to offer the rebels an opportunity to negotiate. The Gatling, with Boulton's scouts as escort, was rushed forward, unlimbered and aimed at the cabins near the cemetery. Howard spun its handle and the gun spat bullets into the log walls of the huts.

The Battle of Batoche had begun.

A few men and some women and children, probably noncombatants who had remained close to the church to avoid involvement in the troubles, ran from the cabins and scuttled through the brush and down into the ravine. There was no answer to the Canadians' fire. Gradually more of the troops came up, and, dropping to their knees, fired over the crest of the hill to persuade any Métis to keep their distance while the guns were brought to a point midway between the church and cemetery.

A white handkerchief fluttered from the door of the parish house and the Canadians ceased firing while General Middleton and some of his staff conferred with the priests.

At this conference, or at some subsequent one, the Métis were betrayed. Despite their denials, there can be little doubt that the priests, embittered by the apostasy of Riel and his converts and by their imprisonment, disclosed to the Canadian command such of the Métis strategy as they knew and, more important, revealed that the rebel force was desperately short of ammunition and food.

The missionaries in their later accounts of the Battle of Batoche insisted that they remained neutral and that they gave no information to the troops, in obedience to a written pledge the Métis had required of them. But against their word stands not only the testimony of the Métis veterans, including Gabriel Dumont, but also the accounts written on the battlefield by Canadian officers, volunteers and newspapermen. "A quarter of an hour," a militiaman wrote, "passed in parley with the priests, from whom it was learned that the enemy numbered about two hundred half-breeds and as many Indians [the estimate was far too high, since the Indians—Poundmaker's—had not arrived] equally divided by the river; they were absolutely without flour, sugar, and tea . . . short of ammunition, especially lead, and many of them dissatisfied with Riel." Wrote another: "From the priests some information was gleaned of the strength and disposition of the rebel forces." And another: "The priests say they are short of ammunition and have only a few cattle." There were many similar statements.

Métis survivors of the climactic battle always complained that they were defeated through the treachery of the priests, and some of them were so bitter that they never became reconciled to the Church. Gabriel Dumont hated the clergy to the end of his life and never ceased to work to nullify its influence among his people.

"We learned," Dumont said, "from a thoroughly reliable source [that] Middleton, even though he had reinforcements, despaired of defeating us, when some traitors whom I don't wish to name advised him that we were almost out of ammunition and that, apart from a few, all the Métis were discouraged. That besides, if the besiegers didn't hurry, aid would soon arrive to reinforce the besieged."

Though Gabriel did not name the "traitors," he made his meaning clear:

These traitors were continually in communication with the enemy and with those of our men whom they persuaded to lay down their arms by offering them a safe conduct.

What contributed greatly to the confusion of our soldiers was that they were refused all religious aid, for themselves, their wives and their children!

Since the troops had advanced as far as the church without encountering resistance, the priests, nuns and the few Métis who had sought refuge with them appeared to be as safe in the parish house as anywhere, and they remained there. Meanwhile Middleton's cannon began shelling the village. Balls struck the Walters and Baker store and house several times, starting fires which, however, did not burn; some of the Métis regarded this as a miracle attributable to the flag which the *Exovidat* had raised on the house: a makeshift cotton banner to which had been sewn a paper portrait of the Virgin. The house used by the *Exovidat* for its meetings, which bore a flag with a portrait of the Christ, also was struck several times but not destroyed.

Occasionally the shelling would bring a few people out of one of the houses, but they were obviously noncombatants. Not a single Métis soldier had yet become visible.

The troops, encouraged, began to move forward beyond the church, with the Gatling, as usual, in the front rank.

Suddenly, less than thirty yards in front of the leading Canadians, fire burst from the steeply sloping hillside right in their faces. For a few moments the troops stood stupidly, gazing at puffs of smoke which appeared to be coming out of the ground itself; then panic seized them and they fled.

An order was shouted to pull back the guns. One of them, caught in brush, could not be extricated immediately and its demoralized crew was about to abandon it when Howard, who had made no move to retreat with his Gatling, silenced the Métis fire in the gun's vicinity and, by maintaining a constant fusillade, held the rebels back while the gun was withdrawn. Virtually alone—the gunner beside him lay moaning, shot through both legs—the Connecticut man held the line for the retreat, and only after the Canadians had reformed at the church did he pull his gun back.

The Canadian command soon discovered what it was up against. The ground was honeycombed with rifle pits, far superior to the ones the Métis had used at Fish Creek. Not only the bank of the ravine, but the meadow below it between the hill and the river contained these pits at intervals of every few yards and they extended almost a mile in depth. They were spread over a front of a mile and a half, from beyond the cemetery to the south to several hundred yards back of the church to the north. It was subsequently discovered that they ranged in size from holes barely large enough for one man, to elaborate trenches accommodating a dozen. Loopholed logs, skillfully camouflaged with dirt and brush, were set at the edge facing the enemy.

The Battle of Batoche lasted for four days, and in all that time, until the last hour or two, some of the Canadians who were in the front rank under almost constant fire never saw a member of the enemy force.

Down in the meadow, behind the hillside rifle pits, Gabriel Dumont rested on one knee and kept his Winchester aimed at the skyline. Now he called orders to the closest of the pits; from man to man they were relayed up the bank to the men in the most advanced positions.

Métis crept from their pits, wormed on their bellies up the slope in communication trenches shielded with brush. Their nondescript clothing blended with the terrain; even if Canadian scouts had dared to peek over the hilltop they probably would not have detected the movement. Previously prepared pits at the edge of the cemetery and in the heavy brush behind the church, at the left and right flanks of the Canadian column, were silently occupied.

The new rebel attack opened from the left, but most of the Métis on that flank happened to be armed only with shotguns and their fire fell short. The Canadians held their ground but could not effectively reply, even with the Gatling, because the enemy was invisible. When a more effective fusillade started on the right flank and almost trapped a battery, further withdrawal was ordered. The first wounded Canadians had been placed in the church; they were now removed and taken to the rear.

A sinister crackling and a sudden hot wind told the Canadians that the enemy had resorted to a favorite trick: they had fired the brush and grass on both sides of the militia column. Soon a dense cloud of acrid smoke rolled over the prairie. Mindful of their experience at Fish Creek, the troops were uneasy: they strained their smarting eyes trying to see the enemy through the murk and saw none, but they saw comrades in their solid line, shelterless on the open plain, methodically picked off. Howard was grimly firing the Gatling into the smoke, without any idea of target or range but with the intent, probably successful, of preventing a Métis charge.

It was now one o'clock in the afternoon. The Canadians

had gone as far as the church but had been driven back. They were not to get that far again for three more days.

Given their advantage of complete concealment, the Métis, the Canadian command feared, could hold out indefinitely if they had food and ammunition. The priests said they lacked these essentials, and it was to be hoped the priests were right, and could be trusted. Otherwise, it was acknowledged sadly, "one rebel was as good as ten volunteers."

Middleton ordered a zareba, an improvised stockade, erected a few hundred yards east of the church and directed that all of the Field Force's animals and equipment be brought up from the overnight camp. In midafternoon Lord Melgund, the representative of the Governor General and Middleton's chief of staff, left suddenly, bound for Ottawa. Again the rumor arose that Middleton was appealing for British regulars, but actually Melgund had left on private business.

The Canadians made one or two more sorties toward the cemetery as the smoke cleared but were easily driven off by the entrenched sharpshooters. The last few hours of sunlight saw only desultory firing by both sides. The Métis were obviously saving ammunition, and the battle, thanks largely to the Gatling, had become a stalemate.

At sunset the troops were slowly withdrawn to the zareba, to the accompaniment of jeers and singing from the Métis line. After the Gatling had been moved back, too, snipers cautiously trailed the Canadians. Howard's entry into the camp brought loud cheering; the volunteers were freely willing to acknowledge that he had saved the advance echelons from destruction and had prevented a catastrophe during the withdrawal to the camp. The short range of the rebels' ammunition kept the pursuers at a safe distance because their guns would not carry to the Gatling or beyond. Howard brought in a souvenir: an ivory-handled knife he had taken from a dead Indian. It had been a United States cavalry saber, cut down and shaped by the Sioux from whose body he got it.

Save for the shaded candle in the hospital tent the stockade was without light. No fires were permitted, so dinner was hardtack and water. Even General Middleton retired in a dark tent. After the men had rolled up in their blankets, the nerve-war tactic Dumont had wanted to try weeks before was employed by the Métis: an intermittent rain of bullets and other missiles plopped into the compound, keeping the men on edge and frightening the hundreds of animals sharing the limited space. The troopers took shelter under the wagons, but many of them had to walk all night among the horses to prevent a stampede.

The zareba had been badly located, fully exposed on the side of a slight rise in the prairie, without a tree or brush for shelter. Unaccountably, it had been placed in a plowed field, and the men and animals stumbled about in choking clouds of dust which obscured what little light there was from the stars.

Firing continued most of the night. It caused few casualties but it kept the disgruntled troops awake. At about midnight a huge rocket burst over the zareba and for a few moments it was brightly illuminated. The Canadians started from their uneasy sleep, bumped their heads on the wagon beds and swore; they rolled out of their blankets but scuttled back under cover as bullets, buckshot and scrap metal rained on them. No one was hurt, though a few of the horses were hit; but the men had another puzzle to keep them awake: Where had the ill-armed Métis obtained the huge flare?

SUNDAY

There was a film of ice on the water pails and the troops were stiff and sore when they were called up at four A.M. Shouts of ribald challenge and some scattered shooting from the Métis greeted the first stir in the camp.

Skirmish lines were flung out at five-thirty and the guns were again pushed forward until their crews could see the village. Steady cannonading reduced most of the houses to rubble. One of the most seriously damaged was the big Batoche house, in the cellar of which about a dozen whites were imprisoned with one recalcitrant Métis, Albert Monkman, formerly a member of Riel's council. The others were telegraph maintenance men, freighters, storekeepers or scouts, for the most part; but included were Riel's former secretary, Will Jackson, who had been judged mentally irresponsible by the council, and his brother, who had come from Prince Albert to find him.

The cannon, firing nine-pound shells, could not be brought low enough on their fixed carriages to bombard the rifle pits on the sloping hillside; the shrapnel shells burst harmlessly in the trees overhead or far beyond the entrenchments. The Métis, meanwhile, were economizing on ammunition and fired much less frequently than they had the day before. The Midland Battalion, taking a lesson from the enemy, dug its own foxholes and was able to hold its position all day without loss. Some effort also was made for the first time to provide concealment for the cannon and the Gatling.

The militia had been instructed on leaving camp to avoid reckless gestures. General Middleton had decided to devote the day to artillery action and, by destroying Batoche, to wear down the morale of the Métis—counting upon the assurances of the priests that the rebels could not withstand siege. The troops did not get within two hundred yards of their furthermost advance of the first day, and there were hours when there was no fire at all from rifles. Middleton, walking among the guns with a cane under his arm, was startled by an impetuous burst of rifle fire. "Hold your fire!" he yelled. "What on earth are you shooting at?" Then, under his breath, he grumbled, "Damned fools!" A Canadian officer heard it, flushed red with resentment.

He did not have enough men, the general insisted, to carry Batoche by storm. He had come on the field with 917 under arms, almost five times the rebel strength; but throughout the campaign he overestimated the enemy's numbers or, as in his conversations with the priests, accepted inaccurate figures without making any effort to check them by espionage.

On Sunday afternoon the Grenadiers were ordered to try a feint—a sudden attack, then a faked headlong retreat. This, it was hoped, might draw the Métis from their pits and into a position which had been secretly occupied by the Ninetieth Battalion. But the maneuver failed; a few nervous and trigger-happy men of the Ninetieth opened fire too soon and betrayed their position, so the Métis held fast in their dugouts.

Gabriel Dumont again spent hours kneeling in the meadow, out of range of the Canadians unless they came over the hill. Behind and before him, clutching the big crucifix, Riel circulated among the men in the pits, exhorting them to keep up their courage for the glory of God. At dawn each day he had led the fighters and their families in prayer in a grove down by the river.

At six o'clock the Canadians again began to fall back to the zareba. The Métis, taking advantage of the fact that the sun was in the eyes of the troops, darted over the crest of the ravine to harass the retreating force and the first important skirmish of the day started in the field before the church. But the Canadians, without shelter, could not make a stand; again the Gatling covered the withdrawal. Meanwhile, in the zareba, the chaplain was starting funeral services for a gunner killed the day before; while he was thus engaged, two more were killed.

The last of the transport had arrived from the camp nine miles east and its wagons were used to strengthen the compound. Several detachments also had been assigned to build earthworks to surround the camp, so the troops retired that night to a much stronger position. They also got some sleep

because the Métis chose not to waste ammunition on a re-
newal of their "nerve war." It was even safe to light fires, and
the Canadians at last had a hot meal and tea.

But the men and their officers were angry. Middleton's decision to win by siege was unpopular; it reflected upon the
courage of the troops, and the indecisive skirmishing and the
discomfort of the nights in the zareba were harder on the
whites than the ordeal was on the Métis. Again the cry arose
from the ranks: Let's get on with it!

MONDAY

The Canadians' timidity had given Gabriel and Louis new
hope. More messengers raced off to Poundmaker, to implore
him to hurry; if Batoche could hold out two or three days
longer there was a chance, the slimmest of chances, that the
invaders could be routed.

But in Poundmaker's camp democracy was functioning as
it always did in that purest of democratic communities, the
Indian band.

Interminable argument absorbed the energies of the Crees.
There were war parties and peace parties, internationalists
and isolationists; and because it had always been so, each had
the right to respectful attention while it pleaded its cause.

Poundmaker, who had made peace with the Blackfeet and
was known from the Missouri to the Mackenzie as a great
chief, was an internationalist; but he had always been
friendly with the whites, had once helped to guide a governor general's party on a Western tour, and temperamentally he was inclined to stand for peace. Still, he was reluctant
to forgo any benefits which might accrue to his half-starved
people from a victory spectacular enough to compel the Government to adopt a more liberal Indian policy. Finally he
took the realistic position: Could the Indians and Métis win?
They couldn't, he told the council of chiefs, because "Riel
has too little powder and cartridge." How he learned this is

a mystery; certainly the Métis messengers were careful to avoid betraying Batoche's weakness.

There were day-long debates about the trustworthiness and fighting qualities of their allies, Big Bear and Riel. The latter's urgent letters were read and reread, analyzed for hidden meanings, for unintentional disclosure of the true Métis situation. They were translated from French into Cree by Riel's envoys, but Poundmaker, suspicious as any statesman, had the translations checked by a white prisoner in his camp.

There was talk about honor. The Crees had accepted and smoked the tobacco sent by Gabriel Dumont; they were pledged.

And because there could be no gainsaying, because no Indian could speak against the honor of the band, the tipis were struck and the camp moved east, toward Batoche. That did not end the arguments, of course; were they fighting someone else's war, would they fight their way, or Dumont's way? It was necessary to pause frequently to discuss these matters.

Democracy was at work, helping to defeat itself.

In Batoche, Dumont moved among the rifle pits and sent his orders flying about the hillside incessantly: Hold your fire, save ammunition! He thought Middleton had sixteen hundred men and could not understand the Canadians' failure to attack, but he took every advantage of their indecision. By moving his men rapidly and secretly over their wide front and spreading their meager fire, he convinced Middleton that the priests' estimate of rebel strength had been, if anything, low.

In the ruined council hut Riel wrote prophecies in his "Commonplace Book" and devised new prayers. In caves dug into the riverbanks on both sides of the stream huddled the women and children, sleeping in straw and subsisting thinly on the last of their provisions. Some were eating horse and dog meat. Hunters, most of them Indians, ranged about the prairie on the west side hunting stray cattle which they drove back to the river and butchered.

The priests and nuns, most of them convinced that they were doomed, prayed incessantly for grace and courage in their martyrdom. The parish house was now in the center of the battlefield, but there were no accommodations for them in the troops' zareba, nor would they have been much safer there. Safety lay west of the river, but to get there they would have had to go through the Métis lines—and Gabriel, for one, probably would not have hesitated to shoot the priests on sight.

The religious did not escape unscratched. Early Monday evening Father Moulin went to the attic of the parish house on some errand, and as he passed an open window was struck by a bullet from a Métis rifle. The shot had not been aimed at him and the bullet's force was spent; he received a painful but not serious flesh wound in the head. His colleagues signaled with an improvised red cross flag; firing stopped and the wounded missionary was taken by Canadian stretcher bearers to the hospital tent in the zareba.

Monday was a tiresome repetition of the day before; nothing happened on the battlefield except that the Canadians were shifted and new units given a taste of Métis marksmanship. At sunset the troops again retired to the crowded, stinking stockade where the dust and manure were now ankle-deep.

Middleton's officers finally got to him with demands that a general offensive be authorized for the next day. Howard, mad with impatience, begged for permission to go forward alone with his gun and clear out the first row of rebel rifle pits.

The general would not assent to an all-out charge, but he did outline new aggressive tactics which he was willing to try.

Word spread through the camp that tomorrow might end the militia's ordeal.

TUESDAY

Early that morning, May 12, Louis Riel told the people gathered in the grove that this could be the day which would decide the fate of their race. His prophetic vision had disclosed, he said, that if the skies were clear, Batoche would survive; but if clouds obscured the sun the Métis cause was doomed.

The women and children gazed overhead, wide-eyed; the men, fidgeting with their guns, glanced covertly at the horizon, at the hot blaze of the sun in the east. There was not even a wisp of cloud in the shimmering blue-green arch of the heavens. The women gave thanks and gratefully mumbled their responses to Riel's prayers. The men laughed and joked. It would be a good day.

General Middleton, with about 150 men including a cavalry detachment, and with the Gatling and one cannon, set out in the morning on a wide sweep around the northeast flank of the rebel position. There he was to create a diversion, under cover of which the main infantry force would attack the center, where the heaviest concentration of Métis riflemen commanded the best route into the ravine.

In midmorning Middleton's gun was heard, but it fired only two or three times and there was no sound from the smaller arms. Lieut. Col. Van Straubenzie, commanding the center force, concluded that something had gone wrong, and did not order the advance.

At noon Middleton and his men returned—the general, according to eyewitnesses, "in a towering rage" because his orders had not been obeyed. In vain his staff protested that a couple of shots from a single cannon could not have been construed by anyone as a diversion.

Nevertheless Middleton's strategy had been worth while. The rebels, after three days of successful resistance on a comparatively narrow front, were alarmed and puzzled by the movement, abortive as it was, and fell into the trap by strengthening that flank of their line at the expense of the center. Moreover, the general now had evidence of weakening resolution among them: a message from Riel. John W. Astley, a surveyor and one of the prisoners in Batoche, mounted and carrying a white flag, had brought it through the lines to Middleton that morning. "If you massacre our families," Riel wrote, "we are going to massacre the Indian agent and others, prisoners." Middleton sent Astley back with a polite reply:

Mr. Riel—I am anxious to avoid killing women and children and have done my best to avoid doing so. Put your women and children in one place, and let us know where it is and no shot shall be fired on them. I trust to your honor not to put men with them.

But neither the general himself, nor the force he had left behind, had taken advantage of the morning's opportunity. At noon, as he lunched grumpily in the stockade, Middleton ordered the troops to take up their static positions of the day before: at the extreme left, toward the cemetery, the Midland Battalion of Port Hope, Ontario, commanded by Lieut. Col. A. T. H. Williams, with Capt. John French's company of scouts; left center, the Royal Grenadiers of Toronto, Lieut. Col. H. J. Grassett; right center, Ninetieth Battalion Rifles of Winnipeg, Lieut. Col. A. McKeand; extreme right, Boulton's and Dennis's scouts, and Howard with his Gatling.

This was an established skirmishing position, from which brief and ineffective sorties had been made by various units for three days. But at least one of Middleton's officers, Williams of the Midland Battalion, had had a bellyful. Williams was the son of a British naval officer and was himself a member of the Dominion Parliament. Soon he would be ordered to move up cautiously, feel out the Métis strength, and retire; but from man to man the word spread that when the order came, Colonel Williams and the Midland would keep on going. Quickly the whispers came back from the Grenadiers and the Ninetieth, promising their support.

For the first time since Saturday the skirmishers were able to reach the church, and General Middleton established headquarters there. Then the Midland got its orders: a "reconnaissance in force" on the left flank.

The Port Hope Battalion leaped up cheering and started on a run for the cemetery and the ravine, with Williams at their head. The command, "Charge!" rolled along the line of the Grenadiers and the Ninetieth and they too jumped up and ran, firing as they went.

General Middleton watched aghast as the troops poured over the crest of the hill. "Cease firing!" he roared. "Why in the name of God don't you cease firing?"

The bugle sounded the command to retire, again and again, but the troops ignored it. Within ten minutes the whole line was in motion. Middleton, realizing at last that his army was out of control, called up the rear echelons to support the charge. From the right flank the scouts and Howard raced to the crest of the ravine and the Gatling's deadly drumbeat was added to the rifles' clatter.

The Midland, Grenadiers and Ninetieth plunged headlong into the first row of Métis pits. Their defenders, unable to reload rapidly enough, were quickly overcome and the Canadians rushed on. Some of the Métis were bayoneted; one, dying, seized a pistol dropped by his attacker and emptied it before he was finished off. A young trooper stumbled over a body in a rifle pit and paused for an instant to stare: the enemy soldier was a dried-up old man, his hair pure white. (He was Joseph Ouellette, ninety-three years old. An-

other defender killed in the final charge, Joseph Vandal, was
seventy-five.)

The Métis held their pits to the last possible moment,
fired their short-range guns, then fled to the next line lower
on the hill, trying to reload as they ran. Many were barefoot;
during days of cramped discomfort in the trenches they had
formed the habit of kicking off their moccasins or boots.

As they ran, some of Batoche's defenders, bareheaded as
well as barefoot, felt raindrops in their faces and glanced up
incredulously. Powder smoke had been drifting into the
ravine and they had not noticed the darkening of the sky.
Now they peered through rifts in the smoke and saw that the
sun was gone. A heavy overcast had brought twilight to Batoche, though it was only three o'clock. This, then, was the
end, as Riel had foretold it; somehow they had offended, and
God had withdrawn his countenance from the Métis. Stumbling on down the hill, some of the warriors sobbed.

Creeping to the mouths of the straw-littered caves in the
riverbanks, the women also watched the darkness come; they
moaned distractedly or sang the Cree death chants they had
heard their mothers sing.

In the chapel of the parish house, led by Father Fourmond, the priests and nuns recited the rosary.

Foot by foot down the hillside the rebels were dislodged
and driven to their trenches in the meadow. Here they
checked the Canadians briefly, and all firing ceased again
when a messenger bearing a white flag rode from the village
and on up the trail to Middleton. It was Astley, with a new
letter from Riel.

"General," Louis wrote, "your prompt answer to my note
shows that I was right in mentioning to you the cause of
humanity. We will gather our families in one place. . . ."
But on the back of the note was a hasty, hysterical scribble:
"I do not like war, and if you do not retreat and refuse an

interview the question remaining the same the prisoners [sic]."

Middleton ignored this note and ordered Astley to remain with the troops. The charge was resumed. Now the Métis fled into the ruined houses and cabins and fired from the windows and the holes in their walls, then to the trees near the river. In this cover, their last stand on the east side of the stream, Gabriel Dumont and seven or eight others held off the foremost unit of the Canadians for about half an hour. Gabriel had cartridges for his Winchester; some of the others were using pebbles, nails, and even soft metal buttons which they shaped with their teeth.

In the Batoche house the Canadians found a pole wedged between ceiling and floor, knocked it out and freed a trap door through which they helped eleven prisoners. They were white-faced, haggard, nearly starved; some of them had not seen daylight in almost two months. They had been fairly well fed in the first weeks of their confinement but as food stocks in Batoche dwindled they had been put on bread and water, and for two days had not even had that.

Captain French, a former Mountie and one of the leaders of the charge, leaned from a window of the Batoche house to cheer his men on, and was promptly shot dead by a Métis sniper.

The militia fought its way from house to house. In the last one, young Private William Hughes of the Ninetieth, the first to enter, found no living foe; but he stumbled over an open casket in which lay a pretty Métis girl, killed by a stray bullet or shrapnel. He judged her to be about fourteen; the body was clothed in a stiff, embroidered burial dress, white and clean. He picked up the casket and moved it to a table beside a wall where it would not be upset by others who might follow him. While he was doing so, Colonel Williams, hero of the charge, borrowed his rifle to fire from the window at snipers.

Within an hour of the start of the attack the major resistance had been crushed, but intermittent firing continued from across the river until about seven o'clock.

Riel and Dumont had vanished. The Canadians moved their camp to Batoche. First the Métis women, then gradually the men, dragged into the village to give themselves up. Only a few ringleaders, Middleton assured them, would be held; but all arms must be surrendered. Some of the men protested. They had no crops; without guns they would starve. But they acknowledged that they should have thought of that before.

The victorious troops raided the cabins and caves for souvenirs that evening, and the nuns of St. Antoine, who had been imprisoned for weeks, took the exercise they had long needed. Chattering like birds, hardly able to believe that they were not, after all, destined to be martyrs, the sisters walked to the Canadians' abandoned zareba. They marveled over the earthworks, clucked about the mess in the compound. They discovered that the troops had left some heavy old kettles with hardly any holes in them, and some splendid empty barrels; these would be useful at the missions. There was also one hen, unconcerned with wars and the fate of peoples, pecking at grain spilled from the horses' feed bins.

The nuns were delighted. They would send faithful Baptiste with a wagon for the kettles and kegs; the hen they carried back themselves. So everyone, except the Métis, got souvenirs of the Battle of Batoche.

Sightseers from the *Northcote,* which was remaining to take away the wounded, had to listen to interminable boasting from their comrades of the land force, and had shamefully little with which to match it, but they, too, were drawn to the souvenir hunt and the guided tours of the battlefield.

One of these wanderers from the steamer strolled into the

grove in which the Métis had met daily to hear Riel. He found a souvenir there, but did not take it.

Nailed to a tree was a cardboard placard, draped in a scrap of white muslin. It was just a rough and ragged board ripped from some packing box, but affixed to it was a cheap, shiny lithograph—the Sacred Heart of Jesus. The chromo had been attached to the card with the pointed tin tags used to designate the brand name on plug tobacco. The afternoon's rain, sifting through the leaves of the poplars, had done some damage: the muslin was moist and the cardboard was becoming stained and limp.

The Canadian found himself strangely moved. He would tell the others about it: he had found a shrine, a cardboard shrine. He went away then, back to ruined Batoche, to the cardboard capital of the New Nation, whence two hundred men in mounted patrols had been sent out to find Riel and Dumont.

If he shared the opinions of most of his fellows, the shrine's discoverer probably reflected that one of those whom the troops sought so eagerly, one of the predestined scapegoats, was only a cardboard prophet. But the other, a fighting man, was solid oak.

It would not have mattered if the Canadian had removed the picture from the grove, for the shrine would never be used again. The beaten Métis, miserably repentant, now shuffled up the hill in long silent lines to seek comfort in the church.

Father Végreville welcomed his prodigal flock; the priests had long been agreed that it was all Riel's fault. He helped them bury their dead—in a mass grave except for "the old one," Joseph Ouellette, for whom Father Fourmond had somehow provided a coffin; they could not have the full rites of the Church, but there were suitable prayers.

Végreville was generous with the small quantity of food

he had been able to obtain from mission stores in the district, and he intervened vigorously with General Middleton to get Government relief.

But the priest was overzealous. He also agreed to act as the Government's commissioner, to receive the submission of the rebels and collect their guns. He got about a hundred weapons; nearly all the rest had previously been surrendered to the troops.

The Métis when necessary could worship at a cardboard shrine, confess each other, and offer their simple prayers directly to their God. Penitent they might be, but they were not yet wholly without spirit, and they did not fancy their priest in the role of agent for their conquerors. A few weeks later, his usefulness at an end, Father Végreville left the district.

Swiftly now the spiritual and temporal power of the Church crumbled. The Métis, destitute and disillusioned, neglected their religious duties, withdrew their children from the parochial school. The young people gave themselves up to dissipation and mocked the priests. Father Fourmond's once prosperous mission of St. Laurent failed and for a time was abandoned. Diocesan headquarters were moved to Prince Albert. The little church of St. Antoine at Batoche, however, survived, and still functions.

"For a while," Father Fourmond wrote, "we had hoped to regain the confidence of the Métis. . . . Like Our Lord, we can but repeat His words: 'How often have I wanted to gather thee, as the hen doth gather the chickens under her wings, and thou wouldst not.' "

Louis Riel, as a disciple of the Ultramontanes, once had shared their dream of re-establishing Catholic New France in the wilderness. As prophet, heretic and Fourmond's "Antichrist," he had destroyed the major stronghold of "the old Roman" in the Canadian West. But perhaps it could be said of the priests, as of Poundmaker's inordinately democratic Crees, that they helped to destroy themselves.

CHAPTER XXV

The Struggle and Flight

TO FULFILL GOD'S WILL

IT was a great grief for Madeleine Dumont that she had never given Gabriel a child. Now, as he ranged furiously through the brush and hunted out the fugitives' caves in the coulees, fruitlessly seeking Riel, she accompanied him with the food, clothing and blankets they had gathered for the Métis youngsters.

They were everywhere, hidden in the brush like rabbits: the big-eyed, dark, Indian-like babies who almost never cried, the self-reliant older boys and girls, reared to accept hardship without complaint, even without question. The Dumonts found Marguerite Riel and her two children in one of the caves. Louis was not there, and she did not know where he could be found; he had left her in the care of relatives and had gone off with some of his councilors. Gabriel and Madeleine left two blankets for her and went on.

They found some children barefoot; Gabriel paused to make moccasins for them from a cowhide. In a clearing where she had collapsed, exhausted, they came upon Madame Vandal, the aged widow of the slain Joseph. Fleeing Batoche,

485

she had been carrying her paralyzed daughter on her back. They ministered to her, gave her food and a fire, and Gabriel found her a horse.

Each night Gabriel would move his own camp, taking his wife farther and farther from Batoche, but each morning at dawn he was off again to look for Riel. The third night, May 15, he took Madeleine to his father's house, several miles from the village. She would be safe there because the elderly Isidore had not participated in the rebellion and was unknown to the Canadians.

Gabriel told the old man that he would never give up, that he would spend the summer in a guerrilla campaign against the despised conquerors—alone, if necessary.

"I am proud that you have not given in," his father said, "but if you stay to kill people you will be looked upon as a fool." He urged Gabriel to escape across the border into Montana.

His son thought it over, finally gave a conditional assent. He had always followed Isidore's advice; now, if he could not find Riel, he would leave.

Probably, his father said, Riel had already surrendered. Then he told Gabriel that Moiese Ouellette, a member of the *Exovidat* and a paroled prisoner of the Canadians, had been entrusted by Middleton with a message for Louis.

Gabriel found Moiese, his brother-in-law, and demanded that he be told the contents of the note and Riel's whereabouts. General Middleton had written: "I am ready to receive you and your council and protect you until your case has been decided upon by the Dominion Government." It meant, Ouellette said, that they would have justice. He urged Gabriel to give himself up.

"Go to the devil!" Dumont stormed. "The Government has sheared you like sheep! It has taken your arms from you and now you are doing just as you are told!"

Ouellette, whose father was "the old one" killed in the defense of Batoche, protested gently. Some of them, he reminded Gabriel, had to consider their children. (He had eleven.) Among those who felt that way, he added, was Louis Riel. The note already had been delivered and Louis had gone "immediately" to Middleton's camp. (This was not quite true; Riel had taken several hours to make up his mind, to write some last letters, and to arrange for the care of his family.)

Gabriel cursed his friend Moiese, the Canadians, and the priests. He had hoped there still might be time to catch his chief and dissuade him. Evidently, he concluded, "the good Lord did not wish me to see poor Riel again. I wanted to advise him not to surrender, but he might well have won me over to his way of thinking."

All was lost now; without Riel the demoralization of the Métis could not be arrested. For Gabriel nothing was left but flight. He knew that he alone did not have sufficient influence to spur the people to continued resistance; and anyway he could not conscientiously urge them to sacrifice their children.

He, however, had no children. His parting words to Ouellette were defiant. "Tell Middleton," he said, "that I am still in the woods. Tell him I still have ninety cartridges to use on his men!"

He sent his nephew Alex to his father's house to tell Madeleine he was leaving; he would send for her when he was safely settled in the United States. And he needed food for the journey. The boy returned with all the food there was—a half-dozen *galettes*. They weighed about three-quarters of a pound each, and might be all he would have to eat on a ride of hundreds of miles.

His horse was the fastest in the region because racing—and betting heavily on the result—was Gabriel's hobby. He sad-

dled up in a secluded spot in the woods while his brother
Jean and a few young men, told the news by Alex, gathered
furtively to say good-by. The date was May 16; Batoche had
fallen four days before.

Gabriel mounted, waved, and rode cautiously out of the
timber, alert for sign of the Canadian patrols. His name was
called and he stopped and jerked his rifle up; but the man
who had hailed him was Michel Dumas, who had ridden with
him to Montana just a year before when they had gone to
St. Peter's Mission to get Riel. Dumas asked if he could go
along; though he was unarmed and, like Gabriel, had only
a few cakes for provisions, Gabriel readily assented.

"We set out," Gabriel said, "by the grace of God." And
it was reasonable to feel that supernatural help might be
needed. The frontier was 275 miles away, but to elude the
hundreds of militiamen and police who guarded every
known trail they were destined to ride about six hundred.
They struck far to the west, seeking the dark shelter of the
Cypress Hills of Saskatchewan and the Sweet Grass Hills or
Trois Buttes on the Montana line; they rode mostly at night,
hiding during the day in the canyons or in Indian or Métis
camps. The trip took two weeks.

Word of Dumont's escape soon spread throughout the
Northwest. Said an old friend, John Andrew Kerr: "He
knows the prairies as a sheep knows its heath. They'll never
catch him." They never did.

While Gabriel and his companion rode south, Louis Riel
sat under guard in a tent beside that of General Middleton
in the Canadian camp.

On May 15 Louis had received the general's note and had
replied. "My council are dispersed," he wrote; "I wish you
would let them [go] quiet and free. . . . Would I go to
Batoche, who is going to receive me? I will go to fulfill God's

will." The note was signed "Louis 'David' Riel, *Exovede.*"

Unarmed, but accompanied by three Métis carrying shotguns, Louis left his hiding place and set off on foot for Batoche. As they neared the river they were discovered by three scouts, Tom Hourie, Bob Armstrong and William Deale. Hourie, a local man, instantly recognized Riel even though his face was haggard, his beard dirty and untrimmed, and his usually neat clothing stained and torn.

The Métis party offered no resistance when Hourie called upon them to surrender, and Riel handed the scout the note he had received from Middleton. "I want to give myself up," he said, "but I fear the troops may hurt me."

Hourie assured him that he would not be molested. While they talked they heard a large party of Boulton's scouts approaching and the three men who had "captured" Louis—his companions were not held—hid him in a coulee until the others had passed.

An effort was made to bring him into the camp secretly, but within a few moments everyone knew that the shabby, dejected "half-breed" who had been escorted into Middleton's tent was the fabulous Louis Riel. Curious militiamen swarmed around the headquarters area and were ordered to disperse.

When the group entered the tent Armstrong said, "General, this is Riel." Middleton, who had been seated at a desk, rose and spoke courteously to the whipped man who faced him. "How do you do, Mr. Riel?" he said, and gestured to a camp stool. "Pray be seated."

The tent was soon besieged by newspaper correspondents, but Middleton would not permit interviews with the prisoner unless Louis assented. The depth of his despondency could be gauged by the fact that, although he usually delighted in opportunities to talk for publication, Riel now flatly refused. Yet he answered Middleton's questions freely.

How could he have dreamed, the general asked, that a few

hundred ill-armed Métis could defeat Canada? And, even if they had, that they could beat Britain, which surely would have intervened?

Wearily, Louis explained again. There had been no hope of defeating Canada or Britain; they had planned only to make a stand, to show strength sufficient to convince the Dominion it must deal honorably with the neglected people of the Northwest—including the whites of Prince Albert who had encouraged the movement until the chips were down. And they would have liked to take a few Mounties or soldiers as prisoners, to serve as hostages.

Yes, he had spoken of Fenian or American intervention; but he had known it would not come. The *Exovidat* had drafted several resolutions on that. The first one, asking outright annexation by the United States, had been discussed a long time, written and rewritten, never finished; another, merely appealing for American friendship and aid, was to have been taken across the line by a mounted courier but never left Batoche.

The records of the *Exovidat,* Middleton told him, had been found in the council house and had been impounded. Louis was glad; the papers would prove that he had not fomented the rebellion, that leadership had been thrust upon him, that he had not wanted bloodshed. (But he had forgotten the damning note to Crozier, before Duck Lake, in his hand and bearing his signature, which had threatened "to commence without delay a war of extermination.")

Louis was nervous that first day. Mindful of the persecution he had suffered fifteen years before—the threats made to kill him, the warrant for his arrest, the ominous pursuit by armed men, his exile—he feared an outbreak of violence amongst the troops, directed at him. But the disciplined Canadians who gathered to stare when he was permitted to leave the tent, under heavy guard, showed respect rather than resentment. To his astonishment he was not even reviled as he passed among the men; and the general and his staff treated him as a gentleman, an equal, and, after a few days, almost as a friend. Louis, a beaten "half-breed" now, was pathetically grateful for this consideration.

In the evening of that first day, General Middleton ordered a tent set up beside his own. This was to be Riel's prison until word came from Ottawa as to what was to be done with him. Captain George H. Young of the general staff was ordered to remain with him day and night, and sentries constantly patrolled the tent, but Louis was not manacled or chained.

Captain Young, a Winnipeg man, had known Louis in 1870; he was the son of the Methodist preacher who had comforted Thomas Scott in his last hours in Fort Garry. The captain was intelligent and scrupulous. He and Riel talked continually, but with one or two exceptions, and then only under orders, Young did not attempt to extract information the prisoner did not want to give. When such questions arose, Young found Louis to be a master of evasion.

They spent eight days together. When they parted Louis had acquired considerable affection for his jailer, and Young at least acknowledged profound respect for him. The captain had learned in their discussions, he said, that "I had a mind against my own fully equal to it," and that Riel was "better educated and much more clever than I was." In one sense, Young's high opinion of Louis's intellect turned out to be unfortunate; it was impossible for him to conceive that this man who had bested him in argument might be mad, so his testimony helped to send Riel to the gallows.

Louis was taken by steamboat to Saskatoon, thence in a heavily guarded wagon caravan to Moose Jaw, and from there by special train to Regina, where the Government had ordered him incarcerated. The Territorial capital had no prison except the guardhouse of the Mounted Police headquarters, so he was put there to await trial.

He had become more cheerful in the camp, reassured by the humane attitude of General Middleton, Captain Young and the troops; but when he learned where he was to be imprisoned he gave way again to despair. There was a strong element of Orangeism among the enlisted men of the Mounties, and the Catholic Métis hated and feared the force—unlike the pagan Indians, who admired it. Métis antagonism had increased since they had come to believe that they had been driven to take up arms because additional Mounties were coming to suppress their constitutional agitation for their rights. Moreover, Louis felt, justifiably, that his crime was important enough to merit trial before a Dominion court in the Province of Manitoba, and not one before the makeshift court of the Territory, presided over by a stipendiary magistrate.

Though he was later to have brief periods of renewed hope, actually when the door of his cell in Regina closed upon him on May 23 Louis Riel knew that he had been delivered into the hands of his enemies and that he was doomed.

"SUCH A PERSON AS I AM"

Unaware of the Batoche disaster which they could have averted or at least forestalled, Poundmaker's slow-moving Crees on May 14 made the biggest haul of the campaign when they captured a train of nearly thirty wagons filled with supplies for the troops and police, and took twenty-two of the freighters prisoner. A few teamsters escaped; some of those who did not apparently were not too dismayed, since they joined in the Indians' celebration and one of them played his fiddle for the party. The same day, in a brief skirmish with some scouts, the Crees killed one and wounded another.

A day or two thereafter Poundmaker learned of the Métis defeat. He immediately dictated a note to one of his white prisoners and had it rushed to Middleton. He asked for confirmation of the report of Riel's surrender, and requested the general to "send us the terms of peace in writing." Middleton retorted promptly that Batoche had fallen, that Riel and most of his councilors were prisoners, and that "I have made no terms with them, neither will I make terms with you." The Canadians would destroy or starve out the Crees unless Poundmaker surrendered unconditionally.

On May 26 Poundmaker and his band, the tall, handsome chief riding stiffly before them, trooped into Battleford to face the humiliation which for some was worse than death. They surrendered their arms; then Middleton arranged a council on the prairie before the fort. Seated in a camp chair, he confronted Poundmaker, who squatted on the ground before him, flanked by his major chiefs. A few paces back the Crees formed a wide semicircle. Imperturbable, they smoked and gazed blankly at their conquerors.

"Is it usual," the general demanded sternly, "for Indians to go about pilfering like rats?"

Poundmaker's lean face, schooled to impassivity, turned to the interpreter. "Tell him," he said in Cree, "I felt I had a rope about my neck, and something drawing me all the time."

Middleton asked who had raided the settlers' homes. Poundmaker replied that he had never advised looting by his young men.

The Englishman put contempt in his voice. "Has a great chief no power?"

"I am not sure that I am a chief," Poundmaker retorted calmly. He went on to explain that when, as chief, he had appealed to the Government for relief for his starving people he had been ignored. It would seem, he said, that he was not recognized as a chief.

Middleton brushed this aside. Why had Poundmaker fought Colonel Otter at Cut Knife?

"When I was sleeping quietly," the chief said, "they came and fired a cannon on me, into my camp. I jumped up and had to defend myself. It frightened me and my children."

The Crees fired first, the general insisted. (Not true, according to eyewitness accounts by veterans of the battle.)

Poundmaker's reply was bland. "I don't know anything at all about it. I only returned the fire when the camp was fired on by the cannon."

Middleton's words now became deliberately insulting. "Poundmaker fired first, because he had a bad conscience. He knew he had done wrong. . . . The only reason he gives for not going to help Riel fight the Queen is that he was afraid, because Riel had not much powder. He told Riel he would join him; then, like a squaw, he was afraid!"

The chief glanced coolly at the general, at the circle of Canadian officers surrounding him, and puffed slowly on his long pipe. "I am sorry," he said. He paused to puff on his pipe again, to let the smoke curl slowly from his mouth and watch it drift away. "I am sorry. I feel in my heart that I am such a person as I am."

Middleton, with effort, controlled his impatience. Poundmaker had been recalcitrant for a long time, he said. He had held out against the treaty terms offered him. . . .

"If I had known then that I was such a great man," his antagonist said gently, "I would have made them recognize me as such."

But why, if his intentions were good, had he not surrendered before Riel's defeat? He had been on the warpath for months!

Poundmaker turned to the interpreter, evidencing boredom. "I've told him I did not intend to do any harm," he said. "Why does he mention this over and over?"

How about the murders of Payne and Fremont? Did Poundmaker know Lean Man, one of the suspected killers?

Yes, he knew him. But he was an Assiniboine, not a Cree. "Did you know that he and his men killed Payne?"

Poundmaker gazed innocently at the general. "Shall I ask him?" he inquired. Then he turned to an Indian beside him, who also was placidly puffing on a pipe, and addressed a few words to him. The smoker, Lean Man, puffed and pondered. He took his pipe out of his mouth and thought some more. No, he told Poundmaker, he didn't know a thing about it.

Poundmaker turned back to the general and shrugged his shoulders.

An elderly Indian came forward, attempted to shake Middleton's hand, and to launch into a speech. Another, a tribal orator, seized the floor. Poundmaker, used to this sort of thing in the councils of head men, listened calmly. There was no hurry, anyway.

"There is a God who made us all," the orator said earnestly to the Canadians. "We borrow this earth from God. When white man and Indian first met we shook hands; no blood on them until now. I suppose the reason we were put here was to help each other. . . ."

They had been told that Riel would bring order and justice to the Northwest, he continued. They had been told that the troops had come "to settle everything." And then, at Cut Knife, they had been fired upon without warning!

Another Cree, Breaking-the-Ice, said he would now like his mother to have an opportunity to speak. He pointed to an aged squaw wearing a blue scarf on her head.

Middleton finally got a word in. "We don't listen to women," he said, with contempt.

Then how was it, one of the Indian speakers quickly rejoined, that orders for the government of the country came from a queen?

For a moment the general was stumped, and his answer, when it did come, was weak. "She has councilors who are men," he said.

Other Indians came forward to harangue the assembly, and Middleton realized that the Indians were getting the upper hand. He announced that the council was at an end. Poundmaker and four of his head men would be held; the others were free to go.

Suddenly two Assiniboines, Itka and Wa-Wanich, pushed their way into the center of the council and calmly confessed their guilt of the slayings of Payne and Fremont. Itka said he had fired in self-defense. "If you want to cut me up in pieces do so, but I beg you to consider my children." Wa-Wanich was a moronic young exhibitionist, extravagantly decked with beads and other Indian finery. His crime, he acknowledged, had been cold-blooded murder, but "I told my people I would give myself up to save them."

Middleton ordered them put under guard, then rose to leave the field. An Assiniboine squaw, true to her sex, managed to get the last word. She waddled out of the crowd and shouted at the general's back. "The Almighty sees!" she cried. "Our children and our country have been taken!"

Big Bear was now the only hostile left in the field. The day before the surrender of Poundmaker, whom Big Bear's band had hoped to join, the latter group raised a Hudson's Bay flag they had taken from Fort Pitt, and discovered to the general dismay that they had hung it upside down. That, it was decided, was a bad omen. Three days later General Strange made his abortive attack on the camp, and, even though he retreated, the Crees fled. They headed into an unmapped wilderness of lake and brush and muskeg to the north, reluctantly dragging along their white prisoners, whose appetites had become a serious expense but whom they did not dare to kill. Now, for the first time, the whites found the going rough. They had little to eat (as did the Indians) and they spent hours wading knee-deep in marshes or streams and scrambling through dense thickets which tore their flesh and ruined their clothing.

Middleton finally decided—much too late—to effect the junction of his own forces and those of Strange, the plan urged upon him weeks earlier by the latter. On June 3 the commanding general, with a detachment from the proven Ninetieth, Midland and Grenadiers and several companies of scouts, met the Alberta column under Strange at Fort Pitt.

A few days after the Frenchman's Butte fiasco, Big Bear and his Crees were overtaken again, this time at Loon Lake. The white force numbered seventy, mostly Mounties, and was commanded by Maj. S. B. Steele of the police, who had been sent by Strange to find the Indians. Three of Steele's scouts were wounded and half a dozen Crees killed in the skirmish which followed, but the Indians escaped by traversing a ford and entering a coulee which the outnumbered whites did not dare approach.

Middleton now rushed his militia companies to the scene but the Crees again escaped, this time by fleeing across two miles of muskeg in which the heavy transport of the troops would have sunk without trace. The Crees were beaten now; they had had to abandon most of their horses and equipment in their flight. But the Canadians could not follow, and on June 9, disgusted, Middleton gave up and withdrew his men. The Indians, he announced, would be starved out. Strange had been sent to the west to head off Big Bear's retreat in that direction, but he could not find the hostiles either, and a couple of weeks later he also withdrew to his base.

Meanwhile, through intrigue with the Woods Crees, Big Bear's white prisoners escaped. After sixty-two days of captivity, they were given a little food, some new moccasins, and on their pledge to help the Woods Crees negotiate a separate peace, sent on their way to Fort Pitt—140 miles distant. They met some troops at Loon Lake and arrived at Fort Pitt June 24.

Big Bear's undisciplined company soon fell apart. Wandering Spirit, the war chief who had led the massacre at Frog Lake, fled or was banished from his own band and joined the Woods Crees. When they came in to surrender at Fort Pitt, Wandering Spirit was with them. After he had erected his lodge on the field before the fort that night and had eaten his evening meal, the war chief thrust back the tipi flap and strode to the center of the camp. He raised his voice in a song to command attention, then he cried out: "All who wish to look on me once more, come now!"

L'Esprit Errant returned to his tipi and sat staring into his fire. Curious neighbors passed in front of the lodge and peeked inside, but none entered. He was not one of their chiefs; and the Woods Crees, less bloodthirsty than their cousins of the plains, had never approved of him anyway.

After half an hour of this, the war chief leaped suddenly to his feet, drew his knife, and thrust it deeply into his side. The blow missed his heart but injured a lung and he fell, bleeding profusely. The other Indians set up an outcry and he was removed to the fort, where his wound was dressed. This saved him to be hanged.

Gradually the other hostile leaders, about a dozen men, drifted in to Fort Pitt to surrender, until all except Big Bear himself were in custody. Three large detachments hunted him throughout the region, and continually came upon his abandoned camps—always a few hours too late.

On July 2 the old chief gave up, but not without a final gesture. With only his youngest son, eight years old, and one councilor for company, he had traveled hundreds of miles under the noses of the police and troops. Now he chose to come not to Fort Pitt or Battleford, but to Carlton, where he surrendered to an astonished Mountie sergeant who was one of the few uniformed men in the Northwest who had not been hunting for him.

Louis Riel was in jail in Regina, Dumont was in Montana; most of the Northwest Field Force was on its way home. With the surrender of Big Bear, a hungry, dirty old Indian in a torn blanket, the Northwest Rebellion was over. The last organized attempt by the primitive races to preserve their strange empire against the encroachment of white civilization had failed.

The defeat doomed some to the gallows and others to prison, which they dreaded more; but the grandeur of their faith and the depth of their anguish lived on in the official record, in the words they spoke when all was lost to them.

"We borrow this earth from God," said the Cree orator whose name is unknown to history. "We were put here . . . to help each other." "Our children and our country have been taken!" cried the old squaw. And Poundmaker, accused of cowardice, answered, "I feel in my heart that I am such a person as I am." The dignity which shaped these words of the great Cree chief sustained him throughout his trial until the judge pronounced sentence: three years in Manitoba penitentiary. Then, for an instant, the heart faltered, the fine head drooped, and a cry of despair was wrung from him. Only a few in the front of the courtroom heard his choked protest: "I would rather prefer to be hung at once than to be in that place!"

FIVE GALLONS OF RYE

Today there is a tendency to gauge the historical significance of events by the number of people involved in them. If the event was a meeting of malcontents, how many attended? If it was a battle, how many died?

But, as a modern writer has pointed out, "the measure of history cannot be taken in square rods or firepower or simple numbers." Sometimes a dozen people can change the course of history; sometimes one. Joan of Lorraine died alone.

By modern standards, casualties in the Northwest Rebellion were so light as to be hardly worth mentioning. In all, some seventy whites were killed and about a hundred and thirty wounded. Middleton's militiamen lost forty killed and one hundred and fifteen wounded; ten per cent of the casualties were officers. At Batoche only eight died and forty-six were wounded. The general thus could, and did, say that his caution had paid off. Of the fifty-four Batoche casualties, thirty-four occurred in the final charge.

A few more members of the Field Force and a few civilians succumbed later to the exertions and hardships of the campaign. One of these was Colonel Williams, who had led the last day's attack at Batoche; he died in Battleford July 4 of fever.

Métis and Indian losses have never been accurately computed. Dumont and the priest who buried the victims testified that only twelve were killed at Batoche, and Gabriel said only three were wounded. But other Métis put the number of wounded at sixteen, and acknowledged that probably a few more were killed; the bodies, especially those of Indians, probably were removed and buried without the knowledge of the priest. The known rebel loss in all engagements totaled only thirty-five dead and eleven wounded, including Indians.

To understand why the loss of so few fighters could have had such calamitous consequences for the rebels, it is necessary to know Indian tradition which, in a crisis, was Métis tradition, too. The sporadic tribal "warfare" of the plains was not war in a modern sense at all, but instead was simple outlawry: sudden raids, a few minutes of disorganized brawling, and headlong retreat. It was every man for himself and few died. Significantly, it was not necessary to kill to "count coup"; it was even more glorious to ride into danger, humble the enemy by striking him down and taking his horse or an article of his apparel, and escape unscratched, than it was to bring back a scalp.

With rare exceptions, contests in the primitive era on the prairie were not between tribes but between bands; seldom were more than a few score men engaged. Indian support of the Métis cause in 1885 was pitifully inadequate, but it was nevertheless a triumph of organization—for Indians. Never before had two Cree chiefs as powerful as Big Bear and Poundmaker made common cause with anyone. Yet there were many other Cree chiefs, almost as strong, who were not interested, who would have been at a loss to understand why, merely because others with Cree blood were fighting for their lives, they should fight, too.

In short, though the concept of honor was vivid in the Indian mind (which meant the honor of manhood, to be preserved so that one's name would live within the band forever; and respect for one's spirit guide, or totem) that of "patriotism" was virtually incomprehensible.

The Métis experience of "war" was similar—a few skirmishes with hostile Blackfeet over horses or hunting rights on disputed buffalo range. Their more intimate contact with the whites had taught them to be race conscious, and they had inherited or borrowed some slight sense of organization, but they had not yet had the time or leadership to develop these concomitants of statehood.

Louis Riel had been the Métis's only prophet of nationalism and Dumont their only military strategist. These two attempted to convert independent tribal communities into an integrated state overnight, skipping all the intervening forms from which disciplined modern society has evolved.

Most of those who fought so shrewdly, so bravely but so hopelessly at Batoche did so simply because they were in thrall to two great leaders. Elsewhere, thousands of Métis and Indians, even more unaware of the basic issues than those on the scene, watched to see what the result would be, quite unperturbed by the fact that unless they pitched in to help, only a miracle could save the rebels. If the rebels were destined to be saved, as these others saw it, a miracle would be forthcoming.

Riel's surrender and Dumont's flight proved that it had all been a mistake. No idea, no matter how noble, was any good unless it worked. As the Red River Métis had subsided into apathy and squalor after their political setbacks in Manitoba, the Northwestern Métis now succumbed almost without a whimper to the undesirable, but obviously invincible, new order.

Canada found, nevertheless, that it had been a costly job to convince the natives that their New Nation was a mirage. The Dominion's direct expenditures for suppressing the uprising, trying the ringleaders and satisfying claims for war damage came to about five million dollars, half of it expended on military operations.

This was money the young Confederation could ill afford, and though Canada had been thoroughly scared and was grateful for victory, the accounts were ruefully scrutinized. They provided interesting and sometimes amusing sidelights on frontier warfare.

The ill-fated venture with the *Northcote* at Batoche brought a claim for $950 damages to the boat; its owners also collected $14,500 for its rental for fifty-eight days. Traders profited enormously; one of them, I. G. Baker & Company, which collected about $18,000 for freighting and supplies, was a Montana outfit. Two new Gatlings cost $2,500 but Howard received only about $400 for his services. Meals purchased for the soldiers while en route cost only about thirty-five cents each, but one hundred and eighty pounds of Myrtle navy tobacco purchased at Prince Albert for the Ninetieth Battalion cost a dollar a pound. Beef, seven cents a pound back East, was seventeen cents in the West, and bread, three cents a pound in Ontario, was double that (or unobtainable) in the Territories.

Not all of those who provided service for the troops were as handsomely paid as the teamsters. A Mrs. Marshall washed eight hundred and ninety blankets for twenty-three dollars, and a Mrs. Watson cleaned a hall, provided half a ton of coal, and bought one two-dollar Bible for the Winnipeg Light Infantry, and submitted a bill for twenty-five dollars.

Lieutenant Colonel Whitehead was reimbursed for the expense he incurred entertaining General Middleton at Selkirk, near Winnipeg. He had rented a "yacht" to take the general off the steamboat and hurry him to town for the official reception, at a cost of six dollars and seventy-five cents. Five gallons of seven-year-old rye came to fifteen dollars, and thirteen dollars bought a hundred cigars. The hors d'oeuvres —ox tongue, turkey, and shrimps—set the Dominion treasury back twenty-seven dollars and seventy cents.

On the other hand, hardtack cost only five cents a pound. In the opinion of members of the Northwest Field Force, happily home and determined to a man never to eat the stuff again, that was a lot more than it was worth.

PART EIGHT

High Treason

CHAPTER XXVI

Instigation of the Devil

THE MOST SERIOUS TRIAL

On July 6, 1885, an information charging high treason was laid against Louis Riel. A complainant was required; to fulfill this formality the indictment was signed by Alexander David Stewart, chief of police in Hamilton, Ontario, and reputedly a member of the Orange Order.

Trial, before Hugh Richardson, stipendiary magistrate of the Northwest Territories, was set for July 20 in Regina. High treason is modern society's greatest crime; under British law the only penalty upon conviction is death. Riel was the only rebellion culprit to face this charge; about seventy were indicted, but most of those who finally were tried were accused of the milder crime of treason-felony, not a capital offense.

A stipendiary magistrate was a barrister of at least five years' experience who served as a part-time judge in the Territories, was paid a stipend for the time he so worked, was appointed by the reigning political powers in Ottawa and continued in office at their pleasure. He was, consequently,

507

a servant of the party in power; moreover, Richardson was the legal adviser to the Territorial Governor.

Treason, as distinct from any other crime, is an offense against the current political regime of the state and the regime therefore becomes an intensely interested party to the proceeding—not as agent for the social community, as in an offense against the moral order such as murder, but in its own right. Acquittal of a treason defendant is an implicit repudiation of the policies of the ruling regime.

There can be little question that the circumstances of Louis Riel's trial were immoral. Whether the trial itself was also illegal has been debated ever since it was held.

Imperial statutes originally required that trials for capital crimes committed in the Territories could only occur in Upper Canada (Ontario) before full provincial courts. But in 1877 the Dominion Parliament, by legislation subsequently affirmed in London, established the stipendiary magistrate system to ease the burden of the provincial judges. This act, which gave the stipendiary magistrates almost unlimited powers, nullified the earlier imperial statute without actually repealing it.

The stipendiary magistrate was permitted to work with a jury of six. This was a reasonable provision in most cases because of the sparse settlement of the Territories; but it was the contention of Riel's counsel that the right of jury trial as won by the Magna Charta and later defined in imperial statutes for capital crimes, meant trial before a full jury of twelve.

The fate of Louis Riel, nevertheless, was given to six men. All were Protestants of Anglo-Saxon stock; the defendant was Catholic and French. Moreover the jurors were unfamiliar with the French language, which Riel and some of the witnesses habitually spoke, and thus were dependent upon translators for much important testimony. Riel himself, in his two speeches, used English, but the necessity for doing so put him at some disadvantage.

Mr. Justice Richardson was no stranger to the problems of the region, and he was fully aware of the historical significance of his present assignment. He was born in England, had been admitted to the bar in Ontario and practiced there until he became counsel for the Territorial Governor in 1876. The defense overlooked, or chose to ignore, a letter he had written in 1880 to the Ministry of the Interior. It urged prompt dealing with Métis grievances because the half-breed colonies had been "latterly subjected to the evil influences of leading spirits of the Manitoba troubles." These "influences" had been circulating in the Saskatchewan "doing at least 'no good.'" This characterization of Métis leadership as evil and up to no good should have cast some doubt upon his fitness to judge the man whom the Métis regarded as the greatest leader of them all.

Yet Richardson's conduct of the trial, at least up to the time he gave his charge to the jury, was above reproach. His charge, while perhaps legally sound (no exception was taken to it on appeal), was definitely prejudicial, and the wording of the sentence would seem to have been unnecessarily cruel.

The information contained six counts listing three overt acts—levying war against the Crown at Duck Lake, Fish Creek, and Batoche. These acts were identically described in the first three counts and the last three, but there was one important difference in preliminary phraseology. In counts one, two, and three, Riel was described as "a subject of our Lady the Queen." In four, five, and six he was said to be merely "living within the Dominion of Canada and under the protection" of the Queen.

Riel, having acquired United States citizenship, was not a subject of the Queen and could not be guilty of violating his "natural allegiance," were it not for the fact that the principle of dual or multiple nationality has long been recognized in international law. Disavowal of allegiance to one's natural sovereign does not automatically make one an alien in the country ruled by that sovereign, and it has always been the law of England that a natural-born subject owes allegiance to the Crown which is intrinsic and perpetual and cannot be lost by any act of his own. (Ironically, as pointed out earlier in this book, this legal principle corresponded to the instinctive sense of dual nationality which the border Métis had always possessed.)

The last three counts charged Riel with violating what has become known as "local allegiance," and of this he could unquestionably have been guilty. It had been established as early as 1600 that an alien living in England and enjoying the protection of the Crown could be convicted of treason for acts committed in the country. Such offenses could range all the way from "imagining the death of the King" to counterfeiting or having carnal knowledge of the Crown Prince's wife.

This principle of "local allegiance" is also recognized in the United States, though under the American act treason can be committed only by levying war and it is not necessarily a capital offense. The congressional statute limits offenders to those "owing allegiance to the United States of America," but this has been interpreted to include aliens living in the country and enjoying the protection of the Federal Government. Thus in both British and United States law, allegiance may be owed by anyone who has been permitted to enter the country on the assumption that he will not jeopardize its security.

The statute under which Riel was tried was Britain's four-hundred-year-old Treason Act, adopted during the reign of Edward III. "When a man do levy war against our Lord the King in his realm," the act said . . .

. . . or be adherent to the King's enemies in his realm, giving to
them aid and comfort in the realm or elsewhere, and thereof be
proveably attainted of open deed by the people of their condition
. . . this shall be one ground upon which the party accused of
the offence and legally proved to have committed the offence,
shall be held to be guilty of the crime of high treason.

The language of the information was traditional and awe-
some. When the court assembled at eleven o'clock on the
morning of July 20, the first business was the reading of the
indictment. Riel, seated beside his counsel, leaned forward
and listened intently as the clerk droned through the long
text: ". . . not regarding the duty of his allegiance, nor having the fear of God in his heart, but being moved and se-
duced by the instigation of the devil as a false traitor against
our said Lady the Queen . . ."

The first two days were taken up with arguments on defense motions. Riel's counsel challenged the jurisdiction of
the court and complained that the information was "double"
because it charged him with the same overt acts both as a
citizen and as an alien. The judge held these objections to be
insufficient and ordered the trial to proceed. Riel, called
upon to plead, said, "I have the honor to answer the court
I am not guilty."

The defense asked for a month's delay to permit it to bring
witnesses which it held vital to Riel's cause—the doctors who
had treated him in two asylums, and three fugitive Métis
leaders, Gabriel Dumont, Michel Dumas and Napoleon
Nault, all of whom were in the United States.

The Métis were willing to appear if they could be guaranteed immunity from prosecution while they served as witnesses and be given safe conduct back to the boundary; but
Crown counsel said no such guarantees could be given to
fugitives who were themselves liable to prosecution for treason. Dumont and Dumas wrote, from Helena, through an
attorney, that they were "very anxious" to help Riel; Gabriel

said he would testify that he alone was responsible for the
rebels' military operations, that the *Exovidat,* not Riel, had
voted to launch rebellion, and that Louis came to the Saskatchewan with peaceful intent. Nault, writing from St. Joe,
offered similar testimony. But without the promise of immunity the three men did not dare to cross the boundary.

One week's delay, sufficient to bring the doctors from the
East, was finally granted.

The trial of Louis Riel opened the morning of July 28
with the selection of six jurors, after five prospective tales-
men had been challenged by the defense and one (the only
Catholic on the panel) by the prosecution. The men finally
chosen were Francis Cosgrave, who was foreman; Harry J.
Painter, Edwin J. Brooks, Walter Merryfield, Edward Erratt
and Peele Dean. Brooks and Painter were merchants; all the
others were farmers.

An organization for Riel's defense which had sprung up
in Quebec provided him with distinguished counsel, headed
by François-Xavier Lemieux, a member of the provincial
legislature and, though only thirty-four, already renowned as
a criminal lawyer. He was assisted by Charles Fitzpatrick,
James N. Greenshields and T. C. Johnstone. The chief prosecution counsel was Christopher Robinson, a brother of the
Lieutenant Governor of Ontario and son of that province's
chief justice; associated with him were David L. Scott and
B. B. Osler, both of Ontario, G. W. Burbidge and T. C. Casgrain. Burbidge, a Nova Scotian, was Deputy Minister of Justice for the Dominion.

Osler opened for the Crown: though there were only six
of them instead of the usual twelve, he said, the jurors he
now addressed were serving in "the most serious trial that
has ever probably taken place in Canada."

The prosecutor outlined the Crown's evidence, making
much of the bombastic note to Crozier, of Riel's offer to
return to Montana if he were indemnified by Ottawa, of his

break with the priests. "The prophet of the Saskatchewan was the cry under which his poor dupes were supposed to rally. . . . I think you will be satisfied before this case is over that it is not a matter brought about by any wrongs so much as a matter brought about by the personal ambition and vanity of the man on trial."

Louis Riel listened eagerly, scribbling notes occasionally on a pad. He sat in a railed dock, with two Mounties on each side. He was again dressed as he liked to be: in black frock coat, with clean white shirt and a black cravat. The barristers and justices were gowned and wore pleated-bosom shirts and white ties. Lieutenant Governor Dewdney of the Northwest Territories had a seat of honor near the bench. Dewdney, militia officers and Mounties were in uniform.

The courtroom was only fifty feet long and twenty feet wide. It was in rented quarters—one of two ground-floor rooms in a two-story brick building owned by a land company and built only two years before. The Territorial Government also rented space in the building for judges' chambers, the clerk of the court and sheriff; Regina as yet had no courthouse. The town itself was only three years old and had but recently been rechristened: originally it was called "Pile o' Bones" because it was a shipping point for buffalo bones.

The Northwest Rebellion and the Riel trial had boomed Regina. The little courtroom was packed. A dozen newspapermen sat at a special press table; among them was Nicholas Flood Davin, editor of the Regina *Leader,* which was publishing daily editions for the first time for the duration of the trial. A section of the spectators' space had been set aside for "the ladies," and they were present in force and dressed to the teeth. Mrs. Middleton, Mrs. Richardson and Miss Osler were among them.

Everyone watched Riel, protagonist in "the most serious

trial that has ever probably taken place in Canada." He was, at last, the historic figure he had always meant to be.

TOO MUCH TO SAY

The first public clue to the plans of the defense came in Fitzpatrick's cross-examination of the first witness, Dr. John Willoughby. He was a Saskatoon physician who had talked to Riel near Batoche at the start of the outbreak. As defense counsel quizzed him closely about what Riel had said, it became apparent that an effort was being made to lay the groundwork for a plea of insanity.

Willoughby said Riel had revealed to him his dream of dividing Canada's Northwest Territories among seven peoples, inviting settlers of each nationality to take up a separate portion of the country. The doctor was led skillfully through a description of this scheme during which Fitzpatrick made it sound more and more fantastic, and then the attorney made his point:

"It appeared to you a very rational proposition?"

"No," the doctor replied, "it did not."

Thomas McKay, Crozier's envoy, was next on the stand and again the cross-examination was designed to show that Riel was irrational when the rebellion began. Greenshields tried to obtain from McKay confirmation of a story that Riel had insisted upon eating cooked blood with his meals, a practice supposed to have been suggested to him in one of his visions. But McKay had not seen this and could not testify to it. He did, however, say that Riel had been subject, when he was present, to sudden inexplicable changes of mood, from fierce excitement to calm courtesy.

From Astley, the surveyor and prisoner at Batoche whom Riel had sent to Middleton with messages, the prosecution elicited damaging testimony. He had seen Riel exercising command over armed Métis, and Louis had told him that he ordered them to fire at Duck Lake. After Fish Creek, Astley said, Riel claimed two victories but said, "We must have another battle." Johnstone, cross-examining, had bad luck with him. When asked if he had not thought Riel's actions eccentric, Astley replied, "He seemed intelligent and in many respects a clever man."

Others among former prisoners of the Métis made it clear that Riel had been the acknowledged brain and soul of the movement. Some of their testimony probably would have been excluded in a stricter court because it was hearsay, and Greenshields finally protested the admission of so much rumor and gossip. Nevertheless the defense was pleased with the first day's work. George Ness, the day's final witness, revealed in Fitzpatrick's cross-examination that Riel had told him the Pope was not legally head of the Church, that "Rome had fallen," that the spirit of God was in himself, and that he could foretell the future.

When court opened for the second day Fitzpatrick sprang another surprise. George Kerr, the storekeeper, had been questioned by the prosecution about the meetings which led up to the rebellion. He had attended the community dinner in January when a purse was presented to Riel, and had contributed a dollar himself. Asked by Fitzpatrick if any speeches were made, Kerr replied, "Yes, Riel proposed the health of our Sovereign Queen Victoria."

But this could not overcome the weight of testimony that Riel had led armed rebellion. Late in the day Thomas E. Jackson, the druggist whose brother had been Riel's aide, proved a damaging witness because of his frankness. Asked by the Crown if he had known of the movement before it became violent, he said, "Oh, yes, and I sympathized with it." But he went on to assert that Riel, and only Riel, had given the orders at Duck Lake. Fitzpatrick got him to say that Louis had urged "purely a constitutional movement," but the attorney's cautious approach to a suggestion that Jackson might have regarded him as mad turned out so badly that the subject was promptly dropped.

General Middleton said most of Riel's conversation with him had seemed sensible; the Métis leader did talk about religion, but to the prosaic old soldier he had appeared to be no more than an "enthusiast." Captain Young, who followed on the stand, also hurt Riel's cause. The defendant had freely admitted his leadership to Young, and perhaps had even claimed some of the credit which should have gone to Dumont for military strategy.

Riel became increasingly nervous as he sensed the direction of his counsel's questions, designed to make him out an irresponsible lunatic, a tool of other persons or of his own delusions. And when Charles Nolin took the stand late in the second day, he finally lost his equanimity. His dramatic attempt to take over the conduct of his own case alienated him from his counsel, almost broke up the trial, and probably helped to cost him his life.

Nolin testified exhaustively to the origins of the movement, admitting that he had participated in its early stages and had approved the invitation to his cousin Louis to come to the Saskatchewan. But, he said, he had withdrawn about twenty days before the Métis took up arms. He was asked by the defense if he had not done in Manitoba in 1869 just what he did in 1885—start with his people and then abandon them; and Nolin admitted that was true, and that in 1875 he had been appointed Minister of Agriculture for the Province of Manitoba, which owed its existence to the man he had abandoned.

The defense scored again when Nolin testified that Riel thought he could prophesy on the strength of reactions in his physical organs, that he had "inspirations that worked through every part of his body," and that he had planned to divide the country up among Prussians, Hungarians, Irish and others. Whenever the word "police" was spoken in Riel's hearing, Nolin said, Louis became "very excited."

At this point Riel suddenly stood up and interrupted the trial. Addressing the bench in a choked voice, he said: "Your Honor, would you permit me a little while—"

Justice Richardson checked him quickly. "In the proper time. I will tell you when you may speak to me, and give you every opportunity. Not just now, though."

"If there was any way," Riel pleaded, "by legal procedure, that I should be allowed to say a word, I wish you would allow me before this witness leaves the box."

"I think you should suggest any question you have to your own counsel," the judge said.

But Riel persisted. "Do you allow me to speak? I have some observation to make before the court."

Worriedly, his counsel intervened. "I don't think this is the proper time," Fitzpatrick objected, and Justice Richardson agreed. "I should ask him," the judge said, "at the close of the case, before it goes to the jury." He again admonished Riel to put his questions through his counsel.

Fitzpatrick now rose to an embarrassing duty. "I think the time has now arrived," he said, "when it is necessary to state to the court that we require that the prisoner should thoroughly understand that anything that is done in this case must be done through us. . . . He must not be allowed to interfere. He is now endeavoring to withhold instructions."

The statute, Richardson pointed out, provided that the prisoner could defend himself personally or by counsel; Fitzpatrick retorted that once counsel had been accepted the prisoner had no right to interfere.

Riel spoke again, jerkily, tense with emotion. "Your Honor, this case comes to be extraordinary, and while the Crown, with the great talents they have at its service [sic] are trying to show I am guilty—of course it is their duty—my counsellors are trying—my good friends and lawyers who

have been sent here by friends whom I respect—are trying to
show that I am insane . . ."

"Now you must stop!" the judge broke in.

"I will stop and obey your court." Riel sat down and bent
his head over his papers.

Richardson again asked him to put his questions through
his counsel, but Louis, obviously feeling it would be useless
because the attorneys were determined to base the case
wholly upon insanity, made no move to do so. Osler spoke
for the Crown: the prosecution would not object to the prisoner putting questions to the witness if his own counsel
would permit it. But Fitzpatrick was adamant, and when he
spoke again his voice was tight with anger and strain:

"For the last two days we have felt ourselves in this position: that this man is actually obstructing the proper man-
agement of this case, for the express purpose of having a
chance to interfere . . . and he must be given to understand
immediately that he won't be allowed to interfere in it or it
will be absolutely useless for us to endeavor to continue."

"Is that a matter I ought to interfere in?" asked the per-
plexed judge. "Isn't that a matter entirely between yourself
and your client?"

Fitzpatrick's temper was now badly frayed. "I don't pre-
tend to argue with the court. It is not my practice, not my
custom . . ."

The judge interrupted soothingly. He knew, he said, that
the prisoner should be required to give all instructions to his
counsel; and he had now been told to do so. "But suppose he
does not, and suppose counsel think fit to throw up the
brief?" he asked.

"We are entirely free to do that," Fitzpatrick said grimly,
"and that is a matter for our consideration at the present
moment if the prisoner is allowed to interfere."

Justice Richardson then got to the heart of the trouble.
"I don't like to dictate to you, but it strikes me that now

an opportunity should be taken of ascertaining whether there is really anything that has not been put to this witness that ought to have been put."

"We have very little desire," Fitzpatrick flared back, "to have questions put which we, in our discretion, do not desire to put!"

Counsel for the Crown, probably inwardly delighted as they saw the defense disintegrate, again intervened to wash their hands of the whole quarrel. They would be happy to have the defendant put some questions. . . .

The judge addressed Riel. "Prisoner, are you defended by counsel?"

He repeated the question three times and finally Riel responded. "Partly. My cause is partly in their hands."

Then, he was told, he must leave it in their hands.

Louis was silent for a few moments, then he raised his head and looked at the judge. His speech, when it came, was one of the best made by him or anyone else in the whole course of the trial.

"I will, if you please, say this." He spoke slowly, picking his way carefully through the English words he had not used for some time. "My counsel come from Quebec, from a far province. They have to put questions to men with whom they are not acquainted, on circumstances which they don't know; and although I am willing to give them all the information that I can, they cannot follow the thread of all the questions that should be put to the witnesses. They lose more than three-quarters of the good opportunities—"

He paused and glanced at his irate attorneys. "Not because they are not able," he said swiftly, "not because they are not able! They are learned, they are talented; but the circumstances are such that they cannot put all the questions. If I would be allowed—as it was suggested, this case is extraordinary!"

He would have the opportunity to speak at the proper time, Justice Richardson assured him.

"But the witnesses are passing, and the opportunities!" Riel protested.

"Tell your counsel."

Louis bowed his head in surrender. All his life he had had so much that had to be said, and now there was so little time before the noose choked off his voice forever.

"I cannot all," he said brokenly. "I cannot all. I have too much to say. There is too much to say."

Court was recessed for a few minutes while defense counsel conferred in an angry little huddle. When proceedings were resumed their chief, Lemieux, could only restate their ultimatum: if Louis were permitted to question the witness, his attorneys would abandon the case.

Judge Richardson was vexed and showed it. The defense, he said, had consistently attempted to put the responsibility upon him. He would not refuse to let the defendant speak, if Louis were aware of the consequences—loss of his counsel of record and appointment of new counsel by the court. He asked the defendant if he understood this; yes, but he still wanted to speak.

Richardson suggested more time for him to instruct his counsel, but Lemieux huffily refused it; they had been amply instructed already. (A few minutes before, Fitzpatrick had said Riel was withholding instructions.)

Louis, desperate now—it was, after all, his neck—tried once more to explain:

"The case concerns my good lawyers and my friends, but in the first place it concerns me—and as I think, conscientiously, that I ought to do this for me and for those who have been with me, I cannot abandon the wish that I expressed to the court, and I cannot abandon the wish that I expressed to retain my counsel, because they are good and learned. . . ."

He was gradually being worn down. "I know it is between them and me," he said despairingly. He thanked the court for its generous treatment, and, at last, he surrendered: "I will assert that I wish to retain them."

But now, beaten, he betrayed what had been his real concern, and in doing so unwittingly disclosed why his counsel could not let him put questions: he would have attempted to upset the whole strategy of the defense. His words were more confused now, but vibrant with his sincerity:

"I cannot abandon my dignity! Here I have to defend myself against the accusation of high treason, or I have to consent to the animal life of an asylum. I don't care much about animal life if I am not allowed to carry with it the moral existence of an intellectual being . . ."

"Now, stop!" Richardson interrupted.

"Yes, your Honor," Riel said. "I will."

He made one more attempt to intervene, when his counsel put their last question to Nolin, but he was quickly quelled. The judge, though fully within his rights, was unhappy. "If it were an ordinary criminal case," he said, "I would not hesitate. But this is beyond the ordinary run of cases that I have had to do with in my entire career."

His distress was justified. It was beyond the ordinary run of cases that any judge had ever had to try.

THE DANGEROUS GROUND

Hour after hour the evidence piled up: Riel with his crucifix, exhorting the Métis to fight; carrying a gun (but never in combat, and no one ever saw it fired); boasting of victories; negotiating with the loyal forces. Worst of all, he was identified as author of the letter to Poundmaker:

Rise. Face the Police. If you possibly can, if the thing is not already done, take Fort Battleford. Destroy it. Save all the goods and provisions and come to us. . . . All that you do, do it for the love of God, under the protection of Jesus Christ, of the Blessed Virgin, of St. Joseph, and of St. John the Baptist. Be certain that faith works wonders.

With the testimony about this letter, given by Robert Jefferson, who had been a prisoner in Poundmaker's camp, the Crown rested. It was late afternoon of July 29; only two days had been required to hear eighteen witnesses.

The first defense witness was Father Alexis André, at first glance a curious choice since he had been one of Louis's most bitter antagonists. But he was valuable if he could help establish justification for the uprising. He admitted he had assisted at numerous public gatherings at which the Métis had reviewed their grievances, that petitions had been sent time after time to Ottawa, that "perhaps we received an answer once" but "it was an evasive answer."

A few minutes of this brought Osler of Crown counsel to his feet in vehement protest. "My learned friends have opened a case of treason, justified only by the insanity of the prisoner; they are now seeking to justify armed rebellion for the redress of these grievances. These two defenses are inconsistent. . . . They have gone as far as I feel they should go."

The objection touched off a battle which continued throughout André's testimony, but the defense managed to get a good deal into the record to show that the Government shared responsibility for the troubles. Still more important was André's testimony about Riel's mental state; when religion or politics were discussed, Louis "lost all control of himself . . . he was a fool . . . he did not have his intelligence." The priest described the conference of the clergy of the district when it was unanimously agreed that on the subject of religion "he was not responsible."

Nevertheless it is doubtful whether André's contributions to the defense made up for what his cross-examination achieved for the Crown. Casgrain elicited from him a full account of his talks with Louis when the latter offered to leave the Saskatchewan and return to Montana if he were given a $35,000 indemnity by Ottawa. This incident provided what was probably the most damaging single sentence of the trial. When André had objected that the Dominion, by buying off Louis, still would not have settled the grievances, Riel, he said, replied, "If I am satisfied, the Métis will be." (Louis meant, the defense tried to show, that his own claim naturally would only be a part of an over-all settlement of Métis demands; but the damage had been done.)

André, in seeking to excuse the priests' inability to control their flock, unwittingly did incalculable harm to the defense contention that the rebel had been mad. Riel gained ascendancy over the Métis, the priest said, because he appeared to be so devout; he was never contradicted by the people and therefore did not get excited with them. "He did not admit his strange views at first. It was only after a time that he proclaimed them and especially after the provisional government had been proclaimed."

Crown counsel glanced slyly at each other. The first witness for the defense had given them, in two sentences, the best supporting testimony they had yet obtained for their claim that Riel's alleged eccentricity had been assumed by him at will, that it was part of a brilliant scheme, immoral but sane.

Philippe Garnot, who had been secretary of the *Exovidat*, described Riel's religious transports, his unusual prayers. "I thought the man was crazy," he concluded. But Robinson got him to say that Riel had come to him with a company of armed men and forced him to join the rebellion, and that the defendant was regarded by all of the Métis as leader of the insurrection.

Father Fourmond testified in more detail about Riel's religious fancies and told of the debate he had had with him.

His account of Louis's sudden change of mood, of his following the priest and helping him into the ferryboat, strengthened the defense claim that the prisoner was unbalanced.

The defense presented only five witnesses and took less than one full day despite the fact that its fourth witness, savagely attacked by Crown counsel, precipitated one of the longest and most acrimonious arguments of the trial.

This witness was Dr. Francois Roy, medical superintendent and one of the proprietors of the asylum for insane at Beauport, Quebec. He had been head of the institution for sixteen years, had known Riel intimately as a patient for nineteen months, and he testified that the defendant had been insane, a victim of "megalomania." What's more, he said, testimony of the previous witnesses and his observations during the current trial convinced him that the disease had recurred, as it was apt to do, and that Riel had been of unsound mind when the rebellion broke out.

Osler's cross-examination started on a hostile note and grew increasingly bitter; Roy soon flared up in response and the two men wrangled for an hour. Inquiring into the staff, Osler asked if the proprietors at Beauport exercised only general supervision, to which Roy responded, "More than that; I am, myself, a specialist."

"A specialist in keeping a boarding house?" Osler asked insultingly.

Roy swallowed his wrath and explained that he was a specialist in treatment of acute mania.

Osler assailed the witness's failure to bring the asylum's records with him and then launched into a long and confusing series of questions about the nature of megalomania, obviously designed to befuddle the French physician, who had been testifying, with difficulty, in English. When, at the suggestion of defense counsel, the doctor insisted upon the use of French for both questions and answers, Osler flared up angrily. Then there was squabbling about the translation, and finally it became evident that everyone—by that time including the harassed physician—was out of his depth in an abstruse discussion of the nature of delusions and whether sound reasoning could proceed from false principles.

Osler tried to make the witness admit that the evidence of Riel's alleged insane acts was consistent with skillful fraud. The doctor, thoroughly outraged by now but still alert, refused. "In the mental condition of the prisoner," he said, "I think he is not [a fraud]."

That was no answer at all, snorted Osler; "can you give me any answer?"

"Put another question or in another way," the doctor retorted.

"If you cannot answer it in English or French I may as well let you go," the exasperated barrister said. It was the first time in the course of the trial that the shrewd cross-examiner had met his match.

Dr. Daniel Clark, Toronto alienist and asylum superintendent, had come to testify as a substitute for another expert, incapacitated by illness. He had been able to examine Riel only three times, but on the basis of those interviews and the testimony he had heard, he said, he believed the defendant was insane. However, he admitted on Osler's cross-examination that either malingering or fraud was "possible" and that Riel might have been capable of judging right from wrong. Fitzpatrick, re-examining, was able to undo only a little of the damage: such judgment of right and wrong would be, of course, "subject to his particular delusions."

On this weak note the defense rested. The Crown called its rebuttal witnesses. Dr. James Wallace, superintendent of an asylum in Hamilton, Ontario, stated flatly that Riel was sane, but retreated in disorder on Fitzpatrick's cross: he should have said only that in his one examination, covering half an hour, he had not discovered symptoms of insanity.

"It would be presumptuous for me," he acknowledged meekly, "to say he is not insane." Dr. A. Jukes, senior surgeon for the Mounted Police, had observed the prisoner since his arrival in Regina, believed him to be sane; but he admitted he knew little about insanity, had never examined Riel with his mental condition in mind, and had never discussed with him the topics which were said to set him off.

Rebuttal testimony for the Crown continued through the next day. Captain Young gave his tribute to Riel's intelligence. General Middleton said again he had not, in his conversations with Louis, thought him insane—"quite the contrary." The Rev. Charles B. Pitblado, a Protestant clergyman who had accompanied Riel to Regina, testified that the prisoner had talked freely with him of his objectives; in the form in which Pitblado repeated them, they sounded reasonable enough. The last two witnesses were Mounties who said Riel had been "polite and suave" in prison, had given no trouble, shown no evidence of unbalance.

That afternoon—July 31, Friday—Fitzpatrick began his long address to the jury for the defense. The fifteen-thousand-word peroration took more than two hours to deliver and continued into Saturday's session. No one could justify the rebellion, he said, "but criminal folly and neglect would have gone unpunished had there been no resistance. It is right for me to say that the Government of Canada had wholly failed in its duty toward these Northwest Territories."

Constitutional agitation had been tried, but what was effective constitutional agitation in Ontario was something entirely different in the Northwest, two thousand miles from Ottawa. Riel had come to help, forsaking his security in the United States and without stipulating that he should be paid for his services. . . .

But, said Fitzpatrick, "I confess I tread on dangerous ground. Either this man is the lunatic that we his counsel have tried to make him, or he is an entirely sane man . . .

and was responsible in the eyes of God and man for every-thing that he has done. If he is a lunatic, we, in the exercise of a sound discretion, have done right to endeavor to prove it. If he is a sane man, what humiliation have we passed upon that man, we his counsel endeavoring—despite his orders, despite his desire, despite his instructions—to make him out a fool."

Even if he were sane, there were redeeming things: he had made no attempt to save himself and abandon others who had been caught up in the movement. "Did he," asked Fitz-patrick, obviously comparing Riel's conduct with that of the Crown's prize witness, Nolin, "did he play the part of the sycophant who comes and kneels at the feet of the Govern-ment, endeavoring to seek a victim among his friends and relations?"

Nevertheless, the defense was convinced it was right in its contention that its client was mad. Fitzpatrick reviewed the whole fantastic dream: Was it consistent with sanity to pick on the British Empire? Even that $35,000 "bribe" had had a lunatic aspect: there had been testimony that Riel hoped to use it to establish a newspaper in the United States to rally foreign help to take the Northwest for the Métis.

Another slap at Nolin: The Crown witnesses, for the most part, had been men with irreproachable motives—"but one has branded himself for all time."

Riel was alien in race and religion "so far as you or I are concerned." He had not been granted trial by jury as under-stood elsewhere, but Fitzpatrick was confident that British principles of liberty were safe anywhere in the hearts of British jurors. "I know that you shall not weave the cord that shall hang him and hang him high in the face of all the world, a poor confirmed lunatic—a victim, gentlemen, of op-pression or the victim of fanaticism."

It was a superb speech and the jurors were moved by it, but its effect had been weakened by the inescapable "treading on dangerous ground," by the admission that, after all, Louis might be sane, and that the defense had conducted the whole case directly counter to his "orders, desire and instructions."

It was weakened still more in the next few moments.

"Prisoner," said Justice Richardson, "have you any remarks to make to the jury? If so, now is your time to speak."

Lemieux leaped up. "May it please your Honors," he said swiftly. "At a former stage of the trial you will remember the prisoner wished to cross-examine the witnesses; we objected at the time, thinking that it was better for the interest of the prisoner that we should do so. The prisoner at this stage is entitled to make any statement he likes to the jury and has been so warned by your Honor, but I must declare before the court that we must not be considered responsible for any declaration he may make."

"Certainly," Richardson replied. "But he is entitled, and I am bound to tell him so."

He nodded to Riel, who sat tensely shuffling his notes as Lemieux spoke. The young barrister sat down and Louis glanced at him, but Lemieux stared straight ahead.

At last the time had come. But so little time—and there was too much to say.

CHAPTER XXVII

To the Place Appointed . . .

PROPHET OF THE NEW WORLD

"I⊤ would be easy," Louis began, "for me today to play insanity, because the circumstances are such as to excite any man, and under the natural excitement of what is taking place today—" He broke off to offer an apology. "I cannot speak English very well, but am trying to do so because most of those here speak English. . . .

"The excitement which my trial causes me would justify me not to appear as usual, but with my mind out of its ordinary condition. I hope with the help of God I will maintain calmness and decorum as suits this honorable court, this honorable jury."

The evidence, he said, had shown that he was in the habit of thinking of God at the start of any venture. "I wish if you —if I—do it, you won't take it as a mark of insanity. . . . Oh, my God, help me through Thy grace and the divine influence of Jesus Christ. Oh, my God, bless me; bless this honorable court, bless this honorable jury, bless my good lawyers who have come seven hundred leagues to try to save my life;

bless also the lawyers for the Crown, because they have done, I am sure, what they thought their duty!"

Today, Louis continued, he was as helpless as he was in the lap of his mother the day he was born. "The Northwest is also my mother, and I am sure that my mother country will not kill me."

He launched into a history of the Métis movement and his own role in it. When he came north from Montana in July, 1884, he had found the Indians suffering from want, found the Métis "eating the rotten pork of the Hudson's Bay Company," found the whites "deprived of responsible government, of their public liberties." He had tried to unite all classes, all parties.

"It has been said that I have been egotistic. Perhaps I am. . . . A man cannot be individuality [sic] without paying attention to himself. He cannot generalize himself, though he may be general."

If he had been allowed to question the witnesses, some subjects—especially his purported "foreign policy," the division of the Northwest among seven nationalities—would have made more sense. He had not meant to spurn his counsel, but to put all his questions through them was not feasible: "I could mention a point, but that point was leading to so many [others]. . . . I could not have been all the time suggesting."

He had written "not books, but many things" which he hoped would be published someday; he trusted in British justice for the return of his papers, impounded by the Crown.

There was that matter of a mission. He had not "assumed" that; Archbishop Bourget had written that he was a man to accomplish great things. Father Primeau of Worcester, his director of conscience, had said, "Riel, God has put an object into your hands, the cause of the triumph of religion in the world; take care, you will succeed when most believe you

have lost." Father Eberschweiler of Fort Benton had blessed
him; "the benediction surrounded me all the time in the
Saskatchewan." Surely it was only through God's active concern and protection that he had escaped all the hazards of
the last fifteen years. "He has kept me from bullets, when
bullets marked my hat. . . .

"Today when I saw the glorious General Middleton bearing testimony that I was not insane, and when Captain
Young proved that I am not insane, I felt that God was
blessing me. . . . I have been in an asylum, but I thank the
lawyers for the Crown who destroyed the testimony of my
good friend Dr. Roy, because I have always believed that I
was put in the asylum without reason.

"Even if I was going to be sentenced by you, gentlemen of
the jury, I have this satisfaction—that if I die I will not be
reputed by all men as insane, as a lunatic!" Of course the
priests had long considered him mad—yet they had said on
the stand that he could "pass from great passion to great
calmness." That was not madness; it showed great control
under stress; "and with the help of God I have that control."

Nolin—"Mr. Charles Nolin"—had not revealed in his testimony that he himself had been a participant, under solemn
oath, with three others, in all the planning which led to the
Métis uprising. "Far from taking them [the Métis plans] as
insane affairs, he was in them under cover of an oath with
four of us. He did not say that in the box!"

But the agitation in the Northwest would have continued
to be constitutional "if, in my opinion, we had not been attacked."

Without presumption, he felt he had the right to say that
he had been libeled for fifteen years. "I know that through
the grace of God I am the founder of Manitoba. I know that
though I have no open road for my influence, I have big influence—concentrated as a big amount of vapor in an engine.
I believe by what I have suffered for fifteen years, by what

I have done for Manitoba and the people of the Northwest, that my words are worth something."

And, though he did not want to give offense, this had to be said: "Yes, you are the pioneers of civilization. The whites are the pioneers of civilization, but they bring among the Indians demoralization."

Even the clergy could not be held blameless. He had been accused of turning against the priests, even of calling Archbishop Taché, his benefactor, a thief. "I have seen him surrounded by his great property, the property of a widow. . . . He bought the land around, and took that way to try and get her property at a cheap price. I read in the Gospel, 'Ye Pharisees with your long prayers devour the widows.' And as Archbishop Taché is my great benefactor, is my father . . . and because there was no one who had the courage to tell him, I did, because I love him."

For this he had been severely rebuked by Father Moulin, who had told him he should have said the archbishop made a mistake, not that he committed robbery. But—

"I say that we have been patient a long time, and when we see that mild words only serve as covers for great ones to do wrong, it is time we are justified in saying that robbery is robbery everywhere, and the guilty ones are bound by the force of public opinion to take notice of it. The one who has the courage to speak out in that way, instead of being an outrageous man, becomes in fact a benefactor to those men themselves and to society."

As to his religious beliefs, what was insane about them? He merely wished to put Rome aside "inasmuch as it is the cause of division between Catholics and Protestants." It might take two hundred years, but someday it would come, "and then my children's children will shake hands with the Protestants of the new world in a friendly manner." He did not want "the evils which exist in Europe" to take root in America.

Visions and prophecies? There was nothing remarkable about them: "we all see into the future more or less." And he had worked at it. The Métis had long known their special skills; an involuntary movement of the muscles in hand, shoulders or legs might portend certain events. Still, he had been uniquely gifted. "If it is any satisfaction to the doctors to know what kind of insanity I have, if they are going to call my pretensions insanity, I say humbly through the grace of God I believe I am the prophet of the new world."

But he did not want to exhaust his listeners. (He had been speaking for about an hour.) "Gentlemen of the jury, my reputation, my liberty, my life are at your discretion. . . . I do respect you, although you are only half a jury; but your number of six does not prevent you from being just and conscientious, does not prevent me from giving you my confidence. . . .

"For fifteen years I have been neglecting myself. My wife and children are without means." Although he had worked, as a guest of the Métis, to help the people of the Northwest, "I have never had any pay. It has always been my hope to have a fair living one day."

But he had said enough. Time now to thank the judge again, and the jury, repeat his apology for imperfections in his English. He had spoken too long; his listeners were bored, fidgety. Nor had the speech been organized as well as it should have been; so much to say, so much of it hard to explain. Too late now to remedy any bad slips; now he had but to end it, end it quickly.

"I put my speech under the protection of my God, my Savior. He is the only one who can make it effective. It is possible it should become effective, as it is proposed to good men, to good people. . . ." He looked about the courtroom. This was the awful moment; the speech was over but the last words were confused and weak; he had run dry in midsentence. He should have stopped before. ". . . And to good ladies also," he said desperately, and slumped into his chair.

THREATS IN DECEMBER

Robinson summed up for the Crown, concentrating his attack upon the defense attempt to show justification for the uprising. The Northwest Rebellion had been "lightly spoken of, lightly written about," he complained; but what was the fact?

"Armed rebellion means the sacrifice of innocent lives, it means the loss of fathers, brothers, sisters, parents, the destruction of many homes, and still more the lifelong desolation of many human hearts; and, gentlemen, we must not allow ourselves for one moment to speak lightly of anything which necessarily involves these terrible consequences!"

Justice Richardson began his charge that afternoon, July 31, but could not finish before court was adjourned at six o'clock. He read the law and portions of the evidence, reserving most of his comment for the following morning.

The jury's responsibility, he then pointed out, was double: first to determine whether Riel was guilty of the overt acts, and second, if he was guilty, to determine whether he was "answerable" mentally.

As for the insanity, the jury would recall that Nolin had told about Riel's demand for $35,000, supporting the Crown contention that the rebellion "was all a scheme of the prisoner's to put money in his own pocket." To be sure, the prisoner had been "very irritable when the subject of religion was brought up."

(Actually the testimony had been that Riel was wholly irresponsible when religion was discussed—not "irritable"—and equally subject to unreasoning excitement over politics, which Richardson did not mention. The judge's milder word may have weakened the impact of defense testimony upon the jury.)

"Then at what date," the charge continued, "can you fix this insanity as having commenced?" The defense theory, the judge said, was that it began in March—"but threats of what he intended to do began in December."

(This was one of the most damaging statements in Richardson's charge and it was very flimsily supported, for it rested wholly upon evidence by Nolin which was far from clear. Riel spoke—in confidence—to Nolin in December about his "plans," but they were plans to leave the country if he could obtain the indemnity he sought from Ottawa. In subsequent testimony *which did not fix the date of their conversations,* Nolin elaborated upon this matter of the indemnity, claiming that Riel said he would buy a newspaper and use it to "raise the other nationalities in the states."

(Nolin was led through a long account of his relations with the movement up to the battle at Duck Lake in March, 1885; then Casgrain, examining for the Crown, suddenly and without prior preparation, asked: "In the beginning of December, 1884, the prisoner had begun speaking of his plans *about taking up arms?"* Nolin replied "Yes," and no elaboration of this answer was sought by Casgrain. Unaccountably, the defense failed to challenge this, nor did it ask the self-righteous Nolin why, if Riel spoke seriously of armed revolt as early as December, he did not break with him until the following March 3.

(Other testimony and documentary evidence indicated that Riel did not decide until March to take up arms. There can be no doubt that he sometimes dreamed, even in Montana, of an armed uprising; but in modern jurisprudence the overt act could only be said to have occurred when he made that fatal decision and publicly incited the Métis to rebel. His thinking, or daydreams he may casually have disclosed to a singularly ill-chosen confidant, did not constitute overt acts. Richardson, by emphasizing the so-called "threats" in December, actually was reaching back to a medieval concept of treason—"imagining the death of the King.")

The justice now reversed himself completely and attacked the insanity defense from the other flank:

"Admitting that the insanity only commenced about the time of the breaking out of the rebellion, what does seem strange to me is that these people who were about him, if they had an insane man in their midst, that some of them had not the charity to go before a magistrate and lay an information . . . that he should be taken care of."

Then Judge Richardson hastily washed his hands. "I only suggest that to you, not that you are to take it as law. I merely suggest it as turning upon the evidence. Having made the remarks I have, I am simply called upon to tell you what is legal insanity."

He set forth the law, succinctly and correctly: the defendant's reasoning must have been proved to their satisfaction to have been so imperfect that he could not know the nature of his act, could not know that he was doing wrong.

"Not only must you think of the man in the dock, but you must think of society at large. You are not called upon to think of the Government at Ottawa simply as a Government, you have to think of the homes and of the people who live in this country, you have to ask yourselves: Can such things be permitted?"

He went on to demolish the argument that Riel's United States citizenship exempted him from the application of Canadian law, then he closed:

"We have the law given to us and we are called upon to administer it. I, under the oath that I have taken, and you, under the oath administered to you Tuesday morning, are to pass between this man and the Crown. If therefore the Crown has not conclusively brought guilt home to the prisoner, say so, say that you acquit him simply by reason of that."

Richardson stopped. Counsel awaited the rest of the usual admonition—that if, on the other hand, the Crown had convinced the jurors of Riel's guilt, it was their duty to convict. But the judge said no more; perhaps subconsciously he realized that he had done enough, or even too much, for the Crown already.

The jury retired and court was recessed; it was two o'clock in the afternoon of August 1, 1885.

Eager chatter began in the spectators' section, then faltered and sank to self-conscious whispering. The people who had been milling around the door stopped suddenly and stared. The attorneys, who had thrust open their gowns and lighted their pipes, went right on talking to each other, but they sneaked embarrassed glances at the prisoner's dock.

Louis Riel had dropped to his knees in the dock and was praying, aloud but softly, in French and Latin.

After a few minutes the hum of conversation grew louder in the courtroom, but whenever it flagged the voice of Riel could be heard, monotonous as an Indian drum, tediously imploring the mercy of God.

Try as they would, the chatterers could not wholly shut out the voice or keep from glancing occasionally at the motionless man on his knees in the dock. They resented it; such public spectacles were bad form, making everyone uncomfortable, especially the ladies.

The voice did not stop, did not even pause, until the jurors came back.

A REASONABLE MAN

At three-twenty the jury returned to the courtroom, shepherded by trimly uniformed men of the Royal Northwest Mounted Police. The judge took his place, glanced at the clerk. "The prisoner will rise," the clerk said. Riel had resumed his chair and was sitting with his head in his hands. Now, slowly, he rose to his feet.

"Gentlemen," the clerk asked, "are you agreed upon your verdict? How say you—is the prisoner guilty or not guilty?"

Foreman Cosgrave was a gentlemanly middle-aged Englishman with a look of intelligence and competence, chin-whiskered, wearing pince-nez secured by a black cord to a disc pinned to his vest. He did not look at the defendant; his grave gaze was fixed upon the judge. His voice was low but clear.

"We find the defendant guilty," he said. Riel swayed momentarily, leaned against the railing.

"Gentlemen of the jury," the clerk said, "hearken to your verdict as the court records it: you find the prisoner Louis Riel guilty, so say you all."

"Guilty," the jurors mumbled.

"Your Honors," Cosgrave said, "I have been asked by my brother jurors to recommend the prisoner to the mercy of the Crown."

"I may say," Justice Richardson replied, "that the recommendation you have given will be forwarded in proper manner to the proper authorities." He thanked the jurors and excused them.

Riel still stood in his place, bracing himself. No one had seen a change in his expression when the verdict was announced, but his body had slumped.

"Louis Riel," Richardson asked, "have you anything to say why the sentence of the court should not be pronounced upon you, for the offense of which you have been found guilty?"

Riel stared into the judge's face. There was a pause before he spoke. "Yes—your Honor—"

Fitzpatrick of defense counsel interrupted. "Before the accused answers or makes any remarks, I would beg leave to ask your Honors to note the objections I have already taken to the jurisdiction of the court."

They had been noted, Richardson said impatiently. Coun-

sel must realize he could not rule upon them. Of course; Fitzpatrick understood. His comment had merely been a safeguard, "to reserve any recourse the law may allow us here-
after."

Riel looked at Fitzpatrick, then at the judge. "Can I speak
now?" he asked timidly.

"Oh, yes," the judge said.

"Your Honors, gentlemen of the jury . . ."

Richardson interrupted bluntly. "There is no jury now;
they are discharged."

"They have passed away before me. . . . But at the same
time I consider them still here." Until now, Louis said, he
had been considered insane, or criminal, or just someone to
be shunned, "so there was hostility, or there was contempt,
or there was avoidance. Today, by the verdict of the court,
one of those three situations has disappeared. I suppose that
after being condemned I will cease to be called a fool, and
for me it is a great advantage. If I have a mission—I say 'if'
for the sake of those who doubt, but for my part it means
'since'—since I have a mission, I cannot fulfill my mission as
long as I am looked upon as an insane being. . . .

"If there has ever been any contradiction in my life it is at
this moment, and do I appear excited? Am I very irritable?
Can I control myself? The smile that comes to my face is not
an act of my will so much as it comes naturally from the
satisfaction that I experienced seeing one of my difficulties
disappearing. Should I be executed—at least if I were being
to be executed—I would not be executed as an insane man.
It would be a great consolation for my mother, for my wife,
for my children, for my brothers, for my relatives, even for
my protectors, for my countrymen. . . ."

He thanked the jurors for recommending him to the clemency of the Crown. It would be easy for him to make "an incendiary protest" on the grounds his attorneys had advanced,
challenging the jurisdiction of the court and the fairness of

his trial. "But why should I do it, since the court has undertaken to prove that I am a reasonable man? Must I not take
advantage of the situation to show that they are right and
that I am reasonable?

"Besides clearing me of the stain of insanity—" He paused
and made a significant change in the sentence. "Besides clearing my career of the stain of insanity, I think the verdict is
proof that I am more than ordinary, that the help which is
given me is more than ordinary. . . . I think I have been
called upon to do something which, at least in the Northwest,
nobody has done yet. And in some way I think that to a certain number of people the verdict against me today is a proof
that maybe I am a prophet, maybe Riel is a prophet, he suffered enough for it!

"I have been hunted like an elk for fifteen years. David
had been seventeen: I think I will have to be about two years
still. But I hope it will come sooner.

"You will excuse me, you know my difficulty in speaking
English—and have had no time to prepare, your Honor—and
even had I prepared anything it would have been imperfect
enough—" His voice stumbled, stopped, began again. "And
I have not prepared, and I wish you would excuse what I
have to say—the way which I will be able to perhaps express
it."

He paused again, took a deep breath. When he resumed,
his phrasing was once more succinct and his voice clear.

"The troubles on the Saskatchewan," he began, "are not
to be taken as an isolated fact. They are the result of fifteen
years' war. The head of that difficulty lies in the difficulty of
Red River. . . ." So much to say, so little time. He spoke,
with clarity and sense, of the creation of Manitoba and his
own services there; but then he jumped suddenly to the Saskatchewan and his own plans to subdivide the country. "If
we cannot have our seventh of the lands from Canada, we
will ask the people of the States, the Italians, to come and

help us as immigrants. . . . I said we will invite the Italians of the States, the Irish of the States, the Bavarians—" His phrasing again was breaking down and his mind was wandering. He began to repeat himself.

His plan had been sent to Pembina; the Fenians would be interested. "And Gabriel Dumont on the other side of the line; is Gabriel Dumont inactive? I think not. He is trying to save me from this box. . . .

"But if there is justice as I still hope—oh, dear, it seems to me I have become insane to hope still! I have seen so many men in my position and where are they?"

The amnesty which had been promised in 1870—"that was no amnesty; it was an insult to me; it has always been an insult!" Besides, it came five years too late, "and took the trouble of banishing me five years more. . . ."

Breathless, he paused, leaning on the railing with his head low.

"Is that all?" Richardson asked, his weariness apparent.

Riel's head came up again. "No—excuse me—I feel weak, and if I stop at times, I wish you would be kind enough—"

He went on. He explained the provisions of the Manitoba Act; they had not been fulfilled. But suddenly he was back on the amnesty, then the indemnity he had sought. He had earned that, he felt, by his services in Manitoba, by his loyalty during the Fenian scare. And he had never received any of the land promised to the Métis, or been compensated for the persecution he had suffered. "I could not even water my horses on the Missouri without being guarded against those who wanted my life. And it is an irony for me that I should be called David!"

He was wandering again, but there still were little gleams of greatness:

"When we gave the land—in giving it to the Canadian Government it does not mean that we gave it, with all the respect that I have for the English population, to the Anglo-

Saxon race; we did not give it only for the Anglo-Saxon race!"

Could there be a special commission to hear his case? And now, suddenly, he revealed that he had known throughout the trial that he was being tried not only for the treason of 1885. Let that special tribunal, he pleaded, inquire first into whether his resistance in 1869 constituted rebellion; let it, above all, answer the question, "Was Riel a murderer of Thomas Scott?"

(When the treason conviction was appealed, Canada's Minister of Justice said, of Riel's leadership in the Northwest Rebellion, "it was a second offense." As the minister should have known and probably did know, it was nothing of the kind. And as for Riel's other concern, Juror Edwin J. Brooks said in a Regina newspaper interview fifty years after the trial: "We tried Riel for treason, and he was hanged for the murder of Scott.")

At last Louis was through. Let the commission decide. "There have been witnesses around me for ten years, about the time they have declared me insane, and they will show if there is in me the character of an impostor. If they declare me insane, if I have been astray, I have been astray not as an impostor, but according to my conscience. Your Honor, that is all what [sic] I have to say." He let himself down in his chair.

Richardson drew a long breath. The long, shapeless, tiresome harangue had exhausted everyone, cost the prisoner some of the sympathy that had been felt for him, and made the judge's task much easier.

Riel's guards nudged him and once more Louis dragged himself to his feet.

"Louis Riel," Richardson said coldly, "after a long consideration of your case in which you have been defended with as great ability as I think counsel could have defended you with, you have been found by a jury who have shown, I might almost say, unexampled patience, guilty of a crime the most pernicious and greatest that man can commit.

"You have been found guilty of high treason. You have been proved to have let loose the floodgates of rapine and bloodshed; you have, with such assistance as you had in the Saskatchewan country, managed to arouse the Indians; and you have brought ruin and misery to many families. . . .

"For what you did the remarks you have made form no excuse whatever. For what you have done the law requires you to answer."

It was true, the judge went on, that the jury had mercifully suggested that he be recommended for the clemency of the Crown, and that his counsel had taken exception to the whole proceeding under which he had been convicted.

"But in spite of that I cannot hold out any hope to you that you will succeed in getting entirely free, or that Her Majesty will, after what you have been the cause of doing, open her hand of clemency to you.

"For me, I have only one more duty to perform, that is to tell you what the sentence of the law is upon you. I have, as I must, given time to enable your case to be heard. All I can suggest or advise you is to prepare to meet your end, that is all the advice or suggestion I can offer.

"It is now my painful duty to pass the sentence of the court upon you. And that is that you be taken now from here to the police guardroom at Regina, which is the gaol and the place from whence you came, and that you be kept there until the 18th of September next; that on the 18th of September next you be taken to the place appointed for your execution, and there be hanged by the neck till you are dead.

"And may God have mercy on your soul."

CHAPTER XXVIII

Deliver Us from Evil

EVERY DOG IN QUEBEC

On August 3, A. G. B. Bannatyne wrote a note to James Wickes Taylor to thank the United States Consul in Winnipeg for a recent gift—some *"chanterelle* [mushroom] soup." "So," his letter said, "I see they have sentenced my poor friend Riel but recommended him to mercy. By Heavens, they ought to string up a number of the Government officials if they hang him!"

He was but one of thousands who felt that way. The news of Riel's conviction brought shocked protest and pleas for clemency from all over the world. The International Arbitration Association cabled promptly from London; in the weeks that followed thousands of people signed petitions in French Canada, the United States and France. Sometimes entire parishes signed: one petition bore 1,850 names. More than eight hundred Chicagoans appealed for remission of the death sentence and more than six hundred signed in Holyoke, Massachusetts. St. Paul, St. Louis, Nashua, Urbana and other United States communities added their pleas.

From Paris came a simple cable: "A woman begs Canadian authorities pardon Riel." It was signed by Juliette Adam, one of the outstanding women of her generation in France—author, publisher of an intellectual review, Republican political strategist and leader of the neo-Hellenist movement in French culture.

A few petitions—and many newspaper editorials—urged that the sentence be carried out. One petition originated in Regina; three of the thirty-eight signers who demanded that Riel hang had been prisoners of Big Bear. An Orange lodge in Ontario, one of many to adopt resolutions, found it necessary to "remind the Government of their duty," and Charles O'Hara, who described himself as a laborer, wrote the Privy Council of Canada that because Louis had had "the murderous audacity of making partisan war against us English-speaking people" he must die.

Execution of the sentence was to be postponed several times, but there never was any real doubt that Riel would hang. As the pressure for clemency grew, as tentative suggestions of a royal reprieve began to come even from important people in London, Ottawa's determination solidified.

The Dominion Government tottered, religious and race hatred swept across Canada like a withering wind, angry speeches in Parliament split parties and wrecked lifelong friendships, Ontario newspapers spoke openly of secession or armed subjection of the clamorous French. The Prime Minister, angrily stamping his foot, made his position clear in an Ottawa interview. "He shall hang," said Sir John, "though every dog in Quebec bark in his favor!"

Meanwhile the trials of other culprits proceeded. More than seventy had been arrested, but fewer than half that number actually came to trial and several were acquitted. Eighteen Métis were convicted of treason-felony or pleaded guilty; they received prison terms ranging from one year to seven. Poundmaker and Big Bear were sentenced to prison for three years on this charge but were released in 1887; broken in spirit, both died soon after they got out.

Eleven Indians were sentenced to hang for murder but three won commutation. The other eight, including Wandering Spirit, who had pleaded guilty, were hanged all at one time on a single scaffold in the Mounted Police courtyard at Battleford on November 27. According to a white witness at the mass execution, the war chief, who had remained mute during his trial, went silent to his death; the Crees, however, say that while the other seven shrieked war songs as the hoods were lowered over their heads, Wandering Spirit hummed a love song to his wife.

Imasees, Big Bear's son, and two or three others who had been associated with the war chief in the agitation for revolt, fled to Montana; Imasees died on the Rocky Boy reservation, a Cree-Chippewa refuge, and is buried there.

Will Jackson, Riel's aide at the start of the movement, was tried for treason-felony a few days before his chief and was acquitted on the ground of insanity. Justice Richardson, who was soon to prove so skeptical of this defense, instructed the jury to free Jackson and it did so without leaving the box. Dr. Jukes testified that Jackson held "peculiar ideas on religious matters" and "the slightest excitement produced a great effect upon him." A few days later he was to testify that the man who originated those same religious ideas and who was even more excitable was, in his opinion, quite sane.

Jackson, to his credit, fought almost as hard as Riel did to get himself convicted. He interrupted the trial twice, once to insist that he had never denied responsibility for anything he had done while he was secretary to Riel, "whose fate, whatever it may be, I wish to share"; and again to protest, "I never considered myself a prisoner of Riel's." But his efforts were fruitless; he was a white man; he must have been mad. The trial took only a few minutes.

Thomas Scott of Prince Albert, the only other white man accused of complicity, was also speedily exonerated by the jury.

During the rebellion and since, the Government's commission had been quietly interviewing Métis settlers and distributing land patents or scrip; by the time Riel came to trial many of the grievances which had caused the revolt had been settled. W. P. R. Street, the chairman of the commission, had had his troubles, but most of them were with Ottawa. At first he was authorized only to list the Métis for adjustment of their claims someday, when Ottawa got around to it. He protested, and was told, he said, "if the half-breeds refused to come before us our duty would have been done and we could not be blamed"; but finally he persuaded the Government to let the commission finish the job, issue scrip to qualified claimants on the spot. It did this in some areas while the siege of Batoche was still on, and unquestionably this resolute action—an astonishing contrast to the fumbling, delays and deliberate provocations of Ottawa—prevented many more Métis from joining Riel's cause.

OUR LADY OF THE SNOWS

Now the cause was dead and he who had given it breath and brain sought only peace for his own tortured soul.

"As things are," Louis wrote his mother, "it is only our Lord who can cope with them." The restraint of imprisonment would be intolerable, he added, "were it not that I am truly resigned and obedient. . . ."

. . . That mortification may be spiritual as well as physical, I open my conscience to my priest and allow him to conquer my likes, my thoughts and my will as he pleases. I have renounced everything as best I can. . . . I am confident that if I surrender my soul to Jesus Christ or to His minister, peace and happiness will be allowed me.

He had, in fact, renounced everything that had given his
life its meaning. Hounded by the priests who had been his
enemies but had now suddenly become his friends, determined to snatch this heretic from hellfire, Louis had brought
himself at last to the ultimate gesture, the ultimate humiliation: he had signed a declaration acknowledging that his
mission had been a delusion.

This document, the most tragic record to be found in all
of the original papers of the Métis movement, was written by
Riel in *"Prison de Regina, 5 Août 1885, Fête de Notre Dame
des Neiges"*—feast day of Our Lady of the Snows. It is headed
by his customary invocation, "Jesus, Mary, and Joseph, save
me!" and addressed to Father Vital Fourmond, "my director
of conscience." The text, which is in French, reads as fol-
lows:

Archbishop Bourget said to me: "God, who has always guided
and assisted you until the present hour will not abandon you in
your most profound sorrows. Because he has given you a mission
which you must accomplish to the full."

My director of conscience tells me that my misfortunes and
missteps come from not having understood my mission correctly.
The religious principle which gave me so much confidence in the
words of Archbishop Bourget now logically induces me to have
the same confidence in the interpretation of those words approved by my spiritual director.

Renouncing, then, all the personal interpretations I have assigned to my mission and which are not approved by my confessor and director, I submit to the Catholic, Apostolic and
Roman Church in making the following declaration:

My father, my confessor, my director of conscience, forgive
please all of my sins and the punishment due for my sins; all of
my faults and the consequences of my faults; all of my offenses
and all that resulted from my offenses—be they against God,
against religion, against society, against my neighbor, against
myself.

The statement was signed, "Your poor penitent, Louis Riel or Louis 'David' Riel," and attested by the signatures of Father Fourmond and Father Louis Cochin.

Louis Riel had made his peace with God and the clergy, and had saved his immortal soul. But the mortal fire within him was already dead. He never again raised his voice when a priest told him to keep still—not even on the gallows while his people waited for the words he had promised to speak, to let them know if he really was to die.

He had hoped, he wrote his mother, to send her a detailed explanation and justification of his life, "but my spiritual director forbids me to send it to you." In depriving himself of this meager satisfaction, he supposed, "I mortify my will, my intelligence and my liberty; and I hope in return God will give me peace."

He devoted most of his time to prayer and writing, composing long letters to his family, friends and sympathizers. As the weeks wore on without a single hopeful development in the struggle to save him, he went to work on his *Dernière Mémoire,* a long statement of the Métis cause which delved into the history of his people, the social and psychological impediments to their integration with white civilization, and their love for their wilderness land.

It was in this work that he wrote of the need for pride, without concern for what fraction of the blood was European or Indian. "We are Métis!" He described the old way of life, the drama of the hunt: "the coursers rearing, neighing, dancing, digging at the ground with eager hooves. . . ." He told of the Métis function in a transitional society: they had maintained good relations with the Indians, had helped to reconcile them to the inevitable; the Métis "at the price of their blood gave tranquillity to the Northwest."

The *Mémoire* was the most eloquent writing Riel ever achieved, notably lucid and moderate when considered with other products of this period—letters and reflections on re-

ligion which were often incoherent. The religious musings
were obsessed with self, but in his political writings he paid
almost no attention to his own fate; of the *Mémoire's* ten
thousand words only a scant two or three paragraphs mention his personal concerns.

He no longer appeared to interest himself more than cur-
sorily in the attempts being made to save his life. His acknowledgment that he had "misinterpreted" his mission may
have left him resigned, but it is unlikely that, as some of his
friends believed, he had become eager for martyrdom. To
the end he would have welcomed a chance to escape, and if
he had escaped he probably would have repudiated the ab-
juration of his mission which Fourmond had wrung from
him.

The defense appealed, as authorized in Dominion statute,
to the Queen's Bench of Manitoba, the Provincial supreme
court. On September 9 the three-judge tribunal decided that
a new trial was not justified and that the conviction must be
affirmed.

The case was then carried to the Privy Council in London,
which was asked to give leave to the defense to present an
appeal; meanwhile Riel's execution was stayed. But on October 24 the judicial committee of the Privy Council announced it had found no ground upon which an appeal
should be permitted.

There remained but two legal ways by which Riel could
escape the noose: an official determination that he was insane, or the clemency of the Crown. Lemieux, still acting as
chief counsel, immediately tried the first, appealing to the
Governor General of Canada to bring about the appointment of a medical commission.

The Marquis of Lansdowne, Governor General, had already had some correspondence with Prime Minister Macdonald about the rising tide of protest over Riel's sentence

at home and abroad. Sir John had tried to allay the Governor's concern: Riel's movement had been, he said, "a mere domestic trouble, and ought not to be elevated to the rank of a rebellion." Lansdowne was not deceived. "I am afraid," he replied wryly, "we have all of us been doing what we could to elevate it to the rank of a rebellion, and with so much success that we cannot now reduce it to the rank of a common riot."

Sir John was persuaded, therefore, that some such gesture as appointment of a medical commission might be expedient. But he did all he could to limit its effectiveness. It could not investigate Riel's delusions, he decreed; its function was solely to determine whether he was sane now. The condemned man was granted a third reprieve to permit this inquiry; the new date for the hanging was November 16.

In a confidential personal letter to one of the two medical commissioners, Dr. Michael Lavell, medical superintendent of the penitentiary in Kingston, Ontario, Sir John made himself clear. The mission to Regina was to be secret, and not a word was to be said until their report was released. Dr. Lavell's colleague would be Dr. F. X. Valade of Ottawa— "he is a reliable man and we have thought it well, for obvious reasons, that there should be a French Canadian on the enquiry." However, Lavell might want to communicate "in cypher" separately from Valade.

"I have told him [Valade]," Macdonald's letter continued, "that as surgeon and warden of the P[enitentiary] you had under your charge criminal lunatics and were, therefore, an expert. I have fully impressed him with this idea—so don't be too modest about it."

After interviewing Riel, Dr. Lavell should see several persons named by Sir John, "and any other persons you like; I should suggest as few as possible—*so soon as you are convinced that Riel knows right from wrong and is an accountable being.*" (The emphasis is this writer's.) Remember, the

Prime Minister warned, that the jury had decided Riel was sane and the judge and court of appeal had approved the verdict; "you cannot, therefore, go behind that verdict." The investigation was merely to determine whether Riel was sane now and could be legally executed. "If—whatever illusions he may have—he still knows right from wrong the law should be allowed to take effect." Dr. Lavell need not devote more than two or three days to the project, Sir John thought.

Despite these precautions the inquiry was not an unqualified success from Sir John's viewpoint. The French Canadian Valade, about whom there apparently had been some misgivings, might have upset the apple cart completely—had not the Government kept his report from the public by unscrupulous falsification of the official record.

On November 8 Dr. Valade telegraphed the Prime Minister:

After having examined carefully Riel in private conversation with him and by testimony of persons who take care of him, I have come to the conclusion that he is not an accountable being, that he is unable to distinguish between wrong and right on political and religious subjects, which I consider well-marked typical forms of insanity under which he undoubtedly suffers, but on other points I believe him to be sensible and can distinguish right from wrong.

This telegram appears in the Canadian Sessional Papers in this form:

After having examined carefully Riel in private conversation with him and by testimony of persons who take care of him, I have come to the conclusion that he suffers under hallucinations on political and religious subjects, but on other points I believe him to be quite sensible and can distinguish right from wrong.

Even Dr. Lavell expressed some doubts. He wired Sir John that Riel gave evidence of "foolish and peculiar views as to religion and general government." However, he said he believed him to be "an accountable being."

Dr. Jukes, the police surgeon, submitted reports to Governor Dewdney and to Macdonald. The report to Dewdney appears in the Canadian Sessional Papers—but, as was Valade's telegram, it was censored. Jukes held Riel to be sane and accountable, but he added, "It must be admitted that he differs systematically from the large majority of mankind" in his religious views. This paragraph was deleted from Jukes's letter before it was printed in the official record.

Valade and Lavell reported on November 8. Louis Riel had eight days to live unless one of three persons in all the world could and would save him. They were the Queen of Britain, the President of the United States, and Gabriel Dumont. Louis himself was putting what hopes he had left on Dumont.

RELAY FROM REGINA

Late in October Lord Carnarvon suggested to his colleagues of the British Cabinet that Riel's case be considered for royal clemency. His was a voice to heed: he had been Colonial Secretary and a sponsor of Canadian Confederation. But the Cabinet was reluctant to act, and definitely rejected his appeal after word came from Ottawa that Sir John's Government would not countenance any interference. Therefore when Queen Victoria received, through the French Ambassador, a plea for clemency initiated by the French colonial press, the Colonial Office replied that Her Majesty had delegated the power of pardon in this instance to the Governor General of Canada.

The Governor General had exercised that power once before to free Riel and Lépine. He could not, in defiance of the wishes of the Dominion Government, employ it again.

James Wickes Taylor wrote the State Department on November 3, "The impression prevails that there will be no further respite of the execution of Louis Riel." He had been reporting frequently on the crisis; in September he had forwarded an appeal written by Riel himself and addressed to President Cleveland in which the condemned rebel challenged Canada's title to the Northwest and urged annexation by the United States. Now Taylor made his last appeal. The Dominion, he contended, had violated its pledge to the Métis in 1870, a pledge which had won it permission from the United States to transport some of Wolseley's supplies south of the boundary. He urged immediate intervention to save Riel while the whole problem of U. S.-Canadian relations in the Northwest was studied.

But the State Department was unmoved by Taylor's pleas, or by the petitions which reached it from French-Canadian communities.

The last hope in Washington rested with a faithful and generous friend of the doomed man—Edmond Mallet. He obtained an interview with Secretary of State Thomas F. Bayard, but Bayard told him the United States would not intervene unless it could be shown that Riel had been discriminated against because of his American citizenship. Disheartened but still trying, Mallet finally got in to see President Cleveland. He made an eloquent plea on political and moral grounds: Riel was an American, unfairly tried by a makeshift court; he was insane; the authority to put a human being to death had been delegated to the state by God and, under the Christian ethic, could not be exercised against one of unsound mind.

The President told Mallet he was "much interested," and agreed to confer at once with Bayard and perhaps the British Ambassador. But late that night the Associated Press office in Washington told Mallet "the President has been constrained to decline interfering."

Riel's friend was broken-hearted and angry. Three weeks after Louis died, President Cleveland, in his message to Congress, said: "The watchful care and interest of this Government over its citizens are not relinquished because they are gone abroad. . . . A fair and open trial conducted with a decent regard for justice and humanity will always be demanded for them." Mallet felt that the United States had failed to live up to this principle, and the protests he inspired brought about a Senate investigation of the Riel incident in 1889.

But there still remained Gabriel Dumont.

He and Michel Dumas had crossed the Montana line about June 1 and had given themselves up to United States troops at Fort Assiniboine, just south of the boundary. The commanding officer of that remote Montana post, at a loss about what to do with them, wired to Washington for instructions. President Cleveland, declaring them to be political refugees and thus entitled to a haven in the United States, ordered them released.

Gabriel hastened to Spring Creek, the most prosperous Métis colony, and set to work immediately to plan the escape of Riel. He visited the other settlements, collected money, horses and men, and in October he was ready: at intervals of every ten to twenty miles from Lewistown, Montana, to Regina, Saskatchewan, four hundred and fifty miles, he had established secret relay stations with fresh mounts, armed men for escorts, and food for the fugitive. Every Métis and Indian camp had been alerted; if Riel once reached any one of them he would have vanished forever from the white man's world. Gabriel, without ever knowing it, recreated within a few weeks the underground railroad of the Civil War and reversed its direction.

That much of the story was well known to Montana Métis

and even to newspapermen; but beyond that all is specula-
tion.

The conspiracy failed, apparently because the Regina jail
break upon which the whole thing rested was foiled. According to associates of Dumont, the plot was betrayed to the
Mounties by a prominent Métis who learned of it through
Riel family connections, one whom they already regarded as
a traitor to their race; but there is no evidence to support
this and the charge may have been inspired only by Gabriel's
hatred for this man. Rumor alone could well have wrecked
the scheme; for a week or two before the date set for the
execution there was talk in Regina that a jail delivery might
be attempted. These tales acquired authority of a sort when
it was observed that the guard in the Regina barracks area
was being strengthened.

Montanans involved in the plot insisted that Riel knew
of it and that his confidence in its success accounted for his
cheerfulness until a week or so before he was hanged. He
may even have been led to believe—as many Métis still believe—that the Canadian Government would connive in his
escape to rid itself of the rapidly developing political crisis;
but he and his friends knew that the Mounties, in whose custody he was, would never be a party to the scheme.

Somehow—when he saw the guard strengthened, or noted
some change in prison routine which was unmarked by anyone else—Louis learned that the loyal Gabriel's plan had
failed. But the other Métis never did learn this, and the Montana colonies thought his escape could occur even as he
walked to the gallows. According to their tradition he was to
reveal, in his last speech, whether he were really going to die.

Louis Riel never made that last speech because the priests
would not permit it. Therefore many of his people in the
United States refuse to this day to believe that he actually
was hanged.

GONE FOR CERTAIN

His mother visited him, accompanied by his brother Alexandre; Marguerite, dying of grief in St. Boniface, could not come. Their third child, a boy, had been born prematurely in October and had lived only a few hours. This loss and her husband's fate had destroyed her will to live; she could not be induced to eat and was slowly wasting away. (She died in May, 1886, of "consumption.")

The plucky Julie, never one to give up hope, returned to St. Boniface convinced that her son would yet escape. All major avenues to clemency had been closed, but desperate measures were still being tried. A. E. Forget, a prominent Regina French Canadian who was to become the first Lieutenant Governor of Saskatchewan, went to Winnipeg to consult with Archbishop Taché; word came back that there still might be a chance.

But on November 6 Louis had written his testament. He again retracted "all that I have said or professed contrary to the doctrine" and asked pardon "for the scandal I have caused." He thanked *"ma bonne et tendre mère"* for her unfailing love, his wife for her goodness and affectionate patience, and begged the latter's forgiveness for the suffering he had caused her. To his children, he wrote, he could leave no gold or silver; he could only pray that God would accept his sacrifice and give them a father's blessing. It was his wish that they be reared in virtue and piety, "firmly and simply, without parade or ostentation," so that they might enter into the Kingdom of God; and he asked them to pray for him. He left the testament in the hands of Father André, whose name he urged his friends always to recall with his own; "I love Father André."

As the day approached, tension grew in Regina. Riel had become a familiar figure during the trial as he was taken through the streets to the courtroom, and there was intense interest in the manner in which he would face death. The precautions taken against a jail delivery, supposed to be secret, were soon common knowledge and added to the excitement.

The gallows had been erected in a fenced enclosure adjoining the guardroom in which Riel was confined, at the southeast entrance to the square. The platform, concealed by the fence, had been placed so that the only access to it was through an upstairs window, which was barred. On November 15 the barracks blacksmith, Sergeant Robinson, cut the bars.

That night Riel wrote his last letter to his mother and a few other notes, some of them suggested by André. He spent most of the night in prayer with the priest; he was calm and showed no sign of fear. At five o'clock in the morning Father André said mass and administered his last communion. Riel then obtained permission to bathe; that much at least he could do, he told André; he was mortified because the garments in which he was to die were not as fine as he would have liked.

The morning was cold and clear. At dawn the people began to assemble in the field before the barracks square. A strong cordon of Mounties had been drawn up around the enclosure and no one without a pass could approach.

At eight-fifteen Deputy Sheriff Gibson appeared at the door of Riel's cell. To him had fallen the unhappy task of officiating; the French-Canadian Sheriff, S. E. Chapleau, was nominally in charge and attended the execution, but took no part in it.

Riel was talking easily with Father André when the deputy appeared. He looked up. "You want me, Mr. Gibson?" he asked. "I am ready."

Gibson stood aside from the door and Riel and André walked into the corridor, where they were joined by other officials and another priest, Father Charles McWilliams, who had been sent by Toronto sympathizers to help Riel in his last moments.

Louis walked upstairs without assistance. André, beside him, was near collapse. Riel's face was set and he moved slowly, but he did not falter. He was hatless and his heavy brown hair was shiny from the brushing he had given it. He wore a short black jacket, dark brown trousers, and moccasins.

The group walked slowly down the hall to the window opening on the gallows platform. The priests and the condemned man knelt. In Riel's hand was a silver-mounted ivory crucifix which he kissed as he prayed. Questioned by Father André he said he forgave his enemies, offered his life as a sacrifice to God, and repented of his sins.

"You do not wish to speak in public?" the priest insisted. "You make that a sacrifice to God?"

"Yes, my father. I make to my God as a sacrifice the opportunity to speak in public in this, my last hour."

The priests placed their hands on his head and pronounced the absolution.

Louis asked God to bless his mother, his wife and children, and others. "My Father bless me," he said, "according to the views of Thy Providence which are beautiful and without measure." It was the prayer he had voiced in the little church at Fort Benton on the fateful day in 1884 when he had started north to the Saskatchewan.

He rose, embraced the priests. His arms were pinioned by his guards; they stooped and passed through the window onto a small ledge above the gallows platform.

Louis Riel looked about him, over the fence surrounding the yard, over the heads of the milling people, to the prairie. It was glittering in the sun, the grass coated with frost. The air was crisply cool. Louis straightened up and breathed deeply. A wonderful morning, the kind of morning a Métis, a wagon man, loved: a morning on which to start a trip.

He remembered a debt, to those who had most recently tried to save his life. "Thanks, Madame Forget and Monsieur Forget," he said.

He went down a few steps to the gallows platform, gently maneuvered by his guards to a position on the trap. His face was dead white and beaded with perspiration.

Father André stumbled along behind. Riel glanced at him. "*Courage, mon père,*" he said.

The priests and Dr. Jukes shook hands with him and Riel said, "Thank you, doctor." The hangman came forward and slipped the noose over his head.

Riel prayed again, in French. "I believe still; I believe in God to the last moment. . . ." Father McWilliams held the crucifix before his face and he kissed it. Father André had turned away to conceal his face; he was crying.

Deputy Gibson spoke. "Louis Riel, have you anything to say before sentence of death is carried out?"

Riel glanced toward Father André, whose back was now turned to him. "Shall I say something?" he pleaded.

"No," the priest said.

"Then I should like to pray a little more."

"Two minutes," Gibson said.

"Say 'Our Father,'" McWilliams suggested. The priest turned to Gibson and whispered an aside: "When he comes to 'deliver us from evil,' tell him then—" He nodded toward the hangman.

Gibson motioned to the hangman to come forward and instructed him in a whisper.

The hangman móved over beside Riel, dropped a white cotton hood over his head, fumbled with the rope, brought his lips close to Riel's ear.

"Louis Riel," he said in a hoarse, angry whisper, "do you know me? You cannot escape from me today!" Quickly he stepped back to his place.

Louis stood firmly erect. The hood concealed whatever

emotion his face may have betrayed when he learned that his callous conquerors had reserved for him one final, incredible indignity: he was to be killed by a man who bore him a personal grudge.

The executioner had waited a long time for this moment. He was Jack Henderson, a Scotch freighter who claimed to have been a prisoner of Riel's in Fort Garry in 1870 with his friend Thomas Scott, though his name does not appear on any of the lists of that period, and to have run afoul of him again in 1885. His outfit was captured during the Northwest Rebellion and he was held for three days, Henderson said; he had been fed on bannocks and water (which was all the Métis themselves had) and had been "abused." He had told Riel then, he boasted, "I'll be the man to put the hangman's knot under your ear."

Henderson was a friend of Tom Hourie, the Mountie scout who was temporarily basking in glory as one of Riel's "captors." When he learned that Louis would be hanged in Regina, the vengeful Scot applied to the Mounted Police for the job of executioner and got it, perhaps with Hourie's help.

The honorarium was eighty dollars, but Henderson said he didn't want the money.

Father McWilliams led the last prayer, in English. Riel's voice was fainter now, but still clear. "Our Father, who art in heaven, hallowed be Thy name. Thy kingdom come. Thy will be done on earth as it is in heaven. Give us this day our daily bread, and forgive us our trespasses, as we forgive them that trespass against us. And lead us not into temptation, but deliver us—"

The trap opened and Riel's body plunged nine feet. It quivered and swayed on the taut rope.

Two doctors stood below the platform. One of them felt the pulse.

"It beats yet, slightly," he said.

"I hope he is without pain?" A newspaper reporter, his voice shrill, asked the question.

"Oh, quite. All sensation is gone."

Father André stood on the steps leading up to the window, his back to the platform; he was trembling. The other priest's head was bowed, his lips moving in prayer. The official witnesses, white-faced and sick, watched the body jerk on the rope, watched it sway in a narrowing arc like a medicine bundle dangling from the pole of the sun dance lodge. At last the bundle stopped.

One of the doctors looked at his watch and felt the pulse. "Dead. Dead in two minutes."

The other doctor put his ear to the chest. "Dead."

Nicholas Flood Davin of *The Leader,* a good newspaperman, chose to cover the execution himself, but he stationed another reporter outside to watch the crowd.

A group of uniformed dignitaries stood at the door of Colonel Irvine's quarters, chatting. The people gossiped and moved about in the field, many of them grumbling because the execution had not been public.

Mounties stood in little clusters on the veranda of the guardhouse, laughing and trading crude jokes. The reporter, though no prude, found it offensive; "their conversation," he complained, "was not edifying."

Their chatter stopped when some sound from within the enclosure warned them that the hanging was about to occur. Their tension was communicated to the crowd and for a few moments there was silence.

The reporter moved into the Mountie group, closest to the fence.

Behind the stockade there was an unintelligible mumble, a scraping of feet; there was a sudden shocking thud.

One of the Mounties turned to a comrade. "Well," he said, "the God damned son of a bitch is gone at last!"

The other man laughed. "Yes," he said, "the son of a bitch is gone for certain now!"

Father André wrote a detailed account of the execution to Lemieux, another to Archbishop Taché. To both he said, "Riel died a saint."

But Regina was more interested in the judgment of Nicholas Flood Davin; more interested, and perhaps a little. disappointed. For, said Davin, the Métis traitor "died with calm courage." Then he added the inevitable tag from *Macbeth* and, just as inevitably, misquoted it:

"Nothing in his life so became him as the leaving of it."

"LOCUM REFRIGERII, LUCIS ET PACIS"

Father André, acting for the Riel family, requested that the body be delivered to him, but did not get it for about a week. Meanwhile ugly rumors circulated in Regina that the corpse had been mutilated.

At about midnight on November 25, André read a funeral mass over the body in St. Mary's Church. The church was full; many who knelt in its pews were Protestants and leading citizens of Regina, and they gave reverent attention to the service.

Riel's body rested in a temporary coffin of black wood, draped in black muslin upon which had been sewn a white linen cross. Two candles burned at the head of the bier and two at the foot, and eight flickered on the altar.

Father André opened the coffin, and at his request the body was viewed by several of the officials and prominent citizens who had come to the service. A few locks of hair had been clipped from the head; there had been no other disfigurement. The moccasins had disappeared. The face was calm, the lips fixed in a slight smile.

The coffin was temporarily lodged under the floor of the church just to the right of the altar. Official custody of it had been given by the Government to Pascal Bonneau, a French-Canadian businessman of Regina. Rumors persisted that an attempt might be made to steal it, so for about a week Bonneau's son, Pascal, Jr., spent every night sitting in a chair above the coffin with a rifle across his knees.

Young Bonneau's vigil ended when arrangements were completed to move the body secretly to St. Boniface. On a bitterly cold night while snow blew wildly through the streets of the little capital and everyone huddled indoors, the youth removed the section of flooring, took Riel's frozen body from the coffin, wrapped it in blankets and carried it on his back about a block to a corner where a sleigh awaited. The corpse was placed in a rough pine box in the sleigh, and, with a Regina citizen named Robert Sinton, Bonneau drove to a railroad siding on which a single box car had been shunted.

Sinton and Bonneau loaded the pine box into the railroad car and Bonneau climbed in to accompany the body to Winnipeg. Sinton signaled with a lantern, a switch engine appeared, and the car was quickly attached to an eastbound Canadian Pacific train. The blizzard shrieked and slapped at the thin walls of the car; young Bonneau huddled over a stove and, in blinking lantern light, watched the pine box dance grotesquely on the lurching floor. Louis Riel was leaving the Northwest.

The day of the execution, the Abbé Dugas, rector of St. Boniface Cathedral, drove in a sleigh to the Riel home in St. Vital. Louis's mother heard the sleigh approach, its runners singing in the crisp snow. She looked out of a window.

The priest climbed slowly from the sleigh, turned to the house, walked a few steps up the path, and paused. He made the sign of the cross over the house. Julie screamed and fainted.

Requiem mass was celebrated at St. Boniface on December 12 and the crowd of mourners overflowed into the church-yard and the street.

Riel was buried in the peaceful, tree-shadowed cathedral yard. In summer it is a serene and tidy park, richly green, bright with flowers and the songs of birds which nest in the soaring twin turrets of the great Gothic church. There is no sight or sound of the prairie.

A simple granite shaft, provided by Quebec sympathizers, stands over the grave. It is inscribed: "RIEL, 16 novembre, 1885."

Louis Riel rests a few steps from the tomb of his grand-parents, Jean Baptiste Lajimodière and Marie Anne Ga-boury. Marie Anne was the pretty bride who had refused to wait in Three Rivers, as brides were supposed to do, while her venturesome lover sought their fortune in the wilder-ness. First white woman in the Northwest, she had died only seven years before the grandson who had dreamed of build-ing, in the country she had dauntlessly invaded and made her own, a strange empire of another race.

Bibliography

Compiled by ROSALEA FOX

CANADIAN AND UNITED STATES GOVERNMENT DOCUMENTS

GOVERNMENT DOCUMENTS, CANADA

CAMPBELL, Sir Alexander. *Le Cas de Louis Riel, Condamné et Execute pour Haute Trahison.* Ottawa, 1885.

Copy of Extracts of Correspondence between the Colonial Office, the Government of the Canadian Dominion, and the Hudson's Bay Company, relating to the Surrender of Rupert's Land by the Hudson's Bay Company and for the Admission thereof into the Dominion of Canada. Ottawa, 1869.

Correspondence and Papers Connected with Recent Occurrences in the North-West Territories. Ottawa, 1870.

Correspondence of the Governor General of Canada, Earl of Dufferin, with the Secretary of State for the Colonies, Earl of Carnarvon, relating to the Sentence of Death Passed on Ambroise Lépine, for the Murder of Thomas Scott, at Fort Garry. Sessional Papers, No. 11. Ottawa, 1875.

Epitome of Parliamentary Documents in connection with the North-West Rebellion, 1885. Ottawa, 1886.

General Table of Subjects of the Report of the Census of the North-West Territories, 1885. Ottawa, 1886.

Half Breed Claims. Sessional Papers, No. 14. Ottawa, 1890.

Hudson's Bay Company Payments. Sessional Papers, No. 50. Ottawa, 1886.

Immigrants' Guide to Manitoba. Ottawa: Department of Agriculture, 1879.

567

Instructions to Surveyors Sent to North-West Territory, 1870. Ottawa: Department of State, 1870.

McDougall, William. *Commission Appointing Col. Dennis, Lieutenant and Conservator of the Peace, Dec. 1, 1869.* Publications of the Canadian Archives, No. 9, Vol. II. Ottawa: Government Printing Bureau, 1915.

Memorandum on Report of the Select Committee to Enquire into the Causes of the Difficulties in the North-West Territory in 1869-1870. Sessional Papers, No. 11. Ottawa, 1875.

Mercier, M. *Discours prononcé à l'Assemblée Législative de Québec, le 7 mai, 1886, sur la Question Riel.* Québec: Imprimerie de L'Electeur, 1886.

Middleton, Gen. Sir Frederick. *Report of Department of Military Defence upon the Suppression of the Rebellion in the North-West Territories, 1885.* Sessional Papers, No. 6. Ottawa, 1886.

Minutes of the Council of the Northern Department of Rupert's Land 1830-1843; Introduction by Isaac Cowie. Reprinted in North Dakota Historical Society *Collections,* IV. Fargo, 1913.

Rapport sur la Répression de l'Insurrection dans les Territoires du Nord-Ouest et Autres Choses s'y Rattachant, 1885. Ottawa, 1886.

Relating to Half Breed Claims. Sessional Papers, No. 116. Ottawa, 1885.

Report of Chief Justice Wood, Respecting Claims Made to Reward Offered for Apprehension of the Murderers of Thomas Scott. Sessional Papers, No. 58. Toronto, 1875-76.

Report of Department of Indian Affairs. Part 1. Sessional Papers, No. 4. Ottawa, 1886.

Report of the Select Committee of the Causes of the Difficulties in the North-West Territories in 1869-1870. Ottawa, 1874.

Riel, Louis. *Papers at Batoche.* Sessional Papers, No. 43h and 43i. Ottawa, 1886.

Summary of Evidence in the Controversy between the Hudson's Bay Company and the North-West Company, from Papers Relating to the Red River Settlement 1815-19, Ordered by the House of Commons to be Printed, July 12, 1819. Reprinted in North Dakota Historical Society *Collections,* IV. Fargo, 1913.

The Queen vs. Louis Riel: Report of Trial at Regina. Ottawa, 1886.

Trials in connection with the 1885 Rebellion. Sessional Papers, No. 52. Ottawa, 1886.

GOVERNMENT DOCUMENTS, U. S.

1836 Description of Métis, in Report of J. N. Nicollet, January 11, 1845. H. Doc. 52, 28th Cong., 2d sess., Serial 464.

HARRISON, President Benjamin. *Message: A Report on the Case of Louis Riel, February 11, 1889.* S. Doc. 1 of the Special Session, 50th Cong., Cong. Serial 2613.

Indian Laws & Treaties, compiled by Charles J. Kappler. S. Doc. 53, 70th Cong., 1st sess., Washington, 1929.

STEVENS, Isaac I., et al. *Reports of Explorations and Surveys to Ascertain the Most Practicable and Economical Route for a Railroad from the Mississippi River to the Pacific Ocean.* H. Doc. 56, 36th Cong., 1st sess.

Survey of the Conditions of the Indians in the United States. Hearings before Subcommittee of the Committee on Indian Affairs, United States Senate, 72nd Cong., 1st sess., Part 23, for the use of the Committee on Indian Affairs. Washington, 1932.

Treaty of Fort Laramie with the Sioux, 1851. S. Doc. 319, 58th Cong., 2d sess., II, Part 2. Washington, 1929.

BOOKS, PAMPHLETS, MANUSCRIPTS, AND HISTORICAL COLLECTIONS

ADAM, G. Mercer. *Sir John A. Macdonald.* Toronto: Rose Publishing Company, 1891.

ADAMS, James Truslow, and Coleman, R. V., eds. *Dictionary of American History.* New York: Charles Scribner's Sons, 1940.

ANDERSON, Edna V. *Art Survey, 1943.* Pamphlet, auspices of American Association of University Women, Lewistown, Montana.

Annual Reports of St. Peter's Mission [Montana] *1884-1886,* translated by Gerald G. Steckler. Spokane: Jesuit Archives, Mount St. Michael's.

ANONYMOUS. *Le mot de la fin. Voici le vote! Conspiration armée contre les métis français. Le chef métis sacrificié aux Orangistes!* etc. Parkman Collection of Canadian History, Widener Library, Harvard University, Cambridge, Massachusetts.

ANONYMOUS. *The Riel Rebellion, 1885.* Montreal: "Witness" Printing House, 1885.

ANONYMOUS. *The Story of Louis Riel, the Rebel Chief.* Parkman Collection of Canadian History, Widener Library, Harvard University, Cambridge, Massachusetts.

ARNOLD, Henry V. *The History of Old Pembina 1780-1872.* Printed by the author, at Larimore, North Dakota, 1917.

BANKS, Eleanor. *Wandersong.* Caldwell, Idaho: The Caxton Printers, Ltd., 1950.

BANKS, Mrs. Samuel. Unpublished book manuscript.

BARBEAU, Marius. *Folk Songs of Old Quebec.* Bulletin 75, Anthropological Series. Ottawa: National Museum of Canada, Department of Mines.

BARBEAU, Marius, and Melvin, Grace. *The Indian Speaks.* Caldwell, Idaho: The Caxton Printers, Ltd.; and Toronto: Macmillan, 1943.

BEGG, Alexander. *The Creation of Manitoba; or, A History of the Red River Troubles.* Toronto: Hunter, Rose and Company, 1871.

——. *History of the North-West.* Toronto: Hunter, Rose and Company, 1894.

BLAKE. *Ministers on Trial,* a speech in the House of Commons on March 19, 1886. Pamphlet.

BLOOMFIELD, L. *Sacred Stories of the Sweet Grass Cree.* Bulletin 60. Ottawa: National Museum of Canada, 1930.

BRENNAN, Margaret. A school copy-book project on the history of Pembina County.

BRUCE, John, and Riel, Louis. *Declaration of the People of Rupert's Land and the Northwest.*

BRYANT, Wilbur F. "Blood of Abel." Hastings *Gazette Journal,* Hastings, Nebraska, 1887.

BURPEE, L. J., and Doughty, A. G., eds. *The Makers of Canadian History: Index and Dictionary of Canadian History.* Toronto: Morang & Company, 1912.

BUTLER, Capt. W. F. *The Great Lone Land.* London: Sampson Low, Marston & Searle, 1873.

CAMERON, William Bleasdell. *The War Trail of Big Bear.* Toronto: Ryerson Press, c. 1925.

CAMPBELL, Marjorie Wilkins. *The Saskatchewan.* New York: Rinehart & Company, 1950.

CARTER, H. Dyson. *Sea of Destiny: The Story of Hudson Bay.* New York: Greenberg, 1940.

CARTWRIGHT, Richard J. *Reminiscences.* Toronto: William Briggs, 1912.

CATLIN, George. *Letters and Notes on the Manners, Customs and Condition of the North American Indians* (2 vols.). Published by the author, London, 1841.

CHAPLEAU, J. A. *La Question Riel.* Pamphlet. Ottawa, 1885.

————. *Execution of Louis Riel.* Pamphlet. Montreal: Imprimerie Générale, 1886.

CHITTENDEN, Hiram Martin. *The American Fur Trade of the Far West* (Reprint edition, 2 vols.). New York: The Press of the Pioneers, Inc., Barnes & Noble, 1935.

CLAY, Charles. *Swampy Cree Legends.* Toronto: Macmillan, 1938.

Collections of the State Historical Society of North Dakota. I. *Tribune,* Bismarck, North Dakota, 1906.

CONSTANTIN-WEVER, Maurice. *La Bourrasque.* Paris: F. Rieder, 1925.

COUES, Elliott W. *New Light on the Early History of the Greater Northwest* (Henry-Thompson Journals). New York: Harper & Brothers, 1897.

CREIGHTON, Donald Grant. *Dominion of the North: A History of Canada.* Boston: Houghton Mifflin Company, 1944.

CULIN, Stewart. *Games of North American Indians.* 14th Annual Report. Washington: Bureau of American Ethnology, Smithsonian Institution, Government Printing Office, 1902-1903.

DELARONDE, M. Alexandre. *L'Ame penitente ou Nouveau Pensez-y-bien* (in the Saulteux language). Franciscaines Missionaires de Marie, 1908.

DELORIA, Ella. *Speaking of Indians.* New York: Friendship Press, 1944.

DENSMORE, Frances. *Chippewa Music.* Bulletins 45 and 53. Washington: Bureau of American Ethnology, Smithsonian Institution, Government Printing Office, 1913.

DIOMEDI, Father A. *Sketches of Modern Indian Life.* Spokane: Jesuit Archives, Mount St. Michael's, 1879.

DOMINION OF CANADA. *Canoe Routes to Hudson Bay.* Ottawa: Department of the Interior.

DOMINION OF CANADA. *Plains Indians.* Pamphlet. A guide to anthropological exhibits, Leaflet 4. Ottawa: National Museum of Canada, 1938.

DUNCAN, David M. *The Story of the Canadian People.* Toronto: Macmillan, 1916.

EBERSCHWEILER, Father Frederick. *A Short History of the Assini-boines* (Written to Father Cataldo in 1886). Spokane: Jesuit Archives, Mount St. Michael's.

——. *A Short History of the Mission of St. Paul, Montana.* Spokane: Jesuit Archives, Mount St. Michael's.

——. *Two Years in Fort Benton.* Spokane: Jesuit Archives, Mount St. Michael's.

FARIES, Ven. Richard. *A Dictionary of the Cree Language.* General Synod of the Church of England in Canada, 1938.

FERNON, Thomas S. *No Dynasty in North America, the West between Salt Waters, Hudson Bay a Free Basin like the Gulf of Mexico, etc.* Philadelphia: Press of Henry B. Ashmead, 1878.

FINNIE, Richard. *Canada Moves North.* New York: Macmillan, 1942.

FRANKLIN, John. *Narrative of a Journey to the Shores of the Polar Sea, 1824.* Bulletin 30, Part 1, A.M.P.P. 102, Record 456. Washington: Bureau of American Ethnology, Smithsonian Institution, Government Printing Office.

FRASER, G. G. *Canoe Routes to Hudson Bay.* Pamphlet of National Development Bureau. Ottawa: Department of the Interior.

GIBBON, John Murray. *The Romantic History of the Canadian Pacific.* New York: Tudor Publishing Company, 1937.

GIRAUD, Marcel. *Le Métis Canadien.* Paris: Institut d'Ethnologie, 1945.

GRANDIN, Mgr., et al. *La Véritable Louis Riel tel que dépeint dans les lettres de sa grandeur Mgr. Grandin, etc.* Montreal, 1887.

HAMILTON, Z. M. *Annual Report of the Secretary of the Saskatchewan Historical Society, 1943-1944.* Regina, Saskatchewan.

——. *The Execution of Louis Riel.* Reprinted from the Winnipeg *Free Press*, 1935.

HANSEN, M. L., and Brebner J. B. *The Mingling of the Canadian and American Peoples.* New Haven: Yale University Press, 1940.

HARGRAVE, Joseph James. *Red River.* Montreal: John Lovell, 1871.

HARPER, Frank B. *Fort Union and Its Neighbors on the Upper Missouri.* Pamphlet published by the Great Northern Railway.

HART, John B. *Report of North Dakota Indian Affairs Commission.* Rolla, North Dakota, 1950.

HAULTAIN, T. Arnold. *A History of Riel's Second Rebellion and How It Was Quelled.* Souvenir number of *Canadian Pictorial and Illustrated War News.* Toronto: Grip Printing and Publishing Company, 1885.

HAVARD, V. *The French Half-Breeds of the Northwest.* Report of the Smithsonian Institution, 1879. Washington: Government Printing Office, 1880.

HEALY, W. J. *Women of Red River.* Winnipeg: The Women's Canadian Club, 1923.

HENDERSON, D. K., and Gillespie, R. D. *A Textbook of Psychiatry.* New York: Oxford University Press, 1932.

HERBERMAN, Charles G., et al. *Catholic Encyclopedia.* New York: Robert Appleton Company, 1907.

HIND, Henry Youle. *Narrative of the Canadian Red River Exploring Expedition of 1857 and of the Assiniboine and Saskatchewan Exploring Expedition of 1858* (2 vols.). London: Longmans, Green, Longmans and Roberts, 1860.

HODGE, Frederick Webb, ed. *Handbook of American Indians.* Bulletin 30. Washington: Bureau of American Ethnology, Smithsonian Institution, Government Printing Office, 1930.

HOWARD, Helen Addison, and McGrath, Dan L. *War Chief Joseph.* Caldwell, Idaho: The Caxton Printers, Ltd., 1941.

HOWARD, Maj. Gen. O. O. *My Life and Experiences among Our Hostile Indians.* Hartford: A. D. Worthington & Company, 1907.

IRELAND, W. W. *Through the Ivory Gate; Studies in Psychology of History.* Edinburgh, 1889.

JEFFERSON, Robert. *Fifty Years on the Saskatchewan.* Battleford, Saskatchewan: Canadian North-West Historical Society, 1929.

JENNESS, Diamond. *Canada's Indian Problems.* Annual Report 1942 of the Smithsonian Institution. Washington: Government Printing Office, 1943.

KANE, Paul. *Wanderings of an Artist among the Indians of North America.* Toronto: The Radisson Society of Canada, 1925.

KAVANAUGH, Martin. *The Assiniboine Basin.* Published by the author, Brandon, Manitoba, 1946.

KELSEY, Henry. *The Kelsey Papers.* Ottawa: F. A. Ackland, 1929.

KENNEY, James F., ed. *The Founding of Churchill* (Journal of

Captain James Knight, 1717). Toronto: J. M. Dent & Sons, 1932.

LaCHANCE, Vernon, ed. *Diary of Francis Dickens.* Bulletin 59, Departments of History and Political and Economic Science in Queen's University, Kingston, Ontario. Ontario: The Jackson Press, 1930.

LARSEN Arthur J. *Minnesota under Four Flags.* Pamphlet, Minnesota Centennial Publications Number 1. St. Paul: Minnesota Historical Society, 1946.

LeCARON, Maj. Henri (T. M. Beach). *Twenty-five Years in the Secret Service: The Recollections of a Spy.* London, 1892.

LeCHEVALLIER, Rev. Father Jules, O.M.I. *Aux Prises avec la Tourmente.* Extracts from *Review* of the University of Ottawa, 1939-1940, Ottawa, 1940.

———. *Saint-Laurent de Grandin.* Vannes: Lafoyle and J. De-Lamarzelle, 1930.

LEE, Charles H., and Cavileer, Charles. *The Long Ago.* Pamphlet. Walhalla, North Dakota, 1898.

LEESON, Michael A., ed. *History of Montana.* Chicago: Warner, Beers & Company, 1885.

LINDSEY, Charles. *Rome in Canada.* Toronto: Williamson & Company, 1889.

Livre de Prières en Langue Sauteuse. St. Boniface, Manitoba: Imprimatur: Adelardus, O.M.I., Canadian Publishers, Ltd., 1945.

LOUNSBERRY, Col. Clement A. *Early History of North Dakota.* Washington: Liberty Press, 1919.

LOWER, Arthur R. M. *Colony to Nation: A History of Canada.* New York: Longmans, Green & Company, 1946.

MACBETH, R. G. *Policing the Plains.* London: Hodder and Stoughton Ltd., 1922.

———. *The Romance of Western Canada.* Toronto: William Briggs, 1918.

MACDONALD, Capt. John A. *Troublous Times in Canada.* Toronto: W. S. Johnston & Company, 1910.

MACKAY, Douglas. *The Honourable Company.* New York: Bobbs-Merrill, 1936.

MACKENZIE, Alexander. *Voyages from Montreal through the Continent of North America.* Toronto: The Radisson Society of Canada, 1927.

MACOUN, John. *Manitoba and the Great North West.* Guelph, Ontario: The World Publishing Company, 1882.

MAIR, Charles. *The American Bison—Its Habits, Method of Capture and Economic Use in the North-West, with reference to Its Threatened Extinction and Possible Preservation.* Ottawa: Royal Society of Canada, 1890.

MANDELBAUM, David G. *The Plains Cree.* XXXVII, Part 2, Anthropological Papers. New York: American Museum of Natural History, 1940.

Map and folder of Regina. Regina, Saskatchewan: Board of Trade.

McINNES, C. M. *In the Shadow of the Rockies.* London: Rivingtons, 1930.

McLENNAN, William, translator. *Songs of Old Canada.* Montreal: Dawson Brothers, 1886.

McNICKLE, D'Arcy. *They Came Here First.* Philadelphia: J. B. Lippincott, 1949.

MEAD, Margaret. *The Changing Culture of an Indian Tribe.* New York: Columbia University Press, 1932.

MELVILLE, C. H. *Life of General Redvers Buller.* London: E. Arnold & Company, 1923.

Memento of St. Boniface, Manitoba. Pamphlet. St. Boniface, Manitoba: Imprimerie de la Liberté, 1938.

MILLER, Joaquin. *History of Montana.* Chicago: Lewis Publishing Company, 1894.

MILTON, Viscount, and Cheadle, W. B. *The North-West Passage of Land.* London: Cassell Petter & Galpin, 1875.

MONTPETIT, André Napoleon. *Louis Riel à la Rivière-du-loup.* Lévis, 1885.

MONTIGNY, B. A. T. de. *Biographie et Récit de Gabriel Dumont.* Montreal, 1889.

MOONEY, James. *The Ghost Dance Religion and the Sioux Outbreak of 1890.* 14th Annual Report. Washington: Bureau of American Ethnology, Smithsonian Institution, Government Printing Office, 1902-1903.

MORICE, A. G., O.M.I. *The Catholic Church in the Canadian Northwest.* Winnipeg, 1936.

———. *A Critical History of the Red River Insurrection.* Winnipeg: Canadian Publishers, Ltd., 1935.

———. *Dictionnaire Historique des Canadiens et des Métis Français de l'Ouest.* Quebec: J.-P. Garneau, 912.

MORICE, A. G., O.M.I. *The Great Déné Race.* Vienna: The Press
of the Mechitharistes, 1928.
———. *History of the Northern Interior of British Columbia.* To-
ronto: William Briggs, 1915.
———. *La Race Métisse.* Winnipeg, 1938.
MORRIS, Alexander. *The Treaties of Canada with the Indians of
Manitoba and the North-West Territories.* Toronto: Willing
& Williamson, 1880.
MORTON, Arthur S. *The New Nation, The Métis.* Ottawa: Royal
Society of Canada, 1939.
MUELLER, Oscar. Notes on interview with Ben Kline, December
2, 1931.
MULVANEY, Charles Pelham. *The History of the North-West Re-
bellion.* Toronto: A. H. Hovey & Company, 1885.
NEWTON, William. *Twenty Years on the Saskatchewan, North
West Canada.* London: Stock, 1897.
NUSSBAUM, Arthur. *A Concise History of the Law of Nations.*
New York: Macmillan, 1947.
NUTE, Grace Lee. *The Voyageur's Highway.* St. Paul: Minnesota
Historical Society, 1941.
O'DONNELL, John N. *Manitoba As I Saw It.* Winnipeg: Clark
Brothers & Company, Ltd., 1909.
OLIVER, E. H., ed. *The Canadian Northwest: Its Early Develop-
ment and Legislative Records* (2 vols.). Ottawa: Government
Printing Bureau, 1915.
"One of the Bunglers." *Reminiscences of a Bungle.* Toronto:
Grip Printing and Publishing Company, 1887.
OUIMET, Adolphe. *La Vérité sur la Question Métisse au Nord-
Ouest.* Montreal, 1889.
PALLADINO, L. B., S.J. *Indian and White in the Northwest.* Lan-
caster, Pennsylvania: Wickersham Publishing Company,
1922.
PAQUIN, Elzear. *Riel; Trágedie.* Parkman Collection of Canadian
History, Widener Library, Harvard University, Cambridge,
Massachusetts, 1886.
PARKER, Arthur C. *The Indian How Book.* Garden City: Double-
day, Doran & Company, 1936.
PARKIN, George R. *Sir John A. Macdonald. Makers of Canada.*
IX. Toronto: Morang & Company, Ltd., 1912.
PIEPER, Ezra Henry. *The Fenian Movement.* Abstract of a thesis,
Urbana, Illinois, 1931.

PRITCHETT, John Henry. *The Red River Valley 1811-1849*. New Haven: Yale University Press, 1942.

Proceedings and Transactions of the Royal Society of Canada, May, 1925.

Proceedings, 1898, of Red River Valley Old Settlers' Association. Fargo: Record Publishing Company.

RIEL, Louis "David," et al. *Family Papers.* Provincial Library of Manitoba, Winnipeg, Manitoba.

RIEL, Louis "David." *Poésies Religieuses et Politiques.* Montreal: L'Etendard, 1886.

ROSS, Alexander. *The Red River Settlement, Its Rise, Progress, and Present State.* London: Smith, Elder & Company, 1856.

SANDERS, Helen Fitzgerald. *History of Montana.* I. Chicago: Lewis Publishing Company, 1913.

Saulteux Hymnal. Oblate Fathers, St. Boniface, Manitoba, 1942.

SCHOOLING, Sir William. *The Governor and Company of Adventurers of England Trading into Hudson's Bay during Two Hundred and Fifty Years 1670-1920.* London: The Hudson's Bay Company, 1920.

SHIPPEE, Lester Burrell. *Canadian-American Relations 1849-1874.* New Haven: Yale University Press, 1939.

SILLOWAY, P. M. *Silloway's History of Central Montana.* Fergus County *Democrat*, Lewistown, Montana.

SINCLAIR, R. V. *Canadian Indians.* A collection of published letters. Ottawa: Thorburn & Abbott, 1911.

SMITH, Harlan I. *An Album of Prehistoric Canadian Art.* Bulletin 37, Anthropological Series, No. 8. Ottawa: Victoria Memorial Museum, Canada Department of Mines, 1923.

Souvenir Booklet on Joseph Rolette from the Memorial Dedication at Pembina, North Dakota, 1937. Pembina, North Dakota, 1937.

Souvenir of 121st Anniversary, Old Pembina, North Dakota, 1818-1939. Grand Forks, North Dakota: Washburn Printing Company, 1939.

SPECK, Frank Gouldsmith. *The Iroquois.* Bloomfield Hills, Michigan: Cranbrook Institute of Science, 1945.

STANLEY, George F. G. *The Birth of Western Canada.* New York: Longmans, Green & Company, 1936.

STEDMAN, Father Joseph F. *My Sunday Missal* (English-Saulteux edition). Brooklyn: Confraternity of the Precious Blood, 1937.

STEWART, George, Jr. *Canada under the Administration of the Earl of Dufferin*. Toronto: Rose-Belford, 1878.

STRANGE, Maj. Gen. T. Bland. *Gunner Jingo's Jubilee*. Victoria, B. C.: Provincial Archives.

SWAN, Elizabeth. Unpublished brief history of the First Catholic Pioneers of Lewistown, Montana, 1878-1906.

TACHÉ, Archbishop Alexandre. *On the Amnesty Question with regard to the North West Difficulty*. Pamphlet. St. Boniface, Manitoba, 1893.

TASSÉ, Joseph. *Les Canadiens de l'Ouest* (2 vols.). Montreal: Imprimerie Générale, 1886.

TENNANT, Joseph F. *Rough Times 1870-1920*, a souvenir of the 50th anniversary of the Red River expedition and the formation of the Province of Manitoba. 1920.

THOMPSON, John S. D. *The Execution of Louis Riel*. Speech of Minister of Justice, Ottawa, 1886.

TRÉMAUDAN, Auguste-Henri de. *Histoire de la Nation Métisse dans l'Ouest Canadien*. Montreal: Editions Albert Lévesque, 1936.

TROBRIAND, Regis de. *Military Life in Dakota*. St. Paul: Alvord Memorial Commission, 1951.

TROLLOPE, Anthony. *North America*. New York: Harper & Brothers, 1862.

TUPPER, Sir Charles. *Recollections of Sixty Years*. London: Cassell & Company, Ltd., 1914.

VAN DEN BROECK, Father V. J. Unpublished sketch of Ben Kline's life.

WADE, Mason. *The French-Canadian Outlook*. New York: The Viking Press, 1946.

WATKINS, E. A., and Faries, R. *A Dictionary of the Cree Language*. Toronto: Church of England in Canada, 1938.

WHITE, Thomas. *The Northwest Rebellion: Facts for the People*. The Government's defense prepared by the Minister of the Interior. Victoria, B. C.: Provincial Archives.

WINTEMBERG, W. J. *Petroglyphs of the Roche Percée and Vicinity*. Section II, 1939. Ottawa: Royal Society of Canada, 1939.

WISSLER, Clark. *Indians of the United States*. Garden City: Doubleday, Doran & Company, 1941.

YOUNG, Rev. Ederton R. *By Canoe and Dog Train among the Cree and Salteaux Indians*. Toronto: William Briggs, 1890.

ARTICLES

ADAIR, E. R. "France and the Beginnings of New France," *Canadian Historical Review*, September, 1944.

ANDERSON, Frank W. "Louis Riel's Insanity Reconsidered," *Saskatchewan History*, III, No. 3, Autumn, 1950.

ANONYMOUS. "First Prairie Wheels," *The Beaver*, June, 1951.

ANONYMOUS. "First Winter," *Scarlet and Gold*, 1940 Annual.

ANONYMOUS. "Last Survivor of Riel's Rebellion," *Current History*, January, 1923.

ANONYMOUS. "Leur Victime," unidentified Quebec newspaper, May 22, 1876.

ANONYMOUS. "A Lost Art," *Scarlet and Gold*, 1940 Annual.

ANONYMOUS. "Métis in St. Paul, 1859," *North Dakota Historical Quarterly*, IX, Nos. 2 and 3.

ANONYMOUS. "Painting Western History," *Scarlet and Gold*, 1940 Annual.

ANONYMOUS. "Riel et le 'Globe,'" *Le Nouveau Monde*, May 27, 1876.

ANONYMOUS. "Saving the Buffalo," *The Beaver*, June, 1948.

ANONYMOUS. "The Story of the Press," *Canadian Northwest Historical Society Publications*, I, Part I, No. 4, 1928.

ANONYMOUS. "Today's History Lesson," *Scarlet and Gold*, 1940 Annual.

ATHEARN, Robert G., ed. "A Winter Campaign Against the Sioux," *Mississippi Valley Historical Review*, September, 1948.

AUDET, Francis-J. "James Cuthbert de Berthier and His Family," *Transactions of the Royal Society of Canada*, XXXIX, Section I, 1935.

BARBEAU, Marius. "Sashes for the Fur Trade," *The Beaver*, June, 1941.

———. "Voyageur Songs," *The Beaver*, June, 1942.

BLEGEN, Theodore C. "Sketch of James W. Taylor," *Minnesota Historical Bulletins*, I, 1915.

BOTKIN, Alex C. "The John Brown of the Half Breeds," *Rocky Mountain Magazine*, September, 1900.

CAMERON, W. Bleasdell. "Christmas at Fort Pitt," *The Beaver*, December, 1945.

———. "Clan McKay in the West," *The Beaver*, September, 1944.

———. "Peaceful Invasion," *The Beaver*, March, 1948.

CHAPIN, Earl V. "Northwest Angle," *The Beaver*, March, 1947.

CHETLAIN, A. Louis. "Red River Colony," *Harper's Magazine*, December, 1878.

CLARKE, Daniel. "A Psycho-Medical History of Louis Riel," *American Journal of Insanity*, July, 1887.

DALRYMPLE, A. J. "Old Saskatchewan Steamboats," *The Beaver*, June, 1943.

DAVIS, Elmer. "Subversion: The Old Story," *Saturday Review of Literature*, April 1, 1950.

GIBSON, H. "L'étude sur l'état mental de Louis Riel," *L'Encephale*, 1886.

GORDON, Daniel Miner. "Reminiscences of the North-West Rebellion Campaign of 1885," *Queen's Quarterly*, January, 1903.

HAMILTON, C. F. "The Canadian Militia: The Northwest Rebellion, 1885," *Canadian Defence Quarterly*, VII, No. 2, January, 1930.

HEWITT, H. W. "Place Called Batoche," *Canadian Magazine*, March, 1916.

KERR, John Andrew. "Gabriel Dumont: A Personal Memory," *Dalhousie Review*, XV.

————. "I Helped Capture Ambroise Lépine," *Canadian Magazine*, May, 1933.

KINGSBURY, George W. "Enos Stutsman," *North Dakota Historical Society Collection*, I, 1906.

KNAPLUND, Paul. "Gladstone on the Red River Rebellion, 1870," *Mississippi Valley Historical Review*, June, 1934.

KNOX, Harold C. "Consul Taylor of Winnipeg," *The Beaver*, June, 1949.

KNOX, Olive. "Red River Cart," *The Beaver*, March, 1942.

LISTENFELT, Hattie. "The Hudson's Bay Company and the Red River Trade," *North Dakota Historical Society Collection*, IV, 1913.

MACBETH, Roderick George. "Louis Riel's Stormy Career," *Canadian Magazine*, January, 1927.

MACDONALD, J. S. "The Dominion Telegraph," *Canadian North West Historical Society*, I, No. 6, 1930.

MACLEOD, Margaret Arnett. "Cuthbert Grant of Grantown," *Canadian Historical Review*, XXI, No. 1, March, 1940.

————. "The Company in Winnipeg," *The Beaver*, September, 1940.

McAstocker, David P., S.J. "Introduction" to *Jesuits in Old Oregon, 1840-1940*, by William N. Bischoff, S.J. Caldwell, Idaho: The Caxton Printers, 1945.

McEwan, Grant. "Robert Sinton—Prairie Pioneer," *The Country Guide* (Canadian), June, 1946.

McFadden, Molly. "Steamboats on the Red," *The Beaver*, June, 1950.

McLean, Elizabeth M. (as told to Constance James). "Our Captivity Ended," *The Beaver*, September, 1947.

———. "Prisoners of the Indians," *The Beaver*, June, 1947.

———. "The Siege of Fort Pitt," *The Beaver*, December, 1946.

Morton, W. L. "The Canadian Métis," *The Beaver*, September, 1950.

Nute, Grace Lee. "Hudson's Bay Company Posts in the Minnesota Country," *Minnesota History*, September, 1941.

———. "Red River Trails," *Minnesota History*, September, 1925.

Oliver, Frank. "The Indian Drum: An Incident in the Rebellion of 1885," *Queen's Quarterly*, Winter, 1929.

Ormsby, Margaret A. "Prime Minister MacKenzie, the Liberal Party, and the Bargain with British Columbia," *Canadian Historical Review*, June, 1945.

Park, Robert E. "Mentality of Racial Hybrids," *American Journal of Sociology*, January, 1931.

Perret, Jules. "Upper Fort Garry Seventy-Five Years Ago," *The Beaver*, December, 1942.

Pritchett, John Perry. "The Origin of the So-called Fenian Raid on Manitoba in 1871," *Canadian Historical Review*, n.d.

Prud'homme, L.-A. "Ambroise Didyme Lépine, en marge de son procès," *Section 1, 1925, Mémoires de la Société Royale du Canada*, in *Transactions*, Third Series, XIX, Sec. 1.

———. "André Nault," *1928, Mémoires de la Société Royale du Canada*, XXII.

———. "La Famille Goulet," *Transactions*, Royal Society of Canada, XXXIX, Sec. 1, 1935.

Racey, E. F. "Skirmish on Patrol," *The Beaver*, March, 1945.

Raven, C. C. "Reminiscences," *Scarlet and Gold*, 1940 Annual.

Reade, John. "The Half Breed," *Transactions*, Royal Society of Canada, Sec. 2, 1885.

RIEL, Louis. "Open Letter," of May 6, 1885, *The Irish World,* November 21, 1885.

REUTER, E. B. "The Personality of Mixed Bloods," *Proceedings,* American Sociological Society, XXII, 1928.

RIDDELL, R. G. "A Cycle in the Development of the Canadian West," *Canadian History,* September, 1940.

ROE, F. G. "Buffalo and Snow," *Canadian Historical Review,* June, 1936.

———. "The Red River Hunt," *Transactions,* Royal Society of Canada, XXIX, Sec. 2, 1935.

ROSS, J. Bethune. "Early Days at Fort Saskatchewan," *Scarlet and Gold,* 1940 Annual.

SANDBORN, Ruth Ellen. "The United States and the British Northwest, 1865-70," *North Dakota History Quarterly,* VI, No. 1, October, 1931.

SHEA, George E., Jr. "Why the United States and Canada Should Be One Country," *Look,* June 6, 1950.

SITTING BULL and Father Genin. "Sitting Bull's Story of the Little Bighorn," *North Dakota Historical Collection,* I, 1906.

SLAUGHTER, Linda W. "Leaves from North-Western History," *North Dakota Historical Collection,* I, 1906.

STANLEY, George F. G. "Gabriel Dumont's Account of the North West Rebellion," *Canadian Historical Review,* September, 1949.

———. "The Half Breed 'Rising' of 1875," *Canadian Historical Review,* December, 1936.

STREET, W. P. R. "The Commission of 1885, to the North-West Territories," edited by H. H. Langton, *Canadian Historical Review,* March, 1944.

THAYER, W. B., "Black as a Preferred Color in Ojibway Art," *Minnesota Archeologist,* April, 1942.

———. "Some Examples of 'Red River Half-Breed' Art," *Minnesota Archeologist,* April, 1942.

THOMPSON, W. T. "Adventures of a Surveyor in the Canadian North-West, 1880-1883," Saskatchewan History, III, No. 3, Autumn, 1950.

TRÉMAUDAN, A. H. de, ed. "The Execution of Thomas Scott," *Canadian Historical Review,* September, 1925.

———. "Louis Riel and the Fenian Raid of 1871," *Canadian Historical Review,* IV, No. 2, 1923.

TRÉMAUDAN, A. H. de, ed. "Louis Riel's Account of the Capture of Fort Garry, 1870," *Canadian Historical Review*, V, No. 2, 1924.

TROTTER, Reginald G. "Some American Influences upon the Canadian Federation Movement," *Canadian Historical Review*, V, No. 3, 1924.

WEEKES, Mary. "The Poundmaker's Strange Ritual," *Trail Riders*, Bulletin 89.

WISSLER, Clark. "The Origin of the American Indian," *Natural History*, September, 1944.

WOLSELEY, First Viscount Garnet Joseph. "A Narrative of the Red River Expedition" (by an Officer of the Expeditionary Force), *Blackwood's Magazine*, December, 1870; January, 1871; February, 1871.

YEIGH, Frank. "Canada's Half-Century Confederation, The Stirring Story of the Dominion, 1867-1917," Lethbridge *Daily Herald*, June 29, 1917.

LETTERS, PETITIONS, AND PROCLAMATIONS

BAKER, William D. Letter of December 30, 1887, reporting condition of Turtle Mountain Indians.

BARNABÉ, Father, and Primeau, Father J. B. Letters about Riel written to Mallet in 1874, 1875, and 1878. Department of Public Health, Rutland State Sanatorium, Rutland, Massachusetts.

BELCOURT, G. A. "Buffalo Hunt," a letter written November 25, 1845, translated by J. A. Burgess, in *The Beaver*, December, 1944.

BOURGET, Ignace, Msg. L'Archbishop de Montreal. Letter of June 2, 1876, to Louis Riel.

DAMIENS, J., S.J. Letter to Wilbur F. Bryant, January 14, 1887.

EBERSCHWEILER, Father Frederick. Letters to J. M. Cataldo, S.J., written in 1886. Jesuit Archives, Mount St. Michael's, Spokane, Washington.

HOLMES, C. Letter to Montana State Historical Library about the Riel family, February 10, 1943.

MACDONALD, Sir John A. Letter to Judge H. A. Lovell, published in "A Secret Mission," in *Queen's Review*, VIII, No. 4, April, 1934.

McDOUGALL, William. Letter to Louis Riel, written December 13, 1869.

"The Memorial and Petition of the People of Rupert's Land and North-West Territory, British America, to His Excellency, U. S. Grant, President of the United States," in *Canadian Historical Review*, XX, No. 4, October, 1939.

O'DONOGHUE, W. B. Letter of March 29, 1871, in *North Dakota History Quarterly*, V, No. 1.

POPE, Sir Joseph. *Correspondence of Sir John Macdonald.* Garden City: Doubleday, Page & Company, 1921.

RIEL, Louis. Letter from Regina prison to his mother, August 22, 1885.

——. Letter of instructions to Ritchot, April 19, 1870.

——. Letter to his brother and brother-in-law, written in 1884 from Saskatchewan, translated by Mrs. Z. M. Hamilton.

——. Letter to his mother on his father's death, February 23, 1864.

——. Letter to J. W. Taylor, U. S. consul at Winnipeg, from Grandin, October 1, 1884.

——. Letter to J. W. Taylor written on the night before Riel was hanged. Provincial Archives, Victoria, British Columbia.

——. Letter to Rev. Father Vital Fourmond, written August 5, 1885.

——. "Petition to His Excellency the Governor-General-in-Council, etc."

——. "Petition to the President of the United States," October 3, 1870, in *Canadian Historical Review*, XX, 1939.

——. "Proclamation to the People of the North-West," March, 1870, in *The New Nation* (Canadian), April 15, 1870.

——. "Proclamation to people of the North-West," April 9, 1870.

TAYLOR, James W. Letter to James D. Porter, Assistant Secretary of State, dated November 3, 1885.

——. "Memorial presented to St. Paul Chamber of Commerce to be presented to Congress on establishment of tri-weekly post-coach service from Fort Abercrombie to Helena and prompt measures for establishment of highway from St. Paul to the Rockies," in St. Paul *Press*, February 25, 1868.

NEWSPAPERS

Anaconda Standard (later *Montana Standard*) (Anaconda, Montana), July 15, 1906.
Avant-Courier (Bozeman, Montana), 1886.
Benton Daily River Press (Fort Benton, Montana), 1882-1889.
Benton Weekly Record (Fort Benton, Montana), 1882-1883.
Boulder Monitor (Boulder, Montana), July 24, 1920.
Christian Science Monitor (Boston, Massachusetts), March 27, 1920.
Glasgow Courier (Glasgow, Montana), March 30, 1942.
Great Falls Tribune (Great Falls, Montana), 1919-1951.
Harlem News (Harlem, Montana), 1950.
Helena Weekly Herald (Helena, Montana), 1882-1885.
Helena Weekly Independent (Helena, Montana), 1885.
Kalispell Times (Kalispell, Montana), October 31, 1940.
Lewistown Daily News (Lewistown, Montana), December 22, 1950.
Lewistown Democrat (Lewistown, Montana), December 31, 1943.
Mineral County Argus (Superior, Montana), 1885-1886.
Minneapolis Sunday Tribune (Minneapolis, Minnesota), August 28, 1949.
New York Times (New York City), January 19, 1947.
Regina Leader (Regina, Saskatchewan), 1885-1886.
St. Louis Post-Dispatch (St. Louis, Missouri), December 12, 1949.
Sun River Sun (Sun River, Montana), 1884-1885.
The Irish-American (New York City), January 19, 1878.
The Leader-Post (Regina, Saskatchewan), July 26, 1935.
Toronto Star Weekly (Toronto, Ontario), March 31, 1951.
Winnipeg Daily Sun (Winnipeg, Manitoba), June 13, 1885.
Winnipeg New Nation (Winnipeg, Manitoba), 1870.

MISCELLANEOUS

Several persons associated with the personages of this book have given the author valuable information in interviews; and he wishes to credit especially Miss Sally Anderson of Lewistown, Montana; Frank Belmore of Perma, Montana; Mrs. Pauline Brennan of Pembina, North Dakota; F. A. Davey of Garnet, Montana; Alex Fyant of Arlee, Montana; W. D. (Dan) Henderson of near Frazer, Montana; Olive Knox of Winnipeg, Manitoba; the T. W. McClellands of Emerson, Manitoba; Charles N. Pray of Great Falls, Montana; Honoré Riel of St. Vital, Manitoba; Father F. J. Saksa of Great Falls, Montana; and George Wright of Great Falls, Montana.

Some persons have written letters of fact and of further sources of information to the author; for such kind encouragement and assistance he wishes to thank J. B. Brebner of New York City; Donovan K. Bryant of Omaha, Nebraska; Ethel Bryant of Lincoln, Nebraska; Hugh Calderwood of Glasgow, Montana; Mrs. Anna B. Carone of Browning, Montana; C. Charron of Prince-Albert, Saskatchewan; Robert Hitchman of Seattle, Washington; L. J. Howard of Choteau, Montana; Mrs. Edmond Mallet of Washington, D. C.; Henri Morrisseau of Ottawa, Ontario; Father Pierre Picton of St.-Boniface, Manitoba; Marjorie L. Porter of Plattsburg, New York; and J. L. Tremblay of Seattle, Washington.

This book is based mainly upon old books and documents, many of which were not easily accessible; hence without the help of librarians, research workers, and writers, the book could not have been written. The author wishes to acknowledge his great debt of gratitude to Mrs. Anne McDonnell, assistant librarian of the Montana State Historical Library, who has continually put him in touch with materials and with persons who have been invaluable to this project.

Also, the author wishes to express his appreciation for the exceptional courtesy of William Norbert Bischoff, S.J., archivist of the Jesuit Scholasticate, Spokane, Washington; Edwin W. Briggs, Professor of Law at Montana State University, Missoula, Montana; Frank P. Bruno, reference assistant at the Boston Public Library, Boston, Massachusetts; Florence H. Davis, head librarian of the State Historical Society of North Dakota, Bismarck, North Dakota; William Lyle Davis, S.J., head of the history department at Gonzaga University, Spokane, Washington; Felix Desrochers, general librarian of the Bibliothèque du Parlement, Ottawa, Canada; Leo-Paul Desrosiers, head librarian of the City of Montreal, Montreal, Canada; James Taylor Dunn, librarian of the New York State Historical Association, Cooperstown, New York; Norman Fee, acting Dominion archivist, Ottawa, Canada; Gerritt E. Fielstra, assistant chief of photographic service, and François X. Grondin, research assistant, Economics Division, New York Public Library, New York City; Norman A. Fox, writer, Great Falls, Montana; Margaret Fulmer, head librarian of the Great Falls Library, Great Falls, Montana; Mrs.

Elizabeth S. Gilbert, head of the reference department, Spokane Public Library, Spokane, Washington; Z. M. Hamilton, secretary of the Saskatchewan Historical Society, Regina, Saskatchewan; Louise M. Hoxie, librarian of State Teachers College, Plattsburg, New York; Willard Ireland, provincial librarian and archivist, Victoria, British Columbia; J. A. Jackson, archivist at the Provincial Library, Winnipeg, Manitoba; Elinor C. Johnson, reference librarian at the Public Library, Moline, Illinois; J. L. Johnston, provincial librarian at the Manitoba Provincial Library, Winnipeg, Manitoba; Kenneth E. Kidd, deputy keeper of the Royal Ontario Museum of Archaeology, Toronto, Canada; William P. Kilroy, research worker at the Library of Congress, Washington, D. C.; William Kaye Lamb, Dominion archivist, Public Archives of Canada, Ottawa, Canada; Gilbert Lekander, secretary to Congressman Wesley A. D'Ewart, Wilsall, Montana; Thomas J. Manning, assistant in the reference division of the Boston Public Library, Boston, Massachusetts; Théophile Martin, assistant secretary of L'Union Saint-Jean-Baptiste D'Amerique, Woonsocket, Rhode Island; Inez Mitchell, cataloguer, Provincial Archives, Victoria, British Columbia; Gabriel Nadeau of Rutland State Sanatorium, Rutland, Massachusetts; Josiah T. Newcomb, librarian at Champlain College, Plattsburg, New York; James C. Olson, superintendent of the Nebraska State Historical Library, Lincoln, Nebraska; Paul North Rice, chief of the reference department, New York Public Library, New York City; Paul P. Sauer, procurator of Oregon Province, Gonzaga University, Spokane, Washington; W. P. Schoenberg, S.J., Gonzaga University, Spokane, Washington; Bessie Sestak, head of the reference department, Great Falls Public Library, Great Falls, Montana; A. W. Sihvon, assistant director, Department of Social Welfare and Rehabilitation, Public Assistance Branch, Province of Saskatchewan, Regina, Saskatchewan; Ellen D. Smith, librarian at the Carnegie Library, Hastings, Nebraska; Lewis H. Thomas, provincial archivist, University of Saskatchewan, Regina, Saskatchewan; Mason Wade, writer, Cornish, New Hampshire; Catherine White, reference librarian at the University Library, Montana State University, Missoula, Montana; Dana Wright, writer, St. John, North Dakota; and the Adjutant General's Office, Washington, D. C.

For translating various materials from French and Latin, the author is gratefully indebted to Mrs. Z. M. Hamilton of

Regina, Saskatchewan; Sister Providencia of St. Thomas Home,
Great Falls, Montana; and Gerald G. Steckler of Mount St.
Michael's Scholasticate, Spokane, Washington.

For reading proof on the manuscript, the editor is indebted
to Mrs. Mandi Bradley of Great Falls, Montana.

The preparation of the index was sponsored by the Montana
Institute of the Arts, an organization of which Joseph Kinsey
Howard was a Founding Member and first chairman of the
Writing Group. (Ed.)

Index